W9-AOV-828

17.50

Taxation and Economic Development in India

PRAEGER SPECIAL STUDIES IN
INTERNATIONAL ECONOMICS AND DEVELOPMENT

Taxation and Economic Development in India

James Cutt

FREDERICK A. PRAEGER, Publishers
New York · Washington · London

The purpose of the Praeger Special Studies is to make specialized research monographs in U.S. and international economics and politics available to the academic, business, and government communities. For further information, write to the Special Projects Division, Frederick A. Praeger, Publishers, 111 Fourth Avenue, New York, N.Y. 10003.

FREDERICK A. PRAEGER, PUBLISHERS
111 Fourth Avenue, New York, N.Y. 10003, U.S.A.
5, Cromwell Place, London S.W.7, England

Published in the United States of America in 1969
by Frederick A. Praeger, Inc., Publishers

Library of Congress Catalog Card Number: 68-55001

Printed in the United States of America

PREFACE

This work had its origins in a doctoral thesis completed for the University of Toronto in July, 1966. The Canada Council financed a summer research trip to India in 1967 to revise the thesis manuscript for publication. The anticipated minor revisions turned into radical reconsideration of the entire project, and the final text bears little resemblance to the original thesis.

The role of taxation in the development Plans in India has not been thoroughly examined since the Report of the Taxation Enquiry Commission in 1953-54. A detailed consideration of the entire tax system in the planning context is, of course, a task beyond the scope of one volume, and, in consequence, this work is limited to a consideration of the major tax devices in terms of the three primary objectives of taxation--growth, redistribution, and stabilization. These three objectives are derived from constitutional and planning aims; a wide range of "sub-objectives"--increasing employment opportunities, curtailing monopoly positions, offsetting regional disparities in growth, etc.--are not considered in any detail.

The ordering of the chapters follows roughly that used in the Indian Budget statements, and in no sense implies any sequence of increasing or diminishing priorities.

Although little emphasis is placed on political considerations, the thesis is predicated on the assumption that tax policy will be implemented by an elected, responsible government which must consider the political implications of changes in, or new forms of, taxation. An initial attempt to consider in a separate and detailed chapter the relationship to tax policy of the Indian social and cultural setting served only to indicate that such a study would be a book in itself. Reference to such implications of tax policy is accordingly made very briefly under the consideration of each particular form of taxation. Attention is directed to the particular Indian institutional setting in Chapter 8.

The completion of the thesis in 1966, and whatever merit it had in its original form, reflected in large measure the patient and constructive direction and guidance of my supervisor, Professor N. K. Choudhry of the University of Toronto. I also wish to acknowledge the assistance of Professors Watkins, Campbell, MacGregor and Hare, all of the University of Toronto.

I received a great deal of help and co-operation in India in the summer of 1967, but wish particularly to acknowledge the assistance of Dr. I. G. Patel, the Chief Economic Advisor to the Ministry of Finance; Mr. N. N. Rampal and Mr. Lachman Dev, both of the Ministry of Finance; Mr. K. Bohr of the International Bank for Reconstruction and Development; Mr. Wasiq Ali Khan, the Secretary of the Central Board of Direct Taxes; Mr. O. P. Vaish, Chief of the Taxation Branch of the Federation of Indian Chambers of Commerce and Industry; Mr. Gauri Shankar, Director, Revenue Audit, Office of the Comptroller and Auditor General in New Delhi; Mr. B. A. Tarlton, Economics Division, the Associated Chambers of Commerce and Industry of India; Mr. S. P. Chopra, Director of Research of the Indian Institute of Public Opinion; Mr. N. A. Palkhivala, a Director of Tata Industries and tax authority par excellence; and Mr. B. S. Bhatnagar, also of Tata Industries.

The errors and inadequacies of the work are, of course, entirely the responsibility of the writer.

The opportunity cost of the work was borne by my family.

CONTENTS

	Page

LIST OF TABLES

Taxation and Economic Development in India

1

FEDERAL FINANCE IN INDIA

The Indian Constitution provides for the division of tax powers between the States and the Union.[1] The division closely follows that established by the Government of India Act (1935). Local authorities are considered to fall under the aegis of their respective State governments and thus have no explicit share in the allocation of tax powers. Under the quasi-federal character of the Constitution fairly wide powers are vested in the States, but residual tax powers belong to the Union.

The Union is allocated exclusive jurisdiction over the following taxes: taxes on income other than agricultural income; corporation tax; customs duties; excise duties except on alcoholic liquors or narcotics; estate and succession duties other than on agricultural land; taxes on the capital value of assets, except agricultural land, of individuals and companies; stamp duties on financial documents; terminal taxes on goods and passengers; taxes on railway freights and fares; taxes other than stamp duties on stock exchange and future market transactions; taxes on the sale or purchase of newspapers and on advertisements therein; taxes on the sale or purchase of goods in the course of interstate trade; all taxes not enumerated in the State List or Concurrent List.

The Concurrent List[2] provides that the Union government and the States have concurrent power to determine the principles on which taxes on motor vehicles should be levied and to levy stamp duty on non-judicial documents.

The State List contains the following taxes which are exclusively under the jurisdiction of State governments: land revenue; taxes on agricultural income; succession and estate taxes on agricultural land; taxes on land and buildings; taxes on mineral rights, subject to any limitations imposed by Parliament; taxes on the sale or purchase of goods, except newspapers; excise on alcoholic liquors and narcotics; taxes on the entry of goods into a local area for consumption, use or sale; taxes on the consumption and sale of electricity; taxes on goods or passengers carried by road or inland waterways; taxes

1

on vehicles, animals and boats; tolls; taxes on professions, trades, callings and employments; taxes on luxuries including entertainments, betting and gambling; capitation taxes; stamp duties other than those specified in the Union List; taxes on advertisements not contained in newspapers.

The Finance Commission

The Constitution also provides for the distribution of certain revenues between the Union and the States. In this matter the Constitution departs from the scheme of the Government of India Act (1935) by creating a Finance Commission. This body was to be formed within two years of the commencement of the Constitution and thereafter at the expiration of every fifth year, or earlier if necessary. The major duty of the Commission, detailed in Article 280, is to make recommendations to the President as to:

(a) The distribution between the Union and the States of the net proceeds of taxes which are to be, or may be, divided between them, . . . and the allocation between the States of the respective shares of such proceeds;

(b) The Principles which should govern the grants-in-aid of the revenues of the States out of the Consolidated Fund of India . . . .

To date four Finance Commissions have reported, the first in 1952, the second in 1957, the third in 1961 and the fourth in 1965. In each case the recommendations of the Commission have been accepted with slight modification by the Union government. The recommendations of the Fourth Finance Commission as accepted by the Union are detailed in Table 1. The Finance Commission Reports provide regular reviews of those tax areas where sharing between the Union and States is prescribed by the Constitution.

The provisions in the Constitution regarding the distribution of revenues between the Union and the States fall into several categories:

1. Article 268 enumerates duties which are levied by the Union but are collected and wholly appropriated by the States; there is thus no problem of sharing in this case. Taxes under this head include stamp duties and excise duties on medicinal and toilet preparations.

2. Article 269 enumerates a group of taxes which are to be levied and collected by the Union but which are assigned to the States within which they may be levied in accordance with

TABLE 1

RECOMMENDATIONS OF THE FOURTH FINANCE COMMISSION

States' Shares	Share of Income Tax	Share of Union Excise Duties	Grants-in aid under Article 275 (1) (Substantive portion)	Share of Estate Duty	Grants in lieu of tax on Railway passenger fares	Additional Duties of Excise in lieu of Sales Tax	
	75 per cent	20 per cent		98 per cent		Income to be assured 97.45 per cent	Distribution of balance
1	2	3	4	5	6	7	8
Distribution	Per cent	Per cent	Rs. Million	Per cent	Per cent	Rs. Million	Per cent
Andhra Pradesh	7.37	7.77	135.1	8.34	9.05	2,352.4	7.42
Assam	2.44	3.32	165.2	2.75	2.79	850.8	1.98
Bihar	9.04	10.03	-	10.76	9.99	1,301.6	6.17
Gujarat	5.29	4.80	-	4.78	7.11	3,234.5	7.43
Jammu & Kashmir	0.73	2.26	65.7	0.83	-	-	-
Kerala	3.59	4.16	208.2	3.92	1.85	950.8	5.65
Madhya Pradesh	6.47	7.40	27.0	7.50	9.85	1,551.7	4.62
Madras	8.34	7.18	68.4	7.80	5.81	2,853.4	11.13
Maharashtra	14.28	8.23	-	9.16	8.98	6,377.7	19.87
Mysore	5.14	5.41	208.2	5.46	3.98	1,001.0	5.21
Nagaland	0.07	2.21	70.7	0.09	0.01	-	-
Orissa	3.40	4.82	291.8	4.07	2.12	851.0	2.58
Punjab	4.36	4.86	-	4.70	7.43	1,751.9	5.01
Rajasthan	3.97	5.06	67.3	4.67	6.40	901.0	3.17
Uttar Pradesh	14.60	14.98	98.5	17.08	18.23	5,758.1	7.83
West Bengal	10.91	7.51	-	8.09	6.40	2,804.1	11.93
Total	100.00	100.00	1,406.1	100.00	100.00	32,540.0	100.00

Source: Reserve Bank of India Bulletin (October 1965), Table 1, p. 1557.

such principles of distribution as may be laid down by Parliament. The only tax presently levied which falls under this head is the estate tax. After allocating 2 per cent of estate tax receipts to the Union territories, the remaining 98 per cent is allocated to the States in the manner recommended by the Fourth Finance Commission and accepted by the Union goverment (Table 1, Column 3).

The taxation of railway passenger fares is also listed under Article 269. Such a tax was, in fact, levied by the Union between 1957-58 and 1960-61 and distributed according to the recommendations of the Second Finance Commission Report in 1957 on the basis of route mileage located in each State. Following the abolition of the tax in 1961, the Third Finance Commission recommended the distribution of a total annual grant of Rs. 125 million in lieu of the States' share of the tax to be divided in such a manner as to place the States broadly in the position they occupied before abolition. The grant of Rs. 125 million is currently under review by the Railway Convention Committee. The Fourth Finance Commission recommended that the amount proposed by the Railway Convention Committee be apportioned to each State on the basis of the latest available statistics of railway route length and the average annual earnings from passenger traffic for three years ending in 1964. The percentage share of each State is shown in Table 1, Column 6.

3. (a) Article 270 provides that taxes on personal income other than agricultural income shall be levied and collected by the Union but shall be distributed between the Union and the States in a prescribed manner. The Fourth Finance Commission fixed the share of the States at 75 per cent and determined the percentage shares of individual States (Table 1, Column 2). The percentage distribution to each State is determined on a weighting system; 80 per cent of the allocation is made according to the population of the particular State and 20 per cent according to income tax collections from that State.

(b) Article 270 also specified certain taxes which shall be levied and collected by the Union but may be distributed between the Union and the States. This group of taxes comprises the Union duties of excise. The division of this case, adopted on the recommendation of the Fourth Finance Commission, allocated to the States 20 per cent of all Union excise duties currently levied (excepting regulatory duties, special excises and duties, and cesses earmarked for special purposes) and such additional duties as might be levied in the next five years. The Fourth Finance Commission recommended that the share of each State be determined on a weighting ratio of 80:20 according to first, population, and second, economic and social backwardness as indicated by the per capita gross value of agricultural production, per capita value added by manufacture, percentage of workers to total population, etc.

The States are also allocated 97.45 per cent of the revenue from additional Union excise duties on six articles;[3] this allocation is in lieu of State sales tax previously imposed on these articles. In this case, 1 per cent of the proceeds goes to the Union Territories, 1.5 per cent to Jammu and Kashmir and 0.05 per cent to the State of Nagaland. In addition the States are guaranteed an amount equal to the income derived by them from the sales tax on the six articles in the fiscal year 1956-57 (Table 1, Column 7). As regards the balance of net collections after meeting the guaranteed amount, the Fourth Finance Commission recommended that this balance be distributed on the basis of the proportion which sales tax revenue collections in each State bear to total sales tax revenues in all States over the years 1961-62 - 1963-64.

The above description of sharing arrangements somewhat exaggerates Finance Commission control over revenue from income tax and excise duties. It is always open to the Union to exclude certain tax revenues or increases in tax revenues from the Commission's jurisdiction. For instance, since 1959 income tax collected from corporations has been redefined as corporation tax and thus excluded from the divisible pool of tax revenue; likewise, increases in excise duties imposed in the emergency budget of 1963-64 were classified as Special Duties and reserved exclusively for the Union. A constitutional means of excluding tax revenue from the jurisdiction of the Finance Commission is provided by Article 270, discussed below:

(c) Article 270 specifies that the Union may levy wholly for its own purpose surcharges on taxes which are levied and collected by the Union but are assigned to or shared with the States under Article 269 and 270. The Union presently exercises this constitutional right in the case of the personal income tax.

4. Finally, Article 275 stipulates grants-in-aid of the revenues of the States by the Union. The Fourth Finance Commission recommended that a total of Rs. 1,406.1 million be provided, first, to fill the revenue gap in the budgets of the State governments where such assistance is necessary to meet non-Plan expenditure, second, to meet State requirements for payment of annual interest on loans outstanding and those likely to be raised in the Fourth Plan, and third, to make a contribution to State sinking funds for public loans. The procedure used in determining grants-in-aid under Article 275 is discussed below.

The Role of the Planning Commission
and the Ministry of Finance

The funds allocated to the States by the Finance Commission amount to only one quarter of the total Union allocation. To understand and interpret State tax policies in the light of Union transfers it is therefore clearly essential to examine the additional sources of transferred funds.

Quite separate from the Finance Commission two other bodies exercise jurisdiction over the allocation of funds to the State governments. These are the Planning Commission and the Ministry of Finance. The isolation on the expenditure side of State budgets of items which are classified as Plan expenditure has as its counterpart on the revenue side receipts from the Union which are related to those expenditures. The Planning Commission is the body responsible for determining the amount and nature of these payments to the States. Such payments have taken the form of loans and of direct grants, the latter sanctioned by Article 282 of the Constitution. Finally, States are given grants-in-aid of non-Plan expenditure where it is considered that such expenditures are of significance for the entire country. Thus, expenditure on malaria control and by border States on police/defense services is subject to reimbursement in part or in total by the Union.

The procedure for determining grants by the Ministry of Finance on behalf of sponsoring departments is relatively clear. Such grants represent simply the sum of all those grants which are given to the States in aid of particular State services of national significance. Their total volume is not large.

The statutory grants-in-aid given under Article 275 and the Article 282 grants and loans are both determined in a residual manner. In the first case the Finance Commission estimates the gap between non-Plan expenditure and non-Plan revenue after allowing for tax revenue assigned from the Union. The residual needs of each State must then be met out of statutory grants. Likewise with the Plan budget the Planning Commission estimates the gap which is expected to arise between Plan expenditure and sources of finance for the Plan other than Union grants and loans. In the procedures used by both the Finance and Planning commissions, the need arises to make forecasts of State Plan and non-Plan expenditure over an ensuing five-year period (and, indeed, annually for Planning Commission purposes) and, in addition, to make projections of State tax revenue at existing rates as well as that resulting from increased rates. In making these forecasts, allowance was made, in principle at least, for the encouragement of administrative efficiency and a greater tax effort on the part of the States. The success of this allowance will be examined in Chapter 2, along with the conflict of jurisdiction arising between the Finance and Planning Commission, and the failure to establish rational and consistent criteria for the allocation of funds to the States.

Ties and Conditions on Transfers

Union transfers to the States can take the form either of assistance to their general financial resources or, alternatively, of assistance for the financing of specific expenditure. This distinction can be referred to as untied and tied assistance, respectively. A further distinction may be made between conditional and unconditional assistance.

The funds transferred to the States as their share of taxes collected by the Union are, under the Constitution, completely untied and unconditional. Only the very tenuous sanction exists of the quinquennial review of the State finances by the Finance Commission. In the case of statutory grants under Article 275 there is likewise no tying to specific kinds or items of State expenditure, and such grants have further come to be looked upon as entirely unconditional.

At the other extreme are the grants made to the States by the Union in respect of non-Plan expenditure which is considered to be of a national character. The States have no discretion in the employment of these grants and the grants are, in fact, computed on the basis of increments to total expenditure on the service. Such grants are, therefore, tied and conditional.

Between the two extremes are the grants and loans made by the Union to assist in the financing of Plan expenditure. Until 1957-58 this assistance was given in respect of specific development projects approved under the Plan. Since then, however, the grants and loans have in general been given in respect of broad heads of service (health, education, irrigation, etc.). Within each of these heads, State governments have full discretion to switch funds from one service to another. Though, in principle, such changes require the consent of the Ministry of Finance, it seems apparent that this consent is virtually automatic. There are a few exceptions to this position. The Union government has retained the right to supervise the use of funds allocated to specific projects such as the education of girls and projects in which the World Bank is involved. Further, the Union has, since 1960, denied State governments the right to transfer, even with Ministry of Finance consent, funds allocated to river valley projects; in 1963 this proscription was extended to cover agriculture and the cooperative sector. With these few exceptions the Union contribution to State Plan financing is untied. Likewise, it is not subject to the

fulfillment of a series of conditions by the States, but is
subject to the over-all condition that the level of Plan expenditure agreed annually and quinquennially for each State be, in
fact, achieved. There is thus a certain amount of financial
discipline imposed on the States at the annual round of negoti-
ations between individual States and the Planning Commission;
though here again it appears the degree of control is very general and permits considerable flexibility on the part of the
States.

Quantity and Pattern of Union Transfers to the States

A complete picture of Union resources transferred to the
States over the planning period to date is provided in Table 2.
Union transfers represented 40 per cent of total State expenditure in the First Five Year Plan period, rose sharply to 48 per
cent in the Second Five Year Plan period, and increased slightly to over 49 per cent in the Third Five Year Plan. The figure
for 1966-67 is comparable to the Third Plan average, suggesting
that State dependence on Union transfers has leveled off after
the very sharp increase between the First and Second Plans.
The very low budgeted figure for 1967-68 may be discounted,
since it reflects a cut in Union loans in a budget geared essentially to short-run stabilization objectives. The share of
transfers within the jurisdiction of the Finance Commission remained at one third of the total over the First and Second
Plans, but declined to just over one quarter of the total in
the Third Plan.

Tax Jurisdiction at the Local Government Level

Although no taxes are constitutionally reserved for local
authorities, the States may assign any of the taxes on the
State List, either in whole or in part, to local bodies. Such
delegation enables State governments to exercise a degree of
supervision and control over the affairs of local bodies. The
taxes traditionally assigned are property taxes, octroi[4] and
terminal taxes, taxes on professions, taxes on vehicles and
animals, and, more recently, entertainment duties.

TAX REVENUE OF THE UNION AND STATE GOVERNMENTS, 1950-51 - 1967-68

General Survey of Revenue Sources

The division of Union tax revenue into constituent items
over the planning period is presented in Table 3. Revenue
accruing to the States over the same period is presented in
Table 4.

The tax revenues of the Union government are mainly derived from three heads: taxes on personal and corporate income, customs, and Union excise duties. In 1950-51, the year before the beginning of the First Plan, net receipts from these three heads accounted for 35.01 per cent, 44.0 per cent, and 18.92 per cent, respectively, of Union tax revenue.[5] Corresponding forecast proportions in the last 1967-68 budget are 23.5 per cent, 29.7 per cent, and 44.5 per cent. Comparing the First and Third plans, taxes on income provided 29.7 per cent of Union tax revenue over the First Plan as a whole, and 27.9 per cent over the Third Plan. Corresponding figures for customs revenue were 43.6 per cent and 25.9 per cent, and for Union excise duties, 22.9 per cent and 43.6 per cent.

Taxes on income have formed a relatively stable proportion of Union tax revenue over the planning period to date, in spite of the increasing States' share in personal tax. It is apparent, however, that the maintenance of this proportion is in large measure the result of the rapid increase in revenue from corporation income tax. Revenue from this latter source has moved from 32.2 per cent of net Union revenue from income tax in 1950-51 to 68.8 per cent in 1967-68; viewed as a proportion of gross income tax revenue--before deduction of the States' share--corporation tax revenue has moved from 23.3 per cent to 54.6 per cent over the same period. The greatest relative decline has taken place in revenue from customs, from 44 per cent of Union tax revenue in 1950-51 to 29.7 per cent in 1967-68. The slight improvement in the relative significance of customs revenue in the forecast for 1967-68 as against the average Third Plan figure--25.9 per cent--reflects the rationalization of the import schedule in the 1965-66 budget and the reimposition of export duties after devaluation. Export duties which constituted 44 per cent of customs revenue in 1950-51 were of negligible revenue significance by 1965-66. These duties were levied in the post-war inflationary period both as revenue duties in monopoly exports of commodities in short domestic supply, and as flexible anti-inflationary tax devices in a period of large export profits.[6] The critical shortage of foreign exchange resulted in emphasis on the promotion of exports and the abolition of virtually all export levies. Following devaluation, export duties were levied on a wide range of goods in order to mop up the adventitious gain accruing to exporters by way of higher rupee realizations on sales abroad. Export duties are expected to realize Rs. 1,400 million in 1967-68, or 20.9 per cent of total revenue from customs duties.

Import duties remain an important source of revenue to the Union government, the more so because customs revenue is not shared with the States. Revenue from import duties has increased fivefold in absolute terms since 1950-51. Since 1945, however, the diminishing relative significance of dutiable

TABLE 2

RESOURCES TRANSFERRED FROM THE UNION TO THE STATES

FORM OF TRANSFER	First Five Year Plan (Actuals)	Second Five Year Plan (Actuals)
I Share of Divisible Taxes and Duties	3,260	7,120
II Grands A. Statutory Grants (within purview of the Finance Commission)	1,030	3,070
B. Other Grants (within purview of the Planning Commission and Ministry of Finance)	1,800	5,390
C. Total Grants	2,830	7,460
III Loans	7,990	14,110
IV Grand Total	14,130	28,690
V Grand Total as a Percentage of Total State Expenditure	40.6[a]	48.3[a]

Note: [a]average of five years.

	THIRD FIVE YEAR PLAN					FOURTH FIVE YEAR PLAN	
1961-62 (Actuals)	1962-63 (Actuals)	1963-64 (Actuals)	1964-65 (Actuals)	1965-66 (Actuals)	Total	1966-67 (Actuals)	1967-68
1,790	2,240	2,590	2,579	2,760	11,959	3,725	3,701
430	680	690	758	747	3,305	1,524	1,488
1,740	1,540	1,620	2,058	2,724	9,682	2,614	2,908
2,170	2,220	2,310	2,816	3,471	12,987	4,138	4,396
4,520	5,240	6,240	6,801	8,214	31,015	9,162	7,288
8,480	9,700	11,140	12,196	14,445	55,961	17,025	15,385
52.0	52.5	50.7	46.6	44.9	49.3a	49.6	40.6

Source: Government of India, Explanatory Memorandum on the Budget of
the Central Government for 1967-68 (New Delhi: Ministry of
Finance, 1967), pp. 107-10.

TABLE 3

TOTAL TAX REVENUE (NET AND GROSS): GOVERNMENT
OF INDIA, 1950-51 - 1967-68

	1950-51 (Actuals)	1955-56 (Actuals)	TOTAL FIRST PLAN PERIOD	1956-57 (Actuals)	1960-61 (Actuals)	TOTAL SECOND PLAN PERIOD
I. TAXES ON INCOME AND EXPENDITURE						
(1+2+3)	1,257.0	1,132.3	5,869.5	1,441.7	1,919.7	8,106.0
Taxes on income other than corporation tax	1,327.3	1,313.5	6,640.7	1,517.4	1,673.8	8,036.8
LESS States' Share	475.2	551.6	2,782.4	587.5	873.7	3,746.7
1. Net Receipts	852.1	761.9	3,858.3	929.9	800.1	4,290.1
2. Corporation Tax	404.9	370.4	2,011.2	511.8	1,110.5	3,792.5
3. Expenditure Tax					9.1	23.4
II. TAXES ON PROPERTY AND CAPITAL TRANSACTIONS						
(1+2+3+4+5)	38.1	25.5	136.9	24.1	134.9	584.4
Estate Duty		18.1	26.2	21.1	30.9	131.2
LESS States' Share		18.6	24.3	24.1	29.1	128.6
1. Net Receipts		-0.5	1.9	-3.0	1.8	2.6
2. Tax on Wealth					81.5	369.7
3. Gift Tax					8.9	26.8
4. Stamps and Registration	18.1	17.2	81.0	21.7	36.8	159.2
5. Land Revenue	20.0	8.8	54.0	5.4	5.9	26.1
III. TAXES ON COMMODITIES AND SERVICES						
(1+2+3+4)	2,274.9	2,956.9	13,729.3	3,471.8	5,246.8	21,256.9
Customs						
Imports	1,077.0	1,279.8	6,483.0	1,405.2	1,546.1	6,984.2
Exports	473.6	377.6	2,643.7	286.7	131.2	1,043.5
Other Revenue	63.7	42.2	218.8	73.1	82.1	377.7
LESS Refunds	42.8	32.6	188.4	32.7	59.1	228.9
1. Net Receipts	1,571.5	1,667.0	9,157.1	1,732.3	1,700.3	8,176.5
Union Excise Duties	675.4	1,452.5	5,172.6	1,904.3	4,163.5	15,539.9
(of which additional excise duties)					336.0	806.5
LESS States' Share		165.7	640.6	182.2	751.0	2,812.3
2. Net Receipts	675.4	1,286.8	4,532.0	1,722.1	3,412.5	12,727.6
Tax on Railway Passengers' Fares					158.9	446.2
LESS States' Share					137.9	421.6
3. Net Receipts					21.0	24.6
4. Other Taxes and Duties	28.0	3.1	40.2	17.4	113.0	328.2
IV. TOTAL NET TAX REVENUE						
(I+II+III)	3,570.0	4,114.7	19,735.7	4,937.6	7,301.4	29,947.3
V. TOTAL GROSS TAX REVENUE						
(including States' Share)	4,045.2	4,850.6	23,183.0	5,731.4	9,093.1	37,056.5

Notes: a includes Stamps and Registration revenue, and Land Revenue, shown
separately for previous years.
b includes projected effect of budget proposals.

12

1961-62 (Actuals)	1962-63 (Actuals)	1963-64 (Actuals)	1964-65 (Actuals)	1965-66 (Actuals)	TOTAL THIRD PLAN PERIOD	1966-67 (Revised)	1967-68 (Budget)
2,288.4	3,123.9	4,140.2	4,572.7	4,537.2	18,662.4	4,880.1	5,085.1
1,653.9	1,859.6	2,586.0	2,665.5	2,718.0	11,483.0	2,800.0	2,900.0
938.5	952.7	1,192.9	1,237.7	1,233.4	5,555.2	1,371.0	1,315.8
715.4	906.9	1,393.1	1,427.8	1,484.6	5,927.8	1,429.0	1,584.2
1,564.6	2,215.0	2,745.9	3,140.5	3,048.4	12,714.4	3,450.0	3,500.0
8.4	2.0	1.2	4.4	4.2	22.2	1.1	0.9
142.1	161.5	170.2	164.9				
42.1	39.4	46.7	54.3	66.6	249.1	67.5	72.5
38.8	38.8	42.2	67.8	67.9	255.5	45.4	69.4
3.3	0.6	4.5	-13.5	-1.3	-6.4	22.1	3.1
82.6	95.4	102.0	105.0	120.6	505.6	122.5	125.0
10.1	9.7	11.2	22.2	22.6	75.8	18.5	15.0
40.5	50.0	49.4	49.7				
5.6	5.8	3.1	1.5				
6,323.2	7,324.4	9,432.9	10,890.4				
1,982.2	2,384.2	3,342.5	4,046.4	5,476.9	17,232.2	4,900.0	5,280.0
126.9	96.0	33.7	24.3	21.4	302.3	1,200.0	1,400.0
78.2	75.0	80.1	42.2	49.0	324.5	35.0	40.0
64.8	95.6	108.9	137.9	157.7	564.9	175.0	180.0
2,122.5	2,459.6	3,347.4	3,975.0	5,389.7	17,294.2	5,960.0	6,430.8
4,893.1	5,988.3	7,295.8	8,015.1	8,979.2	35,171.5	10,302.1	12,140.4
389.6	447.5	431.1	444.9	457.5	2,170.6	465.1	357.7
806.5	1,249.1	1,359.9	1,273.4	1,459.2	6,148.1	2,309.1	2,511.0
4,086.6	4,739.2	5,935.9	6,741.7	7,572.0	29,075.4	7,993.0	9,629.4
114.1	125.6	149.6	173.7	257.4[a]	820.4	289.9[a]	320.0[a]
8,753.7	10,609.8	13,743.3	15,628.0	17,846.2	66,581.0	19,286.1	21,608.4[b]
10,415.0	12,848.4	16,130.0	17,980.0	20,606.7	77,981.1	23,011.6	25,504.6[b]

Sources: Reserve Bank of India, Report on Currency and Finance, 1965-66 (Bombay: Reserve Bank of India, 1967), Statements 80-81; Government of India, Explanatory Memorandum on the Budget of the Central Government for 1967-68 (New Delhi: Ministry of Finance, 1967), pp. 12-13 and Supplement, p. 1.

TABLE 4

TOTAL TAX REVENUE OF STATE GOVERNMENTS,
1951-52 - 1967-68

	1951-52 (Accounts)	1955-56 (Accounts)	TOTAL FIRST PLAN PERIOD	1956-57 (Accounts)	1960-61 (Accounts)	TOTAL SECOND PLAN PERIOD
I. TAXES ON INCOME	570.5	630.8	3,029.0	659.0	1,004.7	4,212.0
Share of income tax	526.5	552.8	2,779.0	579.0	905.8	3,772.0
Agricultural income tax	43.3	76.7	246.0	79.0	94.9	425.0
Profession tax	0.7	1.3	4.0	1.0	4.0	15.0
II. TAXES ON PROPERTY AND CAPITAL TRANSACTIONS	754.0	1,110.4	4,740.0	1,190.0	1,444.1	6,619.0
Estate Duty		18.6	24.0	24.0	28.9	128.0
Land Revenue	479.9	780.1	3,267.0	832.0	971.9	4,550.0
Stamps and Registration.	255.6	290.8	1,354.0	313.0	433.3	1,839.0
Urban Immovable Property Tax	18.5	21.0	95.0	21.0	10.0	101.0
III. TAXES ON COMMODI- TIES AND SERVICES	1,486.0	1,820.1	8,327.0	2,108.0	3,799.0	15,239.0
Union Excise	7.0	165.7	646.0	179.0	751.1	2,809.0
State Excise	494.1	450.9	2,300.0	464.0	531.1	2,420.0
General Sales Tax	544.0	800.6	3,104.0	966.0	1,424.4	5,824.0
Sales Tax on Motor Spirit	45.3	15.4	266.0	10.0	163.0	518.0
Motor Vehicle Taxes	100.9	158.8	651.0	186.0	341.0	1,247.0
Tax on Railway Fares[a]					137.9	426.0
Entertainment Tax	63.9	73.4	319.0	86.0	131.1	523.0
Electricity Duties	33.9	58.2	226.0	69.0	125.1	489.0
Other Taxes & Duties[b]	196.7	97.1	815.0	150.0	194.3	982.0
IV. TOTAL (I+II+III) TAX REVENUE	2,810.5	3,561.4	16,096.0	3,957.0	6,247.8	26,070.0
V. TOTAL STATE TAX COLLECTIONS (Tax Revenue minus share of taxes from union)	2,277.0	2,834.3	12,647.0	3,175.0	4,562.0	19,361.0

Notes: [a]receipts in lieu of this head from 1961-62 are included under grants-in-aid; the Union tax on railway fares was abolished in 1960-61.
[b]includes sugar-cane cess, purchase tax on sugar, tax on passengers and goods, tobacco duties, tax on prize competition and betting, inter-state transit duties, etc.
[c]before tax changes proposed in the 1967-68 budget.

1961-62 (Accounts)	1962-63 (Accounts)	1963-64 (Accounts)	1964-65 (Accounts)	1965-66 (Accounts)	TOTAL THIRD PLAN PERIOD	1966-67 (Revised)	1967-68 (Budget)
1,042.6	1,057.7	1,284.2	1,352.6	1,338.9	6,077.0	1,491.1	1,462.3
943.7	952.4	1,181.0	1,235.9	1,231.7	5,546.0	1,369.5	1,332.0
94.4	95.7	92.6	107.3	98.8	489.0	106.0	109.7
4.5	9.4	10.6	9.4	8.4	42.0	15.6	20.6
1,487.5	1,791.2	1,911.3	1,978.5	1,967.1	9,135.0	1,759.5	1,937.7
38.9	38.9	42.2	67.6	67.8	256.0	45.3	69.5
952.3	1,200.7	1,234.2	1,197.9	1,119.3	5,703.0	879.3	986.9
465.7	522.1	614.1	685.5	741.1	3,027.0	802.5	836.3
30.6	29.7	20.8	27.5	38.9	149.0	32.4	45.0
4,095.8	5,090.6	6,195.1	6,893.1	7,871.5	30,147.0	9,666.0	10,749.4
806.5	1,249.2	1,360.4	1,272.4	1,458.0	6,146.0	2,258.8	2,430.5
585.8	628.1	728.9	845.4	963.7	3,753.0	1,053.4	1,148.7
1,631.4	1,875.2	2,454.1	2,950.9	3,385.7	12,297.0	3,931.2	4,506.5
183.0	213.5	229.0	233.3	292.2	1,151.0	409.4	437.2
379.3	462.9	574.0	593.3	642.2	2,651.0	709.7	765.4
151.0	182.1	225.6	251.1	294.4	1,104.0	342.6	364.3
148.9	194.8	272.9	334.3	353.6	1,305.0	439.0	479.4
209.9	284.8	350.2	412.4	481.7	1,740.0	521.8	617.4
6,625.8	7,939.5	9,390.6	10,224.2	11,177.5	45,359.0	12,916.6	14,132.6[c]
4,836.7	5,699.0	6,807.0	7,648.3	8,420.0	33.411.0	9,243.0	10,300.6[c]

Sources: Reserve Bank of India, Report on Currency and Finance, 1965-66
(Bombay: Reserve Bank of India, 1967), Statement 80; "Finances of
State Governments, 1967-68," Reserve Bank of India Bulletin (August 1967),
Statements 2 and 5.

articles in import composition and the policy of protectionism
and import control have slowed the growth of revenue from import duties. Increases in the rates on luxury items since 1945
have failed to compensate for reductions in duties on commodities essential to industrialization, viz., capital goods, machinery and industrial raw materials. Equally, the scope for
increases in the rates on consumer goods has been limited by
obligations under the General Agreement on Tariffs and Trade
(GATT). Changes in the composition of imports have also had
significant effects on tax yield. The increasing relative significance of imports of food grains--which are free of duty--
and industrial requirements--on which rates are moderate--has
acted to diminish revenue from import duties as a percentage of
import value.[7] The sharp increase in revenue from import duties in 1965-66 reflects largely the rationalization of the import tariff in that year.

        The major reason for the declining relative significance
of revenue from customs in Union revenue is to be found in the
massive expansion of revenue from Union excise duties rather
than in the assortment of factors inhibiting the growth of
revenue from import duties. Net revenue from this source constitutes 44.5 per cent of total Union tax revenue forecast in
the 1967-68 budget, and has increased fourteenfold since 1950-
51. Gross receipts under this head, before the deduction of
States' share, have increased eighteenfold. Of the total revenue forecast of Rs. 1,115.8 million in the 1967-68 budget, basic
duties make up 90.3 per cent, special duties 5.1 per cent, and
additional duties 4.5 per cent. Just over one third of total
revenue forecast (33.5 per cent) comes from duties on petroleum
products, 24.3 per cent from manufactured goods, 11.5 per cent
from tobacco, 11.1 per cent from food and beverages, 8.6 per
cent from metals, and the balance from machinery and transpor-
tation equipment (4.1 per cent), chemicals (3.7 per cent),
cesses on a variety of commodities (2.2 per cent), and vegetable oil and fats (0.74 per cent).

        The vast expansion of revenue from excise duties is ac-
counted for by the extension of coverage to a wide range of
commodities, increased consumption and substantial rate increases. The Report of the Central Excise Reorganisation Committee (hereinafter CERC), indicates that over the period 1953-
54 to 1961-62, the most important factor was rate increases,
accounting for 57.8 per cent of the over-all increases in excise revenue of Rs. 3,310 million. Increased consumption accounted for 19.7 per cent and additional coverage for 21.3 per
cent.[8] For the period prior to 1953-54, the Taxation Enquiry
Commission (TEC) noted that extended coverage and increased
consumption had been most important, the role of rate increases
to that point having been relatively insignificant.[9]

The States' share of Union income tax has increased from Rs. 526.5 million in 1951-52 to a forecast Rs. 1,332.0 million in 1967-68, but the relative significance of this source as a percentage of total States' revenue has dropped from 18.7 per cent to 9.4 per cent. This decline in relative significance has occurred despite the trend towards increasing allocation of income tax revenue--from 50 per cent in 1951 to 66.66 per cent in 1961 and 75 per cent in 1965--and reflects, first, the relatively slow growth of personal income tax revenue to the Union, and second, the more rapid growth of alternative sources of States' revenue, in particular the general sales tax.

The contribution of Union excise revenue to States' revenue began on the recommendation of the First Finance Commission in April 1952 and has grown rapidly; this source provides 17.1 per cent of estimated total States' revenue in 1967-68. This is accounted for by the great expansion of Union excise duties and by the trend towards increasing States' share in their revenues.

Land revenue has declined over the planning period as a proportion of total States' revenue from 17.1 per cent in 1951-52 to a forecast 6.9 per cent in 1967-68. The relative decline of land revenue is even more apparent if the 1938-39 percentage (45 per cent of total revenue of the then nine Provinces[10]) is also considered. Such a mode of taxation tends to be relatively unresponsive to income changes because of the long intervals between assessment revisions dependent on cadastral surveys, and various restrictions on upward revisions of assessment. In India since 1947, despite constitutional re-organization and rising agricultural prices, there has been no program of re-assessment and the increases in land revenue which have occured are in large measure a reflection of the abolition of the Zamindari system and the collection by the State governments of rents previously due to Zamindars.[11]

Revenue from stamp duties has also diminished in relative significance as a proportion of States' revenue from 9.1 per cent in 1951-52 to a forecast 5.9 per cent in 1963-64; for a given rate schedule revenue from this source will generally be relatively unresponsive to income changes, particularly as many duties are nominal and levied on a specific rather than ad valorem basis, and the decline in relative significance would appear likely to continue unless radical rate revisions and general ad valorem assessment are introduced.

In 1951-52 the State excise on alcoholic liquors and narcotics was the second largest contributor to total State revenue, constituting 17.57 per cent as against 19.35 per cent for the general sales tax. In the 1967-68 budget forecast the relative significance of the State excise has fallen to 8.1 per cent. The explanation of this decline, which would initially appear surprising in view of the expansion of other excise taxes, lies in the policy of prohibition. The States are enjoined under the Constitution to implement prohibition (Article 47) and the Prohibition Enquiry Committee (hereinafter PEC) recommended in 1956 the formulation of a program integrated in the Plans to bring about nation-wide prohibition speedily and effectively.[12] Progress under this injunction has been substantial.[13] Economic commentary on prohibition has been, however, almost universally hostile,[14] stressing the loss of revenue and the costs of enforcement, and, in the face of critical revenue shortage, emphasis on prohibition, and hence the consequent decline in revenue, could be reversed. Indeed, by the summer of 1967, it appeared that the momentum of the movement to prohibition had been arrested and even reversed, and it seems likely that the States, with the possible exception of a few intransigents such as Madras, can anticipate increasing revenue under the liquor excise.

The role of the miscellaneous commercial taxes[15] has been of increasing importance in States' revenue since 1951-52, rising from 35.03 per cent of total States' revenue in that year to a forecast 50.7 per cent in 1967-68. Of these taxes the most important is the general sales tax which is forecast in 1967-68 to provide 62.8 per cent of State revenue from commercial taxes, and 31.8 per cent of total State revenue, as against 55.24 per cent and 19.35 per cent, respectively, in 1951-52. The form of sales tax used varies considerably from single-point taxes at the retail level in some States to multi-point "turnover" taxes in others. In general, however, this broadly based source of State revenue, in whatever form employed, has become the single most important source of revenue and appears likely to retain this position in the foreseeable future.

Of the other commercial taxes those of greatest revenue potential are those taxes on commodities or services for which the income elasticity of demand is high. In this group, electricity duties and taxes on motor vehicles and motor spirit would seem likely to become increasingly productive revenue sources. Combined revenue under these three heads has moved from 6.4 per cent of total State revenue in 1951-52 to a forecast 11.8 per cent in 1967-68.

Data on tax revenue accruing to local authorities are not readily accessible and the compilation of the TEC represents the latest available comprehensive review of local finance.[16] In 1951-52 the property tax ("tax on land and buildings") delegated to local authorities by the States constituted almost half the total local rax revenue of Rs. 487.3 million. Octroi and terminal taxes constituted 18 per cent of local tax revenue

and remaining revenue accrued from the local fund cess (surcharge on land revenue); the profession tax; taxes on vehicles
(other than motor vehicles), animals and boats; theatre taxes
(other than State entertainment taxes); tolls and taxes on advertisements (other than in newspapers). In several States the
proceeds of State entertainment duty have been allocated to
local bodies. The growth of revenue from this source, for
which data are available (Table 4), has been substantial, representing a sixfold increase in absolute terms between 1951-52
and 1967-68. The profession tax (Table 4) has, on the contrary, proved to be of almost negligible significance. Local tax
revenue increased by two and a half times between 1938-39 and
1951-52 but this increase is considered largely to reflect the
wider coverage of the later figures and price increases.[17]
Under present tax power delegation procedures the relative
significance of local tax revenue as a percentage of total
national revenue (7.5 per cent in 1951-52) appears likely to
continue to decline.

The recent sample study by Tripathy emphasizes the continued predominance of the property tax in local tax revenue,
and advocates reform via the introduction of progression into
the property tax rate structure on annual value and the use of
local sales taxes.[18]

The Direct:Indirect Tax Ratio

Taxes listed in Tables 3 and 4 under the headings of
"taxes on income and wealth" and "taxes on property and capital
transactions" will be regarded as direct; "taxes on commodities
and services" will be regarded as indirect; this classification
adopts the simple "basis of assessment" criterion, whereby
taxes levied on the receipt of income are termed direct and
taxes levied on expenditure are termed indirect.[19] The Indian
"expenditure tax" which is best seen as a surcharge on income
tax, will be considered under direct taxation.

Table 5 indicates the direct:indirect tax ratio for the
combined revenues of the Union and the States from 1951-52 to
1967-68. The ratio has been diminishing; i.e., indirect tax
revenue has grown more rapidly than direct tax revenue and is
forecast to provide 75.9 per cent of combined revenue in 1967-
68. Table 6 provides comparable ratios for 1962-63 for sixteen
selected countries. The Indian figure is comparable to that of
other countries classified as underdeveloped, and the direct:
indirect tax ratio is, in general, directly correlated with per
capita income.

In the light of the positive correlation of the direct:
indirect tax ratio and rising income the diminishing significance of direct taxation in India would seem to run contrary

to the general rule. The 1952-53 figure of 41 per cent reflects, however, the very high levels of direct taxation during
World War II in India including an excess profits tax and rigorous rates of income taxation. In 1944-45 direct taxation
formed some 45 per cent of total tax revenue of the Union and
the (then) Part A States. The abolition or moderation of
direct tax measures contributed to the declining direct:in-
direct ratio in the 1940's and early 1950's. However, the
major factor providing for the diminishing ratio is certainly
the expansion of Union excise duties and the States' general
sales tax. Excepting the possibility of radical revision of
the direct tax structure, there would appear to be no reason to
expect the present trend toward diminishing revenue significance of direct taxation to be halted or reversed.

Table 7 compares the direct:indirect tax ratio for the
Union and the States in selected years. The ratio diminishes
in both cases, reflecting the relative stagnation of income tax
at the Union level and land revenue at the State level, and the
corresponding expansion of Union excises and the States' sales
tax.

Tax "Burden" or "Sacrifice" in India

The simplest measure of tax "burden" or "sacrifice" in a
national sense is that of the ratio of tax revenue to national
income. Table 8 presents this information for twenty selected
countries between 1950 and 1964. The tax:income ratio, expressed as a percentage, has almost doubled for India over this
period. In this limited sense then, the national tax burden
may be assumed to have doubled. The concept of burden or
sacrifice is, however, most meaningful in a relative sense, and
India emerges very poorly from the comparison. India, indeed,
ranks eighteenth out of twenty. Does it therefore follow, in
some sense, that India is making a lesser tax sacrifice than
almost all the other countries selected?[20]

Tax sacrifice may best be considered as a measure of the
relative importance to the citizens of the resources given up
to government in countries at different levels of income, and
must relate taxes to some index of "ability-to-pay." A
meaningful index of tax sacrifice must, therefore, incorporate
per capita income as well as national income.

Several indices incorporating per capita income have been
proposed.[21] The index proposed by Richard Bird takes taxes as
a percentage of disposable income, all as a percentage of per
capita domestic product.[22] This index was calculated for the
twenty countries dealt with in Table 8, and the results set out
in Table 9. The change in ranking is significant. India,
previously eighteenth, moves to a more respectable ninth equal

TABLE 5

DIRECT TAXES AS A PROPORTION OF TOTAL CENTER AND STATE
REVENUE,[a] 1951-52 - 1967-68

YEAR	Direct Taxes as a Proportion of Total Revenue (Per cent)
1951-52	41.0
Total First Plan Period	38.4
Total Second Plan Period	34.8
1961-62	32.3
1962-63	33.0
1963-64	32.4
1964-65	31.2
1965-66	27.5
Total Third Plan Period	30.7
1966-67 (revised)	25.7
1967-68 (budget)	24.1

Note: [a]Direct taxes are defined as taxes on income, expendi-
        ture, property and capital transactions.
        Indirect taxes are defined as taxes on commodities and
        services.

Sources: Government of India, Explanatory Memorandum on the
          Budget of the Central Government for 1967-68 (New
          Delhi: Ministry of Finance, 1967); "Finances of
          State Governments 1967-68," Reserve Bank of India
          Bulletin (August 1967).

21

TABLE 6

DIRECT TAX REVENUE AS A PROPORTION OF TOTAL REVENUE IN TWENTY OTHER COUNTRIES IN 1964

COUNTRY	Direct Tax Revenue as a Proportion of Total Revenue (Per cent)
Australia	59.5
Austria	38.5
Belgium	38.6
Burma	52.1
Canada	58.3
Ceylon	23.8
Denmark	40.0
France	28.6
Germany, West	51.3
Greece	18.1
Ireland	36.4
Italy	25.6
Japan	57.4
Netherlands	59.8
Norway	26.2
Pakistan	27.8
Philippines	23.6
Sweden	45.8
U.K.	57.7
U.S.A.	67.4

Note: The categories of direct and indirect taxation are identical to those used in the Indian case. Where the particular country has a federal political structure,
total revenue is taken as the combined revenue of the
various tax jurisdictions in that country.

Source: Percentages based on revenue statistics in United
Nations, Statistical Yearbook 1965 (New York: 1966).

TABLE 7

DIRECT TAX REVENUE AS A PERCENTAGE OF TOTAL REVENUE OF
(a) THE UNION GOVERNMENT AND (b) THE STATE GOVERNMENTS
(SELECTED YEARS)

YEAR	Direct Taxes as Per cent of Union Revenue	Direct Taxes as Per cent of State Revenue
1951-52	36.3	47.1
Total First Plan Period	30.4	48.3
Total Second Plan Period	29.0	41.5
1963-64	31.1	34.0
Total Third Plan Period	28.9	33.5
1966-67 (Revised)	26.1	25.1
1967-68 (Budget)	24.1	24.0

Sources: Government of India, Explanatory Memorandum on the Budget of the Central Government for 1967-68 (New Delhi: Ministry of Finance, 1967); "Finances of State Governments 1967-68," Reserve Bank of India Bulletin (August 1967).

23

TABLE 8

TAX REVENUE AS PER CENT OF NATIONAL INCOME:
TWENTY SELECTED COUNTRIES, 1950-64

COUNTRY	1950			1963			1964			Ranking (1964 figures)
	Direct Tax	Indirect Tax	Total	Direct Tax	Indirect Tax	Total	Direct Tax	Indirect Tax	Total	
Australia	10.0	6.6	16.6	12.8	7.3	20.1	12.5	8.5	21.0	12
Austria	8.2	8.5	16.7	15.5	16.2	31.7	12.4	19.8	32.2	1
Belgium	8.6	12.2	20.8	9.5	14.8	24.3	9.4	14.9	24.3	6
Burma	1.8	6.2	8.0	5.1	9.8	14.9	10.8	9.9	20.7	13
Canada	9.0	7.0	16.0	10.9	7.3	18.2	10.5	7.5	18.0	15
Ceylon	3.5	10.8	14.3	5.1	9.8	14.9	5.1	16.3	21.4	11
Denmark	6.7	8.9	15.6	9.2	13.0	22.2	9.0	13.5	22.5	9[a]
France	7.9	16.5	24.4	7.2	18.5	25.7	7.7	19.2	26.9	5
Germany, West	10.4	11.3	21.7	14.0	14.2	28.2	15.0	14.2	29.2	2
Greece	2.9	9.6	12.5	2.9	13.2	16.1	3.0	13.5	16.5	16
INDIA	2.4	4.2	6.6	4.0	9.5	13.5	3.8	8.8	12.6	18
Ireland	6.9	12.4	19.3	8.4	14.2	22.6	8.1	14.1	22.2	10
Italy	3.0	9.3	12.3	5.5	14.3	19.8	5.9	17.1	23.0	8
Japan	9.4	7.4	16.8	7.7	5.7	13.4	7.7	5.7	13.4	17
Netherlands	14.5	13.6	28.1	16.4	10.9	27.3	16.7	11.2	27.9	3
Norway	7.6	11.8	19.4	6.2	16.7	22.9	5.9	16.6	22.5	9[a]
Philippines	1.0	4.3	5.3	2.6	8.4	11.0	2.6	8.4	11.0	19
Sweden	9.9	7.8	17.7	12.5	13.0	25.5	11.0	13.0	24.0	7
U.K.	17.9	14.1	32.0	16.5	11.2	27.7	15.7	11.5	27.2	4
U.S.A.	13.2	3.4	16.6	19.1	6.1	25.2	13.9	6.7	20.6	14

Note: [a] equal ranking.

Source: United Nations, Statistical Yearbook 1965 (New York: 1966).

TABLE 9

TAX BURDEN IN TERMS OF PER CAPITA INCOME, 1964

COUNTRY	Index	Ranking
Australia	3.0	11[a]
Austria	5.9	5
Belgium	2.5	13
Burma	8.4	1
Canada	2.0	14
Ceylon	4.2	9[a]
Denmark	2.7	12
France	4.8	7[a]
Germany, West	4.8	7[a]
Greece	7.9	2
INDIA	4.2	9[a]
Ireland	4.9	6[a]
Italy	6.5	3
Japan	6.0	4
Netherlands	4.9	6[a]
Norway	4.3	8
Philippines	2.1	14
Sweden	3.4	10
U.K.	3.0	11[a]
U.S.A.	1.4	15

Note: [a]equal ranking.

Source: United Nations, Statistical Yearbook 1965 (New York: 1966).

TABLE 10

AVERAGE AND MARGINAL RATES OF TAXATION OVER
THE PLANNING PERIOD

1	2	3	4	5	6
YEAR	National Income at Current Prices Rs.Million	Total Union and State Tax Revenue Rs.Million	Gross Union Tax Collections Rs.Million	State Tax Collections Rs.Million	Average Tax Rate on (3) Per cent
1951-52	99,700	7,387	5,050	2,337	7.4
1952-53	98,200	6,778	4,420	2,358	6.9
1953-54	104,800	6,725	4,200	2,525	6.4
1954-55	96,100	7,204	4,560	2,644	7.5
1955-56	99,800	7,676	4,850	2,826	7.7
1956-57	113,100	8,904	5,730	3,174	7.9
1957-58	113,900	10,450	6,960	3,490	9.2
1958-59	126,000	10,893	7,150	3,743	8.6
1959-60	129,500	12,164	7,840	4,324	9.4
1960-61	141,400	13,504	8,770	4,734	9.6
1961-62	148,000	15,430	10,370	5,060	10.4
1962-63	154,000	18,651	12,670	5,981	12.1
1963-64	172,100	23,246	16,130	7,116	13.5
1964-65	200,100[a]	25,988	17,980	8,008	13.0

Note: [a]provisional figure.

7	8	9	10	11
Marginal Tax Rate on (3)	Average Tax Rate on (4)	Marginal Tax Rate on (4)	Average Tax Rate on (5)	Marginal Tax Rate on (5)
Per cent	Per cent	Per cent	Per cent	Per cent
	5.06		2.34	
--		--		--
	4.50		2.40	
-0.80		-3.33		2.5
	4.00		2.40	
--		--		--
	4.74		2.76	
12.75		7.83		4.92
	4.85		2.85	
9.23		6.61		2.62
	5.06		2.84	
193.25		153.75		39.50
	6.11		3.09	
3.66		1.57		2.09
	5.67		2.93	
36.31		19.71		16.60
	6.05		3.35	
11.26		7.81		4.45
	6.20		3.40	
29.18		24.24		4.94
	7.00		3.40	
53.68		38.33		15.35
	8.22		3.88	
25.38		19.11		6.27
	9.37		4.13	
9.79		6.60		3.19
	8.98		4.02	

Sources: Reserve Bank of India, Report on Currency and Finance 1965-66 (Bombay: Reserve Bank of India, 1967); Government of India, Explanatory Memorandum on the Budget of the Central Government, 1967-68 (New Delhi: Ministry of Finance, 1967); "Finances of State Governments 1967-68," Reserve Bank of India Bulletin (August 1967).

position, while developed countries such as West Germany and
the United Kingdom move substantially downwards in rank. When
tax burden is interpreted in terms of ability-to-pay, it emerges that the poorer countries may be "trying considerably harder," or sacrificing more, than the standard tax:income ratio
analysis would suggest.

It may also be unrealistic to talk of aggregrate tax
burden where different sectors are subject to substantially
different tax burdens. It will be demonstrated at length in
subsequent chapters that the agricultural sector in India is in
a highly favored position in terms of tax liability, and it
would seem useful to return to the old tax:income ratio analysis, but to examine only taxes paid by the urban sector out of
urban income. From 1963-64 figures for tax revenue and national income, this calculation was made for India. The procedure
was as follows: From total tax revenue for the year an amount
was deducted representing direct and indirect taxes paid on
agricultural income. The net tax revenue figure (over three
quarters of the total) was then taken as a percentage of national income minus income earned in agriculture (one half in
1963-64). The resulting figure of 20.6 per cent indicates that
the non-agricultural sector in India is subject to a considerably higher tax burden than is suggested by the usual aggregate
analysis.

A further refinement of tax:income ratio analysis provides
insight into changing tax burdens over the planning period. In
Table 10, tax revenue and national income figures are set out
for the entire planning period to date. The tax:income ratio,
here interpreted as the average tax rate in the year in question, is calculated for gross Union tax collections, net Union
revenue plus State revenue, and State tax collections (i.e.,
State revenue minus Union transfers). The marginal tax rate on
increments in income between years may be obtained from the
national income and tax revenue data, and is set out for all
three categories in Column 11.

The average tax rate rises steadily from 1959-60 on, the
larger part of the increase being accounted for by Union tax
collections. A measure of the increasing tax burden imposed by
both levels of government in India is the marginal rates of tax
imposed in the period after 1959-60. For total tax revenue, the
average of the final six marginal rates (Table 10, Column 6) is
19.3 per cent, for Union gross collections the average is 27.6
per cent, and for State collections, 8.3 per cent. The inference may again be drawn that the resource mobilization efforts,
particularly of the Union government, and the corresponding tax
burden on at least the non-agricultural sector, have not been
inconsiderable--certainly far greater than the prima facie inference suggested by the comparative tax:income ratios.

The Elasticity of Tax Revenue
over the Planning Period

The "elasticity" of tax revenue may be defined as the annual rate of growth of tax revenue other than from changes in tax rates or tax bases. It thus provides a measure of inherent or "built-in" revenue growth, and is of considerable significance in formulating a tax policy for planned development, as in the Indian case. It is, of course, not simple to disaggregate revenue increases into the part resulting from tax changes and the part resulting from built-in growth. The Union government does, in fact, break up each year its increased revenue estimates ex-ante into those two parts, but realized revenue increases differ widely from those anticipated--a perennial source of concern to the Public Accounts Committee--and retrospective classification of revenue increases into the two parts must be based on arbitrary assumptions.

An attempt is made in Table 11 to arrive at some estimates of the built-in elasticity of Union government gross tax collections--including States' share. Column 9 expresses the ex-ante estimate of increased revenue other than from tax changes as a percentage of actual revenue of the previous year. This represents, therefore, a minimum estimation of built-in elasticity, since all of the difference between the estimated and the realized increase in revenue is attributed to an under-estimation of the increase in revenue resulting from tax changes. Excluding the first three years, the average annual rate of growth of Union taxes comes to 3.06 per cent.

The picture is quite different if the entire difference between anticipated and realized revenue is attributed to an under-estimation of the built-in natural growth of revenue at pre-existing rates. Table 11, Column 11 expresses the actual annual increases in tax revenue minus the anticipated increase resulting from tax changes, as a percentage of actual revenue in the previous year. This might then be said to represent a maximum measure of built-in elasticity. Again excluding the first three years, the average annual rate of growth of Union taxes comes out, under this second assumption, to 8.9 per cent.

As a middle course between the two extremes, the ratio of anticipated increase in revenue other than from tax changes to total anticipated increase in revenue was established for each year, and this ratio applied to the actual increase in revenue for the year in question.[23] The results are set out in Table 11, Column 13. Omitting the first three years, and the two subsequent years for which the new estimate of elasticity is not defined, the average built-in elasticity of Union taxes works out to 4.3 per cent.

TABLE 11

ELASTICITY OF UNION TAX COLLECTIONS, 1951-67

	1	2	3	4	5	6
	Gross Tax Revenue			Total Annual Increase in Tax Revenue		
YEAR	Budget Estimate[a] Rs.Million	Revised Estimate Rs.Million	Actual Revenue Rs.Million	Estimated[b] Rs.Million	Actual Rs.Million	Difference Rs.Million
1951-52	4,010	4,910	5,050	190	1,070	+880
1952-53	4,060	4,270	4,420	-850	-630	+220
1953-54	4,240	4,170	4,200	-30	-220	-190
1954-55	4,500	4,520	4,560	330	360	+30
1955-56	4,760	4,830	4,850	240	330	+90
1956-57	5,150	5,560	5,730	320	880	+560
1957-58	6,630	6,780	6,960	1,070	1,230	+160
1958-59	7,120	6,700	7,150	340	190	-150
1959-60	7,000	7,570	7,840	300	980	+680
1960-61	7,940	8,360	8,770	370	880	+510
1961-62	9,080	9,860	10,370	720	1,600	+880
1962-63	10,850	11,590	12,670	990	2,300	+1,310
1963-64	14,430	15,490	16,130	2,840	3,460	+620
1964-65	16,720	17,900	17,980	1,230	2,490	+1,260
1965-66	19,230	20,070	20,350	1,330	2,370	+1,040
1966-67	22,590	22,720	n.a.[e]	2,520	n.a.[e]	

Notes: [a]Coverage: Customs, Union Excise Duties, Corporation Tax, Taxes on Income, Estate Duty, Taxes on Wealth, Expenditure Tax, Gift Tax.
[b]Budget estimate minus revised estimate for previous year.
[c]The ratio is that of the expected increase in revenue other than from tax changes to total expected increase in revenue. This ratio, as a percentage, is then applied to the actual increase in revenue for the year in question, and this final figure is taken as a percentage of revenue in the previous year.
[d]Not defined where one of the expected increases in revenue from tax charges or the increase in revenue other than from tax charges is negative.
[e]Not available.

30

Estimated Annual Increase in Tax Revenue			Actual Annual Increase in Tax Revenue minus estimated increase in revenue from tax changes		Increase in Tax Revenue other than from tax changes in terms of ex-ante ratio[c]	
From tax Changes[a] Rs.Million	Total Rs.Million	Per cent of revenue in previous year	Total Rs.Million	Per cent of revenue in previous year	Total Rs.Million	Per cent of revenue in previous year
312	-122	-3.06	758	19.04	--	n.d.[d]
-450	-400	-7.9	-180	-3.56	-296	-5.86
-10	-20	-0.45	-210	-4.75	-145	-3.28
120	210	4.3	240	5.9	229	5.45
130	110	2.4	200	4.4	150	3.3
330	-10	-0.2	550	11.34	--	n.d.[d]
930	140	2.4	300	5.23	160	2.8
60	280	4.0	150	2.15	156	2.24
230	70	1.0	750	10.5	229	3.20
240	130	1.7	640	8.16	309	3.94
610	110	1.6	990	11.0	246	2.8
670	320	3.1	1,630	16.0	747	7.2
2,640	200	1.6	820	6.0	243	1.92
430	800	4.9	2,060	12.7	1,613	10.0
-60	1,390	7.7	2,430	13.51	--	n.d.[d]
1,020	1,500	7.37				

Sources: Government of India, Explanatory Memoranda on the Budget of the Central Government, 1951-52 through 1966-67 (New Delhi: Ministry of Finance, 1951-66).

Elasticity of tax revenue is often defined in terms of the responsiveness of tax revenue to changes in national income, and it would seem useful to re-examine the above data in terms of this second approach. The "income elasticity" of tax revenue to the percentage change in national income over a chosen period. The relevant change in tax revenue is, of course, that resulting from built-in elasticity; increases in revenue resulting from tax changes are, therefore, as in the previous definition, excluded from the calculation.[24]

The income elasticity of Union taxes was calculated initially for each of the three Plan periods, using the formula specified. For the First Plan period the results were of little value, largely because of the very small increase in national income, and the under-estimation of tax revenue in 1951-52. Using the tax figures from Table 11, Column 8--the minimum revenue estimates--the elasticity coefficient for the First Plan period came to -43.8. Using the figures from Column 10--the maximum estimates--the elasticity coefficient came to 157.5!

For the remaining periods, more satisfactory results were obtained. For the period 1956-57 - 1960-61, the elasticity coefficient calculated, using the minimum revenue estimates, came to 0.4254--indicating that, on the average over the Second Plan, a 1 per cent increase in national income was associated with a 0.4254 per cent increase in Union tax revenue. The picture is a little brighter if the maximum estimates--Column 10-- are used. In this case the coefficient works out to 1.67. If the middle-way estimates of revenue--Column 12--are used, the elasticity coefficient comes to 0.508.[25]

For the remaining period--from 1961-62 to 1964-65[26]--the elasticity coefficients calculated, using the minimum, maximum and middle-way estimates of revenue, came to 0.3918, 1.508, and 0.7811, respectively.

The income elasticity coefficient was next calculated for the entire period from 1951-52 to 1964-65. When very large changes are in question, the problem occurs as to which revenue and income figures to use as the base from which to calculate percentage changes. This problem was resolved by taking as the base for both revenue and income the average of the initial and final values for each.[27] Using the new formula, elasticity coefficients were calculated for the period from 1951-52 to 1964-65 in terms of the three sets of revenue estimates. For the minimum estimates, the elasticity coefficient came to 0.4556, for the maximum estimates, 1.382, and for the middle-way estimates, to 0.79.

In terms of forecasting revenue over time, the estimates of elasticity presented above are of considerable significance. The range arrived at is fairly wide, and it is difficult to say where in that range to find the appropriate figures for elasticity, calculated either with or without reference to national income changes. The middle-way figures offer perhaps a reasonable compromise, reflecting as they do the ex-ante budgetary estimation of the relative importance of tax changes in built-in elasticity.

Of considerably less significance in terms of forecasting revenue is the buoyancy coefficient, measuring the rate of growth of revenue including the effects of tax changes. For historical reasons, however, the buoyancy coefficient was calculated for Union tax collections, combined Union and State tax revenue and State tax collections. Calculations were made using the above formula relating tax revenue to changes in national income.

The results showed surprising consistency. For the period 1951-52 to 1964-65, the buoyancy of Union tax collections came to 1.676, indicating, as in the case of the elasticity coefficient, that, on the average over the period, a 1 per cent increase in national income was associated with a 1.676 per cent increase in Union tax collections, including the effects of budgetary changes in tax rates and bases as well as natural or built-in growth. For combined Union and State tax revenue, the coefficient came to 1.664, and for State tax collections, to 1.637. The similarity of the coefficients for Union and for combined revenue is not surprising in view of the importance of shared Union taxes in State tax revenue, but the relatively high coefficient for State tax collections is somewhat surprising in view of the conventional notion that the growth rate of State tax sources tends to be much less than that of Union taxes. The performance of State tax collections can be accounted for almost entirely by the growth of revenue from the general sales tax.

THE MAJOR INDIAN TAXES: A SUMMARY VIEW

Direct Taxes

The Personal Income Tax

Under the Indian personal income tax the various sources of income are not taxed separately, as would be the case under a "schedular" income tax, but are aggregated on a "global" basis. Elements of a schedular system persist, however, in the

exemption of agricultural income and the concessionary treatment afforded capital gains. Tax is levied at progressive
rates on the total income of all individuals, joint Hindu families, unregistered firms and other associations of persons;
total income for tax purposes is reduced by certain exemptions
and deductions and by a system of personal allowances based on
the taxpayer's family status. Unearned income is subject to
discriminatory rates, and taxpayers whose income exceeds
Rs. 25,000 are subject to payment of "annuity deposits," similar in form to an additional income tax surcharge.

Accretions to capital value--other than in the case of
agricultural land and disposal of house property by small
houseowners--are subject to tax under the personal income tax.
Short-term gains--where the asset is held for less than twelve
months--are fully incorporated in income for tax purposes.
Long-term gains are subject to tax at concessionary rates.

Direct Taxation on the Agricultural Sector

As seen above, agricultural income is constitutionally
excluded from the Union income tax. Seven Indian States levy
a graduated tax on agricultural income, though the tax has
provided a significant revenue source in only three States,
Assam, Kerala and Madras, where large tea plantations are predominant. The major source of revenue from agriculture is land
taxation, until 1967-68 levied in all States. Several States
elected to abolish land taxation in the summer of 1967, largely
on political grounds, and it remains to be seen whether, in the
face of increasing need for revenue, the course of abolition
rather than reform will persist. The existing land tax bases
differ widely, ranging from a simple land area assessment to
various concepts of annual rental value and presumptive annual
income, and classification standards differ as widely as the
tax bases. The rates are fixed within legally prescribed
limits for a settlement period (generally thirty years) by
assessing officers; the prescribed maximum rates vary according
to the tax base employed.

The Annual Wealth Tax and the Expenditure Tax

A tax on net wealth has been in operation in India since
1957 and is levied annually on the taxable net wealth of individuals and Hindu undivided families (HUF); corporations have
been exempt since 1960. Tax rates are graduated but are relatively moderate, reaching a maximum of 2.5 per cent. A wide
range of assets are exempt.

A tax on expenditure was first levied in the 1958-59
budget, and, other than in the two years 1962-63 and 1963-64,
persisted till its abolition in the 1966-67 budget. It is

submitted, however, that an important tax principle is at issue here, and it is proposed to discuss the expenditure tax in some detail. In its form prior to abolition, the tax was levied annually on expenditures incurred by individuals and Hindu undivided families. A basic exempt expenditure allowance of Rs. 30,000 was superimposed on an initial income level exemption of Rs. 36,000; in addition, a broad range of expenditures were exempted from tax. Tax rates were graduated, reaching a maximum of 20 per cent.

Estate and Gift Taxation

Estate tax in India became payable on the capital value of property passing on the death of any person on or after October 15, 1953, in accordance with the provisions of the Estate Duty Act of that year. The definition of "taxable property transfers" has been widened to encompass such transfers as gifts made in contemplation of death or within a short period before death. Above a minimum exemption level of Rs. 50,000 tax rates are graduated reaching a maximum of 85 per cent. A limited group of assets are tax exempt.

The estate tax has been complemented by a tax on inter vivos gifts since 1958. Graduated tax rates are imposed on transfers above a minimum exemption level of Rs. 5,000 by individuals, Hindu undivided families and associations of individuals. The range of exempt assets is considerably wider than under the estate tax, and the rate of progression is also less severe, reaching a maximum of 50 per cent.

Corporation Income Taxation

Corporations are regarded as separate entities for income tax purposes in India and have been subject to income taxation since 1860. Corporations are classified for tax purposes into four major categories, three covering domestic and one foreign corporations. The corporate tax rate structure is complex. Total corporation income--inclusive of a wide range of exempt receipts and deductible expenditures--is subject, according to its place in the four-group classification, to proportional tax rates of between 45 per cent and 70 per cent. Additional taxes imposed on corporations include a penalty tax on distributed profits in the case of public corporations, a capital gains tax to which all corporations are subject and a surtax imposed on all corporations, the total income of which exceeds 10 per cent of the capital base, or Rs. 200,000, whichever is higher.

Indirect Taxes

As seen above, indirect taxes are imposed in India by the Union government and by all the States. The major indirect

taxes are Union customs duties, Union and State excise duties
and State sales taxes. Under the head of Union customs duties
a wide range of commodities are currently subject to either
"revenue" or "protective" duty; the bulk of the duties are ad
valorem. Following devaluation, export duty has been reintroduced on a broad group of commodities; the duties are all
ad valorem. Union excise duties are imposed on a wide range of
commodities and constitute the most rapidly expanding indirect
tax revenue source. Duties are imposed principally at specific
rates and are levied at the manufacturing stage. The basic
duties are supplemented by additional and special excise duties
and by a small group of benefit excises.

     The States levy excises only on narcotics and liquors.
The principal revenue source is the liquor excise levied at
specific rates, though the policy of prohibition has curtailed
the growth of revenue under this head.

     All the States levy a general sales tax. The form of tax
used varies widely, ranging from single-point levies to multi-
point turnover taxes; tax rates vary accordingly from less than
1 per cent to 14 per cent. Tax is imposed on registered
dealers whose total receipts exceed a specified exemption
level.

NOTES TO CHAPTER 1

     1. Constitution, Seventh Schedule, List 1--Union List,
List 2--State List. See also the extensive discussion of the
constitutional division of tax power in: Government of India,
Report of the Taxation Enquiry Commission (hereinafter TEC)
(3 vols., New Delhi: Ministry of Finance, 1953-54), Vol. I,
Chapter 2; and in Harvard University Law School, International
Tax Program, Taxation in India, World Tax Series (Boston:
Little, Brown and Co., 1960), pp. 44-50.

     2. Constitution, Seventh Schedule, List 3.

     3. The additional duties of excise are supplementary
levies imposed by the Union government on certain articles also
subject to standard excise duty. The allocation of resources
in this case is based on Finance Commission recommendations and
is not provided for by the Constitution.

     4. This is a French term describing a tax levied on goods
entering or leaving a town for sale or consumption therein--in
effect, a form of commodity tax. The term is found in several
Continental European countries and in India.

5. Union tax revenue is to be distinguished from Union tax collections, the former being gross collections minus the States' share.

6. TEC, op. cit., Vol. I, p. 32.

7. Ibid., p. 255, and associated diagram on import composition.

8. Government of India, Report of the Central Excise Reorganisation Committee (Delhi: Manager of Publications, 1963), p. 68.

9. TEC, op. cit., Vol. II, p. 258.

10. TEC, op. cit., Vol. I, p. 26.

11. Ibid. The role of the Zamindar was that of a tax farmer, obliged each year to provide a certain agreed amount of tax revenue to the authorities, and in his turn collecting tax from the peasant farmers.

12. Government of India, Report of the Study Team on Prohibition (New Delhi: Planning Commission, 1964). This Report is often referred to as the Tek Chand Report, after its Chairman.

13. Government of India, India 1966 (Delhi: Publications Division, 1966), Chapter 9, pp. 106-10.

14. See, e.g., B. R. Misra, Indian Federal Finance (Bombay: Orient Longmans, 1960), Chapter 18; R. N. Bhargava, The Theory and Practice of Union Finance in India (London: George Allen and Unwin, 1956), pp. 213-21; R. N. Tripathy, Fiscal Policy and Economic Development in India (Calcutta: World Press, 1958), pp. 137-39.

15. The item "other taxes and duties" in Table 4 comprises commodity taxes of various kinds (see Note b) and will be included with the other commercial taxes in calculating proportionate significance.

16. TEC, op. cit., Vol. I, pp. 29-31; Vol. III, pp. 333-416. A thorough examination of the finances of five selected municipalities in Bihar has been conducted by R. N. Tripathy, Local Finance in a Developing Economy (New Delhi: Planning Commission, 1967).

17. TEC, op. cit., Vol. I, p. 29.

18. Tripathy, Local Finance in a Developing Economy, op. cit., pp. 182-98.

19. The origin of these terms is discussed in U. K. Hicks, "The Terminology of Tax Analysis," in R. A. Musgrave and C. S. Shoup, eds., Readings in the Economics of Taxation (London: George Allen and Unwin, 1959), pp. 214-26.

20. A considerable literature has developed which defines "burden" in this simple sense. See H. H. Hinrichs and Richard Bird, "Government Revenue Shares in Developed and Less Developed Countries," Canadian Tax Journal, XIII (September-October 1963), 431-37.

21. See, for instance, H. Frank, "Measuring State Tax Burdens," National Tax Journal, XII (June 1959), 179-85; Richard Bird, "A Note on Tax Sacrifice Comparisons," National Tax Journal, XVII (1964), 303-308.

22.

$$\left[\left(\frac{T}{Y\text{-}T} \right) \; 100 \; \div \; \frac{Y}{P} \right] \; 100$$

i.e.,

where T = Tax revenue,
      Y = Gross National Product
and P = Population.
Bird uses Gross National Product in the first ratio, and Gross Domestic Product in the second. The same convention has been followed in the present work.

23. This is, in fact, roughly the procedure used by the Planning Commission in its studies of Plan financing to arrive at estimates of the yield from additional taxation.

24. The elasticity coefficient is defined as $\Delta T/T$. $Y/\Delta Y$. where T is the initial level of tax revenue, ΔT is the change in tax revenue over the relevant period, Y is the initial level of national income, and ΔY is the change in national income over the same period. See the extensive discussion of this concept of elasticity in R. Goode, The Individual Income Tax (Washington, D.C.: The Brookings Institution, 1964), pp. 287-307; and in G. S. Sahota, Indian Tax Structure and Economic Development (Bombay: Asia Publishing House, 1961), pp. 1-12. The interpretation of the ratio is as follows: a coefficient of, say, 1.5, would indicate that, on average over the period in question, a 1 per cent change in national income was associated with a 1.5 per cent change in tax revenue.

25. The middle-way estimates were made for the years 1957-58 to 1960-61, because of the absence of data for 1956-57.

26. 1964-65 is the last year for which reliable national income estimates are available.

27. The formula thus becomes

$$\Delta T/[(T_1 + T_2)/2] \cdot [(Y_1 + Y_2)/2]/\Delta Y,$$

where T is the change in tax revenue between Period one and Period two, T_1 is tax revenue in Period one, T_2 is tax revenue in Period two, Y is the change in national income between Period one and Period two, Y_1 is national income in Period one, and Y_2 is national income in Period two.

CHAPTER **2** OBJECTIVES
OF TAXATION
IN INDIA

It is the purpose of this chapter to examine the objectives of tax policy in India in the context of planned economic development since 1950. The discussion will thus be in part conceptual and in part historical.

The role of tax policy as a means to further the attainment of planning objectives may be subsumed under three heads: growth, redistribution and stabilization. Each of these objectives will be examined in some detail.

THE GROWTH OBJECTIVE

Reasonably comparable data for 1931-32 and 1950-51 indicate that per capita national income remained virtually unchanged over that period.[1] Against this backdrop of stagnation and in the light of prevailing conditions and assumptions concerning capital:output ratios and the rate of population increase, the First and Second Plans projected that, as compared to 1950-51, national income might be doubled by 1967-68 and per capita income by 1973-74.[2] The Third Plan qualified earlier optimism and laid down as the basic long term objective, to be attained by 1975-76, a cumulative rate of growth of national income as near as possible to 6 per cent per annum so as to secure more than a doubling of national income (from Rs. 140,000 million in 1960-61 to Rs. 340,000 million in 1975-76 at 1960-61 prices) and a 61 per cent increase in per capita income (from Rs. 330 in 1960-61 to Rs. 530 in 1975-76).[3] It is also a fundamental aspect of long run development strategy that the growth process should become self-sustaining within the shortest possible period, and that dependence on external resources should progressively diminish.[4]

If per capita income is to increase, the rate of growth of national income must exceed the rate of growth of population. Population policy is generally considered to be beyond the pale of conventional tax devices, and tax policy will therefore be considered only as a means of affecting the rate of growth of national income. The latter depends on the incremental capital: output ratio by providing incentives to improve productivity,

utilization of excess capacity, etc., its primary significance
lies in increasing the proportion of national income saved and
invested.

Mobilization of domestic resources for investment in both
the public and private sectors is the key to planned growth independent of external assistance. In this context tax policy
may serve directly to mobilize resources for capital formation
in the public sector and indirectly to promote private savings
and investment and redirection of the latter according to Plan
priorities. This goal of tax policy was explicitly recognized
by the TEC:

> . . . we consider that the achievement of increased
> investment on public and private account . . . repre-
> sents the crux of the task with which this Commission
> is charged. This task is to adapt the tax system as
> to enable the maximum practicable rate of investment
> in the public sector to be attained, consistent with
> maintaining and strengthening the incentives to the
> private sector to step up its own rate of investment.[5]

In the absence of foreign aid, investment may be financed
by domestic savings--by the total of household savings, savings
by private and public corporations, and government savings
(defined as a surplus of revenue over current expenditure). To
the extent that this aggregate falls short of the planned total
public and private investment, external assistance and/or deficit financing must be employed. The planned increase in the
investment rate is from 11 per cent of national income at the
end of the Second Plan to 14-15 per cent, 17-18 per cent and
19-20 per cent per annum by the end of the Third, Fourth and
Fifth Plans, respectively. The rate of domestic savings required to finance this investment would have to rise from 8.5
per cent of national income per annum at the end of the Second
Plan to 11.5 per cent, 15-16 per cent and 18-19 per cent by the
end of the Third, Fourth and Fifth Plans.[6] The role of tax
policy in promoting economic growth thus emerges as one of
restraining increases in consumption, i.e., tax policy must
seek to increase the savings:income ratio as national income
increases.

The rate and composition of savings between 1950-51 and
1962-63 in India are indicated in Table 1. The savings:income
ratio has increased over the planning period, from 6.6 per cent
over the First Plan to 9.5 per cent in the first two years of
the Third Plan. Household saving averaged just under 75 per
cent of total saving over the entire period, but fell to 66.4
per cent in the 1961-63 period. Corporate savings as a proportion of national income is of relatively little significance,
particularly relative to other developing countries, and

TABLE 1

RATE AND COMPOSITION OF SAVINGS,
1951-52 - 1962-63 (ANNUAL AVERAGES)

Rs. million at constant (1948-49) prices

	First Plan Period (1951-52 - 1955-56)	Second Plan Period (1956-57 - 1960-61)	1961-62 and 1962-63	1950-51 and 1962-63
1. Government Sector	1,149	1,701	3,340	1,679
Per cent of Total Saving	17.6	17.3	26.6	19.5
Per cent of National Income	1.2	1.5	2.5	1.5
2. Domestic Corporate Sector	402	506	886	510
Per cent of Total Saving	6.2	5.1	7.0	5.9
Per cent of National Income	0.4	0.4	0.7	0.5
3. Household Sector	4,957	7,624	8,339	6,415
Per cent of Total Saving	76.2	77.6	66.4	74.6
Per cent of National Income	5.0	6.6	6.3	5.8
i. Rural Household Sector	1,637	1,852	1,991	1,761
Per cent of Total Saving	25.1	18.8	15.8	20.5
Per cent of National Income	1.6	1.6	1.5	1.6
Per cent of Household Sector Saving	33.0	24.3	23.9	27.4
ii. Urban Household Sector	3,320	5,772	6,348	4,654
Per cent of Total Saving	51.1	58.8	50.6	54.1
Per cent of National Income	3.4	5.0	4.8	4.2
Per cent of Household Sector Saving	67.0	75.7	76.1	72.6
4. Total Saving	6,508	9,831	12,565	8,604
Per cent of National Income	6.6	8.5	9.5	7.8

Source: "Estimates of Saving and Investment in the Indian Economy:
1950-51 to 1962-63," Reserve Bank of India Bulletin
(March 1965), pp. 314-29.

the declining relative significance of household saving is accounted for by the rather sharp rise in government saving in 1961-63. Government saving in this latter period accounts for 26.6 per cent of saving and 2.5 per cent of national income, as against 17.6 per cent and 1.2 per cent, respectively, over the First Plan period, and 17.3 per cent and 1.5 per cent, respectively, over the Second Plan period. This improvement suggests that the conventional development strategy of increasing the saving:income ratio by diverting resources from private consumption to public saving through taxation is, in fact, working well in India. This point, however, requires further examination.

The government sector in India saved 11.9 per cent of its current income--i.e., current governmental expenditure was 98.1 per cent of current revenue--over the First Plan period; for the Second Plan period the figure was 11.2 per cent, and for the first two years of the Third Plan, 15.6 per cent.[7] Nevertheless, the increase in the governmental savings ratio has brought governmental savings to only 2.5 per cent of national income in 1961-63 as against 1.2 per cent over the First Plan. Over the same period, total tax revenue increased from an average of 7 per cent of national income to 12 per cent of national income. It is, therefore, clear that a significant proportion of increased tax revenue has gone to increased governmental consumption expenditure.

To suggest that taxation is only of significance for planned growth if it finds its way into governmental investment expenditure, is to underestimate the importance of much governmental consumption expenditure which is directly developmental or growth-promoting in nature. A broader concept of the importance of taxation as a means of financing growth through public sector expenditure would take into consideration not only governmental saving but all governmental expenditure whether of a consumption (current) or investment (capital) nature, which may be classified as developmental. The significance of taxation is then widened to take into account its contribution to all developmental expenditure, i.e., the role of taxation in financing growth is defined as one of maximizing the incremental ratio of national income minus household consumption and governmental consumption of a non-developmental nature, to national income.[8] Division of expenditures into developmental and non-developmental is now made annually in the Economic Survey which precedes the Union Budget. Total (Union and States) non-developmental expenditure on current account, total tax revenue, total current (tax and non-tax) revenue, and the surplus of both tax revenue and current revenue over non-developmental expenditure, expressed as a percentage, are set out in Table 2. The results indicate that taxation has to some extent been a successful means of channelling increases in

TABLE 2

THE CONTRIBUTION OF CURRENT REVENUE
TO DEVELOPMENTAL SPENDING, 1955-56 - 1965-66

YEAR	1955-56	1960-61	1961-62	1962-63	1963-64	1964-65	1965-66
1. Total Union + States Tax Revenue (Rs. million)	7,676	13,504	15,430	18,651	23,246	25,988	31,784
2. Total Current (tax and non-tax) Revenue (Rs. million)	9,825	17,840	19,154	25,020	30,500	33,270	37,770
3. Total Non-Developmental Expenditure (Rs. million)	5,854	9,530	9,947	14,664	17,600	17,960	20,310
4. Surplus of 1 over 3 (Rs. million)	1,822	4,019	5,433	3,885	5,534	7,892	11,474
5. Surplus of 2 over 3 (Rs. million)	3,971	8,310	9,207	10,356	12,900	15,310	17,460
6. 4 as a proportion of national income (per cent)	1.8	2.8	3.7	2.5	3.2	4.0	5.6
7. 5 as a proportion of national income (per cent)	4.0	5.9	6.2	6.7	7.5	7.7	8.5

Sources: Reserve Bank of India, Report on Currency and Finance, 1965-66
(Bombay: Reserve Bank of India, 1967); Annual Budget Statements of Union and State Governments.

44

income into development expenditure. Other than in the two
years of rapidly increasing defense expenditure from 1962-64,
taxation provided a steadily increasing proportion of national
income to finance developmental expenditure, from 1.8 per cent
of national income in 1955-56 to 5.6 per cent of national income in 1965-66. Including other current revenue, the increase
in the percentage of national income available for developmental expenditure continues even through the 1962-64 period.

The progressive increase in the proportion of national income made available for developmental expenditure over the
planning period through taxation would substantially qualify,
if not contradict, the increasingly popular view that the increase in non-developmental expenditure by the public sector is
a direct function of the availability of tax revenue, and that
the whole policy of increasing the ratio of developmental
spending to national income through increases in taxation is
largely futile.[9]

The fact remains that the whole policy of increasing the
developmental expenditure:national income ratio depends on
restraining the growth rate of non-developmental expenditure
by the public sector below the growth rate of current revenue.
Such a constraint might be provided for statutorily by specifying maximum growth rates for non-developmental expenditure
items, or, more radically, earmarking a specified proportion--
presumably an increasing proportion over time--of current revenue for developmental spending. One variation on the latter
theme would have a portion of current revenue channelled into
a general development fund, as an alternative to earmarking
revenue for specific projects.[10]

In view of the above extension of the original objective
of increasing the saving:income ratio, the role of taxation in
financing growth may be broken down into two parts:

1. (a) Taxation must restrain increments in household
consumption in order to transfer resources to government to
finance developmental spending.

(b) If taxation is to be a useful means of increasing the proportion of national income directed into public
developmental spending, the rate of growth of current non-
developmental spending in the public sector must be less than
the rate of growth of tax revenue. This might best be achieved by general earmarking of tax revenue into a developmental
fund.

2. Given that increases in tax revenue must come from
the addition to private incomes which may be either consumed or
saved, it is essential, through the provision of incentives to

private saving, to minimize the extent to which increased taxation to finance government developmental outlay have an opportunity cost in terms of private savings foregone. Potential
development outlay from increases in income may be seen as a
common pool of resources above increases in household consumption and increases in current non-developmental public sector
spending; it is the object of tax policy to make that common
pool as large as possible by minimizing the diminution in
private saving resulting from taxation.

In sum, the tax system best adapted to the requirements of
planned growth in the Indian economy would appear to be that
which would provide the required resources for government developmental outlay with as small a diminution as practicable
in saving in the private sector, and which is, accordingly,
accompanied by the largest practicable restraint on increases
in household consumption and public sector non-developmental
expenditure. The extent of the restraint on increases in
household consumption will reflect a compromise between the
maximum possible rate of growth of national income and the
desire to improve living standards.[11]

The Growth Objective: Tax Policy to Finance Public Sector Developmental Outlay

Tax Financing of Plan Outlays

The contribution of taxation to developmental expenditure
in the public sector has already been examined at some length.
A related, but distinct, classification of public expenditure
is into Plan and non-Plan expenditure. Plan expenditure of the
Union and States covers only such developmental expenditures as
are specifically included in the appropriate Five Year Plan.
Certain developmental expenditures are therefore excluded, although all expenditure included is specifically developmental
in nature. Plan outlay covers developmental expenditure of
both a current and capital nature, and the contribution of tax
financing to Plan financing represents the extent to which
total tax receipts exceed, over the Plan period, total current
outlays not specifically included in Plan outlay. Since the
entire development process is geared to the series of Five Year
Plans, it might be interesting to set out the contribution of
tax revenue, at both the Union and State levels, to Plan fi-
nancing--it being understood that this role is more specific
and less widely defined than the contribution of tax revenue to
the financing of development outlay in general.

As a means of financing outlays for the Plan, taxation is
supplemented by the surpluses of public enterprises, public
borrowing and miscellaneous capital receipts. Any gap between
resources under these heads and the planned outlay must be met

by deficit financing or external assistance. Table 3 sets out
the scheme of financing the First, Second and Third Five Year
Plans, and the projected means of financing the Fourth Plan.
Tax revenue over the First Plan period proved adequate to finance all current outlays and 29.5 per cent of Plan outlay.
During the Second Plan tax revenue increased rapidly but less
than proportionately to current expenditure: the upshot was a
decrease in the contribution to the Plan of tax revenue at
existing rates and resort to much higher levels of deficit financing and foreign assistance than had prevailed in the First
Plan. Almost half the outlay in the Second Plan was financed
by deficit financing and external assistance; tax revenue contributed only 22.8 per cent of Plan outlay.

In the initial estimates of Third Plan financing, tax revenue was expected to provide 30 per cent of Plan outlay. In
the final analysis tax revenue provided only 25.4 per cent.
The total anticipated tax revenue for the Third Plan was Rs.
22,600 million. The realized total came to Rs. 21,870 million,
a shortfall of only Rs. 730 million. The composition of the
shortfall is, however, interesting, and illustrates very clearly the problem of ensuring that an increasing proportion of tax
revenue is channelled into development expenditure, whether
Plan or non-Plan. Of the initial total projected amount of tax
resources of Rs. 22,600 million, Rs. 5,500 million were expected to accrue as a surplus from current revenue at 1960-61 rates
of taxation, and Rs. 17,100 million were expected to accrue
from additional tax measures--new taxes and extension of existing tax bases and rates. In fact, the balance from current revenue turned out to be negative, (-)Rs. 4,730 million, leaving
a total shortfall from current revenue of Rs. 10,230 million.
Revenue from additional tax sources amounted to Rs. 26,600
million, exceeding the original estimate by Rs. 9,500 million,
and providing for the over-all shortfall of Rs. 730 million.

Forecast tax resources for the Fourth Plan amount to Rs.
60,750 million, Rs. 33,450 as the balance from current revenue
at 1965-66 rates of taxation, and Rs. 27,300 from additional
taxation. The total is expected to provide 37.9 per cent of
the financial resources for the Fourth Plan. It seems clear
that the success of tax financing forecasts will depend on the
degree of control exercised over the growth of non-Plan current
outlay--failing which reliance will again fall on additional
tax measures.

Tax Policy for Increased Revenue

The exigency of raising more tax resources for developmental outlay may be briefly examined under three heads: "Elasticity," "The Comprehensiveness of Tax Bases and New Forms of
Taxation," and "Administrative Efficiency." These headings

TABLE 3

FINANCING OF THE FIRST FOUR FIVE YEAR PLANS

	First Plan Rs.Million	Proportion of Plan Financing Per cent	Second Plan Rs.Million	Proportion of Plan Financing Per cent
1. Balance from Current Revenue	3,240)		110)	
	)	29.5	)	22.8
2. Additional Taxation	2,550)		10,520)	
3. Surpluses of Public Enterprise	1,150	6.0	1,670	3.6
4. Capital Receipts[a]	6,840	34.9	14,390	30.8
5. External Assistance	1,890	12.1	10,490	22.5
6. Deficit Financing	3,333	17.5	9,540	21.3
7. Total Resources	19,600	100.0	46,720	100.0

Note: [a]includes market loans, small savings, annuity deposits, provident funds, and miscellaneous capital receipts.

Third Plan Estimates Rs.Million	Proportion of Plan Financing Per cent	Third Plan Actuals Rs.Million	Proportion of Plan Financing Per cent	Fourth Plan Estimates Rs.Million	Proportion of Plan Financing Per cent
5,500)) 17,100)	30.0	(-)4,730)) 26,600)	25.4	33,450)) 27,300)	37.9
5,500	7.3	6,960	8.1	13,450	8.4
19,400	25.9	21,390	24.8	38,800	24.3
22,000	29.3	24,550	28.5	47,000	29.4
5,500	7.5	11,510	13.2	--	--
75,000	100.0	86,280	100.0	160,000	100.000

Source: Government of India, Draft Fourth Plan Material and Financial Balances 1964-65, 1970-71, and 1975-76 (New Delhi: Planning Commission, 1966).

will be elaborated throughout the essay in the discussion of
increased revenue under the various forms of taxation.

Elasticity Two concepts of elasticity were examined in Chapter
1--the annual rate of growth of tax revenue, and the income
elasticity of tax revenue, which relates percentage changes in
tax revenue to percentage changes in national income. Subsequent discussion will rely largely on the latter definition.

     Increased income elasticity of tax yield--the channelling
of progressively larger percentages of increments in national
income into tax revenue--is essential if taxation is to fulfill
its assigned role in financing growth in India.[12]

     The income elasticity coefficient must exceed unity if the
average revenue:income ratio is to increase over time. For the
planning period to date, the estimates of the income elasticity
of Union tax collections made in Chapter 1 suggest a range from
a minimum of 0.4556 through the middle-way estimate of 0.79, to
the maximum of 1.38. The middle-way estimate, which seems the
most reasonable compromise, implies that the inherent or built-
in income elasticity of Union tax collections is insufficient
to provide an increasing revenue:income ratio over time, and
that the increasing revenue:income ratio to date--manifested in
the buoyancy coefficient of 1.676--is a function of increases
in tax rates, widening of existing tax bases, and the imposition of new taxes.

     A study of the income elasticity of Indian tax revenue
over the period 1951-52 to 1957-58 has been done by G. S.
Sahota.[13] Over the period the coefficient for Union tax collections was found to be 0.613, while that of total tax revenue came to 0.833. Sahota also made estimates of the income
elasticity of individual taxes, and these will be compared
with the estimates of this study in the appropriate sections.

     An income-elastic tax system requires over-all progres-
siveness in the rate structure, in which the marginal rate,
being greater than the average rate, pulls up the average rate
as incomes rise. The subsequent examination of particular
taxes will emphasize the importance of rate modification to
increase progressiveness.

The Comprehensiveness of Tax Bases and the Introduction of New
Taxes The revenue productivity of a tax is dependent not only,
or even chiefly, on its income elasticity, but also on the
width of the tax base relative to national income. If the
coverage of existing tax forms is incomplete--if, in effect,
all those persons and/or things which should technically fall

under a particular tax base are not so included--it should be possible to increase revenue mobilization by widening existing tax bases and curtailing exemptions. It will later be suggested, for instance, that the coverage of the capital gains tax, the annual wealth tax, and the gift and estate taxes in India is inadequate, and that a widening and/or modification of the bases of these three tax measures, and a reform of their rate and exemption structures, would provide increased revenues. The prime reason for the inadequate revenue productivity of the present personal income tax in India is the constitutional exemption of income from agriculture, and radical alterations will be suggested in the present inflexible land tax system with a view to ultimately incorporating agricultural income in the general income tax.

Several new tax devices designed to deal with particular resource mobilization problems in India will also be discussed: these will include means to the mobilization of gold hoards, the extension of the present compulsory savings system, and the possibility of in-kind taxation of the large non-monetized sector.[14]

Administrative Efficiency Where the mobilization of increased revenue for government expenditure is a major tax objective, Adam Smith's canon of "economy" (costs of collection small relative to yield) is of particular significance. This criterion of "administrative efficiency" is generally unexceptionable[15] and may be summarized in the Indian case as requiring that taxes be established in such a manner as to minimize the costs of collection and administration relative to revenue realized, from the viewpoint of both the taxing authority and the taxpayer. Inefficient and ineffective administration directly diminishes net revenue available for other expenditure and indirectly diminishes revenue through inability to eliminate loopholes for evasion and avoidance.

From the general criterion two conclusions may be drawn. First, in a federal State such as India the Central and State governments should be responsible for the methods and types of taxation which each can most efficiently impose and collect, and a process of tax sharing and federal grants should be devised so as to make the revenue accruing to each level of government commensurate with its expenditure responsibilities. The present allocation of tax collection responsibilities in India, detailed in Chapter 1, would appear initially in accordance with this principle of efficiency in collection, in that State collection costs are approximately six times Central costs as a proportion of revenue.[16] A closer examination of the entire structure of Union-State fiscal relations reveals, however, a range of serious problems.

The conflict of roles between the Planning Commission and the Finance Commission must be carefully examined, and some more efficient alternative devised--perhaps the creation of a permanent Finance Commission, or the dissolution of the Finance Commission and the delegation of its functions to the Planning Commission. Further, a rational and consistent set of criteria must be devised to determine the allocation of tax shares to the States in general, and the allocation of States' share between particular States. To date, the absence of a set of criteria for State tax capacity, and tax effort relative to capacity, have discouraged both economy of State expenditure, and the vigorous pursuit of alternative State tax sources and the extension of present sources.

Second, it follows that, given a projected revenue collection, the methods and types of taxation should be chosen so as to minimize costs of administration and collection, i.e., to maximize net revenue. This canon must, however, be qualified in the Indian case by two considerations:

1. Administrative efficiency as part of the objective of growth through public expenditure must be construed relative to other objectives of taxation, viz., growth in the private sector, stability and equity. It might, for example, be administratively desirable and revenue-saving not to exempt certain types of private savings from income tax, but this would conflict with the need to maximize the aggregate of public and private investment.

2. Administrative efficiency must be seen in a dynamic sense, in that expenditure on improved administration in the short run may be amply vindicated in the long run by the increased revenue productivity of a more sophisticated, developed tax system. J. F. Due suggests that the administrative organization be extended till the additional sum spent on administration equals the additional revenue so derived.[17] Such a criterion, although applicable to a developed tax system, might prevent the adoption of necessary administrative reforms in India, which, though costly in the short run, may be essential to the growth of an elastic, productive revenue system in the long run. A subsequent chapter attempts to evaluate tax administration in India and to suggest possible alterations.

The Growth Objective: Implications for
Tax Policy in the Private Sector

Tax Policy and the Allocation of Resources

Under the growth objective in the private sector it is the function of tax policy to provide incentives to private saving and investment. Such incentives should provide both a general incentive to save rather than consume and specific incentives to ensure that saved resources are channelled into investment projects that are consonant with Plan objectives.

Such a role for taxation conflicts with the tax policy principle of economic neutrality. J. F. Due lists the latter as one of the three essential tax principles in a developed country:

> The tax structure must be established in such a
> way as to avoid interference with the attainment
> of the optimum allocation and use of resources
> and, where possible, to assist in the attainment
> of the optimum.[18]

S. Enke has also argued that neutrality is a necessary characteristic of a growth-oriented tax policy in a developing country.[19]

The most recent defense of a neutral tax system is to be found in the massive Carter Commission Report on taxation in Canada.[20] In the view of the Commission, a tax system must avoid concessions to particular types of income. Such concessions are held to be always inequitable, frequently inefficient, distorting the allocation of resources and eroding the tax base.

The contention that taxation should not interfere with the market allocation of resources premises that the market allocation is considered to be optimal. The optimum allocation of resources may be defined in the Indian context of planned growth as the attainment of planning objectives in the various sectors of the economy. The role of taxation may then be defined as that of a diversionary instrument of economic control geared to the attainment of these planning objectives. Such a tax policy would amount to what has been called "fiscal dirigism," defined as a policy aimed at the achievement of planning objectives through the insertion of a variety of incentives and disincentives into the tax system.[21]

Taxation may be employed as a diversionary instrument in several ways:

First, taxation may affect household choice as between savings and consumption and as between the purchase of different commodities. Saving exemptions may be incorporated in direct tax measures and indirect tax rates may be set up to discourage consumption in general and/or the consumption of particular commodities.

Second, taxation may affect the decisions of suppliers of factors of production with respect to the quantity of factor

units they will offer and the direction in which they will
employ those factors. A variety of tax incentives may be introduced into personal and corporate direct taxes to promote
the use of labor, capital and land in accordance with planning
objectives.

Finally, taxation may affect the choice of methods of
production, in that it may affect the relative advantages of
various techniques by changing the structure of input costs.
Corporate tax incentives would be most appropriate for this
purpose.

Incentives and Revenue Productivity

The introduction of a complex system of incentives and
disincentives into the tax system would appear to conflict with
the objective of increased revenue directly through the revenue
cost of the tax incentives and indirectly through the increased
complexity of tax administration.

If the incentive system is successful the level of investment and rate of growth of income and tax receipts should offset the initial direct revenue loss. This conclusion depends,
of course, on the initial premise that the conferral of tax
privileges will induce domestic and/or foreign investors either
to increase their investments in already operating enterprises
or to initiate activities which would otherwise not have been
undertaken. The significance of tax considerations in investment decisions has been subject to extensive debate.[22] It will
simply be suggested here that if tax incentives are employed in
India as an integral part of planning policy, and are sufficient in magnitude, such tax inducements should be a significant determinant in the location and extent of investment.

The indirect loss through enhanced administrative complexity may be more serious. A recent study is pessimistic on
this score:

. . . where an incentive statute called for selective
discrimination in the designation of individual benefit grantees and in the tailoring of benefits to their
individual circumstances, as do most incentive statutes,
a higher degree of administrative efficiency is required than is ordinarily available for these purposes
in most economically less developed countries . . .
the first requirement is that administration be sufficiently experienced and proficient to be entrusted
with broad and discretionary latitude in shaping the
implementation of the statute according to prevailing
development needs. . . . The second requirement is

that the administration be sufficiently expert and
adequately enough staffed to perform satisfactorily
the demanding functions of benefit conferral, sur-
veillance of benefit grantees, and over-all review
of the operation of the statute.[23]

Once it is granted that incentive policies in India should be
integrated in the comprehensive planning program, their administration becomes part of the general capacity of the
Indian government to control and implement planned development.
This capacity may be presumed to be increasing as the Plans
proceed. Equally, it should be possible to circumvent many of
the discretionary administrative obstacles by the use of statutory tax incentives, which come into operation automatically
according to pre-determined movement of economic indicators.

THE EQUITY OBJECTIVE

Equity in taxation is taken to mean taxation in accordance
with "ability-to-pay"; the "benefit" principle may be of specific usefulness in the case of certain taxes such as betterment levies in agriculture--which are assessed specifically
according to benefits conferred by public works--but is of
little value as a general equity criterion in a situation where
the specific benefits of the vast bulk of public sector expenditures cannot be estimated. The major tax base chosen as the
index of ability-to-pay in this study will be a comprehensive
definition of income, widened to mean net accretion (consumption plus gratuitous transfers to others, whether testamentary
or inter vivos plus increase in net worth) over the relevant
tax period.[24] In addition to this broad income base, two other
indexes of ability-to-pay will be used in this study--wealth
and consumption.

There are two aspects of equity under the general heading
of ability-to-pay; those tax-paying units with equal ability
should contribute the same amount of taxes (horizontal equity),
while those with greater ability should contribute more than
those with lesser ability (vertical equity).

The first, or horizontal, sense of equity provides for the
equal treatment of tax-paying units in similar economic circumstances, and has been stressed for India by the TEC.[25] The
principle of equal treatment of equals must, of course, be modified by the structure of selective incentives to personal
saving and investment, to corporate investment in particular
areas, etc., and the principle may therefore be re-defined to
postulate that where such inequality is not a strategically
selected part of tax policy it must be avoided.

Problems which will be discussed under the head of horizontal equity in India include the exemption of agricultural
incomes from the general income tax, the treatment of those
receiving income either totally or partially in kind, the concessionary treatment of capital gains, the treatment of fluctuating incomes, the disparate treatment of inter vivos gifts
and death transfers, and the outstanding, chronic problem of
tax evasion.

The second, and more controversial, aspect of equity is
the treatment of persons and groups in dissimilar economic cir-
cumstances--the problem of equity in the vertical sense. There
are three aspects of the problem of vertical inequalities:
first, inequalities of income, second, inequalities of wealth,
which are aggravated by failure to moderate income disparities,
and third, inequalities of opportunity, which result from the
failure to moderate income and wealth disparities and the inadequacy of taxation of inter-personal transfers (whether inter
vivos or testamentary).

At this point the use of the term "Equity Objective" may
be clarified and justified. A more appropriate title for this
section, which examines the objectives of taxation, might have
been "The Redistribution Objective," since it is primarily with
the question of redistribution that this section is concerned.
However, the cardinal principle (as distinct from objective) of
a tax system is horizontal equity or the equal treatment of
equals, and the overall equity objective is taken to mean that
the tax system must further redistribution, i.e., achieve
vertical equity, but must equally be designed so as to allocate
equal tax burdens on those with equal ability-to-pay, i.e.,
achieve horizontal equity. The over-all objective "Equity" is
thus seen, in sum, to incorporate both an objective (vertical
equity) and a fundamental tax principle (horizontal equity).

A constitutional[26] and long-run planning[27] commitment to
the reduction of inequalities was strongly re-affirmed in the
Mid-Term Appraisal of the Third Plan,[28] and in the Fourth
Plan.[29] The TEC saw an unequivocal role for taxation in this
regard:

We can no longer afford to leave the problem of
equality to the automatic functioning of economic
and social forces. . . . The demand that the instrument of taxation should be used as a means of
bringing about a redistribution of income more in
consonance with social justice, cannot be kept in
abeyance.[30]

One of the arguments against such a role for taxation
would suggest that the redistributive aspect of fiscal policy

be left in large part to government expenditure in the form of
direct transfers to lower income groups.[31] Government expenditure is, however, already spread thinly over many priorities
in the planning process and the inadequacy of expenditure as
the sole means of lessening inequalities was confirmed by the
TEC:

> The extent to which Indian public expenditure brings
> about a reduction in inequalities of economic circum-
> stances and thus helps the tax system to achieve one
> of the objectives which have been suggested for it is
> modest, partly because the total volume of public
> expenditure constitutes a small proportion of the
> total national income and also because the expenditure
> on social welfare and subsidies by way of transfers
> to the lower income groups is of little significance.[32]

The Pattern of Income Distribution

Two recent studies of income distribution in India, by the
Reserve Bank of India[33] and the National Council of Applied
Economic Research (NCAER)[34] differ considerably in their findings on the degree of inequality. The former study covers the
urban and rural sectors over the period 1953-54 - 1956-57; the
latter study refers only to the urban sector for the year 1959-
60. Table 4a presents the evidence of both studies in the form
of income accruing to the top 5 per cent of households and each
decile group of households. The bottom row shows the concentration ratios.[35] Table 4b is based on the Reserve Bank study
and shows the changes in the concentration ratios between 1953-
54 and 1956-57. Table 4c provides some comparative concentration ratios.

The Reserve Bank comparative figures on Table 4c suggest
that the degree of inequality in India is less than an average
of four other underdeveloped countries and an average for seven
developed countries. The comparative position of India would,
of course, be substantially different if the much higher urban
concentration ratio in the NCAER study (Table 4a) were to be
used.[36]

The Reserve Bank study suggests (Table 4b) that the
over-all concentration ratio declined slightly, from 0.349
to 0.341, over the period 1953-57. It is apparent, however,
that this decline is the consequence of a slight fall in the
concentration ratio, from 0.305 to 0.304, in the rural sector
and conceals a sharp increase in the concentration ratio, from
0.378 to 0.421, in the urban sector. Inequality then appears
to be worsening in the more rapidly developing urban sector.
Evidence of the relatively rapid growth of urban incomes is

TABLE 4a

PATTERN OF INCOME DISTRIBUTION IN INDIA:
SHARES OF ORDINAL GROUPS OF HOUSEHOLDS (Per cent)

	Reserve Bank Study (1953-54 - 1956-57)						NCAER Study (1959-60)	
Households	Personal Income			Disposable Income			Personal Income	Disposable Income
	Rural Sector	Urban Sector	All India	Rural Sector	Urban Sector	All India	Urban Sector	Urban Sector
Top 5 per cent	17	26	20	17	24	19	31	29
Top Tenth	25	37	28	25	36	28	42	41
Second Tenth	14	12	14	14	11	14	15	16
Third Tenth	13	10	13	12	11	12	10	11
Fourth Tenth	9	8	9	10	8	9	8	8
Fifth Tenth	9	8	8	9	8	9	7	7
Six Tenth	8	6	8	9	7	8	5	6
Seventh Tenth	7	6	6	7	7	6	4	5
Eight Tenth	6	6	6	5	4	6	4	4
Ninth Tenth	5	4	5	5	4	5	3	3
Bottom Tenth	4	3	3	4	4	3	1	1
Concentration Ratio	0.310	0.400	0.340	0.306	0.382	0.335	0.510	0.500

Sources: P. D. Ojha and V. V. Bhatt, "Pattern of Income Distribution in an
Underdeveloped Economy: A Case Study of India," American Economic
Review, LIV (September 1964), 711-20; "Distribution of Income in
the Indian Economy," Reserve Bank of India Bulletin (September 1962),
1348-63; National Council of Applied Economic Research, Urban Income
and Saving (New Delhi: National Council of Applied Economic Research,
1962).

TABLE 4b

PATTERN OF INCOME DISTRIBUTION IN INDIA:
CHANGES IN CONCENTRATION RATIOS,
1953-54 - 1956-57

	Period I Personal Disposable Income Income		Period II Personal Disposable Income Income	
Rural Household Sector	0.305	0.304	0.304	0.301
Urban Household Sector	0.378	0.368	0.421	0.405
All-India Household Sector	0.349	0.342	0.341	0.335

Source: P. D. Ojha and V. V. Bhatt, "Pattern of Income Distribution in an Underdeveloped Economy: A Case Study of
India," American Economic Review, LIV (September 1964),
figures derived from Table 2, p. 714.

TABLE 4c

INTERNATIONAL COMPARISONS

1. Concentration Ratios in Selected Countries

Developing Countries

Country and Year	Personal Income	Disposable Income
India 1953-54 - 1956-57	.34	.33
Ceylon 1952-53)		
Mexico 1950)		
Mexico 1957) (average)	.47	--
Barbados 1951-52)		
Puerto Rico 1953)		

Developed Countries

Country and Year	Personal Income		Disposable Income
United Kingdom 1951-52	.33)		.29
Germany, West 1950	.45)		--
Netherlands 1950	.45)		.41
Denmark 1952	.44) average .42		.40
Sweden 1948	.44)		.41
United States 1950	.35)		.32
Italy 1948	.40)		--

2. Concentration Ratios in the Agricultural and Non-Agricultural Sectors (Selected Countries)

Country and Year	Rural Sector	Urban Sector
1. India (1953-54 - 1956-57	.31	.40
2. Ceylon (1952-53)	.45	.52
3. Puerto Rico (1953)	.32	.43
4. Italy (1948)	.41	.40
5. Netherlands (1954)	.22	.29
6. Sweden (1959)	.36	.39
7. United States (1950-53)	.41	.34

Source: P. D. Ojha and V. V. Bhatt, "Patterns of Income Distribution in an Underdeveloped Economy: A Case Study of India," American Economic Review, LIV (September 1964), figures derived from Table 4, p. 716, and from Table 6, p. 718.

provided by a recent study of the decade 1950-61 by
V. K. R. V. Rao.[37]

The NCAER study does not provide inter-temporal and international comparative figures but does suggest that the degree
of inequality in the urban sector is considerably more acute
than is indicated in the Reserve Bank study. The concentration
ratio for 1959-60 in the urban sector is estimated by the NCAER
study at 0.510 as against the Reserve Bank estimate of 0.421
for 1956-57. The share of the upper quintile is 49 per cent in
the Reserve Bank study and 58 per cent in the NCAER study.

From the point of view of tax policy it is significant
that the concentration ratios for disposable income are only
slightly lower than for personal income. In the Reserve Bank
study the ratios for personal and disposable income over the
1953-57 period were 0.340 and 0.335, respectively. The equivalent NCAER ratios for the urban sector were 0.510 and 0.500.
The Reserve Bank study suggests that taxation reduced the share
of only the top 5 per cent of all income recipients. The NCAER
study suggests that taxation reduced very slightly the share of
the top 10 per cent.

Distribution of Wealth

Information on wealth distribution is limited, but such
limited evidence as is available--on the distribution of land
holdings, owner-occupied houses and share ownerships--would
suggest a degree of concentration greater than in the case of
incomes. On land holdings, the Committee on the Distribution
of Income and Levels of Living concluded:

> . . . our finding is that both ownership and
> operational holdings are very highly concentrated.
> Also, there was no appreciable reduction in in-
> equality between 1953-54 and 1959-60, in spite of
> the fact that a good deal of land reform measures
> had been enacted during the period. In 1953-54 the
> top 1% of the households owned 17%, the top 5%
> owned 41%, and the top 10% of the households owned
> 58% of the ownership holdings of the households;
> in 1959-60 these proportions were 16%, 40% and 56%
> respectively. The bottom 20% of the households did
> not own any land in either of these two years. . . .
> It appears that the degree of concentration is much
> greater in the urban sector than in the rural.[38]

Figures on the distribution of owner-occupied houses, although
confined to the urban sector, indicate a similar disparity.
The top 10 per cent of home-owning households in the urban
sector were found to account for 57 per cent of the total

wealth held in the form of owner-occupied houses, the top 20
per cent for 73 per cent and the bottom 10 per cent for less
than 1 per cent.[39] Statistics on share ownership indicate an
even greater degree of concentration. The top 10 per cent of
income tax assessees, ranked according to dividend income,
received 55 per cent of total dividend income accruing to
households in 1955-56, while the bottom 10 per cent of assessees received only 2 per cent of dividend income. In 1959-
60 the share in total dividend income of the top 10 per cent of
assessees was 52 per cent while that of the bottom 10 per cent
was 2.5 per cent.[40]

The Relationship of Vertical Equity and Growth

The constitutional and planning consensus on the desirability of reduction in disparities in economic well-being
reflects the normative or esthetic judgment that "the prevailing distribution of wealth and income reveals a degree
. . . of inequality which is distinctly evil or unlovely."[41]
Though this socio-political argument may appear to foreclose
further discussion, it would be extremely short-sighted of
planners in India to consider equity solely in this static,
albeit important, sense. Vertical equity in India must be
interpreted in a dynamic sense. It is only through the rapid
growth of national income that any appreciable increase in the
standard of living of the mass of the people can be effected.[42]
It is a matter of simple arithmetic that if redistributive
measures reduce the rate of economic growth, the absolute share
of income going to the group favored by the redistribution
would, after a time, be less than it would have been with a
higher rate of growth.[43] A dynamic redistributive policy must
then be concerned with the redistribution of a cake which is
growing as rapidly as possible. The relationship between
redistribution and growth is, therefore, of central importance
in the establishment of a redistributive tax policy. This
relationship is characterized by both complementarity and conflict. These may be examined in turn.

With regard to complementarity, it has been argued, first,
that the poverty and apathy of the mass of the Indian people
make it difficult to incorporate them in the productive process
and that redistributive measures will serve to enhance the
productivity of the economic system.[44] Second, the contribution of redistributive finance to political stability may also
be particularly apposite in India.[45] Redistributive finance
may induce a higher rate of private savings by enhancing the
security of the institution of property in a setting of greater
political stability.[46] Third, redistributive finance which
places greater purchasing power in the hands of the mass of the
people may be necessary to provide a sufficiently broad domestic market base to stimulate private investment.[47] It may

contribute to this end particularly by shifting demand from imported luxury items to items which can be produced domestically. The relationship between expected profitability (based on increased consumer demand) and investment, and the consequent role of redistributive finance in underdeveloped countries, has been recently elaborated.[48] The extent to which increases in income are channelled into consumption must, of course, be severely limited by the tax objective of restraining increases in consumption within the requirements of planned investment. A fourth, clearly weaker argument for redistribution in the Indian case suggests that the diminution of inequalities may, in fact, increase the over-all propensity to save by diminishing the "demonstration effect" of luxury consumption expenditure by the very wealthy.[49] A complementary argument that the opportunity cost, in terms of productive private saving foregone, of taxing high incomes may not be substantial because of the propensity of upper income groups to indulge in conspicuous or luxury consumption, or non-productive investment, is widely held.[50] It may be argued that the goals and motivations of the upper income groups in India are not similar to those of their counterparts in Britain during the "Industrial Revolution," when,

> . . . the capitalist classes were allowed to call the best part of the cake theirs and were theoretically free to consume it, on the tacit underlying condition that they consumed very little of it in practice. . . .[51]

The argument on conflict between redistribution and growth emphasizes the effect of redistributive (progressive) taxation on work, and on private saving and investment. Private sector investment was responsible for 40 per cent of planned investment in the Third Plan and is estimated to account for 36 per cent of Fourth Plan investment. Further, private saving finances not only private investment, but a significant proportion of public investment. The effect of redistributive taxation on the flow of private saving and investment is therefore of fundamental importance. The TEC stressed this issue:

> An important question for tax policy is posed by need to strike a balance between the objectives of achieving economic equality through the tax mechanism, and of maintaining unimpaired the flow of investment and savings which make for the continued progress of productive enterprise.[52]

Similarly, a tax policy for development would clearly be self-defeating if it were to lead to a significant reduction in work effort, particularly among upper income groups.

Progressive tax rates are held to dampen the rate of growth first, by reducing the <u>incentive</u> to work, save and invest, and, second, by reducing the <u>ability</u> to save and invest of those groups whose propensity to save is likely to be relatively high.

The case against redistributive tax measures in terms of diminished incentives to work, save and invest is generally unsatisfactory, and much of the argument boils down to psychological conjecture. Equally, the incentive arguments are usually of a partial nature, first, in that they fail to consider the effect of the tax system as a whole, second, in that the role of government as a spender of tax revenue is ignored, and, finally, in that the arguments suggesting a degree of complementarity between redistribution and growth are generally overlooked. However, it will be necessary in the discussion of each of the progressive tax measures to evaluate the incentive arguments. In terms of the ability to save and invest it is indisputable that progressive taxation diverts from private use funds which might have been saved and invested.

The problem emerges as one of distinguishing inequalities which are <u>functional</u> in terms of growth objective from those which are not.[53] Dealing first with inequalities of income, it is submitted that inequality in the treatment of two individuals at the same income level is justified in the event that one saves and invests productively a larger proportion of his income than the other; and that specific exemptions and allowances be permitted under a rigorous progressive scale of income taxation--the object of which is to mitigate vertical inequality--for income saved and invested in a manner consonant with Plan objectives. It may also be contended that inequality in the treatment of two individuals at the same income level is justified in the event that one is engaged in an occupation considered important for the attainment of Plan objectives, and the notion of functional inequalities may thus be extended to include specific incentives and allowances designed to attract labor into key occupations. A dynamic redistributive system tax should, however, seek to drastically curtail non-functional inequalities such as speculative capital gains or inheritance windfalls. In this manner the tax system would, consistent with functional work incentives, seek to eliminate <u>consumption</u> inequalities which are the most disagreeable social manifestation of income inequalities.

The extent of present consumption disparities is indicated in Table 5. The top 10 per cent of urban households accounted in 1959-60 for 26 per cent of total urban household expenditure whereas the bottom 10 per cent accounted for only 3.33 per cent; the corresponding rural figures were 26.77 per cent and 3.40 per cent.

TABLE 5

PERCENTAGE SHARE OF TOTAL CONSUMPTION BY
GROUPS, July 1959 - June 1960 (Per cent)

Fractile Group	Share in Consumption	
	Urban	Rural
0.10	3.33	3.40
10-20	4.66	4.94
20-30	5.67	5.82
30-40	6.34	6.69
40-50	7.44	7.68
50-60	8.30	8.61
60-70	10.21	9.93
70-80	12.17	11.74
80-90	15.88	14.42
90-100	26.00	26.77

Source: Government of India, Report of the Commission on the
          Distribution of Income and Levels of Living (New
          Delhi: Planning Commission, 1964), figures adapted
          from Statement 2, p. 27.

The same type of analysis may be applied to inequalities
of accrued wealth. A rational tax system would treat leniently
functional wealth inequalities based on shares in productive
industry or agricultural land productively employed but would
drastically curtail wealth inequalities based on elaborate
homes or idle land.

Conclusion

The attainment of the redistribution objective requires
the establishment of appropriate exemption levels and over-all
progressivity in the tax structure, combined with a series of
exemptions and allowances designed to maintain functional inequalities. The sharpness of the rates of progression in the
various taxes and the choice of exemption levels will depend
on what is regarded as a "proper state of distribution"; the
establishment of the latter is a political issue--the old benefit and ability theories raise as many questions as they provide answers in this matter--and will be determined by social

choice as reflected in the policy of the ruling party.[54] The
role of the economist in this respect is merely to suggest the
consequences and implications of different exemption levels and
rates of progression. In suggesting tax policy changes to
implement the redistribution objective the degree of progressivity in both direct and indirect taxation must be examined.
Particularly important will be a detailed examination of exemption levels, rate structures, tax bases and administration of
personal direct taxation. The revenue implications, and consequent usefulness in redistribution, of changes in exemption
levels, rates of progression, etc., will be explored for the
individual taxes.

THE STABILIZATION OBJECTIVE

The prevention of inflationary price increases over the
planning period was stated as a long-run planning objective,[55]
was re-affirmed as a short-run objective in the particular
circumstances of the Third Plan,[56] and was ascribed a priority
position in the list of Fourth Plan objectives.[57]

In the context of the planned investment program in India
the stabilization role of tax policy may thus be defined as one
of ensuring that the planned rate and form of economic growth
are not prejudiced by inflation. A corollary of this objective
is that tax policies designed to prevent price increases should
be of such a nature that possible dampening effects of such
policies on the rate of growth of income are minimized. Like
redistributive tax policy, stabilization policy must be defined
in a dynamic sense.[58]

Inflation and Growth

The stabilizing role of tax policy in India is predicated
on the assumption that inflation is detrimental to growth. In
view of the controversial relationship of inflation and economic growth, it is necessary to justify this role of tax policy;
the case for control of inflation as an objective of tax policy
rests on the refutation of the case for the use of inflation as
an instrument of policy in the pursuit of growth.

The Pro-Inflation Argument

A positive relationship between inflation and growth has
been eloquently postulated by Sir D. Robertson:

> . . . a progressive rise in the price level, so long
> as it is not so blatant as to generate social dis-
> order or sap the foundations of contract . . . stimu-
> lates the production of goods; by benefiting the

pockets of the controllers of industry stimulates
also their energies and activies: . . . and this
fillip to production, by adding to the flow of
goods, serves to moderate the very rise in prices
which gives it birth.[59]

Inflation is alleged to promote growth in developing
countries by breaking two key bottlenecks. The first, and less
important, concerns the absence of financial intermediaries and
the consequent difficulty of guiding purchasing power into the
hands of potential entrepreneurs. If governments are willing
to create money the problem of transferring purchasing power
is short-circuited and resources can be directly channelled
into the hands of potential entrepreneurs.[60]

More important is the alleged role of inflation in over-
coming the deficiency of voluntary real saving, particularly
where the fiscal apparatus is inadequate to compel saving of
sufficient magnitude to make possible the desired rate of
growth. Real saving may be increased by inflation in two ways.

First, if money illusion prevails, then, although individual money incomes are rising no more than in proportion to
prices, a larger proportion of current money, and therefore
real, income is saved.

Second, and more important, a rising price level is important for saving because of its unequal incidence. If inflation
is to force a higher level of real saving, it must cause a
shift in real income away from people who tend to save a small
or negligible proportion of their income to people who tend to
save a larger proportion; the money incomes of the former group
must rise less than in proportion to prices while that of the
latter must rise more than in proportion. A. Lewis emphasizes
such a redistribution which increases the share of profits in
national income.[61] Provided these profits are re-invested
Lewis contends, with Sir D. Robertson, that the inflation will
be self-destructive; because of the redistribution voluntary
saving will rapidly catch up to investment and the price rise
will be halted when the additional output of consumer goods
made possible by the capital formation begins to reach the
market.[62] Mr. Kaldor has stressed the importance of inflation,
particularly in a relatively slowly growing economy, in raising
the prospective rate of return on risk investment by a sufficient margin over the supply price of risk capital to induce
increased private investment.[63] With regard to the rate of
inflation considered necessary Lewis suggests an upper limit of
5 per cent increase in prices per annum but would prefer 3-4
per cent,[64] while Kaldor suggests a "slow and steady rate" and
argues that a rate of 4-5 per cent in Britain since 1946 has

been beneficial.[65]   The question at issue is the significance
of the Robertson-Lewis-Kaldor arguments for the Indian case.

The Anti-Inflation Argument

There are several arguments that inflation is not conducive to, and, on the contrary, is detrimental to economic
growth.

First, it has been argued that a very rapid rate of inflation may be necessary to effect a significant increase in the
real rate of voluntary saving through inflationary redistribution.[66]

Second, the crux of the pro-inflation argument is the
alleged high propensity to save of the groups benefiting most
from inflation. In the present relatively inelastic food
supply situation in India, it is probable that food prices
would rise most sharply in any inflationary situation and that
the benefits of inflation may in large measure accrue to a
group whose saving propensity is relatively low.

Third, it is arguable that a degree of inflation of the
order postulated by Kaldor and Lewis may actually cause a
diminution in voluntary domestic saving as a result of loss of
confidence in the monetary unit, and a possible net reduction
in the rate of total (voluntary plus forced) saving.[67]

Fourth, inflation may cause saving to be directed into
non-productive highly liquid forms of investment.[68]   It has
been suggested that the windfall profits and capital gains of
inflation broaden the scope for profitable investment in areas
where "use benefits" are low and "ownership benefits" high,
such as in gold hoarding, the acquisition of certain types of
real estate, inventories, and foreign assets.[69]

Fifth, inflation might have a serious effect on the flow
of foreign capital to India and might encourage a flight of
foreign and domestic capital.[70]

Sixth, it is likely that inflation will hinder the expan-
sion and the diversification of exports.[71] The Third Five Year
Plan drew specific attention to the danger of inflation in
India in this regard.[72]

Inflation and Growth: The Statistical Evidence

A substantial quantity of statistical material is available
on the relationship of growth and inflation in developing countries since 1945.[73] The consensus of these studies is that,
beyond a moderate rate of price increase, up to a maximum annual

rate of 5 per cent, the rate of growth of income has been inversely related to the rate of inflation.

Four of the studies referred specifically to the Indian
case. Growth rates and price movements in India from 1948 to
1953, and from 1950 to 1957, were examined by the U Tun Wai
and Federal Reserve studies, respectively, and the conclusion
of both studies was that India's period of relative stability
was a major factor in the steady rate of growth.

The relationship between growth and inflation between 1950
and 1960 was examined by Madhavan. His findings, summarized in
Table 6, reveal no systematic relationship between inflation
and growth, but indicate that the average growth of national
income was higher in the earlier period of slightly falling
prices than in the later period in which prices rose between
6-7 per cent per annum.

TABLE 6

INFLATION AND GROWTH IN INDIA, 1950-60

Year	Rate of Inflation (Increase per annum in Consumer price index)	Rate of Economic Growth (Increase per annum in NNP[b] at factor cost)
1951-52	4.32	2.82
1952-53	-0.95	3.96
1953-54	1.92	6.03
1954-55	-6.60	2.49
1955-56	-3.03	1.94
1956-57	11.56	4.96
1957-58	4.67	-1.00
1958-59	5.36	7.35
1959-60	4.24	0.51
1951-52 - 1955-56[a]	-0.87	3.45
1956-57 - 1959-60[a]	6.43	2.96

Notes: [a]annual average
         [b]net national product

Source: M. Madhavan, "Inflation and Economic Development: A
         Case Study of India," Indian Economic Journal, Vol.
         10, No. 8 (January 1963), figures adapted from Table
         4, p. 265.

The most recent study is that by the Reserve Bank in June 1967. With regard to saving, the study points out that the growth of real saving slowed down considerably over the Third Plan, particularly in the last two years when the annual rate of increase in prices exceeded 10 per cent. The reasonable inference is that in a period of rapidly rising prices, households prefer to maintain their existing consumption levels at the expense of saving.

Investment appears to have suffered similarly. The Reserve Bank study shows that the real content of investment was sharply reduced over the Third Plan, as investment in financial terms could be realized only at higher prices. A related study[74] indicates that the price rise further resulted in a diversion of resources to those forms of investment which offered scope for large capital gains, such as gold, land generally, and urban house property in particular.

The final conclusion of the Reserve Bank study is that inflation over the Third Plan had a deleterious effect on the Indian balance of payments. The relative inflation in India made it extremely difficult for Indian exports to compete in foreign markets, and, correspondingly, placed Indian imports at a premium.

Inflation in the Third Plan

There are several characteristics of the Third Plan period which have served to make the control of inflation particularly difficult.

First, if food supply per capita does not increase at a rate appropriate to the increase in real income per capita and to the increase in the income elasticity of demand for food, there will tend to be strong upward pressure on food prices.[75] A shortfall in agricultural production was the prime factor in the sharp increase in prices in the Second Plan,[76] and the stagnancy of agricultural production over the Third Plan, and consequent sharp increase in food prices, has been the prime factor in recent inflationary trends.[77] The inflationary process geared to food prices has resulted in a shift in the terms of trade in favor of agriculture;[78] as suggested in the previous section, such a shift implies a redistribution of income to that sector of the economy where the propensity to save is relatively low. Increased food costs also resulted in upward pressure on wage costs.[79]

Second, the emphasis in the Third Plan on investment projects with a comparatively long gestation period[80] would suggest that no short run alleviation of inflationary pressures of the sort implicit in the Lewis model may be anticipated in India.

Third, one of the cushioning factors against inflation during the Second Plan was a widening balance of imports over exports financed by a drawing down of foreign exchange reserves;[81] the Third Plan explicitly stated that the level of foreign exchange reserves would permit no further depletion.[82]

Fourth, the inflationary process was aggravated throughout the Third Plan period by continuing upward pressure on government current expenditures, particularly on defense and food subsidies.

Finally, the 1966 devaluation sharply increased the cost of imported food materials and industrial raw materials.[83]

Table 7a shows the movement of the wholesale price index and that of its constituent parts, Table 7b the compound rate of increase in wholesale prices, and Table 7c the trends in aggregate demand and aggregate supply, all for the entire planning period to date.

Table 7a indicates that the rise in prices began effectively with the Second Plan. The major contributory role of food and raw material prices to the over-all index is apparent from the breakdown of the index into constituent parts. Combining the final column of Table 7a with Table 7b it is clear that the rise in prices accelerated sharply, in effect,

TABLE 7a

THE WHOLESALE PRICE INDEX OVER THE THREE PLAN PERIODS

Per cent change in index

	FIRST PLAN	SECOND PLAN	THIRD PLAN	1966-67
All Commodities	-17.3	+35.0	+32.2	+15.7
Food Articles	-23.0	+38.6	+40.7	+18.4
Liquor and Tobacco	-17.8	+35.7	+24.3	- 4.6
Fuel, power, light and lubricants	+ 2.8	+26.1	+27.5	+ 5.3
Industrial Raw Materials	-24.3	+46.9	+30.1	+20.9
Manufacturer	- 3.4	+24.3	+20.3	+ 9.2

Source: Reserve Bank of India, "Price Trends During the Three Plan Periods," Reserve Bank of India Bulletin (June 1967).

TABLE 7b

COMPOUND RATE OF INCREASE IN PRICES OVER
THE THREE PLAN PERIODS

Percentages

Index	15 years	10 years	Third Plan Period		
	1950-51- 1965-66	1955-56- 1965-66	1960-61- 1965-66	1961-62- 1962-63	1963-64- 1965-66
General Index	2.7	5.9	5.8	1.2	8.9
Food Articles	2.8	6.9	7.1	2.5	10.3
Industrial Raw					
Materials	2.5	6.7	5.4	-3.2	11.5
Manufacturer	2.4	4.1	3.8	2.1	5.0

Source: Reserve Bank of India, "Price Trends During the Three
Plan Periods," Reserve Bank of India Bulletin (June
1967).

TABLE 7c

TRENDS IN AGGREGATE DEMAND AND SUPPLY
OVER THE THREE PLAN PERIODS

Percentages

	First Plan	Second Plan	Third Plan
Growth in Net National Expenditure at current prices	+ 6	+44	+50
Growth in Net National Output at constant prices	+18	+22	+14
Change in Wholesale Prices (1952-53 = 100)	-17	+35	+32

Source: Reserve Bank of India, "Price Trends During the Three
Plan Periods," Reserve Bank of India Bulletin (June
1967).

acquired the characteristics of serious inflation, over the period 1963-64 through 1966-67. Table 7c provides almost the definition of demand-pull inflation, the gap between aggregate spending and aggregate real output widening steadily from 1956-57 through the Second and Third Plans.

Functional Instability

The argument for stable prices is not an argument for price rigidity. A growing economy must have sufficient flexibility in its price structure to induce the movement of real resources into those sectors in which growth is most rapid. The Third Plan recognized this situation by stating that price policy "must ensure that the movements of relative prices accord with the priorities and targets . . . set in the Plan."[84] Such movement of relative prices may be termed "functional"[85] or "policy-oriented"[86] instability. Functional instability is likely to imply not only changing relative prices but also pressure on the general price level, in that the fall in prices in declining sectors is not likely to be as great as the rise in prices in growing sectors.

The problem is to distinguish functional from inflationary increases in the general price level. Perhaps the key distinctions are that a functional rise in prices should be confined to a very limited sector, namely, that area of the economy which is expanding rapidly, and that the movement of prices should be moderate and of short duration. The essence of an inflationary rise in prices, on the other hand, is its pervasive, continuing and cumulative nature.

The distinction between a functional and an inflationary rise in prices is essentially qualitative rather than quantitative. No a priori judgment is therefore possible as to the quantitative limit on price increases beyond which further increases are considered detrimental either to the rate or the pattern of economic growth. The most recent general study of the problem indeed suggests that a rate of price increase from 1 per cent to 5 per cent per annum may, in developing countries, be considered compatible with relative price stability.[87] The approach to the problem must clearly be qualitative and pragmatic.

Tax Policy

Tax policy to control inflation will have to be directed both to the level and composition of aggregate demand, and to problems on the supply side such as inelasticity of food supply, relative immobility of resources, and scarcity of skilled labor.

Policy oriented to supply problems should be geared, first, to promoting increased agricultural productivity, and second, to the provision of tax incentives for labor to work, particularly in key occupations, for firms to operate efficiently and at optimum output in terms of planning goals, and for the transfer of resources toward most desirable activities; in short, toward the elimination of supply inelasticities and the promotion of increased factor mobility.

Conventional fiscal policy for stabilization operates on the level of spending. Tax policy under this head may be either automatic or discretionary. Discretionary changes in the tax structure, i.e., changes in existing tax rates, widening of existing tax bases and the introduction of new taxes-- represent ad hoc policy measures designed for a particular situation. Changes may be effected in the general level of taxation or may be geared to a particular region, commodity, or group of commodities.

Automatic changes in tax receipts reflect the degree of built-in flexibility--defined as $\Delta T/\Delta Y$ where T is tax revenue and Y is national income, and ΔT occurs in the same direction as ΔY--in the tax system. The built-in flexibility of a particular tax will depend on the width of the tax base relative to national income, the responsiveness of the tax base to changes in national income, and the rate structure of the tax. Thus, the wider the base of a particular tax, the more responsive the tax base to changes in national income, and the more progressive its rate structure, the greater will be its built-in flexibility. The impact of built-in flexibility in developed countries has been considerable,[88] although in large measure the result of a broadly based, relatively elastic personal income.[89]

In India the very limited coverage and relatively low elasticity of the present personal income tax clearly limit the usefulness of the income tax as a tool of built-in flexibility; although modifications in the rate structure and coverage should increase the responsiveness of the income tax to aggregate income changes, the major onus of providing built-in flexibility in the immediate future must devolve to indirect taxation. Indirect taxes have a wide base and elasticity studies suggest that revenue is surprisingly responsive to income changes. However, built-in flexibility in indirect taxation is at best an imprecise and unreliable factor owing to changes in tastes, fashions, etc.

The major role in stabilization policy in India would thus appear to fall upon discretionary measures. The latter, however, have some disadvantages. In addition to the need for separate political decisions and administrative actions, discretionary measures have the economic disadvantages of being subject to time lags--raising the possibility of perverse action should a trend change course--and being dependent on forecasts of economic trends.

A possible solution to this problem may lie in the extended use of formula flexibility whereby statutory changes in tax rates (and expenditure levels) are automatically implemented according to the movement of certain objectively identified economic variables or circumstances.[90] In this manner the strength of discretionary action is combined with the immediate responsiveness of automatic measures. Possible uses of this principle in India would include, e.g., pre-determined changes in export duties according to world price movements of primary commodities exported by India, and the introduction of higher excise tax rate structures and/or variations in the degree of progressivity in the personal income tax according to movements in either the domestic wholesale price level or national income.

Built-in flexibility, discretionary measures and formula flexibility are subject to one major criticism in that by exercising an inhibitory effect on private spending in the interests of price stability, they may diminish the rate of economic growth.[91] This difficulty may be at least partially resolved by the incorporation in direct tax stabilization measures of exemptions and incentives to saving, investment and work of particular kinds. In this manner a mix of direct and indirect tax measures would be employed to exercise a maximum inhibitory effect on consumption spending and a minimum inhibitory effect on investment spending. The final object of a development-oriented stabilization policy in India should thus be to control non-functional instability by means which have a minimal inhibitory effect on productive investment.

NOTES TO CHAPTER 2

1. V. K. R. V. Rao, "Changes in India's National Income," Capital: Annual Review of Commerce, Trade and Industry (December 1954), 15-17. See also Government of India, Planning Commission, Third Five Year Plan--A Summary (Delhi: Publications Division, 1962), p. 10.

2. Third Five Year Plan, op. cit, p. 11.

3. Ibid., p. 13.

4. Ibid., p. 11.

5. Government of India, Report of the Taxation Enquiry Commission (hereinafter TEC) (3 vols.; New Delhi: Ministry of Finance, 1953-54), Vol. I, p. 87.

6. Third Five Year Plan, op. cit., p. 13.

7. "Estimates of Saving and Investment in the Indian Economy: 1950-51 to 1962-63," Reserve Bank of India Bulletin, XIX (March 1965), 314-33.

8. This would substitute $\Delta(Y-[C_h + C_{gn}])/\Delta Y$, for $S/\Delta Y$, where Y is national income, S is saving, C_h and C_{gn} are, respectively, household consumption and governmental consumption expenditure of a non-developmental nature, and Δ indicates an increment in the variable.

9. See, for instance, S. Please, "Saving Through Taxation --Reality or Mirage?" Finance and Development, IV (March 1967), 24-32.

10. Please, op. cit., pp. 30-32.

11. The most rapid rate of growth of national income would theoretically be attained if aggregate consumption were restrained by taxation at a level which afforded only an "essential minimum level" of per capita consumption. The notion of the availability for saving of the difference between gross product and that amount required to provide some essential level of living on a per capita basis may be found in J. S. Mill, Principles of Political Economy, ed. W. J. Ashley (London: Longmans Green and Co., 1923), p. 164, and is discussed at length in P. Baran, The Political Economy of Growth (New York: Monthly Review Press, 1962), pp. 22-31. The notion of an "essential minimum" level of per capita consumption implies, of course, a definition of the composition of that minimum level in terms of calories, other nutrients, clothing, fuel, dwelling space, etc. For tax policy this definition would imply rigorous taxation of so-called luxury commodities and services (either domestic or imported). Even when the level of consumption is relatively high and the range of consumer goods and services widely varied, it is possible to arrive at an estimate of an "essential minimum," e.g., the notion of essential consumption used by the Bureau of Labor Statistics in the U.S.A. in compiling the cost of living index.

12. There is virtual unanimity on this aspect of taxation in developing countries. See, e.g., W. A. Lewis, The Theory of Economic Growth (London: Unwin, 1963), pp. 402-4; R. J. Chelliah, Fiscal Policy in Underdeveloped Countries (London: George Allen and Unwin, 1960); A. R. Prest, Public

Finance in Underdeveloped Countries (London: Weidenfeld and Nicolson, 1962), p. 25.

13. G. S. Sahota, Indian Tax Structure and Economic Development (Bombay: Asia Publishing House, 1961).

14. Roughly 40 per cent of consumption of all products in the rural sector is transacted on a non-monetary basis. TEC, op. cit., Vol. I, pp. 65-66.

15. Other than in Adam Smith, this canon finds a place in standard works such as J. F. Due, Government Finance (rev. ed.; Homewood, Ill.: Richard D. Irwin, Inc., 1959), pp. 118; A. R. Prest, Public Finance in Theory and Practice (London: Weidenfeld and Nicolson, 1960), p. 133; and, with special reference to developing countries in S. Enke, Economics for Development (Englewood Cliffs, N. J.: Prentice Hall, 1963), p. 247.

16. Over 1962-65 in India, Union government collection costs averaged 1.9 per cent of revenue; the corresponding figure for the States was 12.8 per cent. "Budget of the Central Government, 1964-65," Reserve Bank of India Bulletin (March 1964), 302-3; "Budget of the State Governments, 1964-65," Reserve Bank of India Bulletin (May 1964), 603-11.

17. Due, op. cit., p. 118.

18. Ibid., p. 103.

19. Enke, op. cit., p. 248.

20. Government of Canada, Report of the Royal Commission on Taxation (Ottawa: Queen's Printer, 1966), Vol. II, p. 11.

21. For a detailed discussion of the term "fiscal dirigism" and its application in West Germany following World War II, see F. G. Reuss, Fiscal Policy for Growth Without Inflation (Baltimore: The Johns Hopkins Press, 1963). For a general discussion of the use of taxation as a diversionary instrument used in the pursuit of economic growth, see National Bureau of Economic Research - Brookings, Foreign Tax Policies for Economic Growth (New York: Columbia University Press, 1966). 1966).

22. See, e.g., J. R. Meyer and E. Kuh, The Investment Decision (Cambridge: Harvard University Press, 1957), pp. 269-77, which presents a bibliography of pre-1956 literature; J. R. Meyer and R. R. Glauber, Investment Decisions, Economic Forecasting and Public Policy (Boston: Harvard University Press, 1964), pp. 273-76, which presents a bibliography of post-1956 literature.

        23. J. Heller and K. M. Kauffman, Tax Incentives for
Industry in Less Developed Countries (Cambridge: Harvard Law
School, 1963), p. 3.

        24. This broad definition of increase in economic well
being was first taken up in the United States by R. M. Haig;
the history of the concept may be found in H. C. Simons,
Personal Income Taxation (Chicago: University of Chicago
Press, 1938). A similar broadened definition of income was
advocated for India by N. Kaldor, Indian Tax Reform (New Delhi:
Ministry of Finance, 1956); the Carter Commission recommended
such a definition for use in Canada, Government of Canada,
Report of the Royal Commission on Taxation (Ottawa: Queen's
Printer, 1966).

        25. TEC, op. cit., Vol. I, p. 147.

        26. Government of India, The Constitution of India
(New Delhi: Manager of Publications, 1967), Part IV, Articles
36-51 (Directive Principles of State Policy), pp. 26-29.

        27. Third Five Year Plan, op. cit., p. 3.

        28. Ibid., p. 5: "In the implementation of plans and
policies there is need for greater emphasis [author's emphasis]
on the special objectives of planned development, in particular
on bringing about reduction in disparities in income and
wealth . . ."

        29. Government of India, Fourth Five Year Plan--A Draft
Outline (New Delhi: Planning Commission, 1966), p. 22.

        30. TEC, op. cit., Vol. I, p. 145.

        31. See, for instance, M. J. Gopal, "Towards a Realistic
Tax Policy for India," Indian Economic Journal, VII (January
1959), 281-326.

        32. TEC, op. cit., Vol. I, p. 42.

        33. P. O. Ojha and V. V. Bhatt, "Distribution of Income
in the Indian Economy," Reserve Bank of India Bulletin (September 1962), 1348-63. The results of this study have been
further elaborated in P. D. Ojha and V. V. Bhatt, "Pattern of
Income Distribution in an Underdeveloped Economy," American
Economic Review LIV (September 1964), 711-20.

        34. National Council of Applied Economic Research
(NCAER), Urban Income and Saving (New Delhi: NCAER, 1962).

35. The concentration ratio is defined as the ratio of the area between the Lorenz curve and the diagonal line, representing equality, to the area under the diagonal. This ratio measures the departure of the Lorenz curve from complete equality, expressed as a ratio to complete inequality (which would be represented by a full right angle under the diagonal). The closer the ratio to unity the greater the degree of inequality.

36. The merits of both studies have been recently debated. See "Pattern of Income Distribution in an Underdeveloped Economy: A Case Study of India," "Comment" by E. Mueller and I. R. K. Sarma, "Comment" by S. Swamy, and "Reply" by Ojha and Bhatt, American Economic Review, LV, No. 5 (December 1965), 1173-88.

37. V. K. R. V. Rao, "Economic Growth and Rural-Urban Income Distribution, 1950-61," The Economic Weekly, XVII, No. 8 (February 20, 1965), 373-78; over the decade total urban income increased by 72.15 per cent as against 39 per cent in the case of rural income. The share of urban income in national income increased from 30.3 per cent to 33.8 per cent. Per capita urban income increased by 43.2 per cent as against 12.6 per cent in the case of rural income. Rural per capita income which was 84.3 per cent of All-India per capita income in 1950-51 declined to 80.5 per cent in 1960-61. Urban per capita income went from 183 per cent to 233 per cent of All-India per capita income in the same period.

38. Government of India, Report of the Committee on the Distribution of Income and Levels of Living (New Delhi: Planning Commission, 1964), pp. 20-21.

39. Ibid., p. 21.

40. Ibid., p. 22.

41. Simons, op. cit., pp. 18-19.

42. The conspicuously large fortunes at the upper end of the scale of economic well being in India may offer in a static sense only a limited field for redistributive finance because the aggregate resources they represent may be small relative to the huge numbers at the other end of the scale.

43. K. E. Boulding, "The Fruits of Progress and the Dynamics of Distribution," American Economic Review, XLIII, No. 2 (May 1953), Papers and Proceedings, 473-83.

44. W. Heller, "Fiscal Policies for Underdeveloped Economies," in United Nations, Taxes and Fiscal Policy in Underdeveloped Countries (New York, 1954), p. 17; C. Cosciani,

"Progressive Taxation in Underdeveloped Counties," Banca Nationale del Lavoro, Quarterly Review, XIII (1960), 303-16; R. Eisner, "Income Distribution, Investment and Growth," Indian Economic Journal, XI (April-June 1964), 400-412.

45. B. M. Russett, "Inequality and Instability," World Politics, XVI (April 1964), 442-54.

46. G. Schmoller, "Zeitschrift für die gesamte Staatswissenschaft," quoted in Simons, op. cit., p. 22.

47. W. Heller, loc. cit.

48. Eisner, op. cit.

49. Cosciani, op. cit., pp. 308-9; J. K. Galbraith, Economic Development (Boston: Houghton Mifflin, 1964), pp. 4-8.

50. See, for instance, H. C. Aubrey, "The Role of the State in Economic Development," American Economic Review (1951), 266-73.

51. J. M. Keynes, The Economic Consequences of the Peace (New York: Harcourt, Brace and Howe, 1920), pp. 19-20.

52. TEC, op. cit., Vol. I, p. 145.

53. "Functional inequalities" are defined in the TEC, op. cit., Vol. I, p. 145, as "inequalities necessary to evoke additional effort or enterprise"; see also D. T. Lakdawala, Taxation and the Plan (Bombay: Popular Book Depot, 1956), pp. 79-80; and U. K. Hicks, "Direct Taxation and Economic Growth," Oxford Economic Papers, New Series, VIII (1956), 302-17; in his speech initiating discussion of the Third Plan (Lok Sabha Debates, August 22, 1960), Mr. Nehru commented: "Incentives are necessary, I agree. But there are many types of incentives, some that are good to society and some that are bad to society . . . I do not want to encourage acquisitiveness in India . . ."

54. It is not intended to elaborate here the problem of obtaining a consistent solution through social choice. R. A. Musgrave, The Theory of Public Finance (New York: McGraw-Hill, 1959), p. 116, footnote 1, provides extensive documentation of the literature.

55. Third Five Year Plan, op. cit., p. 35.

56. Ibid.

57. Fourth Five Year Plan, op. cit., p. 16.

58. TEC, op. cit., Vol. I, p. 162, ". . . the objective of maintaining stability in the economy merges into the larger objective of economic development. The problem . . . is of adapting fiscal and other policies to the end of maintaining an even course of development."

59. D. H. Robertson, Money (Cambridge: Cambridge University Press, 1922), pp. 122-25.

60. G. Maynard, Economic Development and the Price Level (London: MacMillan, 1963), p. 6.

61. W. A. Lewis, The Theory of Economic Growth (Homewood, Ill.: Richard D. Irwin, Inc., 1955), p. 404.

62. Ibid., p. 405.

63. N. Kaldor, "Economic Growth and the Problem of Inflation," Economica, XXVI (1959), 287-98.

64. Lewis, op. cit., pp. 224 and 404.

65. Kaldor, op. cit., pp. 187-88.

66. S. H. Axilrod, "Inflation and the Development of Underdeveloped Areas," Review of Economics and Statistics, XXXVI (1954), 334-38. Axilrod suggests as a typical example that to raise savings from 6 per cent of national income to 8 per cent over a five-year period would require a 10 per cent per annum increase in the price level.

67. Maynard, op. cit., pp. 14-30.

68. Ibid., pp. 34-35.

69. E. M. Bernstein and S. J. Patel, "Inflation in Relation to Economic Development," International Monetary Fund Staff Papers (November 1952), 367-84.

70. G. Dorrance, "Rapid Inflation and International Payments," Finance and Development (June 1965), 65-70.

71. Ibid., pp. 65-67; Maynard, op. cit., p. 13; G. Lovasy, "Inflation and Exports in Primary Producing Countries," International Monetary Fund Staff Papers (March 1962), 38-40.

72. Third Five Year Plan, op. cit., p. 42.

73. U Tun Wai, "The Relation between Inflation and Economic Growth," International Monetary Fund Staff Papers (October 1959), 302-17; Phelps-Brown and M. H. Browne,

"Distribution and Productivity Under Inflation," Economic Journal (March 1960); R. J. Bhatia, "Inflation, Deflation and Economic Development," International Monetary Fund Staff Papers (November 1960), 101-14; Federal Reserve Bank of New York, "Inflation and Economic Development," Monthly Review of the Bank (August 1959), 122-27; A. W. Marget, "Inflation--Some Lessons of Recent Foreign Experience," American Economic Review (May 1960), 205-11; M. Madhavan, "Inflation and Economic Development--A Case Study of India," Indian Economic Journal, No. 8 (January 1963), 257-66; G. S. Dorrance, "The Effect of Inflation on Economic Development," International Monetary Fund Staff Papers (March 1963), 1-31; G. Maynard, "Inflation and Growth--Some Lessons to be Drawn from Latin American Experience," Oxford Economic Papers, New Series, XIII, No. 2 (June 1961), 184-202; G. Dorrance, "Inflation and Growth: The Statistical Evidence," International Monetary Fund Staff Papers (March 1966), 82-102; Reserve Bank of India, "Price Trends During the Three Plan Periods," Reserve Bank of India Bulletin (June 1967), 740-74.

74. V. V. Bhatt, "The Indian Capital Market," The Bankers' Magazine (October 1966), 240.

75. See extensive discussion of this point in G. Maynard, op. cit., pp. 50-60; also, Maynard, "Inflation and Growth in Latin America," Oxford Economic Papers, New Series, XV (March 1963), 63-65.

76. Madhavan, op. cit., p. 264, Table 1.

77. Government of India, Third Five Year Plan: Mid-Term Appraisal (New Delhi: Planning Commission, 1963), pp. 10-12; Government of India, Economic Survey 1966-67 (New Delhi: Manager of Publications, 1967), pp. 36-39. The pressure to inflation from inelastic food supply is one part, albeit a crucial part, of the general problem of relative immobility of resources between sectors combined with relative inelasticity of supply within each sector; the consequence is a proliferation of bottlenecks and inflationary pressure.

78. Reserve Bank of India, op. cit., pp. 763-64; A. M. Khusro, "Inter-Sectoral Terms of Trade and Price Policy," The Economic Weekly (February 4, 1961), 290.

79. Economic Survey 1966-67, op. cit., p. 37.

80. Third Five Year Plan, op. cit., Chapter 4.

81. Ibid., p. 35.

82. Ibid., p. 32.

83. Economic Survey 1966-67, op. cit., pp. 37-38.

84. Third Five Year Plan, op. cit., p. 35.

85. International Monetary Fund, Economic Development with Stability (Washington, D.C.: 1953), p. 5.

86. Third Five Year Plan: Mid-Term Appraisal, op. cit., p. 12.

87. Dorrance, "Inflation and Growth: The Statistical Evidence," op. cit., p. 98.

88. Musgrave has estimated that total budget built-in flexibility (including expenditure variations) in the U.S.A. may be expected to offset 40 per cent of the fluctuations in national income which would occur in its absence, and similar studies in Britain would suggest the prevention of from 30-40 per cent of fluctuations (Theory of Public Finance, op. cit., pp. 505-507).

89. R. Goode, The Individual Income Tax (Washington, D.C.: The Brookings Institution Studies in Government Finance, 1964), records several calculations of the built-in flexibility coefficient ($\Delta T/\Delta Y$) of the personal income tax in the U.S.A., all of which fall between 8-10 per cent.

90. Such a "thermostatic" stabilization policy originates in the British White Paper on Employment Policy, Cmd. 6527 (London, H.M.S.O., 1944, reprinted 1956), pp. 22-24 and Appendix II. The notion has been developed by Musgrave, Theory of Public Finance, op. cit., pp. 512 et seq., Milton Friedman, "A Monetary and Fiscal Framework for Economic Stability," and "The Effects of Full-Employment Policy on Economic Stability," in his Essays in Positive Economics (Chicago: University of Chicago Press, 1953), pp. 117-56; and by E. E. Hagen and A. G. Hart, "Problems in Timing and Administering Fiscal Policy in Prosperity and Depression," American Economic Review (May 1948), 417-51. The concept has now won acceptance as a policy measure in the U.S.A. See the Report of the Commission on Money and Credit (Englewood Cliffs, N.J.: Prentice Hall, 1961), pp. 129-37.

91. This possibility is elaborated by A. T. Peacock, "Built-in Flexibility and Economic Growth," in Stabile Preise in wachsender Wirtschaft, ed., G. Bombach (Tübingen, 1960).

CHAPTER **3** THE PERSONAL
INCOME TAX

DESCRIPTION

Indian income tax laws do not discriminate between different sources of income, as would be the case under a "schedular" type of income tax. Income drawn from agricultural activities, however, is not included in the tax base, the power to tax agricultural incomes being constitutionally vested in the States. Also, while capital gains are included in the definition of income, they are taxed at concessionary rates and must be declared on a separate schedule of the income tax return.[1] The method of taxing capital gains will be examined in detail in the next chapter.

Income from sources other than agriculture and long-term gains--from salaries, interest on securities, property, profits and gains from a business, profession or vocation, and from other sources[2]--is aggregated for purposes of tax liability computation. Thus the Indian system of income taxation may be said to be "global" in principle and, for the most part, in practice. Nevertheless, elements of a schedular system exist in the exemption of agricultural income and the particular treatment of capital gains.

The personal income tax is levied on the total income of all individuals, joint Hindu families, unregistered firms, and other "associations of persons."[3] Total income is the sum of the taxpayer's income under all categories, exclusive of certain exempt receipts which are not included in total income,[4] and reduced by deduction of certain expenditures incurred in earning total income.[5] Certain other receipts are included in the definition of total income but are exempt from tax.[6] Likewise, various expenditures such as life insurance and annuity premiums, employee contributions to pension and provident funds and charitable donations are included in total income but are deductible for tax purposes up to a specified limit.[7]

Income tax is imposed on net income[8] as calculated above subject to a specified amount of tax relief on account of personal allowances. The 1965-66 Budget introduced the use of tax credits in place of personal allowances specified in the form of amounts of exempt income. The tax credit scheme is both

more equitable and more revenue-productive. An exemption takes
the form of a reduction in taxable income and results in a tax
reduction which effectively increases with income, since the
value of an exemption depends on the marginal rate of tax
applicable to the taxpayer. A tax credit affects all taxpayers
in the same amount. Thus the revenue loss resulting from the
use of exemptions is higher than that from the use of credits,
and credits achieve the same results in equity for low-income
groups as would be obtained under an exemption scheme, without
providing extra benefit to higher-income groups whose marginal
rate would have been reduced by an exemption system.

Tax credits under the 1967-68 regulations are as follows:
for an unmarried individual, Rs. 125; for a married individual
with no children, Rs. 200; for a married individual with one
child, Rs. 220; and for a married individual with more than one
child, Rs. 240.

It is further established that no tax shall be payable on
a total income not exceeding Rs. 4,000 for an individual and
Rs. 7,000 for a Hindu undivided family.[9]

Income tax is levied at progressive rates. Super tax,
until 1965 levied separately as a supplement to income tax, is
now fully integrated with income tax. Income tax rates as in
the 1967-68 Finance Act are set out in Table 1. The rates
shown were established in the 1966-67 Budget and were not
changed in 1967-68. Tax rates have been reduced at all levels
since 1964-65, particularly at high brackets, and the degree of
progressivity of the schedule has been considerably reduced.[10]
Equally, exemption levels and tax credits in respect of dependent relatives were increased in the 1966-67 Budget; these increases were unchanged by the 1967-68 Budget.[11] The revenue
cost of these changes was partially offset by a new surcharge
imposed in the 1966-67 Budget, described in detail below.

A diverse group of surcharges imposed on income tax and
super tax was replaced in 1964 by a single Union surcharge.
This device was used to discriminate in favor of earned as
against unearned income, and was retained--at different rates--
in the 1965-66 Budget. The exemption limit for surcharge on
unearned income was doubled in the 1967-68 Budget. The surcharge on earned income is levied at 5 per cent on income
between Rs. 100,000 and Rs. 200,000, 10 per cent for incomes
between Rs. 200,000 and Rs. 300,000, and 15 per cent for incomes above Rs. 300,000. The surcharge on unearned income is
levied at rates of 20 per cent on unearned incomes between
Rs. 30,000 and Rs. 50,000, and 25 per cent on such income above
Rs. 50,000.

TABLE 1

BASIC RATES OF INCOME TAX (1967-68)
BEFORE ADDITION OF SURCHARGES AND
DEDUCTION OF PERSONAL ALLOWANCE TAX CREDIT

(1)	where the total income does not exceed Rs. 5,000	5 per cent of the total income
(2)	where the total income exceeds Rs. 5,000 but does not exceed Rs. 10,000	Rs. 250 plus 10 per cent of the amount by which the total income exceeds Rs. 5,000;
(3)	where the total income exceeds Rs. 10,000 but does not exceed Rs. 15,000	Rs. 750 plus 15 per cent of the amount by which the total income exceeds Rs. 10,000;
(4)	where the total income exceeds Rs. 15,000 but does not exceed Rs. 20,000	Rs. 1,500 plus 20 per cent of the amount by which the total income exceeds Rs. 15,000;
(5)	where the total income exceeds Rs. 20,000 but does not exceed Rs. 25,000	Rs. 2,500 plus 30 per cent of the amount by which the total income exceeds Rs. 20,000;
(6)	where the total income exceeds Rs. 25,000 but does not exceed Rs. 30,000	Rs. 4,000 plus 40 per cent of the amount by which the total income exceeds Rs. 25,000;
(7)	where the total income exceeds Rs. 30,000 but does not exceed Rs. 50,000	Rs. 6,000 plus 50 per cent of the amount by which the total income exceeds Rs. 30,000;
(8)	where the total income exceeds Rs. 50,000 but does not exceed Rs. 70,000	Rs. 16,000 plus 60 per cent of the amount by which the total income exceeds Rs. 50,000;
(9)	where the total income exceeds Rs. 70,000	Rs. 28,000 plus 65 per cent of the amount by which the total income exceeds Rs. 70,000:

Provided that:

(i) no income-tax shall be payable on a total income not exceeding the following limit, namely:

(a) Rs. 7,000 in the case of every Hindu undivided family.

(b) Rs. 4,000 in every other case.

Source: Government of India, Finance Bill, 1967 (New Delhi: Ministry of Finance, 1967), pp. 41-42.

The 1966-67 Budget introduced a flat 10 per cent surcharge on all income tax payments, both under the regular rate schedule and under the surcharge on earned and unearned income. This surcharge was retained in the 1967-68 Budget.

Finally, the 1964-65 Budget abolished the Compulsory Deposit Scheme of 1963-64 and introduced provision for the payment of compulsory "annuity deposits" by all resident personal assessees whose income exceeds Rs. 15,000. The device has been retained in the 1965-66 and subsequent legislation; rates are 5 per cent on income between Rs. 15,000 and Rs. 20,000, 7.5 per cent between Rs. 20,000 and Rs. 40,000, 10 per cent between Rs. 40,000 and Rs. 70,000 and 12.5 per cent over Rs. 70,000.

The complete scale of rates of income tax, surcharges and annuity deposits for married taxpayers with more than one child is detailed in Table 2. The highest marginal rate on earned income is now 66.65 per cent (as against 83 per cent in 1964-65) and 77.94 per cent on unearned income (as against 88 per cent in 1964-65).

Indian tax law provides for the collection of taxes from the taxpayer through one or more of four different processes;[12] first, deduction or withholding at source at the time of payment of income; second, advance payment of tax by the taxpayer himself; third, provisional assessment and demand by the Income Tax Officer; and, fourth, regular assessment and final demand by the Income Tax Officer. Withholding at source--referred to in the U.K. as pay-as-you-earn (PAYE)--is applied to certain types of income, including salaries, interest on securities, and dividends.[13] The term PAYE is used in India to refer to the second method of collection referred to above, viz., advance payment of income tax on incomes not subject to withholding, by taxpayers whose incomes exceed certain minimum limits (Rs. 2,500 for companies and Rs. 5,500 for individuals and other classes of taxpayers).[14] Such advance estimates are computed by the taxpayer himself. Provisional and regular assessments on the balance of tax liability are made by Income Tax Officers.[15]

Income Tax Revenue Productivity

Table 3 sets out total income tax assessments by type of assessee for 1963-64 and the two preceding years. The total income assessed and the corresponding tax demand in 1963-64 were lower than in the previous year, despite the increase in the number of assessees. The declines in income assessed and tax levied were mainly on account of the fall in company income and tax assessment, while the rise in the number of assessments was mainly due to the increase in assessments made

TABLE 2

TAX RATES (INCLUDING SURCHARGES AND ANNUITY DEPOSITS)
PAYABLE IN 1967-68 BY A MARRIED TAXPAYER
WITH MORE THAN ONE CHILD

PRE-TAX INCOME Rs.	ANNUITY DEPOSIT	WHOLLY EARNED INCOME		WHOLLY UNEARNED INCOME	
		AMOUNT OF TAX Rs.	PER CENT OF PRE-TAX INCOME	AMOUNT OF TAX Rs.	PER CENT OF PRE-TAX INCOME
4,500	Nil	Nil	Nil	Nil	Nil
5,000	Nil	11	0.22	11	0.22
6,000	Nil	121	2.02	121	2.02
7,400	Nil	275	3.72	275	3.72
10,000	Nil	561	5.61	561	5.61
12,500	Nil	974	7.79	974	7.79
15,000	Nil	1,386	9.24	1,386	9.24
18,000	900	2,748	15.27	2,748	15.27
20,000	1,000	3,266	16.33	3,266	16.33
24,000	1,800	5,012	20.88	5,012	20.88
25,000	1,880	5,396	21.59	5,396	21.59
36,000	2,700	10,851	30.14	12,204	33.89
40,000	3,000	13,186	32.97	14,946	37.37
48,000	4,800	18,396	38.33	20,838	43.42
60,000	6,000	25,976	43.29	29,826	49.71
70,000	7,000	32,916	47.02	38,251	54.64
72,000	8,000	34,576	48.03	40,076	55.68
100,000	12,500	55,549	55.55	65,167	65.17
200,000	25,000	133,292	66.65	155,870	77.94

Source: Government of India, Memorandum Explaining the Provisions of the
Finance Bill, 1966 (New Delhi: Ministry of Finance, 1966), p. 3.

TABLE 3

INCOME TAX ASSESSMENTS BY TYPES OF ASSESSEES, 1961-62 - 1963-64

Rs. million

Years	Individuals			Hindu Undivided Families			Companies			Unregistered and Registered Forms; Association of Persons; and others			Total		
	Number of Assessments	Income Assessed	Tax	Number of Assessments	Income Assessed	Tax	Number of Assessments	Income Assessed	Tax	Number of Assessments	Income Assessed	Tax	Number of Assessments	Income Assessed	Tax
1961-62	940,246	8,846.0	1,125.8	73,222	968.1	152.4	11,464	4,050.5	1,959.4	47,696	1,889.6	142.2	1,072,629	15,754.2	3,379.8
1962-63	961,841	9,231.2	1,183.5	73,409	951.1	140.6	12,024	3,611.8	1,750.8	56,935	2,328.0	151.1	1,104,209	16,122.0	3,226.0
1963-64	1,036,534	9,591.5	1,158.4	71,536	896.5	128.0	10,315	2,714.8	1,361.4	59,639	2,400.0	170.2	1,178,024	15,602.7	2,818.0

Source: Government of India, All-India Income-Tax Statistics for the Year 1963-64 (Delhi: Manager of Publications, 1967).

on individuals. In 1963-64, individuals contributed 41 per
cent of total tax demand, and companies 48 per cent.

The number of individual income tax assessees have increased over the planning period, from just under 500,000 in
the first year of the Second Plan to 1,036,534 in 1963-64, but
is still limited to a very small proportion of total population.

Table 4 provides estimates of the elasticity of income
tax revenue--other than from corporation income tax--over the
Second and Third Plans and, using Planning Commission forecasts,
over the Fourth Plan. Elasticity is defined as the annual compound rate of growth of tax revenue, as in Chapter 1. Only
maximum estimates are used, i.e., the entire actual growth of
income tax revenue each year minus the budget forecast of increased revenue resulting from tax changes, is attributed to
built-in elasticity.

Over the entire period, from 1955-56 to 1970-71, the
average elasticity of income tax revenue comes to 3.7. It must
be noted, however, that this rather low estimate results largely from the relatively pessimistic estimates of the Planning
Commission for income tax revenue over the Fourth Plan. Taking
the Fourth Plan period alone, the average elasticity comes to
only 1.74; the figure for the Second and Third Plan period
comes to 5.7. Bearing in mind, however, that even this last
figure is a maximum estimate of elasticity, the revenue performance of income tax--exclusive of corporation income tax--is
relatively disappointing. Using the maximum estimates of elasticity, the average for Union tax collections as a whole over
the same period comes to 9.66.

Turning to the income elasticity of income tax revenue, the
coefficients were calculated for the periods, 1955-56 to 1960-
61, and 1960-61 to 1964-65. Over the first of these periods,
the coefficient comes to 0.496, indicating that on average over
the Second Plan period a 1 per cent increase in national income
was associated with a 0.496 per cent increase in revenue. Over
the second period, the coefficient comes to 0.654, indicating a
slight improvement in the income elasticity of income tax revenue over the planning period. These results for income elasticity confirm the results of Mr. Sahota, who found that over the
period 1951-52 to 1957-58, the income elasticity of income tax
revenue--exclusive of corporation tax revenue--came to 0.565.[16]

APPRAISAL OF THE PERSONAL INCOME TAX
IN TERMS OF THE THREE MAJOR POLICY OBJECTIVES

The personal income tax is theoretically perhaps the
most effective tax device for the pursuit of the growth,

TABLE 4

ELASTICITY OF INCOME TAX
REVENUE (OTHER THAN FROM CORPORATIONS),
1955-56 - 1970-71

1 YEAR	2 ACTUAL REVENUE Rs.million	3 INCREASE IN REVENUE OVER PREVIOUS YEAR Rs.million	4 ANTICIPATED INCREASE IN REVENUE BECAUSE OF BUDGET CHANGES Rs.million	5 INCREASE IN REVENUE DUE TO BUILT-IN ELASTICITY (3-4)	6 ELASTICITY COEFFICIENT (5 as per cent of 2)
1955-56	1,313.5				
		203.9	32.0	171.9	13.05
1956-57	1,517.4				
		119.6	57.5	62.1	4.094
1957-58	1,637.4				
		83.1	0	83.1	5.077
1958-59	1,720.1				
		-231.6	0	-231.6	-13.45
1959-60	1,488.5				
		185.3	0	185.3	12.45
1960-61	1,673.8				
		- 19.9	20.0	- 39.9	- 2.383
1961-62	1,653.9				
		205.7	100.0	105.7	6.39
1962-63	1,859.6				
		726.4	390.0	336.4	18.08
1963-64	2,586.0				
		79.5	27.2	52.3	2.02
1964-65	2,665.5				
		52.5	0	52.5	1.967
1965-66	2,718.0				
		-118.0	0	-118.0	- 2.171
(1966-67	2,600.0				
(		- 60.0	0	- 60.0	- 1.154
(1967-68	2,540.0				
(		200.0	0	200.0	3.938
(1968-69	2,740.0				
(		220.0	0	220.0	4.015
(1969-70	2,960.0				
(		240.0	0	240.0	4.054
(1970-71	3,200.0				

Planning Commission Forecasts

Sources: Reserve Bank of India, Report on Currency and Finance 1965-66 (Bombay: Reserve Bank of India, 1967); Government of India, Draft Fourth Plan Material and Financial Balances (New Delhi: Planning Commission, 1966.

redistribution and stabilization objectives. The progressive
rate structure affords a means of curtailing income inequalities, and the combination of progressive rates and, generally,
broad tax base, provides an elastic productive revenue source
and a flexible tool of either automatic or discretionary stabilization policy. The income tax in India is, however, characterized by both low coverage and inelasticity of tax receipts
and the effectiveness of the tax clearly depends on a wider and
more responsive tax base.

In a developing country the usefulness of income taxation
may also be limited by such basic factors as non-monetizatin--
in India some 40 per cent of transactions are of a non-monetary
nature,[17]--a low level of literacy (24 per cent, 34.5 per cent
male and 13 per cent female, in India in 1961),[18] and a general
lack of accounting records among small businessmen, etc. But
these factors cannot adequately explain the present low productivity and inflexibility in the Indian income tax. The
explanation must be sought mainly in factors intrinsic in the
structure and administration of the present tax and in the
attitude of the public to tax liability.

Agricultural Incomes

The constitutional exclusion of agricultural income--43.2
per cent of Indian national income in 1964-65[19]--from the coverage of the Union income tax represents the major weakness of
the present income tax system as a revenue source. This omission is particularly serious in terms of the pool of high incomes, particularly property incomes, in the agricultural sector which escapes progressive income taxation. It is also
likely that the bulk of that portion of the incomes of the
rural population--82 per cent of total population in 1961[20]--
which accrues from activities other than agriculture goes un-
reported and is for all practical purposes exempt from Union
income tax. The present agricultural income taxes and land
taxes are inelastic and inflexible in structure, and Chapter 5
will examine at some length a reformed structure of agricultural taxation which might ultimately be integrated with the present personal income tax. Assessment in monetary terms is
clearly out of the question for that portion of rural incomes
which accrues in kind, and tax measures designed to deal specifically with this situation will be explored at length in
Chapter 8.

Evasion and Avoidance

The second major weakness of the present system is the substantial measure of income tax evasion. Although there is some
controversy over the magnitude of evasion there is unanimity on
the seriousness of the problem.[21] Adequate administration and

enforcement of tax liability remain as an essential first step toward making the effective incidence of the progressive income tax accord with intended incidence, and thus toward the success of the tax as an income-elastic revenue source, a means to the mitigation of inequalities, and as a built-in and discretionary stabilization device. The elimination of corruption on the side of the taxpayer is, of course, conditional on honest and efficient administration of the tax. The degree of integrity in tax administration is difficult to estimate. Such limited evidence as is available--from complaints, etc.--would not suggest that the problem is of serious magnitude.[22] The whole problem of evasion--cause and possible remedies--will be examined in Chapter 11.

Related to evasion is the technically legal issue of tax avoidance, in which an insufficiently comprehensive tax base, or inadequately drafted tax legislation, permit the manipulation of accretions to economic well-being in such a way as to minimize tax liability. Not only is revenue productivity reduced by avoidance but the unequal distribution of opportunities for avoidance detracts from horizontal equity and lowers taxpayer morale and cooperation. The possibility of a comprehensive self-checking personal tax return will be examined in Chapter 11 as means to the elimination of opportunities for avoidance. Related to the proposed self-checking tax return is the whole issue of the definition of income in India.

The Definition of Income

The question to be examined here is whether the present Indian definition of income provides a satisfactory index of ability-to-pay. Professor Kaldor argued in 1956 for the introduction of a wider definition of income in India to embrace all beneficial receipts which increase the taxpayer's spending power, and not merely the conventional forms of income included in the tax base.[23] The Indian Income Tax Act has in the past been framed in terms of the so-called English concept of income which focuses almost entirely on business or commercial income and omits a wide range of other accretions to spending power.

Professor Kaldor's advocacy of a comprehensive income base echoed the earlier defense of such a definition of income by, among others, R. M. Haig[24] and H. Simons,[25] and this broad definition is gaining increasing acceptance among fiscal theorists. The only concession to the broad base made to date in India is the classification of short-term capital gains as ordinary income for tax purposes (1967-68 Budget), and it remains to define a comprehensive tax base.

In terms of horizontal equity and--perhaps more important in India at present--the revenue productivity of the income tax, income must be defined as net accretion, or the change in the spending power of the taxable unit over a specified period of time. Over a given time period, the change in a taxable unit's spending power can be measured as the sum of the following:

1. The market value of the goods and services used by the taxable unit during the given time period to satisfy its own wants, i.e., consumption over the period.

2. The market value of the goods and services given to other tax units during the period, i.e., gifts over the period.

3. The change over the period in the market value of the total net assets held by the tax unit, i.e., change in net worth, which may be either positive or negative over a given period.

Such a base includes all additions to spending over a period without regard to source, intention or form, and whether consumed or saved. As such it represents the theoretical aspiration of an equitable and productive income tax system. In practice, of course, the ideal base must be modified by considerations of administrative feasibility.

By taxing all the net gains, appropriately defined, of the taxable unit over the chosen period, the same result can be obtained as by taxing consumption plus increase in net worth. The tax base would then be defined as the net gains from the following: the provision of personal services; the disposal of property; the receipt of gifts or bequests from other tax units; the receipt of windfalls of any kind; the receipt of such gains as strike pay or social insurance payments; the ownership or property.   The definition of "net" gains implies that losses under any of the heads listed above would be deductible for tax purposes from gains. Net gains can clearly take a variety of forms--the receipt of cash, the receipt of benefits in kind, a change in the value of rights to, or interests in, property, the acquisition of rights to, or interests in, property and the personal use of property which might have been rented to others.

Clearly under such a definition the income base in India would have to be widened to include accrued capital gains, all gifts and bequests, all windfalls, imputed rent on property owned, and all benefits in kind. In practice it would seem administratively feasible to include only realized rather than accrued capital gains (Chapter 4), and to exclude imputed rent. The revised base would, however, include all realized capital gains, all windfalls, all benefits in kind and all gifts and bequests received by the taxable unit.

All expenses, other than personal living expenses, reasonably incurred in the acquisition would, under this broad definition, be deductible in the computation of net gains.

Treatment of Hindu Undivided Families

Avoidance is not always a function of inadequate tax base
definition or tax legislation. There is one particular statutory area of avoidance--the privileged tax treatment of Hindu
undivided families (HUF)--which has been recently shown to
represent very substantial revenue loss to the exchequer.[26]
The HUF enjoys a basic exemption limit of Rs. 7,000 as against
Rs. 4,000 for an individual. The revenue loss involved in
such treatment is aggravated by the possibilities of complete
or partial partition and transfer of assets open to the HUF,
which permit the use of several exemption limits and lower
rates of tax on split incomes.[27]

The Gulati study shows that the HUF, contrary to popular
belief that it is disintegrating under the impact of modern
forces, still accounts for over 10 per cent of total non-
corporate income tax revenue, and that the number of HUF has,
in fact, increased slightly in the last ten years.[28] A calculation made of the maximum tax avoidance available to a HUF,
through varied combinations of complete partition, partial
partition and transfers by gift, shows that by dextrous employment of avoidance techniques a HUF can earn up to Rs. 58,000
without incurring any income tax liability.[29] An aggregative
computation of annual loss of tax revenue to the exchequer on
account of avoidance action of HUF provides an average figure
of between Rs. 800 million and Rs. 1,500 million.[30] The most
disturbing conclusion is a secular increase in this figure
throughout the planning period, because of the annual increases
in the number of families and their total income. The privileged position of HUF would appear to be costly in terms of
revenue sacrificed and difficult to defend on equity grounds.
Mobilization of even the lower estimate of annual revenue cost
--Rs. 800 million--would have increased gross Union income tax
collections in 1965-66 by 25 per cent.

Modifications to the present treatment of HUF might include the removal of the tax incentive, to complete partition
by treating the HUF as a registered firm, the income of which
is allocated among the various partners who are then assessed
on their respective total income including the share of the
firm's income.[31] Again withdrawal of legal recognition of
partial partition would remove a major source of avoidance, as
would the extension of the provisions of Section 16 (3) of the
Income Tax Act covering gratuitous transfers, to transfers
within the HUF in the same manner as they apply to non-HUF
families.

Exemption Levels and Rate Structure

The trend over Union Budgets since 1963-64 has been toward increased personal exemptions and tax credits for dependents, and diminished progression in the rate structure--the effect moderated only very slightly by the widening of the tax base to include short-term capital gains. In the context of the critical need to mobilize resources for developmental spending it is difficult to justify such budgetary changes.

The present personal exemption level of Rs. 4,000 for an individual means that an individual can earn almost ten times per capita income (Rs. 421.5 in 1964-65) before he becomes subject to tax--and that at the minimum rate of 5 per cent. Although it may be arguable that in absolute terms an income of Rs. 4,000 does not represent a large amount--just over $500 --the criterion for taxable capacity in the context of mobilization of resources for development must surely be relative rather than absolute, and in very few countries--Burma being the only example from a sample of twenty developed and developing countries--does the minimum level of taxable income amount to ten times per capita or average income. By setting the exemption at Rs. 4,000, 60 per cent of urban income which provides almost all of Union non-corporation income tax revenue-- is excluded from taxation.[32] A reduction in the personal exemption levels for individuals to Rs. 2,000 would bring another 23 per cent of urban income into the tax net; with a corresponding reduction in the exemption level of HUF from Rs. 7,000 to Rs. 4,000, the immediate annual increase in revenue is estimated to be of the order of Rs. 1,000 million[33]--assuming that the income brought into the tax net is taxed at 5 per cent.

The second major problem is that of very modest rates of tax on middle-income groups, defined as those earning below Rs. 25,000 per annum. The group of taxpayers below this limit comprising 95 per cent of total individual taxpayers, earns over 66 per cent of total income assessed, yet pays just under 29 per cent of total tax.[34] Rates on this group have been reduced substantially since 1963-64, and an individual having a total income of Rs. 24,000 is subject to a marginal rate of only 21 per cent on earned income, or 22.4 per cent on unearned income, including in both cases the effect of the refundable annuity deposit.

As in the case of the basic exemption, there is some disagreement as to the socio-economic argument for increasing rates of tax on these middle-income groups. Again it is argued in absolute terms that those earning Rs. 25,000 are not particularly highly paid, whereas the argument in relative terms

examines the multiple of per capita income which an income of
this magnitude represents.

Table 5 summarizes the argument. The absolute argument
relies on converting all the incomes under examination to a
common rupee base, whereas the relative argument relies on
purely Indian income tax statistics. The former argument,
although clearly the one more commonly used in international
comparisons of tax burden, seems entirely inappropriate in the
context of the capacity of a particular country to mobilize
domestic resources for developmental spending. Turning therefore to the relative argument, there would seem to be a case
for reversing the recent trend toward a diminishing burden on
middle-income groups.

Finally, the recent changes in the income tax rate structure have reduced tax rates on upper-income groups (over Rs.
25,000) and have, in effect, diminished the progressivity of
the rate structure. Wholly unearned income must now amount to
Rs. 70,000--166 times per capita income--before it attracts a
marginal rate of 50 per cent; for wholly earned income the
corresponding income level is over Rs. 80,000.

Diminished progressivity may be expected to reduce the
elasticity of income tax receipts and the effectiveness of income taxation as a redistributive measure. The effectiveness
of income taxation on these two counts depends on the breadth
of coverage and the progressivity of the rate structure. It is
difficult to defend reductions in progressivity unless accompanied by measures to ensure the disposition of enhanced spending power by upper income groups into savings and productive
investment. More logical in the Indian case would be a stiffening of progressivity on the higher income ranges accompanied
by an exemption scheme for savings and investment in certain
directions. In this manner inequalities of consumption would
be drastically curtailed without diminishing private saving and
investment.

The inadequate burden on middle-income groups and the
diminished progressivity of the rate structure may both be
corrected by amendments to the existing rate structure, it
being understood that the income base to which these new rates
should apply is the broad, comprehensive income base previously defined. If incomes below Rs. 4,000 for individuals and
Rs. 7,000 for HUF down to the newly defined lower exemption
limits are taxed at 5 per cent, if incomes between Rs. 4,000
and Rs. 15,000 for individuals, and between Rs. 7,000 and Rs.
15,000 for HUF, are subject to a 2 per cent rate increase, and
all incomes over Rs. 15,000 are subject to a 5 per cent increase, it is estimated that tax revenue from the individual
income tax can be increased in the first year of operation of

TABLE 5

TAX BURDEN OF INDIVIDUAL INCOME TAX RATES

1. ABSOLUTE ARGUMENT

PER CENT OF INCOME TAKEN IN TAX OF MARRIED INDIVIDUAL WITH MORE THAN ONE CHILD (1964)

INCOME Rs.	INDIA per cent	U.K. per cent	U.S.A. per cent	JAPAN per cent	BURMA per cent	MALAYA per cent
10,000	6.9	0.4	nil	12.9	5.8	1.2
20,000	16.8	12.3	8.6	20.0	13.3	3.8

Source: N. Palkhivala, The Highest Taxed Nation (Bombay: Manaktala and Sons, 1965).

2. RELATIVE ARGUMENT

BURDEN OF TAXES ON INCOME IN SELECTED COUNTRIES IN 1964

Country	Level of Income up to which No Tax is Paid (stated as a multiple of Per Capita Income)	Income Taxes Paid as per cent of Various Income Levels			
		10	20	50	100
		times per capita income			
India	11.5	-	2	9	23
U.K.	1.9	28	44	67	78
U.S.A.	1.3	23	35	54	69
Japan	3.4	11	19	31	39
Burma	19.0	-	-	4	11
Malaya	9.8	-	4	12	21

Source: United Nations, Statistical Yearbook, 1965 (New York: 1966).

the new rates by a total of Rs. 1,800 million--Rs. 1,000 million from the lowering of the exemption limit, Rs. 500 million from the 2 per cent surcharge on incomes up to Rs. 15,000, and Rs. 300 million from the 5 per cent surcharge on incomes over Rs. 15,000.

Stabilization: The Question of Formula Flexibility

The suggested measures to broaden the coverage of income tax by widening the tax base definition and reducing exemption levels, and the suggested increases in over-all progressivity in the rate structure and thus income elasticity of tax receipts, should serve to enhance both the built-in flexibility of income tax and its effectiveness as a discretionary stabilization instrument.

The use of the principle of formula flexibility--whereby changes in tax rates are legislated in advance in relation to specified movements of economic variables such as national income--might further increase the effectiveness of the income tax as a stabilization measure. It should be possible to legislate in advance certain increases in the rate structure of the income tax in the event of price movements considered of an inflationary nature. Such statutory increases might be determined by the rate of increase of the wholesale price level and might take the form of either a uniform percentage increase at all rate levels, say, of the order of from 1 per cent to 3 per cent depending on the rate of change in the price level, or the increased rates might be made more severe at higher brackets in order to make the progressivity curve steeper and the reduction in spending power sharper. The effect on spending of the 1 per cent to 3 per cent over-all rate changes would be of the order of Rs. 650 million to Rs. 1,950 million. The increased rates would, of course, be automatically reduced when the rate of price increase fell to a particular level or was of a kind considered non-inflationary. Such policies would be introduced alongside the proposed savings and investment exemption scheme in order to minimize the reduction in investment consequent on stabilization measures.

Fluctuating Incomes: The Question of Averaging

One of the standard arguments used to condemn progressive income taxation in the context of yearly assessment is the discriminatory treatment accorded by this method of taxation to fluctuating incomes. Under a procedure of yearly assessment a taxpayer whose income fluctuates from year to year will pay a greater proportion of his income in tax than a taxpayer having the same average income more evenly distributed from year to year. This is a violation of the principle of horizontal equity. Perhaps more important, the lack of averaging under

a progressive tax increases the likelihood of disincentive effects on fluctuating incomes.

No provision is made in Indian income taxation for averaging incomes and thus eliminating discrimination against fluctuating incomes--except insofar as yearly assessment averages
seasonal incomes within the year. The only mitigating factor
is provision for business loss carry-over for up to a maximum
period of eight years against the profits of a business, profession or vocation.[35] It is suggested that some form of
averaging income be adopted for tax assessment purposes: the
problem is to choose the device most appropriate for India.

Some relatively crude averaging devices have been employed
or suggested at various times. The simplest system, which has
been employed in Wisconsin and in Australia, involved calculation of tax each year on the basis of a moving five-year average.[36] A second relatively crude procedure is the Canadian
system--available to farmers and fishermen--of optional re-
calculation of tax liability on the basis of income over the
previous five years.[37]

A much more thorough system is the cumulative averaging
scheme developed by Vickrey.[38] This system involves the cumulation of a taxpayer's income over his lifetime; tax burden
over time is made completely independent of the distribution of
income over time by the introduction of an interest credit
scheme. Tax due in any year is due on total cumulated income
minus the current value of previously paid taxes; the latter is
established by adding to the total of taxes previously paid an
amount representing interest payments foregone on taxes paid.
This system completely eliminates the discrimination of progressive taxation against fluctuating incomes, but has two
crucial disadvantages in the Indian context.

First, administrative implications are formidable and are
briefly discussed in Chapter 11. Second, the system would
result in considerably diminished responsiveness of tax yields
to fluctuations in income or tax rates; diminished responsiveness is, of course, an inevitable concomitant of averaging, but
is especially significant in the Vickrey system where the averaging period is very long and where equal weight is given to
each year in which income is earned. Diminished responsiveness
involves a diminution of the income elasticity and built-in
flexibility of the income tax, and the gains in horizontal
equity and incentives must be weighed against the diminished
usefulness of the tax in resource mobilization and stabilization.

An alternative scheme suggested by Holt[39] attempts to
retain the advantages of a comprehensive averaging system while

minimizing diminished responsiveness of tax yield to income and
tax rate changes. This scheme employs the moving average concept, though in a novel form which gradually decreases the influence of the older incomes; 67 per cent of weight is given to
incomes received in the last five years. Having established
the weighted average income the appropriate marginal rate at
that income level may be found from the progressive rate schedule for the year. Weighted income is thus taxed at the rates
for the current year; such tax payment, however, is subject to
a "fluctuation adjustment." If current income is above the
average this adjustment is derived by applying the marginal
rate appropriate to average income to the income deviation
above the average. Total tax payable is the sum of the relatively stable portion, determined by applying marginal rates
to average income, and the fluctuation adjustment. In a year
in which current income fell below the average the fluctuation
adjustment would be subtracted from the stabilized tax payment.

The Holt scheme has the great merit in the Indian case of
maintaining income elasticity and built-in flexibility with
only a small sacrifice of the virtually complete equalization
of liability over time obtained by the Vickrey plan. A recent
statistical study by Steger[40] considered the effect of various
averaging systems on revenue productivity, redistributive effectiveness and built-in flexibility. The study showed that a
system similar to that proposed by Holt would cause revenue to
deviate only 1 per cent from that of an annual tax system,
would reduce the redistributive effect of the tax by only 1 per
cent, and would have no perceptible effect on built-in flexibility. A rational comprehensive averaging system of the Holt
variety might be considered useful in the Indian case and is
much to be preferred to the proliferation of piecemeal relief
and special exemptions.

Effects on the Private Sector

It may be argued that a progressive personal income tax
affects growth adversely by diminishing the incentives to work,
save and invest, and the ability to save and invest.

The Incentive Issue

Work Incentives The imposition of an income tax may be said
to have two effects on work incentives; a substitution effect
which induces greater leisure by reducing the relative gain
from work, and an income effect which induces more work in
order to restore income to the pre-tax level.[41] The net effect
depends on the relative preference for work and leisure and on
the degree to which work motivation is based on financial reward. The high exemption level and very low tax coverage in
India would suggest that the income tax is incident on only a

limited number of relatively high salary earners whose work
motivation is likely to be complex.

In a status-conscious society such as India non-monetary
advantages are likely to be of special importance; prestige,
social status, power, the attractiveness of work done, etc.,
all play a part in work motivation. Empirical work done in
Britain and the U.S.A. suggests the predominance of non-
monetary over monetary factors in work motivation and an insignificant reduction in work effort as a result of taxation.[42]
The Indian system of values and aspirations would seem likely
to further diminish the relationship of tax rates and work effort and the summary dismissal accorded the issue by the TEC[43]
would appear appropriate.

It is, however, worth observing that all the empirical
work done to date has examined the effect on work motivation of
an income tax on an income base defined in a very partial way,
usually excluding capital gains, or at best treating them at
concessionary rates, and always excluding the other new elements in the comprehensive definition of income suggested for
use in India. It might therefore be inferred that the absence
of significant effects on work motivation has been a function
of this partial definition, and the consequent exclusion from
the taxable income base of a large part of the income of the
upper-income groups usually examined in the empirical studies.
Under a comprehensive base it seems reasonable to infer that
the substitution effects examined above would become more significant, and it will accordingly be suggested below that specific exemptions and allowances for income earned in occupations considered of priority importance be incorporated in the
personal income tax provisions.

Savings Incentives The financial reward for saving competes
with the desirability of present consumption. The effect of
taxation on this relationship may again be divided into the
substitution and income effects, although the nature of these
effects is more complex than in the case of work incentives.
In the simplest case saving may be considered to be undertaken
simply for the purpose of future consumption; a tax therefore
affects consumer choice between present and future consumption.
A general income tax may be regarded as a tax on wages income
plus interest from savings. By failing to exempt interest from
savings the tax, in effect, raises the price of future consumption (savings) relative to present consumption. The substitution effect will be greater the sharper the progressivity of
the rate schedule.[44]

Since the tax reduces the individual's real income the
income effect may simply be considered to reduce both present
and future consumption and to be neutral in regard to the

propensities to consume and save.[45] On the other hand, it
might be reasonable to widen the income effect to include the
possibility of an individual who has some pre-determined notion of a desirable level of future consumption. Since that
level would be reduced by the tax he might postpone present
consumption (increase saving) in order to maintain the desired
level of future consumption. The inclusion of the possibility
of saving for accumulation does not substantially modify the
analysis, though Musgrave points out that the substitution effect will be reinforced.[46]

The net effect will depend on saving motivation. In India
the latter is likely to be complex; questions of prestige,
status, dowry provision, education of children, provision for
retirement, etc., should all militate against any reduction in
the rate of saving. The penalty imposed on saving by the
standard income tax is, however, high and the present India income tax is of a general nature and is thus subject to the
standard criticism that savings are "double-taxed", in that the
savings "principal" as well as the return on that principal are
both subject to taxation. The possibility of a net adverse effect on savings is clearly present and an exemption scheme to
offset such an effect will be considered below.

Investment Incentives Although only 5 per cent of individual
savings in India goes directly into corporate securities,[47]
the stake of the individual investor as a stock holder in private industry is relatively high; a recent study of 70 selected companies found that individual shareholders owned, by
value, 52.05 per cent of the total value of ordinary shares.[48]

Again a substitution effect and an income effect can be
distinguished. The imposition of a proportional income tax,
without complete loss offset provision, reduces the margin
between prospective return and the risk involved in equity investment. Whether or not this will lead to a switch to low-
risk bonds in the asset portfolio depends on whether the ratio
of probability-weighted returns differs in the after-tax situation. An income tax which does not affect the security and
liquidity of bonds may be considered likely to have such a substitution effect, the more so if tax rates are progressive.
The income effect again may simply be seen as reducing investment in both equities and bonds, or may be extended to include
the possibility of the investor who has a pre-determined notion
of a desirable level of income from assets and who thus is
encouraged to switch a greater proportion of his portfolio to
equities in an attempt to maintain post-tax income from assets
at the desired level. The net effect will depend on the complex issue of investment motivation.

U.S. studies indicate relatively insignificant effects of
taxation on the supply of risk capital either to established or
to new ventures, and a dominant concern with capital appreciation rather than yield.[49] Recent Indian studies provide similar evidence. A 1961 NCAER study concluded:

> . . . The willingness of the public to invest in
> equity shares has not been perceptibly affected
> [by taxation]. The possibility of, and the desire
> for, [concessionarily taxed] capital gains seem to
> be important factors in augmenting the supply of
> investable funds flowing to the market for equity.[50]

A Reserve Bank study of capital issues in the private sector
from 1956-63 would also suggest a lively and apparently un-
inhibited response by the public to new issues of equity capital.[51] The present concessionary treatment of capital gains
would appear to be of considerable significance in diminishing
the adverse substitution effect of income taxation on venture
capital. As in the case of savings incentives, however, the
possibility of a net adverse effect remains, and it will be
necessary to consider devices such as full loss offset and income averaging, which minimize the substitution effect.[52]

An Exemptions Scheme to Promote Saving,
Investment and Work in Priority Occupations

It has been suggested that the present Indian income tax
might exercise some disincentive effect on private work, saving
and investment, and that these disincentive effects are likely
to be more significant with a comprehensive tax base. To this
possibility is added the fact that a progressive income tax
which taxes at higher rates the income of income groups whose
propensity to save is relatively high will diminish the ability
of those groups to save and invest.

The question therefore arises whether there should be a
comprehensive scheme for, at least, the partial exemption from
income tax liability of income saved and invested in certain
specified directions, and/or of income received from certain
forms of employment. The question, in short, is how to permit,
in the interests of economic growth, the continuation of functional inequalities. Discussion on the treatment of capital
gains will be deferred and treated separately.

Present exemptions in India for savings used for specified
purposes cover a limited if widening field. Relief for savings
takes the form of a rebate on income tax in respect of sums
paid as life insurance premiums, contributions to recognized
provident funds, approved superannuation funds and deposits in
the post office under the cumulative time deposit scheme.[53]

Recent budgetary changes have progressively extended the rebate principle. The 1965-66 Budget provided for the deduction from taxable income of 50 per cent of funds directed to the priority areas listed above up to a limit of Rs. 12,500 or 25 per cent of total income, whichever is less, in the case of an individual, and Rs. 25,000 or 25 per cent of total income, whichever is less, in the case of HUF. The 1967-68 Budget extended these limits to Rs. 15,000 or 30 per cent of total income in the case of individuals, and Rs. 30,000 or 30 per cent of total income, in the case of HUF.

Provision was made in the 1965-66 legislation for tax credits to individuals and HUF investing in specified public limited companies. The tax credit amounts to 5 per cent of the first Rs. 15,000 of funds so invested, 3 per cent of the next Rs. 10,000 and 2 per cent of the following Rs. 10,000--making in all a credit of Rs. 1,250 for an investment of Rs. 35,000 by an individual or HUF. The 1967-68 Budget provided for the exemption from tax of dividend income received by any assessee from an Indian company, provided the total dividend income of the assessee does not exceed Rs. 500.[54]

In the 1965-66 Budget interest income on Union government securities was exempted from the unearned income surcharge, and the 1967-68 Budget doubled the ceiling limit on unearned income exempt from unearned income surcharge, from Rs. 15,000 to Rs. 30,000. This latter step was acknowledged as a reform intended to encourage savings, and represents the first step to acceptance of the recommendation by Mr. Bhoothalingam that the distinction between earned and unearned income be abolished.[55]

A piecemeal system of saving-investment exemptions is thus evolving slowly. There is, however, no comprehensive scheme of rebate or exemption for savings and investment such as that employed in West Germany.[56] In the latter case the Savings Premium Law permits a tax credit of 20 per cent of savings held for up to five years in a recognized savings institution, and the purchase of any security considered worthy, including shares in investment funds, is rewarded by a tax premium. Equally, interest and dividends on most investments are not defined as taxable income.

Such a scheme has been suggested for India by R. J. Chelliah,[57] who suggests tax exemptions on various percentages of income invested in a certain manner. The suggested exemption of 20 per cent on purchases of new equity stock would imply that a taxpayer who brought out of current income Rs. 100 worth of new equity would pay tax on only Rs. 80 of that income. Such a scheme--coupled to the present concessionary treatment of long-term capital gains--would appear to have considerable merit in terms of encouraging private savings and their investment in channels deemed worthy under planning objectives.

The enhanced incentives to saving and investment must, however, be weighed against the costs of such a system. The TEC on this topic remarked that "the problem is to find forms of savings to which relief may be attached with the least possibility of abuse."[58] The costs of such a system may be expressed in terms of the effect on resource mobilization for public investment, diminution of inequalities, and stabilization. In terms of resource mobilization an extensive policy of exemptions is directly costly in terms of tax revenue. The sum of investment-oriented tax privileges in Germany has been estimated to have amounted to approximately 10 per cent of total tax revenue from 1939-61,[59] and similar studies in the U.S.A. emphasize the continuing and substantial revenue sacrifice involved in a complex system of exemptions.[60]

The reduced progressivity implied by the exemptions will also diminish the income elasticity of tax receipts--a factor of considerable importance in India. It would, of course, be inaccurate to view this revenue cost in a static sense; insofar as exemptions are successful, incomes and tax receipts may rise more than sufficiently to compensate for the revenue loss which would have occurred at the pre-exemption (lower) growth rate. Nevertheless any such comprehensive scheme of exemptions in India must be defined in terms of the revenue requirements of the public sector.

A possible, somewhat less generous, alternative to the Chelliah scheme might be to offer moderate concessionary treatment to savings committed for a minimum period of five years in pre-determined priority directions. A discount on tax liability arising from the inclusion in total income of the amount of funds committed might be employed, that discount rising from 10 per cent of additional tax liability in the case of funds invested in government bonds to 20 per cent on approved priority industrial stocks. The effect of such a scheme, which requires that the portion of income exempted be not only saved but actually invested in one of the priority areas, would be to penalize consumption and hoarding, but to provide incentives to investment in priority channels.

The suggested stiffening of upper income rates in addition to a scheme of exemptions of the sort proposed by Chelliah, or that suggested above, would offer some alleviation of short-run revenue loss, consequent on the exemption scheme. The rate increases would also compensate for the reduced effectiveness of income tax as a means of diminishing inequalities and as a tool of built-in stabilization.

Similar considerations apply to the introduction of work exemptions. A possible device in this case would be the provision of a system of discounts on tax liability, up to a maximum of 10 per cent of total liability, determined on the basis of a priority scale of employment fields. Such incentives would be compensated--in terms of the revenue productivity of the tax-- by diminished basic exemptions and enhanced rates at all levels of income.

The final issue is that of measures to promote risk investment. The introduction of the proposed system of income averaging would considerably mitigate the discrimination of progressive income taxation against fluctuating income, particularly income from risk investment. The use of full loss offset in the income tax structure would greatly diminish, though not completely eliminate,[61] the substitution effect of income taxation against risk investment.

Conclusion

The effectiveness of the personal income tax in India is greatly diminished by the inadequate definition of income, in particular by the exclusion of agricultural income from the tax base, and by the related problem of substantial avoidance and evasion. A new, wider definition of income was suggested; detailed discussion of the evasion-avoidance issue was postponed until Chapter 11. Further measures to increase the resource mobilization possibilities of the income tax included a curtailment of the privileged position of HUF, lowered exemptions, increased tax rates at all income levels, and sharper progressivity in the rate structure. The broader and more elastic tax base achieved by these changes would also enhance the effectiveness of the income tax as a means of diminishing inequalities and as a tool of automatic and discretionary stabilization. The introduction of formula flexibility should serve to improve the usefulness of the income tax in stabilization policy. The effect of the suggested tax changes on the private sector may be mitigated by a scheme of savings, investment and work exemptions, by complete loss offset for risk investment, and by a scheme of income averaging for tax purposes.

NOTES TO CHAPTER 3

1. Since the 1963-64 Budget, only long-term capital gains (where the capital asset is held for more than one year) enjoy concessionary treatment; since the 1967-68 Budget, short-term gains are simply aggregated with other income for tax purposes, and are not, therefore, declared on the separate schedule.

2. Harvard University Law School, International Tax Program, Taxation in India, World Tax Series (Boston: Little, Brown and Co., 1960), Vol. I, p. 76.

3. The business profits of co-operatives are exempted; for charitable and religious trusts, income derived from property held under trust and from contributions is exempted.

4. Taxation in India,   op. cit. , pp. 159-60.

5. Ibid., p. 161.

6. Ibid., p. 160.

7. Ibid., p. 161.

8. The term "taxable income," though correctly applicable to this quantity, is not used in India because income tax is computed by applying the appropriate rates of tax to total income, and then reducing the tax by that proportion of it which the exemptions and deductions to be subtracted from total income bear to total income. The resulting tax is the same as if the effective rates were applied to "taxable income" as defined in the text.

9. Government of India, The Finance Bill, 1967 (New Delhi: Ministry of Finance, 1967), p. 42.

10. Government of India, Explanatory Memorandum on the Budget of the Central Government in 1965 (New Delhi: Ministry of Finance, 1965), p. 2; the rate of tax on the first slab of income, Rs. 5,000, has been reduced from 6 per cent to 5 per cent; on the slab between Rs. 7,501 and 10,000 from 15 per cent to 10 per cent; on the slab between Rs. 12,501 and 15,000 from 20 per cent to 15 per cent; on the slab between Rs. 20,001 and 25,000 from 35 per cent to 30 per cent; on the slab between Rs. 30,001 and 50,000 from 55 per cent to 50 per cent; and on the slab between Rs. 50,001 and 70,000 from 70 per cent to 60 per cent.

11. Government of India, Explanatory Memorandum on the Budget of the Central Government in 1966 (New Delhi: Ministry of Finance, 1966), pp. 1-2; the basic levels of exempt income for 11 categories of taxpayer were raised by Rs. 500 and the tax credits in respect of personal allowances raised to the levels indicated in the text from the previous levels of Rs. 100, Rs. 175, Rs. 195 and Rs. 215, respectively.

12. Government of India, Outline of Direct Taxes in India (New Delhi: Ministry of Finance, 1960), Chapter 9, p. 71 et seq.

13. Ibid., pp. 10-12; Taxation in India, op. cit., pp. 226, 234 and 241. The Finance Bill of 1967-68 proposed the extension of this system of deduction at source to interest on deposits, loans and other borrowings, fees for professional services and brokerage and commission payable by banks. This suggestion created a storm of protest that increased adminis- trative costs would far outweigh increased collections, and in the final submission of the Finance Bill the Finance Minister restricted the new provisions for withdrawal at source to interest payments and doubled the exemption level for interest payments subject to such withdrawal.

14. Outline of Direct Taxes in India, op. cit., pp. 71- 72; Taxation in India, op. cit., pp. 374-75.

15. Ibid., pp. 72-73.

16. G. S. Sahota, Indian Tax Structure and Economic Development (Bombay: Asia Publishing House, 1961), pp. 12-17.

17. Government of India, Report of the Taxation Enquiry Committee (hereinafter TEC) (3 vols.; New Delhi: Ministry of Finance, 1953-54), Vol. I, p. 189.

18. India 1966, op. cit., Table 28, p. 67.

19. Reserve Bank of India, Report on Currency and Finance, 1965-66 (Bombay: Reserve Bank of India, 1967), p. 58.

20. India, 1966, op. cit., Table 16, p. 21.

21. Government of India, Report of the Direct Taxes Administration Enquiry Committee, 1958-59 (Delhi: Manager of Publications, 1960).

22. Ibid., pp. 231-34.

23. N. Kaldor, Indian Tax Reform (New Delhi: Ministry of Finance, 1956).

24. R. M. Haig, "The Concept of Income: Economic and Legal Aspects," The Federal Income Tax, ed. R. M. Haig (New York: Columbia University Press, 1921).

25. H. Simons, Personal Income Taxation (Chicago: Uni- versity of Chicago Press, 1938).

26. I. S. Gulati and K. S. Gulati, The Undivided Hindu Family: A Study of Its Tax Privileges (Bombay: Asia Publish- ing House, 1962).

27. Ibid., p. 10.

28. Ibid., Chapter 2, p. 13 et seq.

29. Ibid., p. 61.

30. Ibid., p. 83.

31. Ibid., pp. 88-89.

32. Government of India, Report of the Commission on Distribution of Income and Levels of Living (New Delhi: Planning Commission, 1964), pp. 70-71.

33. This estimate is based on the statistics of income distribution provided in Chapter 3 of the Report referred to in Note 32, as is the subsequent estimate of the increased revenue from rate increases.

34. Government of India, All India Income-Tax Revenue Statistics for 1963-64 (Delhi: Manager of Publications, 1967).

35. Taxation in India, op. cit., pp. 211-12.

36. W. Vickrey, Agenda for Progressive Taxation (New York: Ronald Press, 1947), p. 169.

37. This method has been developed by H. Simons, op. cit., p. 154, and by H. M. Groves, Production, Jobs and Taxes (New York: McGraw-Hill, 1944), pp. 84-85.

38. Vickrey, op. cit., pp. 172-97; a variation on this theme which would appear to involve additional disadvantages while offering fewer advantages, has been proposed in J. Bravman, "Equalization of Income Tax," Columbia Law Review, L, No. 1 (January 1950), 9.

39. C. C. Holt, "Averaging of Income for Tax Purposes, Equity and Fiscal Policy Considerations," National Tax Journal, II (December 1949), 349-61.

40. W. A. Steger, "Averaging Income for Tax Purposes; A Statistical Study," National Tax Journal, IX, No. 2 (June 1956), 97-114.

41. R. Goode, "The Income Tax and the Supply of Labour," Journal of Political Economy, LVIII, No. 5 (October 1949), 428-37.

42. Government of the United Kingdom, Royal Commission on the Taxation of Profits and Income, Cmd. 9105 (London:

H.M.S.O., 1954), pp. 91-124; C. D. Long, The Labor Force under Changing Income and Employment (Princeton: Princeton University Press, 1958); Joint Committee on the Economic Report, Impact of the Federal Income Tax on Labor Force Participation (Washington, D.C.: U.S. Government Printing Office, 1953), pp. 153-66; G. F. Break, "Income Taxes and Incentives to Work; An Empirical Study," American Economic Review, XLVII (September 1957), 529-49; C. A. Hall, Jr., Effects of Taxation: Executive Compensation and Retirement Plans (Boston: Harvard University Bureau of Business Research, 1951); T. H. Saunders, The Effects of Taxation on Executives (Boston: Harvard University Graduate School of Business Administration, 1951).

43. TEC, op. cit., Vol. I, p. 154.

44. See R. A. Musgrave, The Theory of Public Finance (New York: McGraw-Hill, 1959), pp. 257-68, for a detailed discussion of the nature of the substitution effect under various forms of tax.

45. Ibid., p. 262.

46. Ibid., pp. 266-68.

47. "Estimates of Saving and Investment in the Indian Economy, 1950-51 - 1958-59," Reserve Bank of India Bulletin (August 1961), pp. 1200-1203, Table IV, p. 1205 .

48. "Survey of Ownership of Shares in Joint Stock Companies as at the End of December, 1959," Reserve Bank of India Bulletin (May 1962), 677-92.

49. J. K. Butters, L. E. Thompson and L. L. Bollinger, Effects of Taxation: Investments by Individuals (Boston: Harvard Graduate School of Business Administration, 1953); J. K. Butters and J. Lintner, Effects of Federal Taxes on Growing Enterprises (Boston: Harvard University Graduate School of Business Administration, 1945).

50. NCAER, Taxation and Private Investment (New Delhi: NCAER, 1961), p. 18.

51. "Capital Issues in the Private Sector," Reserve Bank of India Bulletin (June 1964), 740-55.

52. Musgrave, op. cit., pp. 312-46.

53. Taxation in India, op. cit., pp. 162-63.

54. The legislation does not say that the first Rs. 500 of divided income for those with dividend income in excess of

Rs. 500 is deductible. This must clearly be clarified, since
a rigid interpretation of the wording would lead to results
quite at odds with the new exemption provision.

55. Government of India, First Interim Report on Rationalization and Simplification of Direct Taxation Laws (New
Delhi: Ministry of Finance, 1967).

56. F. G. Reuss, Fiscal Policy for Growth Without Inflation (Baltimore: Johns Hopkins Press, 1963), pp. 111-13;
Harvard University Law School, International Tax Program,
Taxation in the Federal Republic of Germany, World Tax Series
(Boston: Little, Brown and Co., 1959), p. 275; R. G. Wertheimer, "Tax Incentives in Germany," National Tax Journal, X
(1957), 325-38.

57. R. J. Chelliah, Fiscal Policy in Underdeveloped
Countries (London: Allen and Unwin, 1960), pp. 71-73.

58. TEC, op. cit., Vol. I, p. 141.

59. Reuss, op. cit., pp. 138-41.

60. C. H. Kahn, Personal Deductions in the Federal Income
Tax (Princeton: National Bureau of Economic Research, 1960),
Table 2, p. 20, Table 6, p. 29.

61. A tax that is progressive by size brackets of income
will reduce expected gains at a higher rate than losses, even
though full loss offset may be assured (Musgrave, op. cit.,
p. 331).

4 THE TAXATION OF CAPITAL GAINS

DESCRIPTION

The definition of "income" adopted for tax purposes in most countries, e.g., Canada and the United Kingdom, is the accounting concept of income which excludes capital gains. By including capital gains in the definition of income, India has come nearer to the economic definition of income as "the net accretion to spending power between two periods of time," or "consumption during a given period plus increase in net worth." After a false start in 1947-48, a capital gains tax as part of the personal income tax was introduced into the Indian tax system in 1956, following the recommendation of Professor Kaldor.[1]

The initial tax was radically overhauled in 1962 by Morarji Desai, who introduced a distinction for tax purposes between short-term capital gains (where the asset transferred has been held by the taxpayer for not more than twelve months), and long-term capital gains (covering gains on the transfer of assets held for longer than twelve months). In the case of short-term gains, it was provided that income--excluding short-term gains--would be taxed as if it were the total income, and short-term gains would be taxed separately at the average rate applicable to the aggregate of income including short-term gains. Incorporation of short-term gains in total income for tax purposes was thus only partial, and short-term gains were in effect taxed at a concessionary rate. Long-term gains were not to be taxed unless total long-term gains exceeded Rs. 5,000 and, further, were not to be taxed if the taxpayer's total income did not exceed Rs. 10,000. Those long-term gains were to be taxed at a flat rate of 25 per cent or at the rate applicable to short-term gains, whichever was the lesser.

In the 1964-65 Budget, the Finance Minister, Mr. Krishnamachari, further reformed the treatment of long-term gains, while leaving unchanged the treatment of short-term gains. It was provided that a graduated levy replace the flat 25 per cent rate, and that a distinction be made between capital gains relating to lands and buildings and other gains. The former were to be subject to tax at a rate of 75 per cent of the average rate applicable to an assessee's total income, while the latter were to be subject to tax at 50 per cent of that rate.

The 1965-66 Budget introduced only one minor concession relating to the treatment of bonus shares. Tax payable by an equity shareholder in respect of the capital gains represented by the fair market value of the bonus shares allotted to him after March 31, 1965, by a company which is reducing or liquidating its share capital, were to be reduced by an amount of 10 per cent of the face value of such bonus shares.

Left untouched in 1966-67, the capital gains tax was again radically overhauled in the 1967-68 Budget. The concession afforded short-term gains was abolished, and short-term gains are now simply incorporated in other income for purposes of annual tax computation, being treated, of course, as unearned income. As an entirely appropriate corollary, however, short-term capital losses may now be set off against an assessee's ordinary income--i.e., income other than capital gains--in the appropriate tax year. The provisions relating to long-term gains were considerably simplified. Where the assessee's total income from all sources, including long-term gains, does not exceed Rs. 10,000, long-term gains are not taxable. Further, where the assessee's income from all sources exceeds Rs. 10,000, the first Rs. 5,000 of long-term gains remain tax-exempt, and the balance is taxable at 55 per cent in the case of gains relating to lands and buildings, and 35 per cent in the case of other gains.

Gains from the sale of agricultural land are not taxable, gains from the disposal of house property by small house-owners are exempt, and corporations are distinguished from other assessees for tax purposes; the treatment of corporations will be examined in the appropriate chapter.

Finally, for reasons of administrative feasibility capital gains are taxed on a realization as distinct from an accrual basis. In effect, the tax is levied in the year of transfer of property which has appreciated in value rather than in the year of appreciation, should these years be distinct.

Considerable controversy surrounds the rationale and economic effects of capital gains taxation, and it is the purpose of this chapter to examine the taxation of capital gains in terms of the three tax policy objectives in an economy where planned growth depends on a mix of public and private investment.

THE INCLUSION OF CAPITAL GAINS IN TAXABLE INCOME:
HORIZONTAL EQUITY

The comprehensive definition of income posited in Chapter 3 requires on the basis of horizontal equity the inclusion of capital gains in the income tax base as representing, in the same manner as other sources of income, net accretions to spending power.

There are several arguments against the inclusion of capital gains in taxable income:

First, there is the contention that only recurrent and anticipated receipts should be included in income. The argument continues that capital gains are not only irregular, but are also unsought and unexpected and as such do not constitute taxable income.[2]

Even acceptance of the fact that a proportion of capital gains represent "windfall" or unexpected elements in no way diminishes the increase in satisfaction or increase in spending power derived from their acquisition. It is also far from certain that a substantial proportion of capital gains represent unintended, fortuitous receipts. Capital gains differ only in degree from other forms of income and are often deliberately sought; the Indian investment studies referred to previously clearly indicate the importance of the expectation of capital gains in individual investment motivation. In practice capital gains embody substantial elements of personal remuneration, interest, profit and rent, and often represent--particularly under concessionary treatment--an alternative form of the more standard varieties of income.

The contention that the irregularity of capital gains would exclude them from taxable income, especially under a progressive system, is nothing more than an additional argument for some system of averaging, and has no validity as a reason for exclusion or even concessionary treatment.

Related arguments to exclude capital gains from taxable income contend that capital gains taxation represents double taxation of savings; that many capital gains are illusory in real terms; and that gains due to interest rate changes may leave the investor's ordinary income unchanged if the gain is not realized, or, having been realized, is re-invested.

The double taxation of savings argument contends that the taxation of a realized capital gain and the further taxation of the income derived from the re-investment of the net capital gain represents double taxation. This argument merely extends the standard double taxation argument used against any income tax which does not exempt savings, and would not suggest any particular tax status for capital gains income.

The "real capital gains" argument emphasizes that capital gains which represent merely a fall in the value of the mone-tary unit are illusory in that they do not represent a real in-crease in the taxpayer's spending power and thus are not a proper subject of taxation. The argument continues that income taxation generally ignores the positive gains from inflation which accrue to debtors, and that there is no justification for taxing capital gains which are illusory--which do no more than compensate for the rise in the price level--while leaving un-taxed gains from inflation which are real. Taxes on capital gains resulting from inflation, the argument concludes, are in effect taxes on wealth rather than on increments in the value of wealth.

There is no question that, ideally, taxable income should be expressed in real terms; thus, inflationary gains in proper-ty prices would not be taxed, real gains of debtors would be taxed, and real losses of creditors allowed for as deductions. It would, however, represent a radical change in income tax procedures to calculate income tax liability in constant rather than current monetary units, and a wide variety of compensatory adjustments would have to be introduced. The fixed income re-cipient is required to pay a constant or even increasing tax rate on his fixed income in money terms, even though the real value of that income has diminished greatly. Equally, the wage-earner, whose income will almost certainly have increased to some extent with the price level, has to pay tax, on a progres-sive scale and often therefore at a higher effective rate, on his increased money income, notwithstanding the fact that it may be worth less, in real terms, than his initial income. The question, therefore, is whether it is the role of the tax system to deal with the multitude of distributional problems which arise as a result of inflation. A recent Canadian study denies this function to the tax system,[3] and it certainly seems clear that it would be inequitable to introduce compensation for property-owners without at the same time introducing the wide range of associated compensatory adjustments.

The inflation argument against the taxation of capital gains seems then to constitute a case not for the special treat-ment of capital gains, but for certain well-defined exemptions or allowances--such as in the case of a dwelling-house owner who sells and immediately seeks to buy another house[4]--but not to be a decisive argument against the full incorporation of capital gains in income for tax purposes. In any event, in time of inflation the property-owner is likely to be in a

favorable position relative to other taxpayers. The index of
equity prices or some similar index of land prices may be expected to move upward more quickly than the cost-of-living index.

With regard to the final argument on the taxation of capital gains resulting from interest rate changes, there is no
apparent case even for certain exemptions. An appreciation of
capital values which results from a fall in the rate of interest on bonds differs from a capital gain which merely reflects
higher prices, since in this case the capital gain clearly
increases the recipient's spending power over goods and services in a real sense. However, it is also true that if the
proceeds of the gain are re-invested, that re-investment is
necessarily at the new lower rate of interest, and the investor
must invest all or most of the capital gain to maintain his investment income at the previous level. The argument therefore
runs that no additional taxable capacity has been created.

On such occasions, however, the holders of long-term bonds
still gain relative to other savers who save out of current income, or whose past savings are not invested in long-term
bonds. Most savers must accept a reduction in income when interest rates fall, while long-term bond holders are able to
offset the effect of the diminished income by the capital
gains on their existing holdings. As in the case of inflationary gains, failure to recognize the capital gains of bondholders would require a wide range of compensatory adjustments
to those whose savings were neither in bonds nor equities. It
is also worth noting that whereas price trends tend to be in-
exorable and irreversible, periods of falling interest rates
tend to alternate with periods of rising rates, and it seems
reasonable to infer that a taxpayer who is unduly taxed as a
result of a fall in interest rates will be correspondingly fa-
vored--will, in fact, be able to deduct capital losses--as a
result of rising interest rates.

VERTICAL EQUITY

Considerations of vertical equity would also suggest
that capital gains be fully incorporated in taxable income.
Seltzer's detailed study of capital gains taxation in the
U.S.A. has clearly shown that capital gains income is concentrated in the upper income groups.[5] Seltzer goes on to show
that many individuals reach higher income levels mainly because
of capital gains.[6]

The Indian parliamentary speeches introducing the capital
gains tax laid great emphasis on the issue of mitigating inequalities;[7] in amending the tax structure radically in 1964,

Mr. Krishnamachari stated that "the proposed amendments to the
capital gains tax . . . are basically motivated by the socio-
economic objective of reducing the inequalities of incomes and
wealth."[8] Even the TEC, which rejected the use of a capital
gains tax on economic grounds, acknowledged the vertical equity
issue:

> Capital gains . . . constitute one of the factors
> making for inequalities of wealth, especially in
> a developing economy with its increasing measure
> of industrialization and urbanization.[9]

Indian experience with a tax on capital gains in the period 1947-49 suggests that some 70 per cent of total assessed
gains resulted from stock appreciation and realization.[10] Examination of capital gains assessed to tax after 1957 in India
reveals the same percentage.[11] Previously cited figures of the
distribution of dividend income in India indicated extreme concentration of stockholding in a small group of high-income
earners. It seems legitimate to assume that the balance of capital gains income, from real estate appreciation, etc., also
accrues in substantial measure to the upper income groups. Confirmation of the receipt of capital gains by the upper income
groups may be found in the fact that the average rate of tax
liability on capital gains was 22.8 per cent in 1960-61, 22.4
per cent in 1962-63, and 22.2 per cent in 1963-64.[12] In 1963-
64, 84 per cent of individual income assessed to capital gains
tax and 90 per cent of capital gains tax paid were attributable
to income groups earning over Rs. 7,500 per annum; 65 per cent
of incomes assessed and 75 per cent of tax paid were attributable to income groups earning over Rs. 15,000 per annum.[13]

In a period of rising incomes under planned development
capital gains are likely to be of considerable magnitude. If
such gains in India are untaxed or are taxed at significantly
lower rates than other income, the effectiveness of progressive
income taxation as a means of mitigating inequalities would be
seriously curtailed. The question indeed would appear to be not
whether or not the taxation of capital gains in India is necessary on grounds of vertical equity, but whether the present tax
makes any substantial contribution to the diminution of inequalities. It will be suggested that the present rate structure on
long-term gains, the high exemption limit and the list of exempt
transactions constitute the major cause of inadequate revenue
productivity of capital gains taxation; the redistributive objective is similarly compromised. The equity cost of favorable
treatment of long-term gains may be considered particularly important in view of Seltzer's finding that long-term gains tend
to account for an increasing proportion of total net gains as
the income scale is ascended;[14] this latter conclusion has been
recently re-affirmed.[15]

STABILIZATION

By their nature capital gains tend to be irregular and unpredictable over time. Under a progressive tax system without
averaging, this feature of capital gains would substantially
enhance the built-in flexibility of the income tax system.
Henry Simons drew attention to this factor in the 1930's as one
of the major advantages of inclusion of capital gains in the
taxable income base.[16] This point has been more recently
stated by J. E. Head,[17] who emphasizes not only the contribution to automatic stability of capital gains taxation, but also
the role of such taxation in discretionary stabilization policy
in booms sustained by capital gains in real estate and stock
values.

The desirability of increased built-in flexibility and
discretionary stabilizing effectiveness must, however, be balanced against the inequity of discrimination against fluctuating income. The necessary reconciliation might be effected by
adopting in India the previously suggested system of averaging
--for income from all sources including capital gains--on the
Holt model which eliminates the worst discrimination against
volatility while retaining a substantial measure of built-in
flexibility. Such an averaging system is particularly important in the case of volatile capital gains income in that it
avoids the severe penalization of volatility under a progressive tax without averaging and the probable resultant inhibitory effects on private sector saving and investment.

The weakness of the present capital gains tax as a stabilizing weapon in India is, as in the case of income tax, its
very limited coverage--1,331 individual taxpayers in 1960-61,
2,391 in 1962-63 and 3,229 in 1963-64[18]--and measures to increase coverage, such as lowered exemption limits and a diminished list of exempt transactions, are clearly necessary as
part of general income tax reform if the capital gains tax is
to realize its potential as a stabilization device. Given
wider coverage, a more progressive rate structure on income
(including capital gains) would also enhance the stabilizing
effectiveness of the tax.

GROWTH

Resource Mobilization for the Public Sector

An income tax system which taxes capital gains will clearly have a greater revenue productivity than one which does not.
The most curious and indefensible argument used in opposition
to the taxation of capital gains is that the introduction of

such a tax would actually stimulate tax avoidance and so reduce revenue productivity. The TEC employed this dubious argument:

> If a capital gains tax were to be introduced now--
> and it is bound to be levied at rates lower than
> the ordinary income and super-tax on account of its
> [sic] casual or irregular character--there is a
> danger of tax avoidance being stimulated by attempts
> to pass off as capital gains what may otherwise have
> been treated as a part of taxable income.[19]

As Kaldor points out,[20] this argument overlooks the fact that complete exemption of capital gains will afford a much higher inducement to conversion and tax avoidance than diminished liability under preferential treatment. The wider the differential in treatment the greater is the temptation to give income the form and appearance of capital gains. An extensive literature confirms this latter assertion.[21] Any concession made to capital gains will clearly aggravate tax avoidance and directly diminish revenue productivity.

The potential yield of a capital gains tax in India has been a subject of some debate, and opponents of the device have used low yield estimates as a major criticism.[22] One of the justifications offered for the withdrawal of the first capital gains tax in 1949 after two years of operation was that the annual yield was expected to be only about Rs. 10 million.[23] This estimate proved to be inaccurate, the actual yield from assessments for the years 1947-48 and 1948-49 amounting to over Rs. 60 million. Following the re-imposition of the tax in 1957, total yield rose from Rs. 2.1 million in the first year of operation to Rs. 21 million in 1962-63, then fell back to Rs. 13.1 million in 1963-64.[24] The most recent figure amounts to only 0.4 per cent of total income tax revenue in 1963-64 and would seem to confirm the view of critics that the yield does not justify the cost of administering a relatively complex tax. This conclusion, however, is subject to two major qualifications.

First, it is unrealistic to gauge the revenue potential of a capital gains tax on a short-run basis. Mr. Kaldor estimates that the average time lag between accrued and realized capital gains in India is from 10-15 years.[25] Thus even with the inadequate structure of the tax in the 1957-61 period, tax receipts did not reflect the rate of accrual of capital gains over the period and would not do so for 10-15 years. In a period of planned economic development involving large investment programs, extensive and often fortuitous accretions to capital values may be expected, even though they are not reflected immediately in capital values. The problem is to ensure that all avenues of avoidance are sealed so that realized (taxable) gains will encompass all accrued gains in the long run.

Directly following from the previous argument is the
second qualification to the pessimistic conclusion on revenue
productivity. The structure of the capital gains tax in India
is such as to afford completely inadequate present revenue
productivity from currently realized gains, and to ensure,
through a variety of available loopholes, that presently
accrued gains exceed realized gains even in the long run.

Initially it may be said that the tax revised in 1964 and
1967 represents a considerable improvement in terms of potential revenue productivity than did the various forms in operation between 1957 and 1961. The removal of the 25 per cent
limit on long-term gains and the introduction of a graduated
base offer at least the possibility of relatively income-elastic
tax receipts.[26] Equally, there was no justification for the
revenue cost and equity sacrifice involved in the distinction
of short-run gains from other income, and this was finally
recognized in 1967. The only minor cost in the present Indian
system of full incorporation might be a slight diminution in
built-in flexibility if investors are able to use planned realization to offset cyclical fluctuations in the tax rate applicable to their income from other sources,[27] and this problem
would not arise if the suggested averaging system were introduced.

Several deficiences persist, however, in the present tax
structure:

First, long-term gains below Rs. 5,000 in any year are
exempt from tax, and are exempt, whatever their amount, if the
total income of an individual does not exceed Rs. 10,000. The
lowering of the exemption level of gains to Rs. 2,000 and the
exempt total income level to Rs. 5,000 would encompass a much
wider range of taxpayers and increase revenue productivity.

The rate structure might also be modified. The 1967-68
Budget introduced flat rates of 55 per cent and 35 per cent for
long-term gains, above the Rs. 5,000 exemption, relating to
lands and buildings and other forms of appreciation, respectively. Given the suggested lower exemption level, there is a
case for taxing long-term gains at progressive rates, consistent with the treatment of other forms of income (including
short-term gains). The rate of progressivity might begin for
all forms of gain at 25 per cent, but rise more sharply on
gains from land and buildings, and the highest rate of tax on
all forms of long-term gains should be the same as that presently levied on other forms of unearned income. The effect of
these changes on revenue productivity is considered below. It
might also be useful in India to follow the British example of
regarding real estate gains as short-term capital gains unless

the asset has been held prior to transfer for a minimum period
of three years rather than the present one-year period.

Second, the list of exempt transactions contains several
serious loopholes. The first is the constitutional exemption
of land from which agricultural income is derived.[28] The
majority of land transactions are thereby excluded from capital
gains tax and an opportunity for tax avoidance created. The
problem will be considered in the discussion of agricultural
taxation. The exemption of capital gains as a result of the
total or partial division of a HUF[29] is part of the generally
lenient treatment of HUF and creates an avenue of avoidance the
closing of which would increase revenue productivity. Finally,
the most serious loophole is the exemption of capital gains
resulting from the transfer of assets, first, through gift and
inheritance and, second, through the dissolution of a partnership.[30] These two exemptions effectively prevent the equalization of accrued and realized gains in the long run. The latter
exemption may be dealt with by inclusions of such gains in the
present tax. The former, it will be suggested in Chapter 6,
may be dealt with by the incorporation for tax purposes in the
income of the donee or legatee of all gifts and inheritances,
including accretions to capital values of assets transferred.

Potential capital gains tax revenue consequent on changed
exemption levels, modified rate structure and curtailment of
loopholes--particularly the gift and inheritance loophole--is
estimated at between Rs. 120 million and Rs. 200 million per
annum, as against the most recent figure of Rs. 13 million.[31]

The Effect of Capital Gains Taxation
on the Private Sector

The standard argument against gains taxation is that it
inhibits growth in the private sector by diminishing the mobility of capital and the incentive to save and invest.

The Locked-in Effect

Considerable controversy surrounds the discussion of the
locked-in effect, the allegation that a capital gains tax
hinders the free movement of securities in the capital market.
This latter reason, unsupported by any evidence, was adduced
by the Indian Finance Minister in withdrawing the tax in 1949.[32]
The present Indian treatment of capital gains, which permits a
reduction in liability--through concessionary treatment of long-
term gains--if realization is postponed for one year, creates a
situation where there may be a short-run tax inducement to defer
realization of gains. Seltzer's study in the U.S.A. has indicated that changes in the length of the holding period in the
thirties caused substantial postponement of liquidation until

the lower rates became applicable,[33] and the Harvard study of investment habits confirmed the effect of the U.S. six-months holding period in causing deferred realization.[34]

Proponents of the locked-in thesis would go beyond the question of temporary postponement to suggest a long-run tendency of capital gains taxation to freeze investment, particularly among older people if gains are not taxable at death, and thus to act as a kind of permanent brake on the capital market. If the latter allegation could be verified it would constitute a serious indictment of capital gains taxation in an ostensibly growth-oriented tax policy.

Diminished mobility as a result of the locked-in effect may thus occur in the short and/or long run. Such short-run postponement of realization as results from the one year qualifying period for concessionary treatment in India can scarcely be regarded as undesirable. The distinction is intended precisely to promote enterprise rather than speculation. Market activity is not an end in itself, nor is stock turnover an index of capital formation. To the extent that speculation represents a diversion of resources which might otherwise have been productively employed it is inimical to economic growth.

Turning to the alleged long-run built-in brake on the movement of capital, it seems reasonable to postulate that the capital appreciation possibilities offered by new ventures which accord with planned objectives in India will provide a differential which exceeds the capital gains liability resulting from realization of the former stock. The empirical studies examined in Chapter 2 on Indian investment incentives indicated an ample willingness to invest in new government-approved securities regardless of tax considerations of any kind. An empirical study in the U.S.A. which specifically divided the effects of a capital gains tax on the timing of investment decisions into short-term effects (resulting from the tax distinction into short and long-term gains) and long-term "brake" effects concluded that the former (desirable) effects were by far the more important.[35] Of the insignificant minority reporting long-term effects only one case interviewed reported a disincentive to invest in new enterprises. The study concluded:

> . . . our data conspicuously fail to provide empirical support for the charge that the capital gains tax impairs the transfers of capital from seasoned securities to new ventures on any significant scale.[36]

Discussion of the lock-in effect of capital gains taxation frequently excludes discussion of a counter-balancing inverse

lock-in resulting from the deductibility of losses--the usefulness of this latter effect depending, of course, on the period
over which loss offset is allowed. The possibility of deducting capital losses from capital gains tax liability offers an
inducement to sell just as the capital gains tax discourages
selling. Loss offset provisions in India are presently less
than optimal, and their reform will be discussed later in this
chapter.

The present capital gains tax in India contains a long-run
built-in inducement to postpone realization in that capital
gains are not taxable if transferred by gift and inheritance.
This is a serious lacuna which, it has been suggested, is also
costly in terms of revenue, and its suggested removal would not
only further the objective that realized gains equal accrued
gains in the long run but that a major part of any incentive to
postpone realization would be removed.

Some incentive to postpone realization exists, of course,
as long as there is no interest charge on deferred liability.
If there is no such interest charge there will be some disincentive to realization in terms of possible interest earned
on deferred tax payments. The introduction of an interest
charge on deferred payments of tax has been recently advocated
in the U.S.A.[37] The use of such a principle in India would
remove the last disincentive to capital mobility, and, in combination with the removal of the gift and inheritance exemptions would make the yield of the realized capital gains tax
identical to that of a tax on an accruals basis.

An accruals tax is, of course, the ideal type of capital
gains tax but raises formidable administrative problems[38] and
may cause serious horizontal inequity and possible adverse
effects on economic growth through forced realization of assets. It would thus seem, in sum, that while the present capital gains tax in India does contain incentives to diminish the
turnover of capital, the short-run effects may be favorable to
stable planned growth, and the magnitude and economic impact
of the long-run effects are unlikely to be of serious magnitude and may, in any event, be largely offset by some relatively minor reforms.

The Incentive Issue

The economic impact of a tax on capital gains is further
alleged to be detrimental to economic growth by diminishing
the incentive to invest and the incentive and ability to save.
The "locked-in" issue is part of the "incentive to invest";
the latter will now be seen in the wider sense as including
the position of new investors entering the capital market.
The psychological effect of a capital gains tax on investors

(in addition to the effect on real income) is sometimes emphasized, and this factor was submitted as part of the justification for abolishing the capital gains tax in India in 1949.[39]
The point, however, is purely conjectural and there seems no
reason to believe that the resentment engendered by a capital
gains tax will be any greater than that from any other form of
taxation. This is particularly true where capital gains are
treated at a concessionary rate relative to other income. The
buoyancy of investment in India in recent years would scarcely
confirm any adverse psychological effects as a result of the
capital gains tax.

In terms of the over-all (psychological and economic) effects of the tax on investment it may be noted initially that
tax influences constitute only one, and not necessarily the
most important, of the determinants of investment behavior.
After a detailed analysis of the effects of changing rates of
capital gains taxation on investment behavior, the Seltzer
study concluded:

> The major influence upon aggregate capital gains
> realized annually has been neither the tax treat-
> ment nor the general level of prosperity as measured
> by national income. It has been rather the extent
> of changes in prices and turnover of capital assets,
> notably common stocks. Total capital gains have
> varied widely in periods of uniform tax treatment
> and have not always responded even in direction to
> the influence of more or less leniency in tax treat-
> ment.[40]

Insofar as capital gains taxation does influence investment behavior it will be submitted that the present Indian tax structure might have a net detrimental effect on risk investment,
but that a tax structure can be readily devised which should,
theoretically, be directly conducive to risk investment.

The economic impact of a capital gains tax on non-
corporate investment can be viewed, as in the case of a general
income tax, as the sum of an income effect and a substitution
effect. The substitution effect by reducing the return from
risk investment militates against venturesomeness and encourages more conservative security or income-oriented disposition
of capital. This effect is aggravated under a progressive capital gains tax. The income effect would operate to induce
greater venturesomeness in that risk investment for capital
gains offers the best means of recouping the loss in income
caused by the tax.[41] The net effect will be the resultant of
these two forces. Under the present Indian system without
averaging or adequate loss offset provisions,[42] the substitution effect may be expected to be strong and the possibilities

of capital appreciation required to induce risk investment correspondingly larger. It is not practically possible to completely eliminate the substitution effect under a progressive capital gains tax.[43] However, a rational system of averaging and the introduction of complete loss offset provisions over an indefinite period would counter most of the substitution effect of progressive capital gains taxation against risk taking.

There is indeed an argument against an unlimited loss offset provision in that such provision, which in effect makes the government a partner in business losses, would encourage frivolous investment!

As long as capital appreciation is taxed at lower rates than other forms of income there will remain an inducement to obtain income in the former rather than the latter form. This factor will serve to diminish the significance of the substitution effect. The importance of viewing the capital gains tax in terms of the taxation of other income rather than from a hypothetical situation without any taxation can hardly be overstressed.

Because of the short time in which the tax has been in operation no empirical evidence is available in India, but the Butters study in the U.S.A. has provided clear evidence that for investors bent on capital appreciation the income effect prevails over the substitution effect:

> . . . for appreciation-minded investors, the single most important feature of the tax structure is the differentially low rate at which long term capital gains are taxed in comparison with the much higher rates on ordinary income. . . . This differential has stimulated . . . venturesome individuals to shift funds out of relatively conservative investments, offering little or no opportunity for capital appreciation, and into more venturesome types of investments. . . .[44]

The essential issue is not the fact of taxation of capital gains but the favorable treatment accorded relative to other forms of income. Tax policy aimed at encouraging investment would thus maintain such a differential while simultaneously introducing averaging and indefinite loss-offset provisions which greatly diminish the substitution effect against risk-taking.

The effect of a capital gains tax on the incentive to save can also be expressed as the resultant of an income effect (which would induce a greater savings propensity to recoup decline in income from savings caused by tax payment) and a substitution effect (which would induce a switch to consumption). Essentially the same analysis applies in this case as in the case of the incentive to invest, the crucial factor again being the concessionary treatment accorded to capital gains. The return from savings is taxed more heavily as regular income than as capital gains. The income effect would thus again appear likely to prevail over substitution considerations.

There is, however, no question that the ability to save in a sense is diminished by taxation of capital gains. Given the concentration of capital gains in the upper income groups where the propensity to save is higher there is little doubt that a capital gains tax will absorb a higher percentage of savings than a tax with a more general incidence. A recent study contends that a capital gains tax reduces saving by something very close to the amount of revenue produced.[45] The argument reflects a related study[46] which indicates that individuals do not increase their consumption very significantly when they receive capital gains; the corollary follows that individuals will not reduce their consumption significantly when some of these gains are taxed away.

This problem of a diminished supply of saving consequent on a capital gains tax may be obviated by the scheme of exemptions and allowances previously suggested for income saved and invested in priority channels. Such a scheme would apply to capital gains income--acting as a re-investment exemption--as well as to income from other sources, and, combined with the concessionary tax treatment of income from capital gains, should provide a double incentive to private saving and investment. It might also be considered desirable to make the capital gains tax more effective as a means of economic control by providing differential treatment of capital gains income according to the source of income. Capital gains derived from projects which had a high priority in terms of planning goals would be treated more leniently than gains derived from areas considered of less significance. Such differential treatment would apply, of course, only to long-term gains.

CONCLUSION

The capital gains tax in India has been defended as an integral part of a horizontally equitable tax system. By radical revision of exemption levels, the list of exempt transactions, and the rate structure, and, particularly, by the closing of the gift and inheritance loophole, the tax should offer a much higher revenue productivity and should be a more effective means of diminishing vertial inequalities and correcting

inflationary price movements. The effect of such changes on
the private sector should not be serious provided concessionary
treatment of long-term gains--perhaps varied according to the
source of the gain--is maintained, if the savings exemption
scheme is also applied to income from capital gains, and if
adequate averaging and full loss-offset provisions are introduced. Possible restraint on the mobility of capital may be
diminished by an interest charge on deferred tax liability, and
by the sealing of the gift and inheritance loophole.

NOTES TO CHAPTER 4

1. For a study of introductory obstacles and problems,
see R. G. Sarien and O. P. Chawla, "The Capital Gains Tax in
India," Canadian Tax Journal, XI (September-October 1963),
451-57.

2. Government of the United Kingdom, Royal Commission on
the Taxation of Profits and Income, Cmd. 9474 (London:
H.M.S.O., 1955), Majority Report, p. 94. This recommends the
exclusion of capital gains from taxable income, describing a
substantial proportion of capital gains as "neither anticipated
at the time of acquisition nor sought by the recipient."

3. Government of Canada, Royal Commission on Taxation
(Ottawa: Queen's Printer, 1966), p. 349.

4. Such an exemption is specifically provided in India
for a taxpayer who purchases a house within a year of selling
his previous house. Harvard University Law School, International Tax Program, Taxation in India, World Tax Series
(Boston: Little, Brown and Co., 1960), pp. 260-61.

5. L. H. Seltzer, The Nature and Tax Treatment of Capital
Gains (New York: National Bureau of Economic Research, 1951),
p. 122.

6. Ibid., p. 125.

7. Government of India, Finance Minister's Speech,
Special Budget, 1956-57 (New Delhi: Ministry of Finance, 1956).

8. Ibid.

9. Government of India, Report of the Taxation Enquiry
Commission (hereinafter TEC) (3 vols.; New Delhi: Ministry of
Finance, 1953-54), Vol. I, pp. 163-64.

10. N. Kaldor, Indian Tax Reform (New Delhi: Ministry of Finance, 1956), p. 37.

11. Sarien and Chawla, op. cit., p. 457.

12. Government of India, Income-Tax Revenue Statistics for 1963-64 (Delhi: Manager of Publications, 1967), Statement 4.

13. Ibid.

14. Seltzer, op. cit., p. 139.

15. H. H. Hinrichs, "An Empirical Measure of Investors' Responsiveness to Differentials in Capital Gains Tax Rates among Income Groups," National Tax Journal, XVI (September 1963), 224-29.

16. H. Simons, Personal Income Taxation (Chicago: University of Chicago Press, 1938), pp. 221-24.

17. J. G. Head, "The Case for a Capital Gains Tax," Public Finance, XVIII (1963), 220-49.

18. Income-Tax Revenue Statistics for 1963-64, loc. cit.

19. TEC, op. cit., Vol. I, pp. 163-64.

20. Kaldor, op. cit., pp. 31-32.

21. W. J. Casey and J. K. Lassner, Tax-Sheltered Investments (New York: Business Reports, Inc., 1951). Between one third and one half of this study is devoted to procedures using manipulation of capital gains and losses. Joint Committee on the Economic Report, Federal Tax Policy for Economic Growth and Stability (Washington, D.C.: U.S. Government Printing Office, 1955), has a variety of articles on this subject; the best is W. Heller, "Investors' Decisions, Equity and the Capital Gains Tax," pp. 381-84. The British Royal Commission on Profits and Income, Cmd. 9474, op. cit. also dealt with the matter at some length (pp. 368-77). Seltzer's classic work examines tax avoidance via capital gains in Chapter 9, pp. 211-53, discussing all sixteen categories of tax avoidance.

22. Though they usually combine low-yield estimates with protestations of disastrous economic consequences, ignoring the apparent inconsistency between the two lines of reasoning.

23. Finance Minister Mathai, quoted in Kaldor, op. cit., p. 32.

24. Income-Tax Revenue Statistics for 1963-64, op. cit.

25. Kaldor, op. cit., p. 33.

26. A recent American study, H. H. Hinrichs, "Dynamic Regressive Effects of the Treatment of Capital Gains on the American Tax System during 1957-59," Public Finance, XIX, No. 1 (1964), 73-85, shows that a flat tax rate of 25 per cent not only provides a stagnant revenue source, but actually intensifies the inequality of incomes in the upper income brackets, by taxing at a flat rate incomes the capital gains content of which grows progressively larger as the income scale is ascended.

27. The U.S. capital gains tax has been recently criticized on the ground that it permits such manipulation; M. David, "Economic Effects of the Capital Gains Tax," American Economic Review, LIV, No. 3, Papers and Proceedings (May 1964), 288-99.

28. Constitution, Seventh Schedule-List 1, Entry 82.

29. Taxation in India, op. cit., p. 261.

30. Ibid., p. 262.

31. Given the elimination of the major loopholes the whole of capital gains accruing in any year may be considered subject to taxation. The rate of accrual of capital gains per annum in India has been estimated at between Rs. 600 million and Rs. 1,000 million. (Kaldor, op. cit., p. 37; this estimate was made in 1956, and may be considered very conservative.) Given the present full incorporation of short-term gains in income (and the suggested lower general income exemption levels), and the modified rate structure and exemption levels for long-term gains, it is estimated that the average rate on capital gains will be of the order of 20 per cent, suggesting an annual revenue productivity of between Rs. 120 million and Rs. 200 million. Mr. Kaldor suggested a rate structure providing an average effective rate of 40 per cent and an annual yield of Rs. 250-400 million per annum (Ibid.).

32. Ibid., p. 32.

33. Seltzer, op. cit., pp. 167-72.

34. J. K. Butters, L. E. Thompson and L. L. Bollinger, Effects of Taxation: Investments by Individuals (Boston: Harvard Graduate School of Business Administration, 1953), pp. 339-48; 21 per cent of the entire group interviewed and 41 per cent of those with income over $100,000 reported deferred realization.

35. Ibid., pp. 339-49.

36. Ibid., p. 349

37. David, "Economic Effects of Capital Gains Tax,"
op. cit., p. 298.

38. Though a recent proposal by A. J. Merrett, "Capital
Gains Taxation; The Accrual Alternative," Oxford Economic
Papers (New Series), XVI, No. 2 (July 1964), 262-74, suggests a
relatively simple accruals tax whereby annual capital gains tax
payments would be composed of a fixed percentage, say 10 per
cent, of outstanding accrued tax liability equal to the proportion of assets realized. Significantly, the recent Canadian
Royal Commission on Taxation labored long over the requirement
in equity for an accrual basis, but finally opted on grounds of
administrative feasibility for a realization basis.

39. Finance Minister Mathai, quoted in Kaldor, op. cit.,
p. 32.

40. Seltzer, op. cit., p. 180.

41. The definition of the income effect is extended here
--as in Chapter 3--to include the situation in which an investor has some pre-determined notion of a desirable level of income from assets--whether in the form of dividends, interest or
capital gains. As a result of the tax this pre-determined level
would not be realized and the taxpayer might switch a higher
proportion of his portfolio to high-yield risk investment in an
attempt to maintain his income from assets at the desired level.

42. Long-term losses may be set off against long-term
gains of the same year but may be carried forward and set off
against long-term gains of only the subsequent four years.
Oddly enough, the carry forward period for short-term losses is
eight years. Government of India, The Income Tax Act 1961 (as
modified up to October 1, 1965) (New Delhi: Ministry of Law,
1966), Chapter VI, Section 74.

43. R. A. Musgrave, The Theory of Public Finance (New
York: McGraw-Hill, 1959), p. 331, has shown that to avoid all
discrimination the rate of refund must be set to equal the rate
of tax applicable to the expected yield. The subjective nature
of the prospective yield makes this impossible.

44. Butters, et al., op. cit., pp. 41-42.

45. H. Wallich, "Taxation of Capital Gains in the Light of
Recent Developments," National Tax Journal, XVIII (1965), 133-50.

46. J. L. Arena, "The Wealth Effect and Consumption: A
Statistical Inquiry," Yale Economic Essays (1963), p. 294.

CHAPTER **5** THE TAXATION OF
AGRICULTURAL
INCOME

THE CONTRIBUTION OF THE AGRICULTURAL
SECTOR TO RESOURCE MOBILIZATION

Despite the still predominant role of the agricultural
sector in national income[1] and the high and increasing rate of
government expenditure on agriculture over the planning period,[2]
resource mobilization--whether in the form of voluntary savings
or taxation--for developmental expenditure in the private and
public sectors has been relatively low and stagnant.

Evidence on saving would suggest a much lower rate of
saving in the rural[3] than in the urban sector. Evidence on
private household saving reveals that rural household saving
accounted for 38.7 per cent of total household saving 1950-51,
but only 23.1 per cent of household saving in 1962-63. Rural
household saving was 1.7 per cent of national income in 1950-
51, and had fallen to 1.5 per cent by 1962-63; urban household
saving by contrast rose over the same period from 2.6 per cent
of national income to 4.9 per cent.[4]

Inadequate voluntary saving is in no wise offset by an
adequate contribution to tax revenue. Information on indirect
tax liability is again limited to the rural sector in general,
but offers an approximate indication of the relative burden of
indirect taxation borne by agricultural income. Table 1 indicates that indirect taxation constituted 2.9 per cent of rural
household expenditure and 5.9 per cent of urban household expenditure in 1953-54; in 1958-59 the corresponding figures
were 4.4 per cent and 9.3 per cent, respectively. The share
borne by the rural sector is lower in both cases and the relative share of indirect taxation paid by the rural sector diminishes over the period.

More precise evidence is available on the direct tax
burden borne by agricultural incomes. Agricultural income is
exempt from Union government income tax[5] but is subject to tax
by several Indian States which have received constitutional
authorization.[6] Seven States now levy an agricultural income
tax as against twelve in 1953-54 when the TEC surveyed the
question.[7] This reduction is partially due to constitutional

TABLE 1

CONSUMER EXPENDITURE, TAX ELEMENT AND TAX INCIDENCE
IN RURAL-URBAN INDIA IN 1953-54 and 1958-59

		1953-54		1958-59	
		Rural	Urban	Rural	Urban
		Per Capita Rs/month			
I	Consumer Expenditure	21.1	28.9	23.6	32.4
II	Tax Element (Indirect Taxes)	0.62	1.69	1.03	3.03
	1. Central Ind. Taxes	0.38	1.01	0.75	1.97
	2. State Ind. Taxes	0.24	0.69	0.28	1.06
		Tax as per cent of Consumer Expenditure			
III	Tax Incidence (Indirect Taxes)	2.9	5.9	4.4	9.4
	1. Central Ind. Taxes	1.8	3.5	3.2	6.1
	2. State Ind. Taxes	1.1	2.4	1.2	3.3

Sources: 1953-54 figures adapted from Government of India,
Report of the Taxation Enquiry Commission (3 vols.;
New Delhi: Ministry of Finance, 1953-54), Vol. I,
pp. 67-68; 1958-59 figures from Government of India,
Incidence of Indirect Taxation in India, 1958-59
(New Delhi: Ministry of Finance, 1961), pp. 10-13.

revision, but the agricultural income tax has been revoked by
the legislatures of several States and its present use is on
the decline.

The relative stagnancy of revenue from the agricultural
income tax is clearly seen in Table 2. This nominally progressive revenue source has constituted approximately 8 per cent of
State revenue from income taxation throughout the planning period to date, 7.5 per cent over the First Plan, 9.7 per cent
over the Second, and 8 per cent over the Third.

The definition of "capital asset" in the Indian capital
gains tax expressly excludes land from which agricultural income is derived at the time of its disposition;[8] there is

TABLE 2

STATE INCOME TAX REVENUE, 1951-52 - 1965-66

Rs. million

	1951-52 (Accts.)	1955-56 (Accts.)	Total First Plan	1955-57 (Budget)	1960-61 (Accts.)	Total Second Plan
Taxes on Income	570.5	630.8	3,009.7	593.3	1,004.7	4,145.5
i. Share of Union Income Tax	526.5	552.7	2,778.6	535.1	905.8	3,727.5
ii. Agricultural Income Tax	43.3	57.4	226.7	57.3	94.9	403.6
iii. Profession Tax	0.7	1.1	4.4	0.9	4.0	14.4
iv. ii as per cent of i			7.54			9.74

134

Rs. million

1961-62 (Accts.)	1962-63 (Accts.)	1963-64 (Accts.)	1964-65 (Accts.)	1965-66 (Accts.)	Total Third Plan
1,042.6	1,057.7	1,284.2	1,352.6	1,338.9	6,076.0
943.7	952.4	1,181.0	1,235.9	1,231.7	5,544.7
94.4	95.9	92.6	107.3	98.8	489.0
4.5	9.4	10.6	9.4	8.4	42.3
					8.04

Source: Reserve Bank of India, Report on Currency and Finance, 1965-66 (Bombay: Reserve Bank of India, 1967).

no equivalent tax either in the varied State agricultural income taxes or in the land taxes.

The major source of revenue from agriculture is land taxation; as in the case of agricultural income taxation the record is one of stagnancy, inflexibility, and diminishing relative burden. The power to impose land taxation is reserved exclusively to the States under the Constitution--though a very small and declining source of land revenue devolves to the Union government from the centrally administered areas or Union Territories.[9] The declining significance of land revenue was clearly indicated by the TEC which stressed that receipts from land revenue as a proportion of total revenue (Center and States) had fallen from 73.1 per cent in 1918-19 to 8.6 per cent in 1953-54. More recent figures show a similar trend; land revenue as a percentage of total revenue declined to 4.13 per cent in 1965-66. Table 3a and 3b show the findings of the TEC and the later figures.

Planning Commission estimates of revenue from the land tax at both the Union and State levels are not optimistic. The anticipated total level of land revenue over the Fourth Plan period is Rs. 6,665 in aggregate, or roughly Rs. 1,300 each year.[10]

A study covering the period 1950-59 confirms the above findings of an inadequate relative tax burden on agriculture.[11] On the basis of estimates of national income by the Central Statistical Office and calculation of direct and indirect tax burdens, A. Mitra arrived at the figures set out in Table 4. He concluded:

> . . . the tax complex of the country is made up of two disparate fiscal systems. In the agricultural sector, barely 4% of the aggregate income flows out to the state in the form of taxation. Outside agriculture, on the other hand, the government's tax claims are in the neighborhood of 10%. The current average tax revenue for the nation as a whole--about 8% of national income--tells only part of the story and conceals the significant reality of two parallel tax structures.[12]

Final confirmation of the argument for additional taxation of the agricultural sector on grounds of inter-sectoral inequity, i.e., that the relative tax burden on the agricultural sector is lower than on the urban sector, is to be found in a recent comprehensive study of inter-sectoral tax burdens in India by V. P. Gandhi.[13] Gandhi defines a new index of relative tax burden which takes into account both the ability-to-pay side (by incorporating in the index per capita taxable

TABLE 3a

LAND REVENUE AS A PERCENTAGE OF TOTAL
(CENTER PLUS STATES) TAX REVENUE

Year	Percentage	Year	Percentage
1793-94	69.0	1881-82	35.5
1808-09	61.1	1891-92	36.5
1818-19	73.1	1901-02	33.9
1839-40	70.6	1911-12	31.3
1850-51	66.5	1938-39	16.1
1871-72	42.8	1953-54	8.6

Source: Government of India, Report of the Taxation Enquiry
Commission (3 vols.; New Delhi: Ministry of Finance,
1953-54), Vol. III, p. 216.

TABLE 3b

LAND REVENUE AND TOTAL TAX RECEIPTS IN INDIA

Rs. million

	1951-52	Total First Plan Period	1956-57	1960-61	Total Second Plan Period
State Land Revenue	479.9	3,290.4	926.6	971.9	4,645.7
Central Govt. Land Revenue	20.0	54.0	5.4	6.9	26.1
Total Land Revenue	499.9	3,344.4	932.0	977.8	4,671.8
Total Tax Revenue (Center plus States)	6,380.5	35,765.9	8,604.9	13,549.2	55,727.0
Land Revenue as per cent of Total Tax Revenue	7.8	9.2	10.8	7.2	8.3

Rs. million

1961-62	1962-63	1963-64	1964-65	1965-66	Total Third Plan Period
952.3	1,200.7	1,234.2	1,197.9	1,119.3	5,704.4
5.6	5.8	3.1	1.5	2.6	18.6
957.9	1,206.5	1,237.3	1,199.4	1,121.9	5,723.0
15,379.5	18,549.3	23,133.9	25,852.2	29,021.7	111,936.6
6.5	5.8	5.3	4.6	4.1	5.1

Source: Reserve Bank of India, Report on Currency and Finance, 1965-66
(Bombay: Reserve Bank of India, 1967).

TABLE 4

TAX BURDEN IN THE INDIAN ECONOMY

	1950-51	1951-52	1952-53	1953-54	1954-55	1955-56	1956-57	1957-58	1958-59
1. Direct Tax Burden on Agriculture (per cent of agric. income)	1.2	1.1	1.4	1.4	1.8	2.0	1.8	1.8	1.7
2. Indirect Tax Burden on Agriculture (per cent of agric. income)	2.2	2.4	2.3	2.2	2.2	2.2	2.1	2.1	2.0
3. Total Tax Burden on Agriculture (per cent of agric. income) = (1+2)	3.4	3.5	3.7	3.6	4.0	4.2	3.9	3.9	3.7
4. Tax Burden on Non-Agricultural Sector (per cent of non-agric. income)	9.9	11.2	9.3	9.1	10.1	10.2	10.9	13.4	12.8
5. Total Tax Burden on Agriculture (per cent of total tax revenue)	25.3	23.1	24.9	28.0	24.0	24.4	24.5	19.2	21.8

Source: Ashok Mitra, "Tax Burden for Indian Agriculture," in R. Braibanti and J. Spengler, eds., Administration and Economic Development in India (Durham, N.C.: Duke University Press, 1963), p. 289.

income, a factor to allow for progressive tax rates, and a
variety of related factors which affect tax capacity, such as
wealth per capita, and the degree of inequality of wealth and
income distribution), and the benefit side (by incorporating
benefits received from government expenditures), and concludes:

> All of these pieces of evidence in combination
> lead to the inescapable conclusion that the agri-
> cultural sector is being inadequately taxed in
> comparison to the nonagricultural sector and that
> the tax burden on the agricultural sector should
> be raised in the interest of inter-sectoral equity
> and to reduce the outflow of funds from the non-
> agricultural to the agricultural sector. The
> latter is essential if the process of industriali-
> zation is not to be jeopardized in the short run.[14]

GROWTH

In terms of the evidence on resource mobilization from
agriculture, the growth objective of taxation in the agricultural sector may be defined in two parts. First, a reformed
tax system should seek to siphon off an increasing proportion
of the increases in agricultural income[15] consequent on the
program of public investment in agriculture; the system should
provide, in short, a productive and elastic source of revenue.
Second, not only must the resource mobilization role of taxation of agriculture be carried out with the passive qualification of minimum adverse consequences, but taxation must be so
fashioned as to complement positively the expenditure programs
designed to increase agricultural productivity. The urgency
of increasing agricultural productivity is such that the incentive issue becomes of the highest importance.

EQUITY

The resource mobilization argument for the taxation of
agricultural incomes has been stated as an argument on grounds
of horizontal equity, in effect as indicating the need to correct a serious inter-sectoral inequity by taxing agricultural
income in the same fashion, or to the same extent, as non-
agricultural incomes.[16]

The case is reinforced by considerations of inter-sectoral
vertical inequity, in other words, by the need to mitigate
serious inequalities of income within the agricultural sector.
The problem of inequalities of wealth (mainly in terms of land
ownership) in the agricultural sector will be examined in Chapter 7. Tables 4a and 4b, Chapter 2, indicate the distribution

of income in India as between the rural and urban sectors. The
approximation of "rural" distribution to cover "agricultural"
distribution is used in this case. Table 4a indicates that the
degree of inequality on average over the period was considerably less in the rural than in the urban sector. Moreover, as
Table 4b suggests, the concentration ratio in the rural sector
actually fell slightly between 1953-54 and 1956-57.

The fall in the concentration ratio in the rural sector
may, however, be attributed to various land reform measures and
the consequent break-up of large farms, rather than to tax
policy.[17] Indeed the Reserve Bank study (discussed in Chapter
2) stresses the relative ineffectiveness of tax policy as a redistributive device in the rural sector; the total income of the
rural high-income group (incomes exceeding Rs. 3,000 per annum)
was diminished as a result of taxation by only 3.7 per cent
while that of its urban counterpart was reduced by 7.3 per
cent.[18] Table 4a (Chapter 2) indicates that the concentration
ratio for disposable income in the rural sector was .306 over
the period studied as against .310 for personal income. Table
5 (Chapter 2) indicates that in 1959-60 the degree of inequality of consumption in the rural sector was considerably sharper
than in the urban sector.

In sum, the degree of inequality in the rural sector,
though less than in the urban sector, remains significant and,
at present, is only very slightly mitigated by taxation. The
relative sharpness of consumption inequalities in the rural
sector suggests that the degree of inequality of income distribution cannot be readily defended on functional grounds.

This conclusion is again confirmed by the Gandhi study,
which shows that the upper income group in the agricultural
sector--defined as those earning over Rs. 3,600 per annum--paid
between 6 per cent and 7 per cent of its annual income in taxes
between 1950-51 and 1960-61, whereas the upper income group in
the non-agricultural sector paid over 17 per cent. Defining
marginal tax burden in the same way as in Chapter 1 of this
study--i.e., as the ratio of additional taxes to additional income over a given time period--Gandhi further shows that the
marginal tax burden on the income group in the agricultural
sector was 7 per cent compared to 13 per cent in the non-
agricultural sector over the period 1950-51 to 1960-61.[19]

STABILIZATION

The limited coverage of the agricultural income tax and
the inflexibility of the land tax would imply that the contribution of such taxes to stabilization policy through affecting
the level of aggregate demand is minimal. Wider coverage and

sharper progressivity in the agricultural income tax and a more
elastic base and rate structure in the land tax would increase
the stabilizing effectiveness of these taxes on the demand
side.

The most important contribution of agricultural taxation
to stabilization lies, however, on the side of supply. A major
cause of inflation in India in the planning period has been an
inelastic food supply. The promotion of increased agricultural
productivity may be seen therefore not only as a qualification
to the tax objective of increased revenue mobilization from
agriculture but also as a crucial contribution of agricultural
taxation to the prevention of inflation.

MODES OF AGRICULTURAL TAXATION

The Agricultural Income Tax

The theoretically most effective means of combining the
tax objectives of increased and elastic revenue productivity,
diminished inequalities, and enhanced flexibility and consequent stabilizing effectiveness, with the provision of a comprehensive assortment of incentives, allowances and exemptions
designed to promote agricultural productivity, would be a progressive agricultural income tax based on ascertained net in-
come--supported by the necessary accounting records--with a
series of specific exemptions and allowances for re-investment,
land improvement, etc.

The history of attempts to levy taxation on agricultural
incomes in India has, however, not been encouraging. Except
for the periods 1860-65 and 1869-73--nine years in all--agri-
cultural incomes have been exempt from Union income tax and,
until 1935, from any levy on income whatsoever. In 1925 the
Indian Taxation Enquiry Commission observed:

> There is no historical or theoretical justification
> for the continued exemption from the income tax of
> incomes derived from agriculture. There are, how-
> ever, administrative and political objections to the
> removal of the exemption at the present time.[20]

Nothing was done until 1935 when the Government of India
Act empowered the provinces to levy taxes on agricultural incomes, and removed agricultural income from the tax jurisdiction
of the Union government. In 1938 Bihar became the first State
in India to levy an agricultural income tax. Tables 5a, 5b and
6 show, first, total returns from agricultural income tax in
all States using the measure between 1940 and 1963, second,
sample scales of progression in 1953-54, and third, returns in

TABLE 5a

RECEIPTS FROM AGRICULTURAL INCOME TAX, 1940-66

Rs. million

State	1940-41	1945-46	1950-51	1951-52	1952-53	1953-54	1954-55	1957-58	1958-59	1959-60	1960-61	1961-62	1962-63	1963-64	1965-66
Assam	3.9	4.9	7.9	9.1	10.8	8.9	6.9	22.4	29.9	25.7	27.5	28.8	33.1	41.1	28.4
Kerala	–	–	–	–	–	–	–	18.3	18.1	19.8	23.5	24.6	23.5	22.5	22.7
Travencore Cochin	–	–	5.0	9.9	9.6	9.0	9.0	–	–	–	–	–	–	–	–
Madras	–	–	–	–	–	–	15.4	13.0	8.6	15.4	13.5	14.2	13.6	11.6	12.3
West Bengal	–	–	6.3	6.4	6.1	6.3	6.4	11.7	8.9	8.8	8.3	8.0	7.2	7.2	10.8
Uttar Pradesh	–	–	13.8	10.0	7.1	5.8	3.6	5.3	6.1	8.8	8.8	6.6	2.2	0.6	3.2
Mysore	–	–	–	–	–	–	–	5.4	10.3	7.3	7.1	5.9	7.1	4.5	15.8
Coorg	–	–	–	0.3	1.4	1.5	1.0	–	–	–	–	–	–	–	–
Bihar	1.5	3.1	6.9	5.7	4.6	3.5	2.2	1.4	1.7	2.6	5.1	4.7	7.8	4.4	2.2
Orissa	–	–	1.0	1.3	0.7	0.8	0.8	0.3	0.3	0.3	0.4	0.5	0.3	0.5	0.7
Rajasthan	–	–	–	–	–	–	1.5	0.2	0.2	0.3	0.3	0.6	0.4	0.5	0.2
Andhra Pradesh	–	–	–	–	–	–	–	–	–	0.1	0.3	0.4	–	–	–
Hyderabad	–	–	–	1.1	0.3	0.5	0.5	–	0.1	0.1	0.1	0.1	–	–	–
Madhya Pradesh	–	–	–	–	–	–	–	–	–	–	–	–	–	–	–
Bhopal	–	–	–	–	–	–	0.2	–	–	–	–	–	–	–	–
Vindhaya Pradesh	–	–	–	–	0.1	0.1	0.3	–	–	–	–	–	–	–	–
Jammu & Kashmir	–	–	–	–	–	–	–	–	–	–	–	–	–	–	–
TOTAL	5.4	8.0	40.9	43.6	40.5	37.7	47.8	78.0	84.2	89.2	94.9	94.4	95.2	92.9	96.3

Note: Blanks indicate either the disappearance of a state after consolidation or its non-existence prior to consolidation. Dashes indicate that no agricultural income tax was levied.

Sources: "Agricultural Income Tax in India," Reserve Bank of India Bulletin (August 1963), 1022-33; Government of India, Report of the Taxation Enquiry Commission (3 vols., New Delhi: Ministry of Finance, 1953-54), Vol. III, Table 1, p. 199.

TABLE 5b

SAMPLE SCALES OF PROGRESSION IN THE
AGRICULTURAL INCOME TAX, 1953-54

Tax Burden according to State (Rs.)	Income Group (Rs.)	5,000	10,000	25,000	50,000	100,000
Bihar		164	633	3,914	12,352	34,695
Uttar Pradesh		219	688	3,031	10,469	32,968
Travancore-Cochin		164	633	3,798	12,664	37,039

Source: Figures from Government of India, Report of the Taxation Enquiry Commission (3 vols.; New Delhi: Ministry of Finance, 1953-54), Vol. III, Table 2, p. 202.

TABLE 6

STATE INCOME TAX SOURCES

(Rs. million)

State	Type of Tax	1960-61 (Accounts)	1963-64 (Revised)	1965-66 (Accounts)
Andhra Pradesh*	Share of Income Tax (a)	70.3	92.2	95.0
	Agric. Income Tax (b)	0.3	0.1	-
	Profession Tax (c)	-	-	-
Assam	a	21.2	29.1	30.1
	b	27.5	41.1	28.4
	c	1.1	1.2	1.6
Bihar	a	86.5	99.9	114.9
	b	5.1	4.4	2.2
	c	-	-	-
Jammu and Kashmir**	a	9.8	8.3	8.6
	b	-	-	-
	c	-	-	-
Kerala	a	31.7	43.3	43.7
	b	23.5	22.5	22.7
	c	-	-	-
Madras	a	73.4	97.2	100.1
	b	13.5	11.6	12.3
	c	-	-	-
Maharashtra	a	64.5	156.1	165.2
	b	-	0.5	2.5
	c	-	-	-
Mysore	a	44.7	61.9	63.2
	b	7.4	4.5	15.8
	c	-	-	-
Orissa	a	32.4	41.0	42.4
	b	0.4	0.5	0.7
	c	-	-	-
Rajasthan	a	35.6	47.5	48.9
	b	0.3	0.5	0.2
	c	-	-	-

(Rs. million)

State	Type of Tax	1960-61 (Accounts)	1963-64 (Revised)	1965-66 (Accounts)
Uttar	a	142.3	174.0	177.6
Pradesh	b	8.3	0.6	3.2
	c	-	-	-
West Bengal	a	112.0	142.5	148.9
	b	8.5	7.2	10.8
	c	-	-	-
TOTAL (all	a	905.8	1,180.7	1,231.7
States including	b	94.9	93.5	98.8
those not using	c	4.0	7.1	8.4
the agricultural				
income tax)				

Notes: *agricultural income tax abolished in 1964-65 Budget.
          **agricultural income tax introduced in the 1966-67
          Budget, where it was expected to produce Rs. 0.1
          million.

Sources: "Finances of State Governments 1967-68," Reserve Bank
          of India Bulletin (August 1967); Reserve Bank of
          India, Report on Currency and Finance, 1962-63 (Bom-
          bay: Reserve Bank of India, 1964); Reserve Bank of
          India, Report on Currency and Finance, 1966-67 (Bom-
          bay: Reserve Bank of India, 1968).

---

individual States now using the agricultural income tax--in-
cluding returns from Andhra Pradesh where the tax was recently
abolished--relative to other sources of income tax revenue. By
the time of the report of the TEC in 1953-54, twelve states were
employing the tax, but in only five cases--Bihar, Assam, West
Bengal, Uttar Pradesh, and Travancore-Cochin--was revenue significant, and even in these cases the return was relatively inflexible and stagnant (Table 5a). This was true in spite of a
substantial measure of progression (Table 5b). The States Re-
organization Act of 1956, and the Constitution (Seventh Amendment) Act of 1956 reduced the number of States, eliminating as
individual entities five of those levying agricultural income
tax. At present, eleven of the sixteen States levy agricultural
income tax but in only seven of these cases does the tax make a

significant contribution to direct tax revenue (Tables 5a and
6). In none of the individual cases illustrated, nor in the
aggregate, is agricultural income tax the flexible, elastic
revenue source which might be expected in a progressive income
tax.

The rate structures of the present agricultural income
taxes are indicated in Table 7, and the rates of super-tax on
agricultural incomes, levied in only four States, Bihar, Kerala,
Madhya Pradesh and Mysore, are indicated in Table 8. The rate
of progression is relatively mild except in Orissa. Table 9
presents an analysis of tax receipts in three states, Assam,
Kerala and Madras, which were responsible for 70 per cent of
agricultural income tax revenue in the last three years. The
revenue possibilities of the tax are, in fact, indicated very
clearly by the case of Madras which only introduced the tax in
1954-55, and has since seen revenue multiply twenty-fold. The
concentration of revenue in these three States, however, can
be attributed to the fact that plantations, mainly tea, are
predominant there.[21] The incidence study of agricultural income tax (Table 9) in the above three States confirms that in
Assam and Madras the greater part of agricultural income tax
revenue is derived from high (presumably plantation) income
groups. Kerala, however, is a much more hopeful case in terms
of comprehensive coverage with almost as much revenue derived
from the three lowest brackets as from the top two. The number
of relatively small agricultural incomes assessed is also much
greater than in the other two States, and the experience of
Kerala may serve as a prototype for other States.

The present agricultural income taxes in India would appear
in general to be of little consequence as means to the attainment of the three major tax objectives. Few specific incentives
are incorporated in the taxes and the only sense in which the
taxes may be said to promote productivity is in the negative
sense that such limited taxes can scarcely exercise disincentive
effects. With the single exception of Kerala, the agricultural
income tax has only been successful where the unit of agricultural operation has been of the plantation variety.

It would appear that present administrative difficulties
preclude the immediate extension of coverage and enhanced progressivity which would be necessary if the agricultural income
tax is to become an effective means of implementing tax objectives. Assessment problems are at present almost insuperable
except in the plantation type of farm unit.[22]

The replacement of the present inflexible land taxes by
agricultural income taxes would thus appear to be, of necessity,
a long-run objective. The TEC found it difficult to conceive
of any immediate substitute of comparable revenue productivity

TABLE 7

RATES OF AGRICULTURAL INCOME TAX IN INDIA
(Rates of levy in nP. per rupee of
Agricultural Income)

State	Bihar	Assam	West Bengal	Orissa	Uttar Pradesh	Kerala	Madras	Mysore	Madhya Pradesh (Bhopal)	Maharashtra	Jammu and Kashmir
Exemption Limit Rs.	3,000	3,000	3,000	5,000	3,600	3,600	3,600	3,500	3,000	36,000	3,000
Income Ranges											
On the first 1,500	Nil	Nil	Nil			Nil		Nil	Nil		
" 1,800					Nil						
" 3,000				Nil							Nil
" 3,600							Nil				
On the next 1,400							5				
" 2,000				3							
" 3,200					5						
" 3,500	5	4	5			5		3	6		
" 2,500		8									
" 2,500		12									
" 2,500		15									
" 2,500		19									
" 5,000	11	24	8	6	10	11	15	6	9		
" 5,000	16		12	9		18	20	9	9		
" 5,000	22		19	16			25	12	19		
" 5,000				22			30	15	19		
" 5,000				29							
" 5,000				36							
" 5,000				44							
" 7,000											8
" 10,000					25			18			11
" 10,000					40						
" 15,000				50				21			
" 15,000				62							
" 15,000				69							
" 15,000				72							
" 15,000				75							
" 30,000		30									20
" 50,000		34						25			
On Balance	25	38	25	78	60	25	45	40	25	50 (Flat rate)	25

Notes: [a] In the States of Assam, West Bengal, Kerala, Madras and Madhya Pradesh, the rates are applicable to individuals, Hindu undivided families, firms, other associations of persons, i.e., excluding companies. In other States the rates are applicable to all assessees.
[b] The table indicates that the initial tax-free slab next to the exemption limit varies from Rs. 1,500 - Rs. 3,600, with the exception of Maharashtra which imposes a flat rate of 50 nP./rupee above Rs. 36,000.

Source: "Agricultural Income Tax in India," Reserve Bank of India Bulletin (August 1963), 1022-33.

TABLE 8

RATES OF SUPER TAX ON AGRICULTURAL INCOMES
(Rate in nP. per rupee)

	Bihar	Kerala	Madhya Pradesh	Mysore
On the first 25,000 of the total agricultural income	Nil	Nil	Nil	Nil
On the next 10,000 " " "	6		6	
" " " " "	9		9	
" " " " "	13		12	
" " " " "	16		15	
" " " " "	19		19	
" 15,000 " " "	22	12	22	
" " " " "	25	16	25	
" " " " "	28	22	28	
" " " " "		28		
" 25,000 " " "				9
" " " " "				12
" " " " "				15
" 30,000 " " "	31		31	
On Balance	33	34	33	25

Note: The blanks serve to distinguish the different slabs of income for tax
purposes in the various States.

Source: "Agricultural Income Tax in India," Reserve Bank of India Bulletin
(August 1963), 1022-33.

TABLE 9

INCIDENCE[a] OF AGRICULTURAL INCOME:
ASSAM, MADRAS AND KERALA, 1960-61
(In Rs. 1,000)

Grades of Income	Total Income Assessed	Total Agricultural Income Tax Collected	Col. 3 as per cent of Col. 2
1	2	3	4
ASSAM			
3- 5	529	9	1.7
5- 10	176	21	11.9
10- 15	167	30	18.0
15- 20	298	60	20.1
20- 30	580	150	25.9
30- 40	340	81	23.8
40- 50	364	108	29.7
50-100	3,281	1,093	33.3
100-200	5,268	2,197	41.7
Above 200	68,019	25,250	37.1
TOTAL	79,022	28,999	36.7
MADRAS			
Up to 5	15,848	266	1.7
5- 10	20,438	836	4.1
10- 15	5,109	487	9.5
15- 20	2,274	275	12.1
20- 25	1,488	226	15.2
25- 30	1,037	178	17.1
30- 40	1,635	417	25.5
40- 50	1,032	334	32.4
50- 60	574	187	32.6
60- 70	488	163	33.3
70- 80	350	59	17.0
80- 90	680	259	38.1
90-100	595	192	32.2
Above 100	18,819	7,587	40.0
TOTAL	70,367	11,416	16.2
KERALA			
Up to 5	39,487	2,123	5.4
5- 10	51,800	2,858	5.5
10- 25	31,004	2,481	8.0
25- 50	16,038	1,570	9.8
50-100	6,888	1,329	19.9
100-200	16,518	7,398	47.7
Above 200	3,361	896	26.7
TOTAL	165,096	18,655	11.4

Note: [a]The term "incidence" in this case is that used in the
Reserve Bank study. More correct would be the term "impact incidence," i.e., legal or intended incidence, which
may, of course, differ widely from final incidence or
"effective incidence."

Source: "Agricultural Income Tax in India," Reserve Bank of India
Bulletin (August 1963), 1022-33.

to the land tax as a source of State finance, in spite of their considerable enthusiasm for agricultural income taxation in terms of equity and as a long-run part of Union income taxation.[23]

The partial replacement of land revenue by agricultural income taxation was accomplished in the former State of Travancore-Cochin--now Kerala--where the old land tax was abolished in 1945 and a nominal uniform rate land tax on area substituted. This was, however, coupled with the use of a progressive agricultural income tax, and the new formula yielded more revenue than the previous land tax.[24] The extension of this formula depends, however, on the administrative feasibility of an income tax levied on farmer's incomes. The TEC considered this issue and concluded that the success of the agricultural income tax was largely accounted for by features peculiar to Travancore-Cochin, such as the relative homogeneity of the land and the preponderance of large holdings.[25] The study concluded that the extension of the principle was not feasible at that time and for most States would involve considerable revenue loss because of the enormous number of small holdings.

The only practicable present procedure, then, would seem to be the reform of the land tax base to accord with some notion of, at least, presumptive income or output, the long-run intention being the transition from land taxation to agricultural income taxation and the integration of the latter with the Union income tax. To fulfil the three major tax objectives a revised land tax system would have to be determined on a standardized base, be flexible in response to changes in prices and output, be capable of personalization in terms of the individual circumstances of the taxpayer, and be adaptable to a comprehensive series of incentive and disincentive devices designed to promote agricultural productivity.[26]

The Present Land Tax System

The historical development of land taxation and the evolution of the Zamindari, Mahalwari and Ryotari varieties of assessment procedures have been well documented.[27] It is proposed here only to examine present procedures: Table 10 indicates land revenue and total tax revenue derived by individual States from 1960-61 to 1965-66; the inelasticity of land revenue relative to other tax sources is apparent from the statistics. At present in India there is a wide variety of land tax bases, classified by the TEC as: net assets or economic rents; net produce or annual value; rental value; capital value; gross produce; and a variety of empirical ad hoc procedures.[28] In Punjab, Uttar Pradesh, Madhya Pradesh and the temporarily settled areas of Bihar, Orissa and West Bengal, assessment of land revenue is based on "net assets," determined by estimating the gross produce, valued at the average price of a crop for a specified period ("commutation price") and deducting the land-lord's estimated costs. In Madras the assessment is based directly on the value of the "net produce," determined by de-ducting cultivation expenses and certain adjustments for bad seasons from gross produce valued at the commutation price. Originally, gross produce was the basis of assessment in all parts of India, and is still the basis of assessment in Assam.

The standards of classification to be used by assessing officers in determining the basis of assessment are as varied as the tax bases. In some cases these standards are prescribed by law to include pre-determined factors, in others the judg-ment of the assessing officer is relied upon. A wide and varied group of factors--soil fertility, crop yield, climate, proximity to markets, etc.--is included in classifying the villages for land tax purposes.[29]

Assessment is determined for a "settlement period"--nor-mally thirty years, though a shorter period may be specified by the State government--and rates of tax are fixed by assessing officers for the settlement period within limits prescribed by law. Where assessment is based on net assets or net produce, the maximum limits on the rates of tax range between 25 per cent and 50 per cent. Where Zamindari tenure has been abol-ished, the rate of tax now generally amounts to 100 per cent of the settled rental value (since rent previously paid to Zamin-dars is now paid directly to the State government as land reve-nue). In Assam the rate of tax is 10 per cent of the gross produce; in other areas where gross produce is the basis of assessment, the tax is one sixth of gross produce. With the maximum prescribed rates the range and type of rate structure vary widely.[30]

The conglomerate of classification system, tax bases and rate structures in the present land tax clearly fails to meet the requirements of revenue productivity, equity and stabiliza-tion; nor does the present system directly promote increased agricultural productivity. Indeed, dissatisfaction with land taxation on both revenue and equity grounds led nine States to announce in 1967 varying degrees of land tax curtailment, rang-ing from exemption for small landholders to outright abolition. The nine States involved were Bihar, Haryana, Madras, Mysore, Orissa, Punjab, Rajasthan, Uttar Pradesh, and West Bengal.[31] The subsequent disintegration of the coalition administrations in most of these nine States has made the actual fate of land taxation in these States uncertain.

When a particular form of taxation manifestly fails to discharge its intended objectives, the obvious alternatives are

TABLE 10

LAND TAX AND TOTAL TAX REVENUE, 1960-61 - 1965-66

State	Tax Revenue		1960-61	1961-62	1962-63	1963-64	1964-65	1965-66
Andhra Pradesh	Land Revenue	(a)	93.0	88.4	164.9	164.7	165.0	141.2
	Total Tax Revenue	(b)	555.4	550.3	688.0	778.1	794.5	912.6
Assam	a		27.7	29.0	32.0	34.9	47.2	54.9
	b		171.2	182.5	226.0	268.8	301.0	307.1
Bihar	a		87.6	99.7	154.1	105.0	112.2	120.5
	b		479.7	520.2	635.9	660.0	713.0	829.5
Gujarat	a		43.9	50.8	68.0	60.4	61.8	73.2
	b		378.7	435.5	482.0	537.9	555.9	674.6
Jammu and Kashmir	a		6.9	7.2	6.9	7.6	8.0	4.4
	b		38.3	44.7	54.8	60.6	71.2	68.0
Kerala	a		14.0	15.8	11.2	6.0	12.9	26.5
	b		262.4	286.2	342.8	414.6	437.7	501.6
Madhya Pradesh	a		96.5	98.8	96.3	101.5	105.7	70.0
	b		391.2	417.8	480.7	580.7	633.7	682.3
Madras	a		49.8	44.7	44.1	44.8	47.1	67.6
	b		544.3	554.8	691.4	794.9	833.9	1,038.7

154

State	Tax Revenue	1960-61	1961-62	1962-63	1963-64	1964-65	1965-66
Maharashtra	a	87.7	68.9	72.9	78.2	73.4	55.8
	b	799.4	796.5	1,034.7	1,254.2	1,286.6	1,530.1
Mysore	a	44.0	49.5	52.0	78.8	78.3	55.7
	b	333.5	365.6	435.6	529.5	547.2	606.3
Orissa	a	20.6	28.1	27.9	30.7	31.2	28.7
	b	148.0	174.8	236.9	278.3	285.0	327.5
Punjab	a	42.5	41.7	56.6	50.9	45.0	39.8
	b	343.9	367.9	461.8	559.3	556.3	708.8
Rajasthan	a	71.5	84.7	94.1	83.0	88.5	48.9
	b	256.0	290.5	353.2	403.2	418.8	708.8
Uttar Pradesh	a	222.3	215.3	251.3	248.9	222.9	241.0
	b	871.9	870.1	1,009.3	1,093.1	1,105.2	1,325.5
West Bengal	a	63.3	71.1	78.4	86.2	86.3	70.2
	b	673.9	673.3	806.4	948.7	959.3	1,185.3
TOTAL	a	971.9	994.3	1,200.7	1,181.6	1,185.5	1,119.3
	b	6,247.8	6,530.7	7,939.5	9,161.9	9,499.5	11,177.5

Sources: "Finances of State Governments 1964-65," Reserve Bank of India Bulletin (May 1964); "Finances of State Governments 1967-68," Reserve Bank of India Bulletin (August 1967).

abolition or reform. Given the critical need for revenue
sources to meet increasing expenditures of both a Plan and non-
Plan variety at the State level, the current move to large-scale
exemptions from, or abolition of, land taxation, would seem
economically unwise if politically opportune. The subsequent
section of this chapter will explore some avenues of reform.

A Reformed Land Tax System

Given the necessary standardization of land classification
procedures, the first essential step in the reform of Indian
land taxation would seem to be the definition of a standardized
tax base which is sufficiently flexible to fulfil the specified
requirements. Such a base would have to correspond in some
pre-determined manner with presumptive net income or output[32]--
the long-run goal remaining, of course, to base the tax on
ascertained net income. Of the various tax bases employed in
India perhaps the concept of "net produce" used in Madras most
closely corresponds to presumptive net income. There are, however, many variations and refinements on the theme.[33]

The tax base chosen in the Indian case must be defined in
terms of its economic consequences; it has been argued that on
grounds of growth and stabilization, tax policy in agriculture
must be such as to promote increased agricultural productivity.
Thus the goal of tax policy in agriculture should be to levy
taxes in such a manner as to leave the reward for additional
effort undiminished, i.e., to minimize the "substitution effect"
of taxes; indeed it is necessary that the tax should penalize
under-utilization or inefficient utilization of land. This
criterion would suggest that presumptive income be defined not
in terms of actual output but in terms of productive capacity
or the output which the land should yield if managed with
average efficiency. The tax would thus be based on potential
output in relation to some regional average.[34] Thus the inefficient farmer whose production is less than the average for
the region and/or for the type of land concerned would be
penalized, whereas the efficient farmer would be correspondingly encouraged; the tax would also promote the transfer of land
from inefficient to efficient hands and would penalize heavily
under-utilization, absentee ownership, etc.

The case for a tax on potential as distinct from actual
output is re-inforced by the existence of a substantial margin
of "slack" or unutilized capacity in the agricultural sector
in India. Gandhi has argued that "slack" exists in several
forms--that average farm productivity is far below best performance yield, that there is large-scale abuse and/or underuse
of resources devoted to agriculture, and that the increasing
income of farmers over the planning period has been largely
channelled into consumption rather than into capital formation.[35]

The tax might be made <u>progressive</u> in terms of land holdings, though remaining proportional in terms of potential output for any given land size. In this way not only is the vertical equity criterion satisfied but there will be a sharp
inducement to either the utilization of large land holdings--
which are most likely to be held idle--or to the break-up of
such large holdings into smaller units which would presumably
be worked more efficiently. Allowance under the productive
capacity criterion would have to be made for reduction or remission of land revenue in the event of extensive crop failure.
Most States presently provide such allowances.[36] The land size
exemption limit and the rate of progressivity would be determined by considerations of equity, revenue productivity, and
the attitude of the government toward land holding. The rate
of progressivity may indeed be employed as an instrument of
land reform.

The proposed progressive land tax is in accordance with a
movement of opinion away from the present roughly proportional
rate structures. A conference held in 1959 on Taxation and
Optimum Land Utilization[37] recommended making land revenue progressive with the size of holdings. K. N. Raj[38] has also proposed a progressive scheme in which land tax is doubled on
holdings above five acres, an additional tax is imposed on
agricultural rents--collected at source from tenants--and a
surcharge is imposed on holdings above five acres under commercial crops. I. M. D. Little's proposed scheme is considerably
more involved;[39] the proposed tax is based entirely on size of
holding and has 27 tiers of graduation, reaching a maximum of
Rs. 30 per acre on holdings above 30 acres.

A. M. Khusro has suggested a simpler scale;[40] he suggests
leaving present rates constant for all holdings below five
acres (at approximately Rs. 3 per acre), raising present rates
on holdings between five and ten acres to Rs. 5 per acre, and
raising present rates on holdings of ten acres and over to
Rs. 10 per acre. The suggested scale of progression in relation to approximate imputed average farm income on these three
area brackets rises from 3 per cent on lowest groups to 23 per
cent on highest groups. Khusro's latest scheme meets some of
the political objections to the land tax by suggesting the
exemption of holdings under five acres--thus exempting the vast
majority of land taxpayers but <u>only 25 per cent of acreage</u>--and
increased progressive rates on holdings above the five acre
limit. The highest suggested rate--50 per cent above the
present highest rate in every State--would come into effect on
all holdings above ten acres, thus removing the incentive to
minimize tax burden by sub-dividing holdings.[41]

The proposed tax structures are not, however, directly
related to income or output and might tend to become almost as

inflexible as the traditional proportional tax. The variation
on this theme--suggested above--which would make tax rates
proportional in terms of output but progressive in terms of
land acreage would offer much greater flexibility as well as
incentives to increased productivity.

Flexibility

Tax yield under a reformed flexible land tax must clearly
be responsive to price and production changes. A stable yield
has in the past been regarded as an attribute of land revenue;
this characteristic becomes a serious deficiency in the Indian
setting where a vigorous program of agricultural development is
being undertaken. The resource mobilization and equity objectives require that part of the increase in agricultural income
must be appropriated by sufficiently flexible revenue instruments.

The only flexibility device employed at present in India
is provision in a few States for reduction or remission of land
tax in the event of constant and severe price declines.[42] The
TEC proposed a decennial revision of the land revenue assessment (after standardization) with reference to changes in the
price level. This contrasts with the present system of revision every thirty or forty years. The method of revision proposed by the TEC "should be such that it can be carried out
more or less automatically on the basis of the price levels
without the intervention of an elaborate administrative machinery operating in small units over long periods at dispropor-
tionate cost."[43] Land revenue adjustments were to be made in
accordance with the change in price of the predominant crop
in the particular area in question, and price changes of less
than 25 per cent were to be ignored.[44] This procedure does
not, however, provide for adjustments to changes in the level
of production or short-run price changes, and more frequent
revisions by means of an easily applied automatic formula would
be more effective and more equitable.

What would appear to be necessary are, say, five-year
adjustments of regional average rated capacity to take account
of general growing conditions and annual adjustments according
to movement in prices. The required responsiveness might be
achieved by the introduction of what has been called "structural flexibility," defined as "the automatic variation of tax
collections with changes in prices or production, a variation
having its source in the structure and administration of the
tax rather than in deliberate adjustments in the tax rates or
exemptions."[45] The five-year re-assessment of productive
capacity norms might also be used to incorporate the present
varied and unproductive group of betterment levies and

irrigation charges for improved capacity resulting entirely
from public developmental expenditure.[46]

The upward adjustment of "potential output" norms has incentive implications, which should not, however, be serious in
that the desired flexibility is to be achieved through over-all
regional average adjustments in the level of assessments rather
than through individual adjustments according to each taxpayer's
output. Effectively the marginal tax rate on output remains as
zero for the individual farmer but is positive with respect to
farmers in the aggregate.

Personalization

The final requirement of a system of land taxation in the
process of transformation into a system of agricultural income
taxation is that the tax be related by allowances and exemptions to the personal circumstances of the taxpayer. The
proposal to this point is only related to individual circumstances in terms of the amount of land possessed. A possible
method of personalizing the tax might be to raise the average
exemption limit by one acre for every two children up to a
maximum of four acres. The introduction of such a qualification would help to expunge the in rem character of the tax--
the organic cause of the rigidity and inelasticity which
characterize the present system.

Incentive Devices

The basic incentive built into the proposed system is a
short-run incentive to efficient cultivation. It might also
be considered desirable to provide inducements to long-run
improvements of land. Exemptions or preferential treatment--
perhaps in the form of deliberately frozen production norms for
tax purposes--might be granted for improvements in and structures on the land. Though such incentives are usually the in-
advertent and capricious result of long delays in cadastral
surveys and tax assessments, there is no reason why they might
not be specifically incorporated in the proposed system for
India.[47] Similar devices might be employed to direct agricultural effort into the production of particular crops.[48] At
present in India the rates for land under cultivation of tea
are slightly lower than for other crops,[49] and the principle
might be elaborated and extended.

Capital Gains

The direct income taxation of agriculture might be completed by the introduction of a capital gains tax on the transfer of land.[50] The basic purpose of such a tax would be to
siphon off a portion of increased land values at the time of

transfer and to discourage land speculation. Rates should thus
be highly progressive, ranging from very moderate rates on improved, efficiently worked land to penal rates on increments in
value of unimproved land.[51] Such a capital gains tax would be
levied in addition to the State stamp duty required on the
transfer of property.

Tax Treatment of Landlords and Tenants

The tax system proposed is conceived basically in terms of
assessment of owner-cultivators, and requires modification in
terms of the still predominant divorce of ownership from cultivation in India.[52] If only landlords are taxed according to
productive potential there is the likelihood of backward shifting of the tax burden to tenants in the form of higher rents.
Security of tenancy may also become an issue in this case. It
might be argued that the landlord should be viewed as a tax-
withholding agent, in which case rental adjustments to shift
some of the tax to the tenants might be sanctioned. Control of
rental terms may indeed be a convenient tool for regulating the
extent of tax shifting and relative burden on landlords and
tenants. It may be argued that no rental or tenancy adjustments
be allowed on the grounds that rent income is sufficiently great
to bear the full burden and/or that absolute tenancy security
is an irrevocable axiom. On the other hand such a policy may
prove inequitable and inefficient under the proposed system in
that a landlord may be prevented from taking any measures which
would increase productivity.

The present arrangements in India are, as in all aspects
of land taxation, varied and generally imprecise. The most
common procedure would appear to be the imposition of the entire
tax on the landowner and the use of an increasing array of rent
control and tenancy security devices to prevent backward shifting.[53] Rents are in several cases specified as fixed proportions of land revenue, and as previously indicated, where the
Zamindari system has been abolished the land revenue due is 100
per cent of previous rent to the Zamindar. This present system
might well act as a serious brake on land improvement under the
proposed tax system.

There would appear to be two possible solutions. First,
the total tax might be assessed as at present on the landlord
and the proportionate distribution of burden considered most
desirable achieved by means of a standardized system of rent
control. A satisfactory system here would involve a knowledge
of the allocation of production costs.

Second, and probably more satisfactory, the tax might be
assessed against both landowners and tenants having presumptive
income over a specified exemption level. The landowner would

be assessed with the full burden of the tax, as would tenants
for their particular piece of land. The landlord would, of
course, receive his rent from the tenants, and the latter would
receive a tax credit in respect of rental obligations. It
would be possible to incorporate in both suggested schemes
discriminatory treatment of rental (unearned) as against cul-
tivator's (earned) income.[54]

Land Reform

The process of land reform which tends to reduce the size
of large holdings may appear to run contrary to the development
of a reformed land tax system based on some notion of presumptive or potential income and the evolution of land taxation
into agricultural income taxation. Assessability certainly
becomes more difficult the smaller is the holding, and a recent
study shows that the yield from the present agricultural income
tax has declined substantially in areas--such as Bihar, West
Bengal and Uttar Pradesh--where large land holdings have been
broken up and/or the intermediary system abolished.[55]

To use the land reform program as a pretext for the delay
of land tax reform measures would be to under-estimate the
possibilities of assessing relatively small income earners--as
in Kerala--and also to misunderstand the purpose of land reform.
It is not the purpose of land reform in India to reduce the
size of the average holding to that of an untaxable entity. It
is the purpose of that program to eliminate the unproductive
and grossly inequitable intermediary system, to eliminate absentee landlordism and to redistribute land with the objective
of imposing a ceiling on holdings. The first two purposes do
not represent any great fiscal loss and the size of holdings
envisaged in the Plan should provide ample scope for presumptive, if not direct, assessment.

The average ceiling enacted in the state legislatures has
been in the order of 25 to 30 acres,[56] a size that should not
offer tremendous obstacles to assessment on the base proposed
above. The emphasis in the Plan on consolidation of holdings
and cooperative farming and the considerable achievements in
these areas[57] are often insufficiently stressed. Such developments facilitate the solution of assessment problems in agricultural taxation. The primary objective of land reform in
India was stated as follows:

> . . . to remove such impediments to increase in
> agricultural production as arise from the agrarian
> structure inherited from the past. This should help
> to create conditions for evolving as speedily as
> possible an agricultural economy with high levels of
> efficiency and productivity.[58]

An Alternative Proposal

The proposed scheme of taxing agriculture in terms of potential income is subject to one serious argument on equity grounds. If vertical equity is a major objective, it is argued that progressive rates should be levied on realized or ex-post as distinct from potential or ex-ante income, and that the scheme proposed gives priority to productivity incentives at the cost of the optimal system for the attainment of vertical equity. In the Indian context this priority may perhaps be considered a justifiable one; the base differs little in the above sense from many of the present land tax bases which are levied ex-ante regardless of actual output.

The following alternative proposal reflects concern over this equity issue, and represents in general terms a suggestion made to the writer by Dr. I. G. Patel, the Chief Economic Adviser to the Ministry of Finance in New Delhi.

Farmers whose holdings exceeded 50 acres should fall within the present standard income tax net. This would presumably involve a constitutional amendment allowing the Union to at least collect income tax from specified categories of farmers, or the States would themselves have to levy and collect an income tax on the same basis as that levied by the Union. Fewer than 1 per cent of rural households, but more than 15 per cent of land area would fall into this first taxable category.[59]

Holdings below 1 or 2 acres would be exempt, thus excluding up to 60 per cent of rural households, but only 6 per cent of area, from the tax net. This exemption, perhaps extended to include holdings up to 5 acres (covering 75 per cent of rural households and 17 per cent of area) would meet many of the present political objections to agricultural taxation. For these small farmers, a certain amount of tax revenue--insignificant on an individual level but substantial in the aggregate--might be obtained from registration fees and stamp duties on property transfers.

For all remaining holdings a system of land taxation made progressive by size of land holdings, but having for administrative reasons relatively few slabs in the scale of progression, should be introduced. This last aspect of the proposal is very similar to the most recent proposal by Khusro, previously outlined.

Two final observations may be made on the problem of the direct taxation of agriculture. First, there will remain in the agricultural sector, regardless of which of the above schemes is introduced, a pool of taxable capacity in kind,

particularly among small landholders. A proposal to incorporate some of this untapped pool is outlined in Chapter 8.
Second, the present stamp and registration tax system--on all
transactions and property, including agricultural--is of considerable significance, providing Rs. 741 million to the States
in aggregate in 1965-66. An enhanced degree of progression
might be introduced into State agricultural taxation by setting
up a sharply progressive scale of registration fees for agricultural land, and an associated scale of rates of stamp duty
on transfers of agricultural land.

THE EXAMPLE OF JAPAN

The potential of the agricultural sector as a means of
financing development may be illustrated by the experience of
economic development in Japan between 1880-1920. This period
of "forced draft" development has been well documented.[60] Between 1881-1920, farm output increased by 77 per cent; the
estimated rise in output per farm worker was 106 per cent.[61]
This expansion of output and doubling of farm labor productivity was attained chiefly through improved techniques, including
more liberal use of fertilizer, improvement of rice strains,
improvements of water and pest control, and in cultivation,
transplanting and weeding. The significance of this technolog-
ical change from the Indian point of view is that the emphasis
was on land-saving and capital-extensive and small farm improvements introduced into a framework of hand agriculture.

In the period as a whole national income rose by 75 per
cent, and 40 per cent of this increase is attributed to agriculture and fisheries. Significantly, however, "there is ample
evidence that there was only limited improvement in the levels
of living of the farm population."[62] The landlord's share of
farm income was augmented and farm tenancy increased (from 31
per cent of cultivated land in 1873 to 45 per cent in 1915)
because of the land tax reforms of 1873 when the old feudal
levies in kind were replaced by a tax payable in money. This
reformed land tax was the means of siphoning off and utilizing
most of the increase in agricultural productivity for capital
accumulations and industrial development.

The new tax was based on the assessed value of farm land,
and, unlike the previous collections in kind, did not vary with
fluctuations in the farmer's harvest; fixed at 3 per cent initially, reduced to 2.5 per cent between 1876-1899, the tax
seems to have amounted to about 13 per cent of the value of a
normal crop. The land tax accounted for 86 per cent of total
tax revenue in 1875-76, 45 per cent in 1893-94, and 22 per cent
in 1906-07, by which time industrialization was well under way.
The relative burden on agriculture declined slowly to 9.7 per

cent of agricultural income as against 4.3 per cent of non-
agricultural income in 1930.[63]

Such a scheme is not, of course, directly transferable to
India, and compromise solutions would have to be reached on
such matters as the Indian desire to raise the consumption level
of the rural population, and to reduce rather than augment
tenant farming. The severely regressive tax structure employed
in Japan would not be politically acceptable in India. The
vertical inequity of the Japanese system which relied on taxing
the peasant heavily via the land tax and the general consumer
via high excise duties,[64] while placing a relatively light burden on the landlord and industrial-merchant class,[65] would also
be politically unacceptable in India. It might also be economically unsuccessful; in Japan, "the dependability of profit re-
ceivers in the burgeoning secondary sector left fiscal policy
here essentially free to disregard the dangers of potential
luxury spending, speculation, or non-productive investment, and
to concentrate on containing the broad mass of consumption."[66]
It might be optimistic to expect the same co-operation from
merchant-industrial and landlord groups in India.

The other sense in which the Japanese tax system was regressive also has relevance for the Indian case. The relatively
severe burden on agriculture in Japan has been illustrated, and
it is likely that such a radical change in tax policy in India,
directing the greater part of the direct tax burden onto the
agricultural sector, would be politically and administratively
very difficult. The fact remains, however, that the agricultural sector at present is contributing an inordinately small
proportion of both the indirect and direct tax burden, and a
substantial increase in this contribution could not be deemed
excessive or inequitable.

In short, although the philosophy and practice of forced
draft development in Japan via regressive taxation and reliance
on the investing propensities of the high-income groups is not
directly transferable to India, the potential of the agricultural sector as a source of funds for development expenditure
emerges as an example for Indian fiscal planners. The similar
process in Russia in the 1890's of financing industrialization
through taxation of agriculture also illustrates the possibilities of reformed agricultural taxation.[67]

CONCLUSION

The relative tax burden on Indian agriculture has been
shown to be slight. The objectives of growth, equity and stabilization require both enhanced resource mobilization for public
spending and increased agricultural productivity. A long-run
means of reconciling these objectives would be offered by the

use of an agricultural income tax based on ascertained net income and qualified by a series of exemptions and allowances for
reinvestment, etc. Assessment problems in the short run suggest
that the first step to a solution might lie in a reformed land
tax structure which, though progressive in terms of land size,
would be proportional in terms of average potential output for
each land size. This tax base would be refined by the introduction of structural flexibility and a series of exemptions
and personal allowances. The potential of the agricultural
sector as a means of financing development is illustrated by
the experience of Japan at the turn of the century.

NOTES TO CHAPTER 5

1. In 1964-65, agriculture accounted for 43.2 per cent
of Indian national income, as against 49 per cent in 1950-51.
Reserve Bank of India, Report on Currency and Finance, 1965-66
(Bombay: Reserve Bank of India, 1967), p. 60. Agriculture
includes animal husbandry, forestry and fisheries.

2. The Third Five Year Plan total outlay on agriculture
was Rs. 12,810--14 per cent of total Plan outlay--as against
Rs. 6,670 in the Second Five Year Plan--11 per cent of total
Plan outlay. In the Fourth Five Year Plan, the projected outlay on agriculture is Rs. 42,740--18 per cent of total Plan outlay. Government of India, Planning Commission, Third Five Year
Plan--A Summary (Delhi: Manager of Publications, 1962), p. 69;
Government of India, Fourth Five Year Plan--A Draft Outline
(New Delhi: Planning Commission, 1966), p. 41. The general
head of agriculture includes agricultural production, animal
husbandry, dairying and fisheries, forests and soil conserva-
tion, community development, co-operation, land reform, and
agricultural labor.

3. It would, of course, be very difficult to discover
the rate of saving from purely agricultural incomes. The best
available approximation is evidence for the rural sector which
is predominantly agricultural, encompassing about 65 per cent
of national income as against 43 per cent for agriculture.

4. "Estimates of Saving and Investment in the Indian
Economy: 1950-51 to 1962-63," Reserve Bank of India Bulletin,
XIX (March 1965), 314-33.

5. Constitution, Seventh Schedule, List 1, Entry 82.

6. Constitution, Seventh Schedule, List 2, Entry 46.

7. The Government of Uttar Pradesh announced in June 1967 its intention to replace land revenue by an agricultural income tax, the replacement to be phased over a five-year period (Hindustan Times, June 28, 1967). The fall of the Uttar Pradesh Government and the imposition of President's Rule in 1968 would seem to make unlikely the implementation of the tax reform.

8. Harvard University Law School, International Tax Program, Taxation in India, World Tax Series (Boston: Little, Brown and Co., 1960), p. 261.

9. Constitution, Seventh Schedule, List 2, Entry 45.

10. Government of India, Draft Fourth Plan Material and Financial Balances, 1964-65, 1970-71, and 1975-76 (New Delhi: Planning Commission, 1966).

11. Ashok Mitra, "Tax Burden for Indian Agriculture," in R. Braibanti and J. Spengler, eds., Administration and Economic Development in India (Durham, N.C.: Duke University Press, 1963), pp. 281-303.

12. Ibid., p. 290.

13. V. P. Gandhi, Tax Burden on Indian Agriculture (Cambridge: Harvard University Law School, International Tax Program, 1966).

14. Ibid., p. 195.

15. Non-monetary incomes are, of course, not subject to present modes of taxation and will be dealt with separately in Chapter 8.

16. The TEC elaborated the anomalies and inequities resulting from disparate treatment of agricultural and non-agricultural incomes. Government of India, Report of the Taxation Enquiry Commission (hereinafter TEC) (3 vols.; New Delhi: Ministry of Finance, 1953-54), Vol. III, pp. 222-24.

17. "Distribution of Income in the Indian Economy," Reserve Bank of India Bulletin (September 1962), 1348-63.

18. Ibid., Table 3, p. 1357.

19. Gandhi, op. cit., p. 135.

20. Indian Taxation Enquiry Commission (1925), cited in TEC, op. cit., Vol. III, p. 198.

21. "Agricultural Income Tax in India," Reserve Bank of India Bulletin (August 1963), 1022-33.

22. Ibid., p. 1023, emphasizes that systematic maintenance of farm accounts is an essential pre-condition of assessment.

23. TEC, op. cit., Vol. III, pp. 209, 221.

24. V. R. Pillai, "A Basic Tax on Land (the Travancore Experiment)," Indian Journal of Agricultural Economics, V, No. 1 (March 1950), 185-90.

25. TEC, op. cit., Vol. III, p. 208, para. 4

26. The reform of land taxation is dealt with in detail in H. P. Wald and J. N. Froomkin, eds., Agricultural Taxation and Economic Development (Cambridge: Harvard University Law School, International Tax Program, 1954); H. R. Wald, Taxation of Agricultural Land in Underdeveloped Economies (Cambridge: Harvard University Law School, International Tax Program, 1959); TEC, op. cit., Vol. III, pp. 179-330.

27. See, for instance, TEC, loc. cit.; Taxation in India, op. cit., pp. 89-90.

28. TEC, op. cit., Vol. III, p. 185. The variety of tax bases is detailed in Appendix A, 263-84.

29. Ibid., p. 263.

30. Settlement periods and rate structures for each State or area in each State are detailed in TEC, op. cit., Vol. III, Appendix B, pp. 285-96.

31. Economic Times (Bombay), July 19, 1967.

32. This principle is generally employed in the Ghanaian income tax. When the income tax was subjected to basic reforms in 1961 a presumptive income rule was introduced. For traders and similar business activities, the figure of taxable income cannot be less than 2.5 per cent of gross turnover. Likewise professional men are taxed on figures based on typical incomes for the particular occupations unless records demonstrate that the liability should be less. J. F. Due, Taxation and Economic Development in Tropical Africa (Cambridge: M.I.T. Press, 1963), pp. 34-35.

33. See, for instance, R. D. Stevens, "A Review of Measures of Farm Income for International Use," Indian Journal of Agricultural Economics, XVIII (October-December 1963), 1-20, where six standard measures of farm income are elaborated: net

farm benefit, net farm income, family earnings, operator's net earnings, labor income, and management return--on an ascending scale of sophistication.

34. Since 1951, South Korea has levied its land income tax on the basis of a standard assessment keyed to the average or normal productive capacity of a region; the tax specifically exempts output which exceeds the standard assessment. W. Heller, "The Use of Agricultural Taxation for Incentive Purposes," in Agricultural Taxation and Economic Development, op. cit., pp. 222-44; see the development of the notion of a tax on productive capacity in N. Kaldor, "Role of Taxation in Economic Development," in Essays in Economic Policy (2 vols.; London: Duckworth, 1964), Vol. I, pp. 225-54. Gandhi has recently suggested a "graduated faculty tax" based on potential output for use in India; Gandhi, op. cit., pp. 217-22.

35. Gandhi, op. cit., pp. 143-72.

36. Taxation in India, op. cit., p. 91.

37. The papers presented at the conference are published in the Indian Journal of Agricultural Economics, XV, No. 1 (January-March, 1960), Proceedings of the 19th Conference, 27-54 and 250-58.

38. K. N. Raj, "Resources for the Third Plan: An Approach," The Economic Weekly, Annual Number (January 1959), 30-34.

39. I. M. D. Little, Tax Policy and the Third Plan, Institute of Economic Growth, 1959, mimeograph, reproduced in Prices and Fiscal Policies--A Study in Method, ed. P. N. Rosenstein-Rodan (London: G. Allen and Unwin, 1964), pp. 30-76.

40. A. M. Khusro, "Taxation and Agricultural Land--A Proposal," The Economic Weekly, Annual Number (February 1963), 275-82.

41. A. M. Khusro, "Should Land Revenue be Abolished," Economic Times (Bombay, June 16 and 17, 1967).

42. TEC, op. cit., Vol. III, Appendix A, pp. 263-84.

43. TEC, op. cit., Vol. III, p. 228.

44. Ibid., p. 229.

45. H. P. Wald, Taxation of Agricultural Land, op. cit., p. 152.

46. The variety of betterment levies and irrigation rates is described in TEC, Vol. II, pp. 225-59 and 326-30, and is criticized in A. Mitra, op. cit., pp. 296-98.

47. Note, e.g., the use by Australia and New Zealand of a graduated tax on unimproved land values. (Heller, op. cit., p. 225.)

48. As an instance of this technique, Chile employs a penalty tax on newly planted vineyards in an attempt to discourage domestic production of wine. (Heller, loc. cit.)

49. TEC, op. cit., Vol. III, p. 264.

50. The extension of the wealth tax base to include agriculture is suggested in Chapter 6.

51. Denmark and Portugal levy highly progressive land value increment taxes at the time of transfer. (Heller, op. cit., p. 229.)

52. It was estimated in 1947 that 75 per cent of the cultivated land in India is cultivated by tenants with varying status; P. Irani, "Structure and Taxation of Agriculture in India and Pakistan," in Wald and Froomkin, op. cit., pp. 368-95. This percentage may be expected to decline continuously under the land reform program.

53. Government of India, India 1964 (Delhi: Manager of Publications, 1965), Chapter XVII, details the arrangements made in each State.

54. In Brazil rents are taxed more heavily than owner incomes. Any holding not exceeding 20 hectares is exempted from land tax if the owner cultivates it alone or with the aid of only his family and owns no other real estate. (Heller, op. cit., p. 229.)

55. "Agricultural Income Tax in India," op. cit., p. 1029.

56. Government of India, India 1966 (Delhi: Manager of Publications, 1967), p. 246.

57. Ibid.

58. Third Five Year Plan, op. cit., p. 95.

59. Government of India, National Sample Survey, First Report in Land Holdings, Rural Sector, Eighth Round (New Delhi: Cabinet Secretariat, 1958).

60. The definitive work is B. F. Johnston, "Agricultural Productivity and Economic Development in Japan," Journal of Political Economy (December 1951), 498-534; almost as comprehensive is, G. Ranis, "The Financing of Japanese Economic Development," Economic History Review, Second Series, XI, No. 3 (April 1959), 440-54. See commentary in W. Heller, "A Survey of Agricultural Taxation and Economic Development," in Agricultural Taxation and Economic Development, op. cit., pp. 147-48. See also, Nobutaka Ike, "Taxation and Landownership in the Westernization of Japan," Journal of Economic History, VII, No. 2 (November 1947), 160-82, for an account of the lot of the peasant under the system.

61. These productivity figures--accepted by Johnston, Ranis, etc.--are based on official statistics the accuracy of which has been questioned in a recent study. J. I. Nakamura, "Growth of Japanese Agriculture, 1875-1920," in W. W. Lockwood, ed., The State and Economic Enterprise in Japan (Princeton: Princeton University Press, 1965), pp. 249-324. Nakamura suggests a rate of growth of agricultural productivity only half as great as that in the official estimates, and his findings--though presumably open to debate--may be seen as qualifying the conclusions by Johnston and others on the effectiveness of land taxation as a means of mobilizing increments in agricultural productivity.

62. Johnston, op. cit., p. 501.

63. Ranis, op. cit., Table 6, p. 448.

64. Ibid., p. 446; excise duties constituted 10 per cent of total revenue in 1870, 21.8 per cent in 1880, 28.6 per cent in 1890, 18.7 per cent in 1910, 31.6 per cent in 1920 and 37.4 per cent in 1930--the duty on Sake alone constituted 20 per cent of total revenue at the turn of the century.

65. The income tax appeared in 1887 at the low rate of 3 per cent. Revenue from this source was negligible before 1900 and deductability of interests and dividends made the tax severely regressive.

66. Ibid., p. 449.

67. T. H. Von Laue, "The High Cost and the Gamble of the Witte System: A Chapter in the Industrialization of Russia," Journal of Economic History (1953), 156-72; A. Gerschenkron, "The Rate of Growth in Russia since 1885," Journal of Economic History, Supplement VII (1947), 144-74; A. Baykov, "The Economic Development of Russia," Economic History Review (December 1954), 137-49.

6

AN ANNUAL TAX ON NET WEALTH

It is proposed to examine the incidence of an annual wealth tax on income and/or capital, to describe the present Indian tax, to evaluate the tax in terms of the criteria previously established, and, finally, to suggest changes and modifications in the present Indian tax.

Incidence on Income and/or Capital

The choice of income--broadly defined--as the primary index of ability-to-pay does not preclude the use of other, supplementary indices in the tax structure. The major alternative bases are wealth and consumption--the latter defined either "directly" through an expenditure tax, or "indirectly" through the taxation of commodities and services.

The State land taxes in India have relied, and in some cases continue to rely, on a wealth (property) base. The first section of this chapter is concerned with a quite different concept of wealth taxation--that of taxing net wealth, or the value of assets minus liabilities at a specified point in time. It is, in fact, arguable that a net wealth tax of the low rate variety imposed in India is more properly seen as an addition to the income tax structure than as a tax on capital itself. Examples of the latter type of taxation would be a capital levy or an estate tax; the distinction lies in the question of recurrence. Mr. Kaldor drew this distinction in 1942:

> The fundamental criterion for determining whether
> a particular tax falls on capital or on income,
> is not whether it is levied on the one or the other,
> but whether it is singular (a once-and-for-all pay-
> ment) or recurrent.[1]

In his detailed study of capital taxation in India, I. S. Gulati arrives at the same distinction.[2] Because of its recurrent and predictable nature the Indian net wealth tax is better seen as a tax intended to be paid from the annual yield from capital (whether in the form of money income, psychic income or expected

appreciation in value),[3] than as a tax on the principal itself.
The tax at present low rates is envisaged accordingly as an additional tax on property incomes, which should serve to increase
the progressivity of the personal income tax, to alleviate aggravation of wealth inequalities, and to tax property which is
not used to earn income--such as idle land--but which will not
to any great extent diminish existing inequalities of wealth.

While the similarity between a net wealth tax of the Indian
sort and an additional income tax on property incomes is appar-
ent--given a rate of return on capital of 5 per cent, a net
wealth tax of 1 per cent is equivalent to a 20 per cent tax on
income from capital, a 2 per cent wealth tax to a 40 per cent
income tax, a 3 per cent wealth tax to a 60 per cent income
tax, etc.--there are certain conceptual differences which should
not be overlooked.

First, the wealth tax falls on the entire lump sum of
wealth, regardless of whether that wealth is productively employed, whereas an income tax applies to wealth only in a marginal sense--to the annual increment in wealth. This distinction might have considerable significance for the taxpayer's
psychological reaction to the two forms of tax, the seeming
higher rate of the income tax and its incidence only at the
margin presumably making the incentive effects of the income
tax more serious. Further, this distinction is particularly
important in that all net wealth taxes presently in operation
exclude from the tax base "human capital," or the capital value
of expected future earnings. This latter point will be further
discussed in the consideration of the equity aspects of the net
wealth tax.

Second, the wealth tax includes in its base types of property which either do not yield a current income taxable under
the standard income tax, say, interest on cash holdings, or are
not taxable at all without some imputation system, say, psychic
income.

Finally, the relative wealth tax burden on holders of
securities will differ sharply according to the rates of return
on different securities.

Description

A tax on net wealth has been in effect in India since
April 1, 1957; the tax was introduced as part of the integrated
system of direct taxation recommended by Mr. Kaldor. Unlike
the novel expenditure tax, the wealth tax had been widely
applied previous to its introduction in India. Annual taxes on
net wealth of the sort defined above are presently levied in
twelve other countries: Sweden, Norway, Denmark, Finland, West

Germany, the Netherlands, Switzerland, Luxembourg, Ceylon, Pakistan, Columbia and Uruguay.[4] Japan adopted a net wealth tax in 1950 in accordance with the recommendation of the Shoup Mission, but repealed the tax in 1953.

The Indian net wealth tax is levied annually on the tax-able net wealth--the aggregate value of all assets owned by the taxpayer minus liabilities[5] on the valuation date, March 31 each year or the final date of the year or years adopted by the taxpayer for purposes of income tax declaration--of individuals and HUF. Corporations were originally included within the pur-view of the tax at a uniform rate but were exempted in 1960. Individuals and HUF are subject to exemptions of Rs. 100,000 and Rs. 200,000, respectively, beyond which the tax is progres-sive, ranging from 0.5 per cent on the first slab (up to Rs. 400,000 for an individual and Rs. 300,000 for a Hindu undivided family) to 2.5 per cent on the highest slab. The progressivity of the tax has been substantially increased since 1957 by reducing exemption levels and increasing tax rates.[6] Table 1 indicates the present rate structure.

In Sweden, Denmark, the Netherlands and Ceylon, a "ceiling" is specified in the combined income-wealth tax system, so that the average or marginal joint rate of income and wealth tax does not exceed a specified percentage of income. No such ceiling is specified in India.[7]

Besides the basic wealth tax levied on the net wealth of individuals and HUF, an additional wealth tax was introduced in the 1965-66 Budget--and since retained--to be charged on the value of lands and buildings, other than business premises, and rights therein possessed by individuals and HUF in areas with a population exceeding 100,000. The tax is calculated at pro-gressive rates applicable to successive slabs of the amount by which the value of such property exceeds a certain initial exemption, determined by the population of the area in which the property is situated. Table 2 details the additional tax rates.

The tax base for the basic wealth tax includes property of every description, movable and immovable--in effect, in-cluding real property (land and buildings), tangible personal property (jewelry, household furniture, automobiles, etc.), and intangibles (stocks, bonds, mortgages, bank deposits, etc.), but excluding a valuation of human capital, represented by the discounted value of the flow of expected future earnings--although certain classes of assets are specifically exempted from tax liability.[8] These include short-term interests (where interest in property is available for less than six years), lands, buildings and other assets used in agriculture (this exemption is based on a constitutional limitation),[9] profes-sional equipment, assets used in scientific research, patents

TABLE 1

WEALTH TAX RATES, 1967-68

							Rate of Tax
(a)	In the case of every individual:						
	i.	On the first Rs.	100,000	of net wealth			Nil
	ii.	On the next Rs.	400,000	"	"	"	0.5 per cent
	iii.	" " " Rs.	500,000	"	"	"	1.0 per cent
	iv.	" " " Rs.	1,000,000	"	"	"	2.0 per cent
	v.	On the balance of net wealth					2.5 per cent
(b)	In the case of every HUF:						
	i.	On the first Rs.	200,000	of net wealth			Nil
	ii.	On the next Rs.	300,000	"	"	"	0.5 per cent
	iii.	" " " Rs.	500,000	"	"	"	1.0 per cent
	iv.	" " " Rs.	1,000,000	"	"	"	2.0 per cent
	v.	On the balance of net wealth					2.5 per cent

Source: Government of India, Finance Bill, 1965 (New Delhi: Ministry of Finance, 1965), p. 50.

TABLE 2

LEVY OF ADDITIONAL WEALTH TAX ON THE VALUE OF
URBAN IMMOVABLE PROPERTY IN CERTAIN CASES

The initial exemption will be as follows:

i. Where the assessee has any property situated in an area with a population exceeding 1,000,000 — Rs. 500,000

ii. Where the assessee has any property situated in an area with a population exceeding 800,000 but not exceeding 1,000,000 and there is no property in the area at (i) above — Rs. 400,000

iii. Where the assessee has any property situated in an area with a population exceeding 800,000 and there is no property in any area at (i) or (ii) above — Rs. 300,000

iv. Where the assessee has any property situated in an area with a population exceeding 100,000 but not exceeding 400,000 and there is no property in any area at (i) or (ii) or (iii) above — Rs. 200,000

The rates applicable to the excess will be as under:

On the first Rs. 200,000 of the excess:	Nil
On the next Rs. 500,000 of the excess:	1 per cent
On the next Rs. 500,000 of the excess:	2 per cent
On the next Rs. 500,000 of the excess:	3 per cent
On the balance of the excess:	4 per cent

Source: Government of India, Memorandum Explaining the Provisions in the Finance Bill, 1965 (New Delhi: Ministry of Finance, 1965), p. 26.

and copyrights, property held in trust for charitable and
religious purposes, miscellaneous personal assets (the original
exemption of jewelry up to Rs. 25,000 was withdrawn in the
1963-64 Budget), and a variety of exemptions to encourage the
direction of savings to specified areas.

Annuities, pensions in respect of past services, and
amounts credited in provident funds and insurance policies are
exempt, as are a variety of government securities, ten-year
treasury savings deposit certificates, fifteen year annuity
certificates, deposits in post office savings banks, post office
cash certificates, post office national savings certificates,
post office national plan certificates, twelve-year national
plan savings certificates, and, since the 1963-64 Budget, ten-
year defense deposit certificates and twelve-year national defense certificates provided that such securities have been held
for a minimum period of six months from the date of issue. Corporate shares are subject to tax; an original five-year exemption in respect of shares held in new industrial corporations
was withdrawn in 1962, but restored in the 1965-66 Budget.

Administration and procedure under the Wealth Tax Act
closely parallel administration and procedure under the Income
Tax Act, and the income tax authorities also serve as wealth
tax authorities.[10]

Revenue Productivity

Returns of the Indian tax on wealth since its inception in
1957 are detailed in Table 3 in relation to total taxes on
property and capital transactions, and total Union tax revenue.
The revenue productivity of the wealth tax has fallen somewhat
short of the estimates of N. Kaldor, who forecast a yield of
Rs. 200-250 million per annum,[11] and I. S. Gulati, who envisaged a yield of Rs. 520-570 million per annum.[12] Wealth tax
revenue constituted 1.1 per cent of total Union tax revenue in
1960-61, and has declined in relative significance since then;
in 1965-66, wealth tax revenue accounted for only 0.67 per cent
of total Union tax revenue. Revenue forecasts for the Fourth
Plan period anticipate that annual revenue from the wealth tax
will rise to Rs. 170 million by 1970-71, and that total wealth
tax revenue over the Fourth Plan will amount to Rs. 770 million.[13]

Wealth taxes have generally constituted a very small proportion of total tax revenue, although the Indian tax seems
particularly unproductive. In Ceylon (1964-65), Uruguay (1965),
and Denmark (1958-59), the net wealth tax constituted 2.0 per
cent, 2.6 per cent and 2.5 per cent, respectively, of total national tax revenue. In Pakistan (1964-65) the relative revenue
significance--0.8 per cent--is similar to the Indian figure.[14]

TABLE 3

WEALTH TAX REVENUE, 1957-58 - 1965-66

Rs. million

Tax	1957-58 (Accts.)	1958-59 (Accts.)	1959-60 (Accts.)	1960-61 (Accts.)	Total Second Plan Period	1961-62 (Accts.)	1962-63 (Accts.)	1963-64 (Accts.)	1964-65 (Accts.)	1965-66 (Accts.)	Total Third Plan Period
Wealth tax	70.4	96.7	121.1	81.5	369.7	82.6	95.4	102.0	105.0	120.5	505.5
Total taxes on property and capital transactions	106.1	149.1	170.2	134.9	584.4	142.1	161.5	170.2	164.9	198.3	767.0
Total Union tax revenue	5,753.3	5,530.6	6,424.4	7,301.4	29,947.3	8,753.7	10,609.8	13,743.3	15,628.0	17,846.2	66,581.2

Source: Reserve Bank of India, Report on Currency and Finance, 1965-66 (Bombay: Reserve Bank of India, 1967).

The reasons for the disparity between realized and projected returns would appear to be first, the lack of adequate registration of property transactions and a consequent large measure
of evasion,[15] second, the excessively high previous and present
exemption limits, and, third, inadequate progressivity in the
rate structure in the early years of the tax.

The progressivity of the tax was substantially increased,
particularly in the 1964 Budget, by reduced exemptions and increased rates, and the 1965 Budget imposed a progressive surcharge on urban property. These changes should make the tax
considerably more income-elastic and thus more suitable as a
means of siphoning off an increasing proportion of increasing
property incomes and reaching the expanding ownership of physical and monetary capital which accompany the progress of the
development plans.

The present rate structure is sufficiently progressive for
a tax which is essentially aimed at <u>income</u> from property rather
than property itself, and it is, in fact, conceivable that an
individual in the highest income brackets, deriving--as seems
likely--a high proportion of his income from property, would be
subject to the equivalent of a marginal rate on income of over
100 per cent. However, the present move toward the removal of
the distinction between earned and unearned income in the Union
income tax--by reducing the surcharge on unearned income--will
diminish the progressivity of the personal income tax. The
Finance Minister will then have two basic alternatives to restore progressivity; he can either increase progressive rates
on all income, or he can, in effect, maintain the steeper progressive rates on unearned income by increasing wealth tax
rates. It will be suggested below that wealth tax rates remain,
but that the slabs of wealth to which they apply be drastically
modified.

On exemption levels there is immediate scope for substantial reform. Although the present exemption for individuals--
Rs. 100,000--represents a halving of the exemption prior to the
1964-65 Budget, the exemption level is still 270 times per
capita income, a generosity exceeded only by Ceylon and Pakistan. Wealth tax assessments for 1963-64 show 10,545 individual
assessees out of a total of 26,278 falling between the assessable wealth categories of Rs. 200,000 and Rs. 300,000; these
10,545 assessees accounted for 20 per cent of assessable wealth
but only 6 per cent of wealth tax revenue.[16] An exemption
level for individuals of Rs. 50,000 would broaden the tax base
considerably, but would not add greatly to tax revenue. More
significant would be a downward adjustment of all wealth slabs
in the manner indicated in Table 4. Entirely the same slab
structure should apply to HUF. The maximum rate would now apply

TABLE 4

REVISED WEALTH TAX SLAB STRUCTURE
FOR INDIVIDUALS AND HUF

i.	On the first Rs. 50,000 of net wealth	Nil
ii.	On the next Rs. 50,000 of net wealth	0.5 per cent
iii.	On the next Rs. 100,000 of net wealth	1.0 per cent
iv.	On the next Rs. 100,000 of net wealth	1.5 per cent
v.	On the next Rs. 100,000 of net wealth	2.0 per cent
vi.	On the balance of net wealth	2.5 per cent

to all wealth exceeding Rs. 400,000 instead of the present
Rs. 2 million. The estimated increase in revenue from these
modifications to the slab structure would be between Rs. 150
million and Rs. 200 million in the first year.[17]

In one instance there may be a case for introducing a new
exemption--the case of an assessee with taxable wealth but very
low current income. Such an exemption would be on equity
grounds, and might take the following form; no taxpayer would
be liable to wealth tax unless his annual income from all
sources exceeded Rs. 5,000. Since such an exemption by definition would be applicable in general only to low wealth holders,
the effect on revenue is unlikely to be significant.

Mr. Kaldor has also suggested that a low exemption for
wealth taxation--perhaps encompassing sections of the community
not presently touched by income taxation--would offer an administratively feasible and highly productive revenue source.[18]

The present list of exempt personal assets is fairly generous,[19] though the removal of jewelry (up to a value of Rs.
25,000) from the list of exempt assets in the 1963-64 Budget
closed one serious loophole in the coverage of the tax; the
1965-66 surcharge on urban property other than business premises
is also likely to prove a productive short-run revenue source
and a long-run disincentive to such investment. Perhaps the
most costly remaining exemption is the unlimited exemption provided for all articles intended for household and personal use;
a strictly limited list of exempt household assets would serve
to discourage excessive expenditure on consumer durable goods.
Since a wealth tax is likely to affect the pattern of consumption according to which consumption goods are taxable, the inclusion of a wide range of consumer durable goods would provide
a necessary--and easily enforceable--disincentive to consumption

which, in the Indian context, may reasonably be held to be
conspicuous.

The most significant exemption of all is, of course, the
exclusion of agricultural property from the wealth tax base on
constitutional grounds. To this point, the States have not
demonstrated a willingness to introduce an agricultural wealth
tax, although such a tax was suggested in Kerala in 1967.[20]
Other than through a constitutional amendment which would allow
the Union to bring agricultural property under the Union wealth
tax net, the best solution would be a coordinated and consistent
introduction of wealth taxes at the State level, the taxes to
be collected by the Union and the proceeds from each State sur-
rendered to the State Government in question.

The exclusion of corporations from the tax base also removes a large and potentially productive part of the tax base.
Kaldor has advocated the re-introduction of the wealth tax on
corporations on the ground that corporation incentives would be
promoted by a tax which assessed what the corporation took out
of the economy--its capital base--rather than what the corporation put into the economy--its annual income. Suffice it to
note that even a very low rate wealth tax on corporations would
provide a substantial revenue source, the tax base of which is
likely to increase more rapidly than individual wealth, and
which would be administratively relatively simple once a taxable corporate capital base is defined.

A second exemption, based on income, has been suggested
above. Such an exemption would be simple to administer if income and wealth tax returns were submitted jointly. This points
to another aspect of the revenue significance of the wealth tax
--as a check on income tax returns. Indeed, this cross-check
role--to be elaborated in Chapter 11--is a decisive argument
for the wealth tax in India. The wealth tax will be defended
as an integral part of a comprehensive personal direct tax
return. The lack of a central registration and checking system
is the prime cause of income and wealth tax evasion, and the
need for a Central Records Office has been stressed by several
studies of Indian taxation and will be elaborated, along with
the related administrative problem of valuation, in Chapter 11.

Finally, it has been noted that the wealth tax base in
India, as elsewhere, excludes human capital. The issue here is
primarily one of equity, and will be explored in the appropriate
section of this chapter.

Shifting

The contribution of the wealth tax to equity and stabilization, and its effects on the private sector, depend on where

the burden of the tax lies. The general assumption of the remainder of this chapter is that the tax is not shifted, but
falls directly on assessed wealth holders. Due has pointed out
that some shifting may occur if real estate mortgage holders
pass on the tax in the form of higher interest rates, or landlords in the form of higher rents.[21]

Stabilization

The contribution of the annual wealth tax to stabilization
is likely to be of less significance than that of a comprehensive tax on income, in that property values, in general, are
less volatile and flexible than other income sources. However,
the recently increased progressivity and consequent income
elasticity of the tax will contribute to the built-in flexibility of the tax structure. The suggested reduced exemption
levels and increased coverage might be of even more significance. The fact that a low rate annual tax on wealth is most
likely to be defrayed from current income rather than capital
will also enhance the stabilizing effectiveness of the tax.
The latter will depend on the extent to which payments are met
from current consumption spending rather than saving. A combination of diminished exempt personal assets (so increasing the
forms of consumption which will increase future tax liability),
and exemptions for certain forms of saving, would tend to increase the likelihood that the tax payment would be met by
reduced current consumption, and would raise the possibility of
employing the wealth tax as a discretionary stabilizing device.

Equity

The role of the annual wealth tax in furthering the equity
objective was clearly stated in the preamble to the 1964 Budget,
in which wealth tax progressivity was substantially increased
and tax exemptions halved.[22] There are several parts to the
over-all equity objective. First, a wealth tax may actually be
intended to reduce the concentration of wealth. Though such a
goal has been explicitly stated in India, the nature of the
wealth is such that while it might help to prevent the worsening
of wealth concentration, it is unlikely to actually diminish the
present concentration. Another form of wealth tax--a capital
levy--would be necessary to realize this objective, and the
feasibility of such a levy will be discussed in the second
major section of this chapter.

Second, the wealth tax, seen essentially as an addition to
the upper reaches of the personal income tax, is intended to
contribute to increased progressivity in the personal income
tax, and thus to help mitigate present inequalities of income.
The wealth tax is particularly useful for this purpose since it
is addressed to highly concentrated property incomes, and offers

one means of assessing <u>accrued</u> capital gains each year. This
is the real significance of the Indian wealth tax in terms of
vertical equity.

Finally, in terms of horizontal equity, a wealth tax offers
a balancing factor in a tax system which relies heavily on the
taxation of current income. A limitation of income taxation is
its discrimination against persons who have not yet accumulated
as against those who have.

Turning explicitly to the vertical equity justification of
the net wealth tax in India, there is clear evidence of the concentration of income from property. In 1963-64, 100,987 individuals and HUF were assessed on the basis of income from
dividends, and only 20,818 on the basis of interest from securities. Dividend income is concentrated very heavily among income recipients over Rs. 25,000 per annum; the degree of concentration of income from securities in the over Rs. 25,000 per
annum group is less marked but still considerable. Some 207,959
individuals and HUF were assessed on the basis of property income (defined as rent and interest on physical capital). Again,
although there are a large number of assessments in the range
Rs. 3,000 to Rs. 15,000 per annum, income received and tax
payed is highly concentrated again in the group over Rs.
25,000.[23] Although there will clearly be considerable overlapping between these groups, even an arbitrary summation indicates that property income generally in India accrues to a
very small segment of the population; it has been shown that
even within this small group property income is highly concentrated.

This conclusion is confirmed by the recent findings of the
Committee on the Distribution of Income and Levels of Living
that the distribution of wealth (and thus of property incomes)
was more highly concentrated than the distribution of income
generally.[24] Additional taxation of property income would
clearly serve to tax more heavily upper income groups and thus
to supplement a reformed and comprehensive income tax in mitigating inequalities of income distribution.

Mr. Kaldor would add to the previous argument the notion
that additional taxation of property incomes is justified on
an equity basis on the principle that the possession of property is a measure of economic well-being quite apart from the income earned from that property:

> The main argument in equity for the (annual tax
> on wealth) is that income taken by itself is an in-
> adequate yardstick of taxable capacity as between
> incomes from work and incomes from property, and
> also as between the different property owners. The

basic reason for this is that the ownership of
property in the form of disposable assets endows
the property owner with a taxable capacity as such,
quite apart from the money income which that property
yields.[25]

This principle is acknowledged in the relief afforded to
earned income in the Indian income tax structure. Such relief,
however, is a relatively crude fiscal device by comparison with
an annual wealth tax which permits specific treatment of different types of assets and thus adjustment of tax liability
according to broader Plan objectives and priorities and in
terms of the particular circumstances of each taxpayer. The
argument that a wealth tax is inequitable in that property may
not directly yield money income merely serves to emphasize the
inadequacy of the definition of income used in computing economic well-being and consequent ability to pay taxes. As
Mr. Kaldor emphasizes:

If a property does not yield money income, it
must either yield an equivalent psychic income
to the owner or it must be held in the expectation of a certain appreciation in value which
makes it at least as attractive to the holder as
other property on which a current money return is
obtained.[26]

Defining income in the broad sense as encompassing not
only money income but psychic income or the expectation of
capital appreciation, an annual wealth tax appears to be a
necessary supplement to the standard income tax. However, it
has been argued at some length that redistribution is only a
meaningful objective in the context of growth. Accordingly,
the redistribution objective in wealth taxation must be qualified by the condonation, indeed positive encouragement, of
functional wealth inequalities. Into this category would fall
the restoration in the 1965-66 Budget of the five-year exemption for shares purchased in new industrial undertakings, and
the variety of exempted savings forms, such as annuities,
savings certificates, etc. Such a list of exempt assets might
be modified over time to include all functional wealth categories, and might usefully be disaggregated to specifically
include certain categories of stocks and securities and to
exclude others.

Two issues remain to be discussed under the general head
of equity. First, there is the question of taxing human capital. Such a procedure has been advocated in the U.S.,[27] and a
variety of devices suggested to estimate the discounted present
value of an individual's expected future income stream. The
basis in equity of such a suggestion is ungainsayable. A true

account of a person's net wealth should include the capital
value of the person himself; otherwise, the tax discriminates
against the small property owner compared to the propertyless
but highly skilled professional individual who is likely to
receive a large annual income, and who may or may not accumu-
late property. There are technical difficulties with the proposal; which interest rate should be used in discounting?
Would the additional revenue so derived significantly exceed
the initially high administrative costs of such a scheme? The
most important question, however, is one of equity. By estimating what a person should earn, is he then to be taxed if he
decides not to work to maximum expected potential? Such a tax
would be consistent with the balance of the wealth tax which
essentially taxes income from property even if that property
is left idle--thus providing an incentive to use the property
to its potential--but raises some rather fundamental questions
of human rights when applied to the capital value of the actual
taxpayer himself. On this ground, and on grounds of administrative feasibility, the inclusion of human capital in the
wealth tax base is not recommended for use in India at present.

        The second issue is that of the taxpayer who has taxable
wealth but very low income. It was suggested in the previous
section of this chapter that this problem be resolved by a
two-tier exemption system, excluding from wealth tax liability
all taxpayers whose annual income from all sources does not
exceed Rs. 5,000.

                    Effect on the Private Sector

Savings

        It has been argued that the present wealth tax will tend
to be met out of annual accrual from property. The question
then arises--given that the tax will be defrayed from current
income--whether it will be largely met at the expense of current consumption or whether the tax will reduce saving from
property income. The problem here is that, like the standard
income tax which taxes saved income and also the income from
those savings, an annual wealth tax is not neutral between consumption and saving. Every addition to capital, except insofar
as a particular use of savings has been exempted from wealth
taxation, increases tax liability, whereas consumption other
than on durable goods included in the tax base, does not. It
is thus not sufficient to argue that the tax will affect current consumption and saving in the ratio of the given propensities to consume and save at the margin. Wealth taxation discriminates against savings and a tax on annual net wealth might
thus seem to diminish directly not only the ability but the
incentive to save. In the situation (less likely under the
proposed income exemption) of a taxpayer with insufficient

income to pay his wealth tax assessment, the tax will be paid directly from capital.

The theoretically detrimental effect on private saving is mitigated by two factors. First, a wealth tax discriminates against saving only insofar as additions to capital are subject to tax liability. A carefully devised system of exemptions and allowances can remove the discrimination against saving in areas considered as of priority importance. The present Indian tax employs a comprehensive list of savings exemptions of this nature. Second, a tax on wealth will discriminate against various forms of consumption expenditures which increase tax liability. It has been argued that the removal of the jewelry exemption and the surcharge on urban property would discourage "conspicuous" consumption and that a more rigorous definition of exempt personal assets would curtail spending on consumer durables. Such an effect might conceivable benefit saving indirectly by lowering the average propensity to consume as a result of a diminished "demonstration effect."

Investment

A wealth tax does not rest directly on the gain from investment, affecting accumulated wealth rather than marginal increments to that wealth. Whereas an income tax (without complete loss offset) discriminates against high-risk, high-yield equities, a wealth tax actually offers a direct incentive to such investment. The yield of a particular piece of property does not affect wealth tax liability, so that a given amount of wealth attracts the same wealth tax whether it is invested in equities yielding 10 per cent, in bonds yielding 5 per cent, or is kept idle and entirely unproductive. Much as the proposed agricultural income tax provides an incentive to productivity by taxing according to average potential earnings, so the wealth tax penalizes the unproductive use of investment funds and offers a direct incentive to use the funds in the most productive manner possible.

An income tax, unless by a system of imputed returns, cannot reach the non-monetary advantages of low-risk, low-yield investment; by taking all assets equally, regardless of yield, the wealth tax may be considered to impose a penalty on, and therefore discourage investment in, low-yield areas. The wealth tax amounts to a carrying charge on assets, and makes the financial yield from hoarding negative rather than zero; taxpayers are provided with an incentive to maximize the difference between the uniform carrying charge and gross yield, in order to maximize net yield on the investment. Finally, a net wealth tax, by definition, automatically allows losses to be offset against taxable wealth up to the full extent of the investor's net wealth.

The incentive to invest in equities will be further
stimulated by such measures as the recent five-year exemption
from tax of shares in new industrial undertakings. Such a
measure might reasonably by extended to purchases of new issues
from established corporations, and the whole suggested policy
of exempting certain assets from wealth tax would complement
the built-in incentive offered to investment by the tax.

The wealth tax will only impinge indirectly on the incentive to invest insofar as income expected from investment is
intended for further accumulation (and hence wealth tax liability) rather than current expenditure. This effect is unlikely
to outweigh the stimulus to equity investment previously described.

Work

A wealth tax is unlikely to have significant effects on
work incentives. The effect on work incentives could only occur
if work income were intended for saving or taxable consumption.
The decisive factor again is the absence of any direct burden
on marginal earnings, so that the substitution effect in favor
of leisure is minimized. In the over-all resultant effect on
work, the income effect--here re-interpreted as a wealth effect
(describing the attempt by the taxpayer to restore his wealth
to its pre-tax position)--is thus likely to be of greater relative significance than in the case of an income tax. The in-
directness of the wealth tax burden, and the psychological
effect of seemingly low rates, would also tend to minimize any
adverse effects on work incentives.

Conclusion

It has been argued that an annual tax on wealth should make
a substantial and increasingly significant contribution to the
tax objective of mobilizing resources for the public sector,
particularly through the suggested exemption and slab modifications which would widen tax coverage and increase tax rates on
"middle wealth," and through the increased progressivity of the
present tax which should raise the income-elasticity of tax
returns; that the probable defrayal of tax liability from current income might make the tax an additional tool of discretionary stabilization; that disincentive effects on productive
saving should be substantially offset by a structure of exemptions; and that conspicuous consumption should be curtailed by
a strict limitation of exempt personal assets; that the tax has
a theoretically positive inducement effect on risk investment
which may be enhanced by extending present incentive provisions;
and finally, that what amounts to an additional tax on property
incomes, which are highly concentrated, would further the objective of mitigating inequalities.

THE POSSIBILITY OF A CAPITAL LEVY

Unlike an annual wealth tax a capital levy is a once-for-all impost of such a magnitude that it is not payable from property income and is therefore intended to be defrayed from accumulated wealth. It is thus a genuine tax on capital. Such a tax carries an implicit, and perhaps explicit, understanding by the government that the measure will not be repeated. Thus it is likely to be paid out of capital not only because of its magnitude but because the assurance of non-recurrence is likely to induce assessees to spread the incidence of the tax by a relatively small diminution in spending over a period of time rather than to meet liability by a drastic curtailment of current spending habits. The present Indian estate tax is, in effect, a personalized capital levy which recurs once in each generation; immediate discussion will be limited to the use of a general once-for-all capital levy.

The possibility of a capital levy was much discussed in the U.K. and the U.S. after both world wars as a means of reducing accumulated war debt in one drastic step.[28] The case for a capital levy in India can be stated in terms of the contribution of such a tax to resource mobilization for the public sector and to the mitigation of inequalities of wealth.

Revenue Productivity

Estimates of tangible wealth in India are available from several recent studies.[29] The results of the Datta-Prakash study for 1949-50 and the Reserve Bank estimates for 1960-61 are summarized in Table 5. The value of reproducible tangible wealth almost doubled over the period studied, from Rs. 170,860 million in March 1950 to Rs. 321,640 million in March 1961. Significantly, however, the share of the household sector declined relatively. The household sector accounted for 71 per cent of tangible wealth in 1950 and 60 per cent in 1960-61. The corresponding figures for the organized private sector were 12 per cent and 15 per cent and for the government sector 17 per cent and 25 per cent.[30] This change reflects the increasing significance of the basic facilities provided by the government sector in the economy. The fact remains that household sector reproducible tangible wealth has increased by approximately 61 per cent over the period; organized private sector reproducible tangible wealth has increased by 135 per cent.

The value of the total reproducible tangible wealth owned presently by the household and organized private sectors amounted to Rs. 240,000 million. The value of land in 1961 is recorded as Rs. 202,410 million, an increase of approximately Rs. 25,000 million over the 1950 figure.[31]

TABLE 5

ESTIMATE OF TANGIBLE WEALTH IN INDIA

Sector	Estimate of tangible wealth--depreciated cost at current prices	
	1949-50	1960-61
I. AGRICULTURE, ANIMAL HUSBANDRY AND ALLIED ACTIVITIES		
1. Agricultural implements including tractors	3,630	8,600
2. Livestock used in farms	24,280	27,020
3. Sheds, barns, etc.	8,880	13,660
4. Improvement of land and irrigation works: private	13,040	24,150
5. Improvement of land and irrigation works: public	2,290	13,650
6. Plantations other than tea plantation, etc.	200	350
7. Forestry and fishery	120	400
SUB-TOTAL	53,360	87,830
II. MINING AND MANUFACTURING (LARGE SCALE)		
1. Mining	1,110	1,830
2. Electricity generation and transmission	2,400	11,740
3. Tea plantations	1,330	2,820
4. Other factory establishments: private	12,060	32,360
5. Other factory establishments: public	1,270	7,670
SUB-TOTAL	18,160	56,420
III. SMALL ENTERPRISES	7,630	12,000
IV. TRANSPORT AND COMMUNICATIONS		
1. Railways	15,740	27,460
2. Communications	930	1,980
3. Vehicles	2,810	6,390
4. Transport animals	3,560	3,940
5. Shipping and navigation companies	180	1,350
6. Airways companies	170	420
7. Other transport companies	480	640
SUB-TOTAL	23,870	42,180
V. CAPITAL OUTLAY IN GOVERNMENT ADMINISTRATION	7,070	18,100

Sector	Estimate of tangible wealth--depreciated cost at current prices	
	1949-50	1960-61
VI. TRADE AND COMMERCE		
1. Wholesale and retail trade	17,040	32,600
2. Banks, Cooperatives, Insurance companies, etc.	680	1,380
SUB-TOTAL	17,720	33,980
VII. HOUSE PROPERTY		
1. Urban: Private	26,440	43,810
2. Rural: Private	17,610	27,320
SUB-TOTAL	44,050	71,130
VIII. REPRODUCIBLE TANGIBLE WEALTH	170,860	321,640
IX. VALUE OF LAND	178,540	202,410
X. TOTAL TANGIBLE WEALTH	349,400	524,050

Sources: "Estimates of Tangible Wealth in India," Reserve Bank of India Bulletin (January 1963), p. 10; Government of India, Report of the Commission on the Distribution of Income and Levels of Living (New Delhi: Planning Commission, 1964), pp. 19-22.

More recent information is available on the value of intangible wealth held in the form of Union government and State securities and bank deposits. Deposit liabilities of scheduled banks totalled Rs. 25,580 million at the end of 1964.[32] The total internal debt of the Union government as of March 1965 stood at Rs. 49,870 million.[33] The corresponding figure for the State governments--deducting loans from the Union--stood at Rs. 10,490 million.[34]

There are no estimates available of the value of share ownership in India. The Committee on the Distribution of Income found that the total paid-up capital of non-government companies stood at approximately Rs. 12,000 million.[35] This is clearly an underestimate of the present market value of share capital--the index of equity prices increased 64 per cent between 1952 and 1964[36]--but may suffice as a first approximation.

The final component of wealth is the estimated present value of
gold holdings in India--at Indian market price--of Rs. 30,350
million.[37]

Summing up these estimates of tangible and intangible
wealth a figure for total private wealth of Rs. 570,680 million
is derived; this is certainly a low estimate, given the indubitable but determinate increase in the market value of land since
1961 and the underestimation of the value of share capital.

In 1963-64, some 26,278 individuals and HUF were assessed
for wealth tax purposes. The exemption at that point was Rs.
200,000. If the exemption for purposes of the capital levy
were made the same as that proposed for the reformed net wealth
tax--Rs. 50,000--it is estimated roughly that the number of
assessees would rise to around 50,000. The total of wealth
exempt from the capital levy would then be 50,000 times Rs.
50,000 or Rs. 2,500 million, leaving a total of Rs. 568,180 as
taxable wealth.

A capital levy at a moderate rate, say, 5 per cent, on
taxable wealth would therefore have a potential yield of Rs.
28,409 million, almost twice the total of Union tax revenue in
1965-66 (Rs. 17,846.2 million). The once-for-all productivity
of a capital levy would thus be substantial; this might be increased by graduating rates according to the type of asset
taxed, say, by taxing unused (or abused) land and property more
rigorously.

As a means of pump-priming or injecting a once-for-all
massive dose of public spending into the economy, or as a device to provide immediate substantial revenue in the context of
a national emergency of some kind, the capital levy must receive serious consideration. The capital tax structure of West
Germany provides an interesting example of the use of a rigorous capital levy. In attition to a net worth tax,[38] similar to
the Indian annual wealth tax, and a federally-determined but
municipally-collected real property tax,[39] the German government employs a capital levy as the major component of the Equalization of Burdens law designed to accomplish some measure of
equitable distribution among the population of West Germany, of
the war and post-war losses which had affected the citizens to
a very uneven degree.[40] The capital levy amounts to 50 per cent
of the net worth of individuals and entities subject to the levy
computed as of the date of the currency reform (June 21, 1948),
and is payable with interest from 1949 to 1979. Including the
interest payment the total burden of the levy amounts to considerably more than 50 per cent of the taxpayer's net worth as
of June 1948.

A similar impost of 50 per cent of net worth--above an exemption of Rs. 50,000 for 50,000 taxpayers in the Indian context, with payment spread over twenty years, would provide, without interest payment, an addition to total Union tax revenue of approximately Rs. 14,200 million per annum over the twenty-year period.

The type of levy which might be imposed in India would accordingly depend on whether the purpose of the levy was to secure an immediate injection of revenue for some specific purpose--in which case the proportion of wealth taxed would have to be moderate--or whether the levy was viewed as an addition to revenue over, say, a ten or twenty-year period and as a radical means of redistribution of wealth--in which case a much more severe rate might be applied.

Equity

The attractiveness of a capital levy as a productive revenue source is reinforced by redistributive considerations. All the statistical evidence available points to extreme concentration of wealth in India. Information available on the distribution of land holdings, owner-occupied houses and dividend incomes has already been detailed in Chapter 2. If the figures on wealth distribution in the form of land, owner-occupied houses and shares can be regarded as representative of wealth distribution as a whole, the conclusion emerges that disparities in wealth distribution are even more acute than in income distribution and that the tax objective of mitigating relative inequalities of wealth would be furthered by a capital levy even of a simple proportionate nature. It is also arguable that in India and developing countries in general, property ownership may be so unequally distributed as to constitute a threat to political and social stability, and that a drastic fiscal measure such as a capital levy is necessary and preferable to confiscation or other extreme devices.

The Case Against a Capital Levy:
Economic Effects on the Private Sector

The economic effects of a capital levy may be divided into short-term and long-term. In the short run there is no question of adverse incentive effects due to anticipation of tax liability; the usefulness of a capital levy in this respect is that it is unanticipated. There remains the question of the liquidity of wealth and the extent to which assessees can meet liability without selling substantial proportions of their property. This problem would be most acute in the event of a severe, say, 20-50 per cent capital levy which would necessitate vast property sales, consequent depression of prices, and a considerable degree of disorganization and inequity; the depression of equity prices would probably have an immediate adverse effect on investment. Such a situation might be further complicated by the necessity for many taxpayers to borrow to meet tax liability.

Short-run difficulties in meeting immediate assessment under a severe capital levy would suggest in the Indian context that if the purpose of the tax is to meet some immediate financial emergency, then the rates should be moderate, say, of the order of 5 per cent, and that if the purpose of the tax is to secure a radical redistribution of wealth and a massive, although not necessarily immediate, addition to revenue, then an installment system of payment on the German model would be least disruptive economically.

In the long run the effect of a capital levy on private saving and investment will depend on the extent to which the ability and incentive to save and invest are affected by the levy. Abstracting from the question of the expenditure of tax revenue, the incentive effect of a capital levy can be seen as the resultant of a wealth effect and a substitution effect. The accumulated wealth of the taxpaper is diminished by the levy and the wealth effect would operate by encouraging the taxpaper to restore his former position by increased saving and investment. The substitution effect would operate by making saving and investment (and conspicuous consumption of articles which increase liability under a capital tax) relatively less attractive than consumption of articles not subject to tax. In theory, the great merit of a once-for-all tax is that it will have no substitution effect on future behavior; liability, once ascertained, is unaffected by future behavior. The unhindered action of the wealth effect would thus imply that a capital levy should provide a positive inducement to saving and investment in an attempt to recoup losses.

A beneficial effect on investment is likely in the event of a moderate capital levy, say, of not more than 5-6 per cent of net worth, linked specifically to a national emergency of some kind. Such a levy would probably be viewed as an extension of the annual wealth tax--designed to impinge slightly on principal as well as accrual--for a specific non-recurrent purpose and might be expected, through the wealth effect, to stimulate equity investment or at least to have no serious adverse effects. In the event of a radical capital levy, say, in the order of 30-50 per cent, it would be unrealistic to dicsount a substantial substitution effect. Despite assurances of non-recurrence a major capital levy would seem likely to have an adverse psychological effect on saving and investment, particularly in fixed illiquid and conspicuous assets. This adverse psychological effect would be greater the shorter the time period permitted

for payment. Insistence on immediate or relatively prompt payment would add the problems of liquidation in a falling market
to the suggested psychological reaction to a severe impost and
would compound resentment, uncertainty and opposition. Even a
fairly general arrangement for spreading liability over, say,
thirty years as in the German case, would seem unlikely to
dispel entirely the adverse psychological effect of the levy
on saving and investment. This point would seem to be particularly apposite in the Indian case where a substantial amount of
private sector co-operation is required for the attainment of
investment goals in the planning process. The magnitude of the
psychological effect is, of course, unpredictable and the resultant of the wealth and substitution effects correspondingly
undeterminate.

The only reasonably safe conclusion would seem to be that
adverse effects on saving and investment are more likely the
more rigorous the levy and the shorter the period permitted for
payment. This conclusion is reinforced by political considerations. A major capital levy with a short payment period is a
drastic and radical fiscal device which seems certain to engen-
der more opposition and resentment than less extreme measures.
Perhaps no other tax measure is as susceptible to the label of
confiscation.

Finally, considerations of administration would seem to
preclude the use of a severe capital levy with a short payment
period. There is at present in India no comprehensive record
of capital assets and their value. Crude measures of agricultural land values are available under present State land tax
administration and the present valuation procedure under the
annual wealth tax on non-agricultural property affords estimates of the value of the latter. There is, however, no central
valuation register and under the present system immediate general valuation under a severe capital levy would be an administrative task, success in which might reasonably be considered
doubtful. Present valuation procedures--refined by some of the
administrative reforms discussed in Chapter 11--should be able
to cope with an immediate moderate levy and to deal with a
severe levy with a relatively long payment period.

Conclusion

The use of a capital levy in India may be defended on
grounds of revenue productivity and equity. Contrary arguments
in terms of adverse effects on saving and investment, political
objections, and administrative complexity, do not seem compelling in the event of a moderate levy designed to meet a specific,
non-recurrent purpose; they would, however, appear to be of substantial but not critical important in the event of a severe levy
with a relatively long payment period, and would seem to present

decisive obstacles to the use of a severe levy with a very short payment period.

A moderate levy to meet an emergency situation might be a legitimate additional fiscal weapon in the Indian context. The alternative is a miscellaneous collection of new taxes and tax increases such as those resorted to by Mr. Desai in the emergency situation of 1963.[41] It has been argued that a severe capital levy is only feasible in India if payment is arranged on an installment basis over a period of twenty-five to thirty years. The question arises, however, whether a severe installment levy is the best method of obtaining an additional revenue source from accumulated wealth and mitigating inequalities of wealth distribution. The alternative policy would be to reform and tighten the existing tax structure of three capital taxes--the annual tax on wealth, the estate duty, and the gift tax.

The estate duty and gift tax will be examined in detail in Chapter 7. For the present it may be suggested that an integrated gift and estate tax structure set up so as to eliminate present loopholes, and levied at progressive rates would effect resource mobilization and wealth redistribution comparable to that from a capital levy, but spread over a much longer period of time. Equally, the estate and gift tax mix is an established part of the tax structure, and reform and tightening of existing weapons can be expected to induce less resentment and reaction--both political and economic--than the introduction of an entirely novel measure. This point is reinforced by the fact that the estate and gift taxes have a specific rather than general incidence, and thus have no general psychological impact. The cost of the estate:gift tax mix in terms of private sector co-operation is thus likely to be much less than under a capital levy. Finally, the capital levy--particularly a severe capital levy--is a once-for-all measure, part of the virtue of which lies in a pledge of non-recurrence. The present annual wealth tax:estate tax:gift tax mix is a permanent component of the direct tax system and thus offers a built-in long-run means of preventing the growth of wealth disparities in the future.

Despite the attractiveness of the gift:estate tax procedure, however, the two procedures may not be alternatives, as the above argument might suggest, but complements. The essential feature of the wealth:estate:gift tax mix is its gradualism. The immediate increments to revenue are relatively small and unpredictable and the redistributive impact spread over a long period of time. If the need for substantial revenue increases in the next twenty to thirty years is critical, and if the disparities of wealth are considered to be of immediate consequence and to be inadequately moderated by the gradual approach to capital taxation, then the role of a capital levy might be

seen, first, as providing a guaranteed revenue increment over
the crucial development period, and, second, as a means of
effecting, in a relatively short period of time, a reduction in
wealth disparities to a level considered more appropriate in
terms of the consensus of opinion on equity.

Having acquired a substantial addition to revenue and
having reduced the magnitude of wealth disparities to more
manageable proportions, future capital taxation could be more
easily delegated to a wealth:estate:gift tax mix. The only
major obstacle to such a policy is the problem of an adverse
psychological effect on private saving and investment. The
Indian government would have to endeavor to alleviate such uncertainty by a public education program, perhaps a constitutional guarantee of non-recurrence, a scheme of exemptions for
"functional" wealth inequalities, and a variety of inducements,
through expenditure programs and tax incentives of various
kinds, to saving and investment in the private sector.

In sum, the capital levy may be a useful addition to Union
fiscal weapons in two distinct forms; first, in the form of a
moderate levy, payable immediately, and designed to finance an
emergency situation; and, second, in the form of a more severe
levy, payable by installments over twenty to thirty years, and
designed to provide a substantial revenue increment over the
payment period, and to effect a radical diminution in disparities of wealth.

THE EXPENDITURE TAX

In the 1966-67 Budget, the expenditure tax in India was
abolished on the ground that its revenue productivity did not
justify its administrative costs. Consideration of the tax in
some detail is, however, in the opinion of the writer, of more
than historical interest. The expenditure tax, seen (like the
net wealth tax) as an adjunct to the personal income tax, is of
peculiar significance in the developmental context because of
its inducement to saving, and its role as an integral part of a
self-checking structure of personal direct taxes. The writer
therefore strongly disagrees with the decision of the Indian
government to abolish the expenditure tax, and offers in the
following pages a defense of the role of an expenditure tax,
and proposals for the reform of the structure of the tax used
until 1965-66.

In this short consideration of the expenditure tax it is
not proposed to enter into the extensive debate on the relative
merits of the expenditure or income base for direct taxation
in terms of equity and the effects on private sector, work,
saving and investment.[42] In any event, the possibility of a

substantial immediate replacement of the income base by an expenditure base in India is precluded by administrative considerations. Perhaps the only virtually unanimous conclusion of
the debate has been that problems of administration are more
intractable under the expenditure base. Several of the original
proponents of a tax on expenditure abandoned the concept at the
stage of practical application.[43]

Mr. Kaldor himself has acknowledged the formidable administrative problems in substituting on a large scale the expenditure base for the income base;[44] his critics have emphasized
the "host"[45] or "legion"[46] of administrative difficulties, and
H. Simons concludes:

> A feasible type of spending tax would appear to
> involve all the present problems of estimating
> annual income and those of measuring net annual
> saving or dissaving as well.[47]

The examination of an expenditure tax in India will accordingly be confined to the role of such a tax essentially as a
supplement to or surtax on income taxation on the upper income
ranges. This is the role which Mr. Kaldor envisaged for the
tax in India, and the role which the Indian tax as legislated
was basically intended to fulfill. It is proposed to describe
the expenditure tax in India in its last year of operation,
1965-66, and to appraise the tax in terms of revenue productivity, equity, stabilization and its effect on the private sector.

Description

A tax on personal expenditure was first levied in India on
April 1, 1958. In the 1962-63 Budget, Mr. Desai withdrew the
measure on the grounds that the tax had made an insignificant
contribution to resource mobilization and was ineffective as a
stabilization device.[48] Reintroducing a revised version of
the tax in the 1964-65 Budget, Mr. Krishnamachari emphasized
the contribution of the tax to the mitigation of inequalities
of income and wealth.[49]

The revised tax remained unchanged in the 1965-66 Budget,
and was levied annually on expenditure incurred by individuals
and HUF during the base year (the base year is the same as that
for income tax purposes, usually expiring on March 31).[50] The
tax was based upon world-wide expenditure, expenditure within
India, or expenditure outside India from Indian sources, according to the residence and citizenship status of the taxpayer.[51]
With regard to married persons, each spouse was taxed separately on expenditure incurred by him for his own benefit and out
of separate funds. However, an individual was subject to tax
on expenditure incurred by him on behalf of his dependents, and

also on expenditure incurred by his dependents. A spouse was subject to tax on expenditure made on his behalf, or on behalf of his dependents, by the other spouse.[52]

Corporations were not subject to tax; neither was any taxpayer whose income from all sources received by him and his dependents in the base year--net of income and capital gains tax--did not exceed Rs. 36,000.[53] An individual taxpayer and his dependents were entitled to a single standard expenditure allowance of Rs. 30,000. The basic expenditure allowance for a HUF consisting of the manager and his wife and children was also Rs. 30,000; another Rs. 30,000 was permitted for each additional coparcener up to a maximum family allowance of Rs. 60,000.[54]

There was a broad list of expenditures exempt from tax: expenditures for expenses wholly and exclusively for purposes of business or employment, i.e., expenditure incurred in earning income; investment expenditure either in connection with a business or in the nature of personal investment in deposits, loans, shares, securities, insurance policies, etc.; miscellaneous expenditures covering books, works of art and livestock; charitable expenditures; expenditures by way of gifts, trust and settlements; expenditures on Union State and Local Authority taxes; and miscellaneous expenses, cost of legal proceedings, expenditure on marriage, medical treatment, maintenance of parents, and education outside India, up to specified limits.[55]

Expenditure out of agricultural income was not exempt from tax. There was a compulsory five-year averaging or "spreading" period for expenditure "of a capital nature" on the purchase of bullion, precious stones, jewelry, furniture and other household goods, automobiles and other conveyances for the personal use of the taxpayer.[56] Taxable expenditure was thus defined as total expenditure incurred by a taxpayer during the base year, other than the standard allowance and exempt expenditure, plus attributed expenditure incurred by others, and expenditure from previous years added through spreading.

Taxable expenditure was taxed at progressive rates rising from 5 per cent to 20 per cent on successive slabs of Rs. 12,000. The highest slab rate of 20 per cent on expenditure over Rs. 84,000 was not scheduled to become applicable until August 1, 1967. Table 6 indicates the rates of expenditure tax prevailing in 1965-66. Progressivity was much less than in the 1958-62 version of the tax, where rates rose sharply from 10 per cent on the first Rs. 10,000 of taxable expenditure to 100 per cent on expenditure over Rs. 50,000.[57] Administration and procedure under the Expenditure Tax Act closely parallel administration and procedure under the Income Tax Act, and Income Tax Officers are ex-officio Expenditure Tax Officers.[58]

TABLE 6

THE RATES OF EXPENDITURE TAX FOR
INDIVIDUALS AND HUF

i.	up to Rs. 36,000	nil
ii.	exceeding Rs. 36,000 but not exceeding Rs. 48,000	5 per cent
iii.	exceeding Rs. 48,000 but not exceeding Rs. 60,000	7.5 per cent
iv.	exceeding Rs. 60,000 but not exceeding Rs. 72,000	10 per cent
v.	exceeding Rs. 72,000 but not exceeding Rs. 84,000	15 per cent
vi.	exceeding Rs. 84,000	20 per cent

Source: Government of India, Explanatory Memorandum on the
         Budget of the Central Government for 1965-66 (New
         Delhi: Ministry of Finance, 1965), p. 32.

Revenue Productivity

Table 7 indicates returns from the expenditure tax since
its inception in 1958, relative to personal income tax returns.
In spite of the sharp progressivity in the rate structure in the
early years of the tax, returns proved to be relatively insignificant and inelastic--both in terms of natural revenue growth
and in relation to the growth of national income. It is, of
course, worth noting that the stated primary purpose of the tax
was to divert private funds from conspicuous consumption to
saving; low revenue productivity, combined with minimal evasion
and avoidance, and comprehensive coverage, would suggest that
the tax had been successful in increasing the private savings
ratio.

There are several reasons for doubting that low revenue
productivity in both versions of the expenditure tax--Mr. Krishnamachari's tax which was intended to produce Rs. 15.5 million
in 1964-65 produced only Rs. 7.5 million--has been a measure of
induced private savings. The major reason for low revenue productivity has, in fact, been the very narrow coverage of the
tax. In 1961-62 (prior to its suspension in the 1962-63 Budget),
the total number of assessees (individuals and HUF) was only
807. Following suspension, the number of assessees declined to

TABLE 7

EXPENDITURE TAX RECEIPTS, 1958-59 - 1965-66

Rs. million

	1958-59 (Accts.)	1959-60 (Accts.)	1960-61 (Accts.)	1961-62 (Accts.)	1962-63 (Accts.)	1963-64 (Accts.)	1964-65 (Accts.)	1965-66 (Accts.)
Expenditure Tax	6.4	7.9	9.1	8.4	2.0	1.2	4.4	4.2
Personal Income Tax (including State's share)	1,720.1	1,488.5	1,673.8	1,653.9	1,859.6	2,586.0	2,665.5	2,718.0

Source: Reserve Bank of India, Report on Currency and Finance, 1965-66 (Bombay: Reserve Bank of India, 1966).

199

348 in 1962-63 and 42 in 1963-64.[59] It seems likely that the
coverage of Mr. Krishnamachari's 1964-65 tax was less than in
1961-62.

Turning specifically to the tax reintroduced in 1964-65,
low coverage may be attributed, first, to the high initial income exemption; second, to a generous standard expenditure
allowance; and third, to a complex and comprehensive series of
exempt categories of expenditure.

The Rs. 36,000 total income exemption level has been
labelled by Mr. Kaldor the "most serious defect of the tax."[60]
In particular, dis-saving from accumulated wealth might go
exempt from expenditure tax, if the total income--net of all
taxes on income--of the assessee did not exceed Rs. 36,000.
Equally, this provision made it possible for a taxpayer to
telescope his spending into particular years in which his income is kept low enough to exempt him from the expenditure tax.

Superimposed on the income exemption was the standard deductible allowance of Rs. 30,000. It would certainly not have
been administratively feasible to check all small or moderate
expenditures, but an exemption base of Rs. 30,000--ten times the
income tax exemption limit--seems inordinately high. Mr. Kaldor
suggested Rs. 10,000--without any income exemption.[61] There is
no "functional" justification for such a large basic exemption.

Initially easier to justify was the list of functional
exemptions--expenditures incurred in earning income, expenditures of an investment nature, etc., and the list of exempt
personal and family expenditures. There were, however, within
the general headings of exempt expenditures several allowances
the nature and/or scale of which might be subject to question,
particularly in that they had no counterpart in the income tax
laws. Anomalous exemptions of this nature included expenditure
from an entertainment allowance up to Rs. 7,500; an unlimited
exemption for acquisition of immovable property; an unlimited
exemption for the purchase of livestock, books, works of art,
or products of cottage industry; election expenses within the
limit fixed by law; and exemptions up to Rs. 5,000 for medical
or marriage expenses.[62] Perhaps the most alarming exemption--
certainly the one which offers the greatest opportunity of
abuse--was that of any expenditure by way of gift, donation,
settlement, or trust. Gifts were and remain subject to a very
moderate gift tax (Chapter 7) but clearly offered a relatively
simple means of avoiding expenditure tax liability; trusts, of
course, are a classic means of avoiding expenditure, estate
and gift taxation. In sum, the comprehensive and generous
exemptions under the expenditure tax reduced tax coverage to
insignificant proportions, and rendered the tax ineffective as
a revenue source.

The rate structure under the expenditure tax was very moderate relative to the sharply progressive scale from 1958-62. The highest rate of 20 per cent compares with 100 per cent in the 1958-62 version of the tax, and the 300 per cent top rate proposed by Mr. Kaldor.[63] Although Mr. Kaldor's rate scale may seem a trifle exuberant, particularly in that the tax is envisaged merely as a supplement to income taxation, it is arguable that the present moderate--almost token--progression will neither deter private consumption, and so increase private savings, nor provide an elastic or productive source of revenue.

Reduction of the income exemption to Rs. 10,000 and of the basic expenditure allowance to Rs. 10,000, the elimination of the gift and inheritance loophole, and the use of a rate structure starting at 5 per cent on expenditures between Rs. 10,000 and Rs. 20,000, and rising by 5 per cent on each Rs. 10,000 slab to a maximum rate 45 per cent on expenditures over Rs. 90,000 would offer in terms of 1960-61 income statistics an annual revenue productivity of approximately Rs. 250-300 million.[64]

Finally, the expenditure tax, like the wealth tax, is an integral part of a cross-checking personal direct tax return, and its abolition removes a vital check on the validity of other personal tax returns.

Equity

The contribution of the expenditure tax to the vertical equity objective was adduced specifically by Mr. Krishnamachari in reintroducing the tax in 1964. The contribution of the Indian form of expenditure tax to the mitigation of inequalities is essentially to complement a comprehensive progressive income tax--which provides partial exemption to income saved and invested in certain directions--as a means of curtailing inequalities of consumption. An expenditure tax has the additional role of diminishing inequalities of consumption which result from dis-saving.[65] In this latter role the tax complements indirect taxes on articles purchased by high-income groups. The income level exemption in the 1965-66 Indian tax prevented effective penalization of dis-saving, and it is arguable that the high standard allowance, wide range of exempt expenditures and only slightly progressive rate structure minimized the contribution of the tax to the mitigation of general consumption inequalities.

The assessment of an expenditure tax on consumption is, of course, an intended contravention of the maxim of horizontal equity. In the pursuit of growth the tax is intended to discriminate between individuals whose propensities to save and consume differ. Horizontal equity was, however, unnecessarily compromised in the 1965-66 tax by the blanket Rs. 30,000

standard allowance. No provision was made for tax assessment
on a per capita basis; Kaldor suggested calculation of tax
liability according to expenditure per capita in the family
(the maximum allowable division being into 5 units) rather than
total expenditure of the family unit.[66] An alternative method
of varying tax liability with family size would be to replace
the Rs. 30,000 allowance by an initial basic exemption, say,
Rs. 10,000, supplemented by Rs. 3,000 slabs of allowable expenditure according to family size up to a total maximum allowance,
including the basic exemption, of Rs. 25,000.

Stabilization

The role of a progressive expenditure tax in stabilization
policy in India is to supplement the progressive income tax,
and indirect taxes on articles with a high income elasticity of
demand, as means of controlling inflationary price increases by
containing increases in aggregate demand. Like indirect taxation, the personal expenditure tax is peculiarly well suited to
this role in India in that its restraining effects are limited
to consumption demand, and exercise no direct restraint on
savings and investment.

An income tax even with partial savings exemptions will
inevitably be defrayed partly at the expense of saving. The
more an income tax is paid at the expense of potential savings,
the higher the tax has to be to secure a given restraint on
consumption spending; and the higher the taxes are the greater
the likelihood that they will be paid at the expense of savings.

A progressive expenditure tax may thus offer a necessary
and efficient method of supplementing income taxation, particularly on the higher income ranges, as a discretionary or automatic built-in stabilizing device. Pre-determined sharp statutory increases in expenditure taxation--under the head of
"formula flexibility"--would offer a useful stabilizing tool
with a negligible opportunity cost in terms of private savings
foregone. Again, of course, the narrow tax base and modest
progressivity of the 1965-66 tax in India limited its role as
a stabilizer.

Effect on the Private Sector

In defending the introduction of an expenditure tax (of
the surtax variety suggested above) in India, Mr. Kaldor emphasized the role of the tax in increasing the saving:income ratio:

As the consumption standards of the masses . . . in
India are so near to the bare minimum level, the
reduction in the propensity to consume of the well-
to-do classes appears to me as an indispensable

requirement for sustaining a high rate of income
growth. . . . A graduated progressive tax on
personal expenditure is . . . the ideal instrument
for attaining this end.67

The introduction of an expenditure tax as a surcharge on
income tax increases the relative attractiveness of saving
against consumption at the margin. The "substitution effect"
of an expenditure tax should act therefore to increase the
savings ratio. The extent of this substitution effect will be
greater the sharper is the progressivity of the tax. This substitution will be greater or less according to the purpose for
which income is saved. If savings are for the purpose of retirement spending, when the taxpayer will presumably be in a
low spending tax bracket, or if savings are desired for their
intrinsic value or "psychic income," the substitution effect
will be substantially increased. If, on the other hand, savings
are intended to finance consumption expenditures in the near
future which might move the taxpayer into a higher spending tax
bracket, the substitution effect may be largely offset.

It might also be reasonable to distinguish a "consumption
effect" whereby the taxpayer desires from a given income to
maintain his pre-tax level of consumption. In this event the
residual income available for saving is diminished. Of course,
such a policy would diminish absolute income in the following
year by the amount of interest income foregone through diminished saving. The strength of this effect will depend on which
of his savings or spending levels the taxpayer is most anxious
to maintain.

With regard to the incentive to invest in equities a progressive income tax must offset its inherent discrimination
against risk-taking by special exemption or incentive devices
such as those suggested in Chapter 3. The progressive expenditure tax has no "built-in" discrimination against risk except
insofar as income from risk investment is intended for consumption in years in which the taxpayer is in a high spending bracket. If investment has some "psychic" value, or is intended for
spending in retirement, the expenditure tax should have no
effect on risk investment. A similar analysis would apply to
work incentives; unless work motivation is predominantly for
the purpose of short-term consumption the "substitution effect"
of leisure for work at the margin is likely to be outweighed by
the "income effect" of working harder in order to be able to
maintain pre-tax saving and consumption levels.

Conclusion

The use of a progressive expenditure surcharge in India
has been defended on the following grounds: First, the measure

should serve to curtail the extent to which increases in income
are consumed rather than saved, and thus to increase the savings:
income ratio. Second, the tax would appear to offer a useful
supplementary revenue source; revenue productivity might be
greatly enhanced by, in particular, more rigorous definition of
exemptions and allowances, and by sharper progression. As a
part of a cross-checking personal direct tax system, the tax
contributes to the administrative efficiency of the whole gamut
of personal taxes. Third, an expenditure surcharge should further the reduction of inequalities of consumption and, by acting
solely on consumption, should offer an additional discretionary
or automatic stabilizing device. Finally, the tax would appear
to have negligible disincentive implications with regard to investment and work.

On these grounds, it is submitted that the expenditure tax
be reintroduced into the Indian tax system.

NOTES TO CHAPTER 6

1. N. Kaldor, "The Income Burden of Capital Taxes,"
Review of Economic Studies, IX, No. 2 (1942), reproduced in
R. A. Musgrave and C. S. Shoup, Readings in the Economics of
Taxation, American Economic Association Series (London: George
Allen and Unwin, 1959), pp. 393-415.

2. I. S. Gulati, Capital Taxation in a Developing Economy
(India) (Calcutta: Orient Longmans, 1957), p. 11.

3. N. Kaldor, Indian Tax Reform (New Delhi: Ministry of
Finance, 1956), p. 19.

4. Information on Sweden is available in Harvard University Law School, International Tax Program, Taxation in Sweden,
World Tax Series (Boston: Little, Brown and Co., 1959), pp.
617-52; on West Germany in Harvard University Law School, International Tax Program, Taxation in the Federal Republic of West
Germany (Chicago: Commerce Clearing House, 1963), pp. 152-67;
on Ceylon in R. Goode, "New Systems of Direct Tax in Ceylon,"
National Tax Journal, XIII, No. 4 (1960), 329-40; on Norway in
J. Fisher, "Taxation of Personal Income and Net Worth in Nor-
way," National Tax Journal, XI (March 1958), 84-93. The whole
issue has been recently surveyed in N. Tanabe, "The Taxation of
Net Wealth," International Monetary Fund, Staff Papers, XIV
(March 1967), 124-68.

5. Harvard University Law School, International Tax Program, Taxation in India, World Tax Series (Boston: Little,

Brown and Co., 1960), p. 405; Chapter 14 (pp. 399-442) provides a detailed description of the tax.

6. All countries presently using a net wealth tax have a rate schedule low enough for the tax to be payable out of current income. If one assumes an average rate of return on capital of 5 per cent, a wealth tax whose highest marginal rate is less than 5 per cent will theoretically be payable out of current income (though not if one allows for subsistence consumption expenditures). In fact, the present Indian highest rate fo 2.5 per cent--equivalent to an income tax of 50 per cent on the assumption of an interest rate of 5 per cent--is the most severe presently levied. The next highest rate is 2.3 per cent, in Denmark; several countries use 2 per cent as the highest rate, and Japan used 3 per cent before the abolition of the tax in 1953. (Tanabe, op. cit., pp. 139-40.)

7. Ibid., pp. 140-41.

8. Taxation in India, op. cit., pp. 406-10.

9. Constitution, Seventh Schedule, List 1, Entry 86, and List 2, Entry 85.

10. Taxation in India, op. cit., pp. 417-20.

11. Kaldor, Indian Tax Reform, op. cit., Appendix C.

12. Gulati, op. cit., Chapter 7, Appendix 6.

13. Government of India, Draft Fourth Plan Material and Financial Balances (New Delhi: Planning Commission, 1966).

14. Tanabe, op. cit., p. 142.

15. Kaldor, Indian Tax Reform, op. cit., p. 1.

16. Government of India, All-India Wealth Tax Statistics for 1963-64 (Delhi: Manager of Publications, 1966).

17. Estimate arrived at by applying the rate structure to the wealth total (for 1963-64) in each new slab, and deducting present revenue from these slabs.

18. Kaldor, Indian Tax Reform, op. cit., p. 19.

19. Taxation in India, op. cit., p. 410.

20. Economic Times (Bombay), July 23, 1967.

21. J. F. Due, "Net Worth Taxation," Public Finance, XV (1960), 310-21.

22. "The proposed amendments to . . . the wealth tax . . . are basically motivated by the socio-economic objective of reducing inequalities of income and wealth." "Government of India Budget, 1964-65," Reserve Bank of India Bulletin (March 1964), 283.

23. Government of India, Income Tax Revenue Statistics for 1963-64 (Delhi: Manager of Publications, 1967).

24. Government of India, Report of the Commission on the Distribution of Income and Levels of Living (New Delhi: Planning Commission, 1964), pp. 19-24.

25. Kaldor, Indian Tax Reform, op. cit., p. 20.

26. Ibid., p. 22.

27. E. R. Rolph and G. F. Break, Public Finance (New York: Ronald Press Co., 1961), pp. 196-200.

28. See e.g., A. C. Pigou, "A Special Levy to Discharge War Debt," Economic Journal (1918), 38-58; J. R. Hicks, U. K. Hicks and L. Rostas, The Taxation of War Wealth (Oxford: Oxford University Press, 1941), pp. 180-285; U. K. Hicks, Public Finance (London: Pitman, 1947), Chapter 13--a review of wealth taxation and the capital levy.

29. Committee on Distribution of Income, op. cit., pp. 19-22, also Table 3.22, p. 81; "Estimates of Tangible Wealth in India," Reserve Bank of India Bulletin (January 1963), Table 2, p. 10.

30. Committee on Distribution of Income, op. cit., p. 20.

31. Ibid. This figure is arrived at by applying to the 1950 value of land the index of the increase in prices of agricultural commodities, and is probably a serious under-estimate.

32. Reserve Bank of India Bulletin (March 1965), p. 364.

33. Ibid., Table 6, p. 297 (revised estimate).

34. "Finances of State Governments," Reserve Bank of India Bulletin (May 1964), 585.

35. Committee on Distribution of Income, op. cit., Table 4.1, p. 84.

36. Reserve Bank of India Bulletin (March 1965), p. 401.

37. The derivation of this estimate will be explained at length in Chapter 8, Section 1.

38. Harvard University Law School, International Tax Program, Taxation in the Federal Republic of West Germany, op. cit., pp. 152-67.

39. Ibid., pp. 167-74.

40. Ibid., pp. 174-76.

41. "Government of India Budget for 1963-64," Reserve Bank of India Bulletin (March 1963), 286-304.

42. The debate begins with Mr. Kaldor's resurrection of the old Mill-Fisher-Pigou-Marshall notion of a tax on spending; An Expenditure Tax (London: George Allen and Unwin, 1959). Later contributions include: A. R. Prest, "The Expenditure Tax and Saving," Appendix 2, Chapter 2, in Public Finance in Underdeveloped Countries (London: Weidenfeld and Nicolson, 1962), and review of Kaldor's book in the Economic Journal, LXVI (March 1956), 116-20; R. A. Musgrave, review of Kaldor's book in American Economic Review, XLVII, No. 1 (March 1957), 200-205; E. Cary Brown, "Mr. Kaldor on Taxation and Risk Bearing," Review of Economic Studies (October 1957); M. A. Willemson, "The Effect upon the Rate of Private Savings of a Change from a Personal Income Tax to a Personal Expenditure Tax," National Tax Journal, XIV, No. 1 (1961), 98-103; R. Solo, "Accumulation, Work Incentives and the Expenditures Tax," National Tax Journal, IX, No. 3 (1956). Mr. Kaldor's proposals for such a tax in India are detailed in Indian Tax Reform, op. cit., Chapter 4, and are attacked in O. Prakash, "An Indian View of the Expenditure Tax," Manchester School, XXVI (January 1958), 48-67, and in D. T. Lakdawala, "An Expenditure Tax," Indian Economic Journal, III, No. 4 (April 1956), 331-40; Mr. Kaldor deplores the Indian tax as a pale shadow of his recommended version in, "Tax Reform in India," in Essays in Economic Policy (2 vols.; London: Duckworth, 1964), Vol. I, pp. 217-19.

43. J. S. Mill, Principles of Political Economy (London: Longmans, Green and Co., 1923), Chapter 11, Section 4; A. C. Pigou, A Study in Public Finance (London: Macmillan, 1947), Chapter 10, pp. 118-26 (especially pp. 123-24); A. Marshall, "The Equitable Distribution of Taxation," in A. C. Pigou, ed., Memorials of Alfred Marshall (New York: Kelley and Millman, Inc., 1956), pp. 345-52--Marshall labels the expenditure tax a "utopian goal" (p. 351).

44. Kaldor, An Expenditure Tax, op. cit., Chapter VII, pp. 191-223 (especially summary on p. 222).

45. Musgrave, op. cit., p. 203.

46. Prakash, op. cit., p. 57.

47. H. Simons, Personal Income Taxation (Chicago: University of Chicago Press, 1938), p. 228.

48. "Government of India Budget for 1962-63," Reserve Bank of India Bulletin (April 1962), 530.

49. "Government of India Budget for 1964-65," Reserve Bank of India Bulletin (March 1964), 283.

50. Taxation in India, op. cit., pp. 423-25 and pp. 425-26.

51. Ibid., p. 423.

52. Ibid., p. 424.

53. Ibid., pp. 424-25.

54. Ibid., p. 432.

55. Ibid., pp. 427-30.

56. Ibid., pp. 426-27.

57. Ibid., p. 433.

58. Ibid., pp. 433-34.

59. Government of India, All-India Expenditure Tax Statistics for 1963-64 (Delhi: Manager of Publications, 1966).

60. Kaldor, "Tax Reform in India," op. cit., p. 27.

61. Kaldor, Indian Tax Reform, op. cit., pp. 45-46.

62. Taxation in India, op. cit., pp. 427-30.

63. Kaldor, Indian Tax Reform, loc. cit.

64. This estimate is based on information from Tables 3.7-3.16, Committee on Distribution of Income, op. cit., pp. 70-74. Total income accruing to the percentage of the population whose income exceeded Rs. 10,000 was first obtained. An allowance of Rs. 10,000 expenditure per household was then

deducted from the total sum liable to tax. Allowing for the sealing of exemptions and for inducements to saving as a result of the tax, it was presumed that roughly 50 per cent of income remaining to the relevant population segment would be spent on taxable articles. The average rate of tax under the new scheme was taken to be 20 per cent.

65. Mr. Kaldor is particularly enthusiastic about this role. (Indian Tax Reform, op. cit., p. 40 text and footnote 1.)

66. Ibid., pp. 44-45.

67. Ibid., p. 42.

CHAPTER 7   ESTATE AND GIFT TAXATION

THE PRESENT SYSTEM

It has been argued that inequality in India has three aspects: inequality of income; inequality of wealth; and the perpetuation and aggravation of income and wealth inequalities through gift and inheritance. The latter is the cause of perhaps the most serious, certainly a non-functional, form of inequality, namely, inequality of opportunity. The Preamble to the Indian Constitution specifically establishes equality of opportunity as a fundamental constitutional goal. Against this constitutional injunction, and in the light of the critical problem of mobilizing every available revenue source for public spending, it is proposed to examine the estate and gift tax structure in India.

Description

Estate tax in India became payable on the capital value of all property passing on the death of any person on or after October 15, 1953, in accordance with the provisions of the Estate Duty Act of that year. The tax is a simple so-called mutation duty charged directly on the value of property changing hands at death, irrespective of the destination of that property or its distribution among the beneficiaries; it is patterned after the single comprehensive duty imposed in the United Kingdom since 1949.

The Constitution gives the Union government exclusive jurisdiction over estate taxation on all property except agricultural land; jurisdiction over the latter is reserved to the States.[1] Almost all the States have, however, delegated the power to tax agricultural land within their respective borders to the Union government;[2] in accordance with the recommendations of the Fourth Finance Commission, 98 per cent of such revenue is returned to the States, 2 per cent going to the Union Territories. With respect to estate duty on agricultural land, 100 per cent is assigned to the particular State within which it is collected.[3]

Estate duty is levied on the "principal value" of the estate which passes or is deemed to pass at death. Principal value is defined as the price at which the property could be sold on the open market at the time of the decedent's death, diminished by deductions for liabilities and debts of various kinds, and allowances such as funeral expenses up to Rs. 1,000.[4] Property liable to tax includes not only that actually passing at the decedent's death, but also property in which the decedent's death produces a change of beneficial interest, and property of which the decedent was competent to dispose, even if he did not actually dispose of it. Further, all gifts made in contemplation of death and conditional on death occuring (donationes mortis causa) are deemed to pass on the death of the donor; equally, all gifts of property made within two years of death are, with a few specific exceptions, subject to estate duty.[5]

The major items exempt are works of art, heirlooms, scientific collections, household goods and implements, and, since the 1964-65 Budget, a house or part of a house used exclusively by the deceased for his residence, situated in a place with a population exceeding 10,000, subject to an upper limit of value of Rs. 100,000.[6] The 1966-67 Budget provided that the estates of deceased members of the police force killed in border fighting should be exempt from estate duty.[7] No estate duty is chargeable on the passage at death of a house, in which the decedent has resided till death, to a spouse, son or daughter, or brother or sister of the decedent.[8]

Provision is made in the Estate Duty Act for the problem of "quick succession." Where the Central Board of Direct Taxes is satisfied that estate duty has become payable on any property passing on the death of any person, and that subsequently within five years estate duty has again become payable on the same property, or part thereof, passing on the death of the person to whom the property devolved on the first death, the amount of estate duty assessed on the second passage of property is reduced as follows:

Where the second death occurs within
one year of the first death,   by 50 per cent;

Where the second death occurs within
two years of the first death,   by 40 per cent;

Where the second death occurs within
three years of the first death,   by 30 per cent;

Where the second death occurs within
four years of the first death,   by 20 per cent;

Where the second death occurs within
five years of the first death,   by 10 per cent:

Provided that where the value on which the duty
is payable of the property on the second death
exceeds the value on which the duty was payable
of the property on the first death, the latter
value shall be substituted for the former for the
purpose of calculating the amount of duty on which
the reduction under this section is to be calculated.[9]

The 1964 Budget provided for a radical revision of the
estate tax rate schedule. Steep progression was introduced
rising from 4 per cent on estates valued above the exemption
level of Rs. 50,000 and below Rs. 100,000 to 85 per cent on
estates over Rs. 2,000,000; the previous rate schedule provided
for a maximum rate of 40 per cent on estates over Rs. 5,000,000.
By such changes it was hoped to almost double estate tax revenue in 1964-65. Further rate adjustments, involving slightly
greater progressivity, were introduced in the 1966-67 Budget.
Table 1 indicates the rates of estate duty in operation in
1967-68; no changes were introduced in the 1967-68 Budget.

Estate taxation is administered and collected by Controllers of Estate Duty who are appointed by the Union government
and perform their functions under the general supervision of
the Central Board of Revenue. Appellate procedures are conducted by Appellate Controllers, appointed by the Union government, and by the Central Appellate Tribunal.[10]

The Indian government was subject throughout the 1950's to
considerable criticism concerning its failure to supplement the
estate duty with a tax on inter vivos gifts.[11] In response to
such advice, in particular the Kaldor recommendations, and in
spite of the hesitancy of the TEC,[12] a gift tax was imposed by
the Union government under the Gift Tax Act of April 1, 1958.[13]

The tax is levied each year on individuals, HUF and associations of individuals, the tax liability of a particular
donor being determined by his residence status.[14] A gift is
defined as any voluntary transfer of existing property--includ-
ing any interest in property, real or movable--for less than
full consideration in money or money's worth.

Certain categories of gifts are exempt from tax, in particular, gifts to the Union government, a State government or any
local authority; gifts to charitable institutions; gifts of
insurance policies or annuities to dependents, other than wives,
subject to a maximum value of Rs. 10,000 in one year for each
donee; "reasonable" gifts to the donor's children for the purpose of their education; "reasonable" gifts to employees or
dependents of deceased employees in respect of services rendered, and a few other minor categories. The 1965-66 Budget

TABLE 1

ESTATE DUTY RATES, 1967-68

In the case of any property which passes or is deemed to pass on the death of the deceased--

(1) where the principal value of the estate does not exceed Rs. 50,000

Nil;

(2) where the principal value of the estate exceeds Rs. 50,000 but does not exceed Rs. 100,000

4 per cent of the amount by which the principal value of the estate exceeds Rs. 50,000;

(3) where the principal value of the estate exceeds Rs. 100,000 but does not exceed Rs. 200,000

Rs. 2,000 plus 10 per cent of the amount by which the principal value of the estate exceeds Rs. 100,000;

(4) where the principal value of the estate exceeds Rs. 200,000 but does not exceed Rs. 350,000

Rs. 12,000 plus 15 per cent of the amount by which the principal value of the estate exceeds Rs. 200,000;

(5) where the principal value of the estate exceeds Rs. 350,000 but does not exceed Rs. 500,000

Rs. 34,500 plus 25 per cent of the amount by which the principal value of the estate exceeds Rs. 350,000;

(6) where the principal value of the estate exceeds Rs. 500,000 but does not exceed Rs. 1,000,000

Rs. 72,000 plus 30 per cent of the amount by which the principal value of the estate exceeds Rs. 500,000;

(7) where the principal value of the estate exceeds Rs. 1,000,000 but does not exceed Rs. 1,500,000

Rs. 222,000 plus 40 per cent of the amount by which the principal value of the estate exceeds Rs. 1,000,000;

(8) where the principal value of the estate exceeds Rs. 1,500,000 but does not exceed Rs. 2,000,000

Rs. 422,000 plus 50 per cent of the amount by which the principal value of the estate exceeds Rs. 1,500,000;

(9) where the principal value of the estate exceeds Rs. 2,000,000

Rs. 672,000 plus 85 per cent of the amount by which the principal value of the estate exceeds Rs. 2,000,000.

Source: Government of India, The Finance Bill, 1966 (New Delhi: Ministry of Finance, 1966), pp. 21-22.

exempted gifts of property to places of public worship approved for purposes of the exemption.[15]

The two most important exemptions are, first, gifts from an individual to his or her spouse in one or more previous years up to an aggregate maximum of Rs. 50,000--reduced from Rs. 100,000 in the 1964 Budget, and, second, the basic exemption for each individual in each year of Rs. 10,000 covering gifts to all donees--reduced to Rs. 5,000 in the 1964-65 Budget but restored in the 1966-67 Budget.

With regard to rates the 1964-65 Budget changes included more severe progression at the upper levels, providing for a maximum rate of 50 per cent on the slab over Rs. 345,000 as against 40 per cent on the slab over Rs. 500,000 on the previous schedule. The 1966-67 Budget substantially reduced progressivity in the rate structure, while retaining the maximum rate of 50 per cent. Table 2 indicates present gift tax rates.

The 1964-65 reforms also introduced a degree of sophistication into the gift tax structure by the inclusion of a provision to the effect that the value of the gifts made to the same donee in the relevant previous year and during any one or more of the four years immediately preceding such previous year should be aggregated for the purpose of rate computation.[16] A crude averaging device, limited to gifts to a particular donee, was thus introduced into the tax structure.

The averaging provision was withdrawn in the 1966-67 Budget on a somewhat narrow administrative pretext:

> . . . it is a measure whose practical utility is not established, specially if the time and trouble it involves on the part of both the administration and the assessees are taken into account.[17]

A fundamental part of the usefulness of the gift tax has thus been sacrificed; this whole question of averaging gifts and integrating gift and estate taxes will be explored at some length later in this chapter.

A gift of property other than cash is valued at the rate at which, in the opinion of the gift-tax officer, it could be sold in the open market. Special rules are prescribed for goods that cannot be sold in the open market, the Central Board of Revenue being the ultimate valuation authority.[18] Administration of the gift tax is quite distinct from that of estate taxation, and is conducted by income tax authorities under procedures similar to those used for the income and wealth taxes.[19] Appeal procedure is also similar to that under the income tax.[20]

TABLE 2

GIFT TAX RATES, 1967-68

(1)	Where the value of all taxable gifts does not exceed Rs. 15,000	5 per cent of the value of such gifts.
(2)	Where the value of all taxable gifts exceeds Rs. 15,000 but does not exceed Rs. 40,000	Rs. 750 plus 8 per cent of the amount by which the value of such gifts exceeds Rs. 15,000.
(3)	Where the value of all taxable gifts exceeds Rs. 40,000 but does not exceed Rs. 90,000	Rs. 2,750 plus 10 per cent of the amount by which the value of such gifts exceeds Rs. 40,000.
(4)	Where the value of all taxable gifts exceeds Rs. 90,000 but does not exceed Rs. 140,000	Rs. 7,750 plus 15 per cent of the amount by which the value of such gifts exceeds Rs. 90,000.
(5)	Where the value of all taxable gifts exceeds Rs. 140,000 but does not exceed Rs. 190,000	Rs. 15,250 plus 17.5 per cent of the amount by which the value of such gifts exceeds Rs. 140,000.
(6)	Where the value of all taxable gifts exceeds Rs. 190,000 but does not exceed Rs. 340,000	Rs. 24,000 plus 20 per cent of the amount by which the value of such gifts exceeds Rs. 190,000.
(7)	Where the value of all taxable gifts exceeds Rs. 340,000 but does not exceed Rs. 490,000	Rs. 54,000 plus 25 per cent of the amount by which the value of such gifts exceeds Rs. 340,000.
(8)	Where the value of all taxable gifts exceeds Rs. 490,000 but does not exceed Rs. 990,000	Rs. 91,500 plus 30 per cent of the amount by which the value of such gifts exceeds Rs. 490,000.
(9)	Where the value of all taxable gifts exceeds Rs. 990,000 but does not exceed Rs. 1,490,000	Rs. 241,500 plus 40 per cent of the amount by which the value of such gifts exceeds Rs. 990,000.
(10)	Where the value of all taxable gifts exceeds Rs. 1,490,000	Rs. 441,500 plus 50 per cent of the amount by which the value of such gifts exceeds Rs. 1,490,000.

Source: Government of India, The Finance Bill, 1966 (New Delhi: Ministry of Finance, 1966), p. 23.

It is proposed to examine Indian taxation of gratuitous transfers--whether by <u>inter vivos</u> transfer or testamentary devolution--first, in terms of the significance of the taxes as means of resource mobilization for public spending; second, in terms of the contribution of the tax to the mitigation of inequalities of opportunity through off-setting the perpetuation from one generation to another of inequalities of income and wealth; third, in terms of the role of such taxes in stabilization policy; and, finally, in terms of the effects of the present system on the private sector. In the light of the contribution of the present system to resource mobilization and equity, the possibility of a radical re-appraisal of the whole form and structure of gratuitous transfer taxation will be examined at some length, and the economic implications of the reformed system briefly discussed.

Revenue Productivity

Estate and gift taxes have not as yet proved to be productive sources of revenue in India. Table 3 sets out revenue from the two taxes on gratuitous transfers from 1958-59--when the gift tax was introduced--until 1965-66. Revenue from both taxes increased sharply following the 1964-65 Budget changes, but the aggregate of revenue still amounts to less than 0.33 per cent of total (Union plus States) tax revenue.

Revenue forecasts reflect the recent tax reforms, but anticipate that combined estate and gift tax revenue will still provide only 0.3 per cent of total (Union plus States) tax revenue over the Fourth Plan. By 1970-71, it is expected that estate duty will bring in Rs. 80 million per annum, and gift tax Rs. 40 million.[21]

It is submitted that within the present conceptual framework the revenue productivity of transfer taxation might be greatly increased by policy changes in two areas. First, revenue may be substantially increased by a reform of the structure of progression in both taxes and, particularly, by the moderation of available exemptions, allowances and loopholes of various kinds. Second, a necessary reform in the structure of transfer taxation is complete integration of gift and estate taxes. The present complete separation of the two taxes in India provides the clearest opportunity for tax avoidance.

The rate of progression in the Indian estate tax until the 1964-65 reforms was moderate to the point of being ineffectual. A recent sample study done in Maharashtra indicated that the high exemption of Rs. 50,000 exempted 620 out of the 870 estates studied. The low rates of tax on those estates which were subject to taxation resulted in an average tax rate of only 6 per

TABLE 3

GIFT AND ESTATE TAX REVENUE, 1958-59 - 1965-66

Rs. million

		1958-59	1960-61	1961-62	1962-63	1963-64	1964-65	1965-66
i.	Estate Duty	27.0	30.9	42.1	39.4	46.7	54.3	66.6
ii.	Gift Tax	9.8	8.9	10.1	9.7	11.2	22.2	22.7
iii.	Total (Union & States) Tax Revenue	10,901.2	13,549.2	15,379.5	18,549.3	23,133.9	25,852.2	29,023.7
(i+ii) as per cent of (iii)		0.34	0.29	0.34	0.26	0.25	0.30	0.31

Source: Reserve Bank of India, Report on Currency and Finance, 1965-66 (Bombay: Reserve Bank of India, 1966).

217

cent.[22] A general survey of estate duty assessed in 1962-63 and 1963-64 is set out in Table 4.

On the three grades of estates indicated the average rate of tax in 1962-63 was 3.6 per cent, 11.2 per cent and 20.1 per cent, respectively, and the over-all average rate on taxable estates, 7 per cent. The corresponding percentages for 1963-64 were, 3.3 per cent, 11.8 per cent and 25.1 per cent, for an over-all average on taxable estates of 8 per cent.

The 1964-65 and 1966-67 Budget changes raised the scale of progressive rates to one comparable to that in use in other countries, but there remains considerable scope for rate varia- tion, changes in the tax slabs to which rates are applicable, and reduction of exemptions, particularly in the light of the available evidence on inequality of wealth distribution, and the size of the potential tax base--the total of accumulated private wealth--an approximate estimate of which was attempted in Chapter 6.

The revised tax structure still exempts from taxation estates below a value of Rs. 50,000. There would seem little justification for this very generous exemption which, as the Maharashtra study indicates, places the majority of estates beyond the pale of taxation. Table 4 indicates that less than 4,000 estates in total in India were assessed in 1963-64.

Given fairly moderate rates on the first brackets there would appear to be no reason to exempt estates above say, Rs. 10,000. Equally, the introduction in the 1964-65 Budget of exemption for residences up to a value of Rs. 100,000 would appear to offer an obvious inducement to expenditure on private housing; a more moderate allowance, say, up to Rs. 50,000, would suffice in this case. Tax rates from the proposed exemp- tion level of Rs. 10,000 up to Rs. 50,000 by Rs. 10,000 brackets might be 5 per cent between Rs. 10,000 and Rs. 20,000, 7.5 per cent between Rs. 20,000 and Rs. 30,000, 10 per cent between Rs. 30,000 and Rs. 40,000, and 12.5 per cent between Rs. 40,000 and Rs. 50,000. An appropriate rate for estates over Rs. 50,000 would then be 15 per cent rather than the present 4 per cent. The present scale of progression would thus be significantly raised at the lower end. At the other end of the scale there seems no reason why the rates should not be correspondingly raised so that the present maximum of 85 per cent would come into operation on estates over Rs. 1,000,000 instead of over Rs. 2,000,000 as at present. The maximum might then be raised to 90 per cent on estates over Rs. 2,000,000. The revenue im- plications of these changes will be examined at the end of this section.

TABLE 4

ESTATE DUTY ASSESSED, 1962-63 - 1963-64

Grade of Estate	1962-63			1963-64		
	No. of Estates	Value of Total Property (Rs.million)	Estate Duty Assessed (Rs.million)	No. of Estates	Value of Total Property (Rs.million)	Estate Duty Assessed (Rs.million)
Up to value of Rs. 500,000	3,464	453.9	16.35	3,793	482.6	16.36
From Rs. 500,000 to Rs. 1 million	104	71.5	7.98	102	69.6	8.25
Above Rs. 1 million	49	92.5	18.66	40	111.4	28.03
Total	3,617	617.9	42.99	3,935	663.6	52.64

Source: Government of India, All-India Estate Duty Statistics, 1963-64 (Delhi: Manager of Publications, 1966).

In terms of revenue productivity the present gift tax
structure is considerably weaker than that of estate taxation.
The aggregate allowance for gifts by an individual to his or
her spouse was reduced from Rs. 100,000 to Rs. 50,000 in March
1964, but would still seem excessively generous. Though special provision must clearly be made for an assessee's spouse,
the present very generous allowance presents an obvious method
of avoiding estate taxation and might be reduced to around
Rs. 20,000. Equally the annual exemption of Rs. 10,000 offers
another way of drastically reducing the ultimate estate tax
burden by small gifts over a period of years. There seems no
justification in terms of the urgency of increased resource
mobilization for exempting gifts over Rs. 1,000 each year.

These problems are compounded by a gift tax rate structure
with a modest degree of progressivity flattening out at a very
moderate maximum. Tax rates were substantially increased in
the 1964-65 Budget, but were reduced again in the 1966-67 Budget. The merit of the 1966-67 reductions is that gift tax
rates on transfers of between Rs. 50,000 and Rs. 1.5 million
are now identical to estate tax on similar transfers made in
the form of bequests. However, the maximum gift tax rate stays
unaccountably at 50 per cent, while the progressivity of the
estate tax continues to rise to reach a maximum rate of 85 per
cent. The incentive to give away large sums before death in
order to avoid the rigorous upper bracket rates of estate tax
thus remains.

Table 5 sets out gift tax assessments for 1962-63 and
1963-64.

In 1962-63, the average tax rates on the three categories
of gifts indicated were, 4.3 per cent, 7.2 per cent and 18.4
per cent, respectively, and the over-all average rate on gifts
was 6 per cent. The corresponding figures for 1963-64 were,
4.2 per cent, 6.6 per cent and 15.2 per cent, with an over-all
average rate of 5 per cent.

Reviewing the new Indian gift tax in 1959, N. Kaldor--on
whose specific recommendation the tax was introduced--felt
almost bound to disown parentage, on grounds of the excessive
exemptions and absence of averaging.[23] The different exemption
lists and the disparate rate structures of the gift tax and
estate duty constitute major demerits from the point of view of
revenue productivity. As long as the two taxes are not integrated, opportunities for avoidance--and thus the reduction of
revenue productivity--will remain.

TABLE 5

GIFT TAX ASSESSED, 1962-63 - 1963-64

Range of Taxable Gifts	1962-63			1963-64		
	No. of Assessees	Value of Taxable Gifts (Rs. million)	Gift Tax Assessed (Rs. million)	No. of Assessees	Value of Taxable Gifts (Rs. million)	Gift Tax Assessed (Rs. million)
Up to Rs. 100,000	7,292	126.2	5.33	8,247	129.6	5.45
Between Rs. 100,000 and Rs. 500,000	334	61.7	4.56	319	54.7	3.84
Above Rs. 500,000	23	23.9	4.40	10	8.7	1.32
Total	7,649	211.8	14.29	8,576	193.0	10.61

Source: Government of India, All-India Gift Tax Statistics, 1963-64 (Delhi: Manager of Publications, 1966).

The Revenue Cost of Separate Assessment
and Disparate Rate Structures

Gift tax liability in India is computed separate and apart from liability under estate taxation. The taxes are not even administered by the same body, estate duty being administered by the Controllers of Estate Duty and gift tax by the income tax authorities. Virtually the only administrative connection between the two taxes in India is the credit allowed against estate duty for gift tax previously paid on property included in the estate.[24] Thus an identical act of transfer is treated in two quite separate ways according to the time at which the transfer is effected. The increased administrative complexity of separate treatment is compounded by the dual system of rates and exemptions.

More important, the dual system of rates and exemptions has drastic direct consequences on revenue productivity. First, gifts may be removed from the highest estate tax brackets to the much more moderate maximum gift tax bracket. The difference between the maximum rates of 50 per cent in the case of the gift tax and 85 per cent in the estate tax offers a clear opportunity for substantial tax savings on large transfers before death. Second, the disparity in rate structure is complemented by a much broader and more generous structure of exemptions under the gift tax. The annual exemption and the generous marital allowance under the gift tax offer opportunities to further diminish the size of the estate and thus reduce ultimate estate tax liability.

The failure to integrate the two transfer taxes is particularly costly in terms of revenue productivity in the case of progressive transfer taxes such as those in India. Separately taxed inter vivos transfers will divide the estate into compartments and will thus greatly diminish the average rate of tax payable on the whole. Under progressive rates each portion of the estate given away prior to death will not only be subject to a lower rate of tax than it would if taxed in the composite estate, but by reducing the size of the estate, provides for a lower rate of progression on the remainder. This effect on progression would occur even if the rates and exemptions of the two taxes were identical, provided that the taxes were administered on a non-integrated basis. A lower rate maximum and higher exemptions under the gift tax operate, however, to aggravate this effect on revenue productivity.

The final revenue cost of separate tax treatment of gifts and estate results from the standard practice--to which India is no exception--of regarding gift tax as a liability of the donor. The result of this procedure is that whereas estate tax is paid out of the tax base and is thus levied gross on the

whole assessed estate, gift tax is paid from funds separate
from the tax base and is thus levied on the net amount transferred. Transfer tax revenue is reduced in two ways as a result of net rather than gross assessment of gift tax liability,
i.e., by the exclusion of tax liability from the tax base.
First, gift tax is paid at the expense of the residual estate
of the donor and thus reduces the final size of the estate
against which estate tax will be levied. Second, gift tax is
leviable on a smaller base.[25] This revenue cost would occur
even if there were an identical rate structure in both gift and
estate taxation and even if tax rates were of a proportional
nature. The problem is aggravated substantially in the Indian
situation, first, by the disparate rate structure where estate
tax rates are higher, and second, by the progressive rate structures of both taxes.

The Revenue Cost of the Failure to Cumulate Gifts

Progressive rates of gift taxation necessitate the use of
averaging. If gifts are not cumulated over time and the tax is
administered on a simple annual basis the tax on a gift to a
particular donee can be drastically reduced simply by spreading
the gift over time. The fraction of the gift given each year
will be subject to a lower rate of tax on the progressive scale
than it would as part of the whole. In recognition of this revenue cost a limited degree of averaging was introduced in the
1964 Budget providing for the aggregation of gifts to a given
donee over a four-year period. This reform may be seen in
retrospect as a minor palliative rather than a complete cure.
It would still have been possible by spreading gifts over a
longer period than four years to reduce the gift tax burden on
the transfer. Equally the averaging procedure was limited to
gifts to a particular donee. The door has thus opened to tax
avoidance by spreading gifts over a number of donees. In any
event even this minor cumulation was abandoned in the 1966-67
Budget.

Given continued separation of gift and estate taxation and
the persistence of a dual structure of rates and exemptions it
would be possible to minimize revenue loss under the gift tax
by introducing a more sophisticated form of averaging such as
that employed in federal gift taxation in the U.S.[26] In this
latter case the tax rate applicable to gifts in a particular
calendar year, in excess of exclusions and exemptions, by the
same donor is calculated on the basis of the aggregate of gifts
made since the inception of the cumulative gift tax in June 1932.

The revenue cost in India of the anomalous dual system of
rates and exemptions could be removed by applying an identical
system of rates and exemptions to both estate duty and gift
tax, and the loss of revenue through net assessment of gift tax

could be eliminated by gross assessment--the inclusion of tax liability in the tax base. Equally, the present revenue cost of inadequate gift cumulation could be reduced by the introduction of a more sophisticated averaging system of the sort used in the U.S. The problem would remain, however, of the effect on progression, and thus on total transfer tax revenue, of separate assessment of gift and estate liability, and consequent failure to incorporate the final estate in the cumulated total of gifts.

A Completely Integrated Cumulative Tax

The above difficulties could be resolved by the introduction of a single, unified transfer tax applicable to all transfers whether inter vivos or at death. The taxpayer would be required to cumulate all gifts above specified allowances and exemptions from the inception of the scheme. Each year current tax liability might be calculated in the following manner. Tax due on the total cumulated gifts would be calculated at current rates, in effect, as though all gifts had been made currently; credit would then be allowed against total current liability for all previous gift tax payments, incorporating an additional allowance for interest on taxes previously paid. The difference would represent net current gift tax liability. Calculation of total accrued liability on all gifts from the current rate table has the effect of applying current rates to all previous gifts as well as current gifts and thus compensates for the possibility of changing rate structures over time. On the occasion of death the estate would simply be regarded as the final gift, and tax liability computed in an identical manner to annual gift tax liability. By employing such a method of computation the tax burden would be identical whether property were given away in a series of steps prior to death, or entirely at death, or by some combination of both procedures. All the avenues of avoidance examined above would be closed and the artificial inducement to give property away prior to death removed.

Potential revenue productivity would thus be substantially increased by a reform which actually reduces the administrative complexity of the system by bringing the administration of both taxes under one head and by removing the anomalous distinction between bequests and gifts of various forms.

Using the suggested rate structure for estate duty as the rate structure for the integrated tax, and a general exemption level of Rs. 10,000 for lifetime transfers, the annual revenue productivity of the integrated tax is roughly estimated at Rs. 1,300 million.[27]

Equity

The acceptance in India of the ethical justification for
rigorous taxation of gratuitous receipts is attested by
Mr. Krishnamachari's Budget speech in 1964 when he indicated
that the primary justification for the substantial increase in
the structure of progressive rates was the objective of mitigating inequalities of incomes and wealth.[28] The role of transfer taxation is essentially to prevent the perpetuation of inequalities of income and wealth from one generation to another,
and thus to diminish inequalities of opportunity. The estate
duty rate structure, though much lighter than income tax rates
in the lower brackets (largely as a result of the initial high
exemption), becomes more severe than income tax rates on higher
brackets. Gift tax rates, though substantially increased in
the lower brackets in the 1964 Budget, still remain lower than
income tax rates at both ends of the scale. The evidence provided by the Committee on the Distribution of Income[29] of
severe inequalities of income and wealth, particularly the
latter, would suggest the need for more rigorous transfer taxation to curtail the transfer of assets from one generation to
another.

The reforms suggested in the gift and estate tax structure
for purposes of increased revenue productivity would serve
equally to improve the effectiveness of transfer taxation as a
means of alleviating inequalities. Of particular importance
would be the complete integration of the gift and estate tax
base, diminished exemptions, and a rate of progressivity such
as that suggested for the present estate duty.

The previous discussion of the need for integration of
estate and gift taxes on grounds of resource mobilization and
administrative simplicity may be read as constituting an argument for the adoption of the principle of horizontal equity in
transfer taxation. The present Indian tax structure distinguishes quite arbitrarily between transfers according to the
time at which these transfers are made.

In a crude attempt to prevent tax avoidance resulting from
disparate tax rates, the Indian estate duty includes a variety
of gifts (made within two years of death, or in contemplation
of death, or with donor's interest reserved) in the estate
taxable at death.[30] But, in effect, the more tax authorities
try to limit the scope for avoidance by extending the period
prior to death in which inter vivos gifts are taxable at estate
tax rates, or the more they extend and elaborate the category
of gifts defined as part of the taxable estate, the greater is
the element of chance in determining total tax liability on any
given amount transferred, and the more arbitrary tax incidence
becomes.

At present in India if a gift is made, say, two years and one day before death, it is subject only to gift tax rates, and the subsequent death of the donor does not affect tax liability. Were the gift to have been made a few days later, the death of the donor would bring the transfer into the taxable estate at much higher rates. Since the exact time of death is unpredictable the present difference in treatment of transfers results in greatly disparate treatment of a transfer by donors equal in all respects except their exact date of decease, and is thus contrary to the maxim of horizontal equity. This criticism would be equally relevant if transfers were taxed as income of the donee or legatee; disparate treatment would distinguish identical accretions simply on a chronological basis.

Stabilization

Gratuitous transfer taxation is generally seen as a stable rather than flexible instrument of taxation. The stabilizing effects of direct taxation were shown to depend on the built-in flexibility of tax revenue. For built-in flexibility to be significant, the coverage of the tax must be substantial and tax revenue must be responsive to changes in national income, and must increase in the same direction as national income increases to provide the required stabilizing effect. The present high exemption levels would seem to preclude significant coverage; the relatively small number of gifts and estates presently taxed has been shown in this chapter. Given the possibility, however, of widening coverage by the proposed diminished exemptions, it remains to consider whether the progressive structure of gift and estate taxation might provide for revenue responsiveness in relation to national income changes.

Estate duty revenue in any one year will depend on the number of taxable estates falling liable to duty in that year. Though in the long run, say, over two or three generations, the number of estates falling liable to estate taxation may vary substantially in relation to population changes, secular variations in mortality statistics, and changes in the distribution of wealth and income, in the short run the number of estates falling liable to tax is likely to be predictable and relatively stable. Equally, estate taxation revenue will depend on factors other than national income changes, such as increasing administrative competence and the prevention of avoidance and evasion. It would seem highly unlikely that there will be any direct short-run relationship between estate duty revenue and national income, or, in terms of elasticity, that there will be any immediate positive responsiveness of estate duty revenue to increases in national income.

Revenue from inter vivos gift taxation would also seem likely to be a stable rather than a flexible element in total

personal direct tax revenue. As in the case of estate duty
initial exemptions and a complex list of exempt gift categories
greatly diminish the potential coverage of the tax.

An integrated cumulative tax base and drastically curtailed
exemptions might, of course, increase coverage substantially.
The question again, however, is whether any short-run relationship to changes in national income may be postulated. It is
true that gift tax revenue, unlike estate tax revenue, is tied
to the capricious factor of individual inclinations rather than
to the predictable mortality of estate owners, but such volatility is unlikely to bear direct or predictable relation to
movements in national income.

In sum, it seems highly unlikely that transfer tax revenue
--which is seen essentially as a tax on the stock of capital
rather than on income--will bear any direct short-run relationship to movements of national income. The proposed integration
is unlikely to modify the situation. Transfer taxation is
therefore likely to be of little consequence in stabilization
policy.

Effects on the Private Sector

Until the 1964-65 Budget the rate structure of Indian gift
and estate taxation was relatively very moderate. In examining
the Indian estate tax in 1953-54, the TEC pointed out that
"Indian rates are lower than foreign rates for almost every
bracket."[31] Confirmation of the relatively mild impact of
estate duty in India may be found in the evidence of average
tax rates provided in Table 4. The average rate was 7 per cent
in 1962-63 and 8 per cent in 1963-64. Corresponding average
gift tax rates were 6 per cent and 5 per cent, suggesting a
less than devastating impact.

However, the 1964-65 and 1966-67 Budget changes introduced
a more severe rate structure in both taxes; rates are now comparable to rates in other countries and, unlike the previous
inconsequential rates, might be expected to evoke reaction in
the private sector.

The Ability to Save

The first argument used against transfer taxation is that
such taxation is paid in large measure out of private savings,
and thus diminishes the ability to save in the private sector.
The argument would be that such taxation is progressive in
nature and redistributive in intent and is largely incident on
the upper income groups whose propensity to save is highest.
Regardless of whether the income of the estate is sufficient to
meet tax liability or whether liquidation of a proportion of

assets or the contracting of a loan is necessary to meet tax
liability, payment of the tax represents a diminution in net
accretions to the legatee or legatees. Since the recipients of
substantial legacies are, in general, likely to belong to the
upper income groups with a relatively high propensity to save,
estate duty would appear to represent largely a draft on resources which would otherwise have been saved by the private
sector.

J. M. Keynes regards estate duty as a tax on upper income
groups largely met out of savings.[32] So does A. C. Pigou,[33]
and in a recent article H. S. Bloch accepts the consensus.[34]
The same conclusion would apply to inter vivos gift taxation.
The high exemption limit places donors assessed to tax un-
equivocally in the high income groups, and the low rates would
generally permit the tax to be paid out of current income and
thus substantially at the expense of potential savings.

The diminution in potential private savings must be
balanced against the equity and resource mobilization objectives of such tax measures. Although this factor may reasonably be presumed to have been insignificant prior to the tax
reforms of March 1964, the radical alteration in the exemption
limit and the whole scale of progression in the 1964 Budget
would seem likely to make the problem of private savings depletion of more importance. It would seem necessary to extend the
concept of functional inequalities to the case of transfer
taxation. The drafting of a list of exemptions to estate duty
might include provision for very moderate treatment of such
assets as plant and machinery being productively utilized, or
certain types of farm land being efficiently operated, etc. In
this way transfer taxation would operate to diminish inequalities of unproductive wealth.

The Incentive to Save

Liability to transfer taxation may affect the incentive to
save of potential transferors. Given the savings motivation of
provision for dependents by transfer either inter vivos or at
death, the effect of transfer taxation may be seen as composed
of two parts, a substitution effect which would make present
consumption relatively more attractive than saving intended for
transfer, and a wealth effect which would induce a higher rate
of saving in order to maintain after tax the minimum considered
necessary for the care of dependents. The net effect on the
incentive to save is indeterminate, but there are some considerations which would suggest that the substitution effect will
not be substantial.

It is likely that liability to transfer taxation, particularly to estate duty will be heavily discounted; the actual

time of incidence is indeterminate, and even if such considerations do after a certain period in life weigh heavily, that period is likely to be at an age when radical departures from spending and saving habits are generally unattractive. Equally, even if tax liability is anticipated at a comparative early age when changes in behavior are more likely, it seems probable that such anticipation will impinge to a large extent on conspicuous consumption, on lavish spending for homes, land, imported vehicles, etc. In the general case the incentive to save is unlikely to be significantly impaired by anticipation of transfer tax liability. This will be particularly likely if exemptions are drafted on the "functional" basis suggested above.

The Incentive to Work

The effect of transfer taxation on the incentive to work, assume responsibility, etc., can also be, in all probability, disregarded. The influence of such taxes on work incentives is indirect, unlike the income tax, and because of its remoteness is likely to be heavily discounted. Again the substitution effect in increasing the relative value of leisure as against work is unlikely to be significant, and, to the extent that tax liability is considered at all, is likely to be outweighed by the wealth effect, which would lead to increased work in order to maintain a desired level of transfer.

The Incentive to Invest

Of more significance is the effect of the anticipation of transfer taxation liability on the asset composition of investment. Again substitution and wealth effects can be distinguished. The substitution effect would lead to a more conservative pattern of investment by diminishing the relative gain from risk investment; this effect will be greater the more progressive the rate structure of the tax. On the other hand the wealth effect would induce a higher proportion of risk investment in the asset portfolio in the attempt to maintain the after-tax value of the estate. The net effect is again indeterminate, but some initial considerations would militate against movement to more conservative portfolios.

The wide slabs of wealth against which a particular marginal rate of tax applies would tend to neutralize discrimination against risk-taking and provide for automatic loss offset.[35] Other considerations such as the tendency to discount heavily estate tax liability, and the unpredictability and probable tendency to exaggerate the remoteness of liability would militate against tax considerations affecting individual investment decisions to any significant extent. Insofar as tax considerations are relevant, the introduction of complete loss

offset would suggest the predominance of the wealth effect and
a consequent beneficial effect on risk investment.

There are, however, two further arguments relevant particularly to large estates, which would suggest that the inducements, first, to maintain sufficient liquidity to meet tax
liability and, second, to the formation of trusts, might lead
to a diminution of risk investment.

The liquidity problem has two aspects. First, there is
the possibility of forced liquidation of an estate to meet
estate tax liability. Second, should the problem of forced
liquidation prove to be overstated, this might imply the maintenance of asset structures in a more liquid form than would
have been the case in the absence of impending tax liability.
Such liquidity has implications for economic growth in that
assets held in cash, savings accounts, government securities
and other liquid forms are withheld from equity investment.

With regard to forced liquidation Indian government regulations as to payment of estate duty are fairly rigorous. Payment, in cash or check or specified securities, is due on the
date of death but generally is not payable until the filing of
an account, which must be done within six months by the execu-
tors. Additional duty is due on assessment and demand by the
Controller of Estate Duty. In the event of excessive sacrifice
the Controller may postpone payment, but an interest rate of
4 per cent or any higher rate yielded by the property is
charged.[36] Provision also exists for payment, in four equal
annual installments or in eight equal semi-annual installments
on the same interest rate basis as for postponed returns. A
minor concession is made by permitting an allowance--a valuation
deduction--for depreciation in value of the estate resulting
directly from the decedent's death; this would include such
factors as loss of business "goodwill." But this is offset by
the refusal to allow for any effect on the price of the estate
as a result of putting the entire property on the market at one
time.[37]

Experience in the U.S. would suggest that forced liquidation is not a serious problem. A study done in 1949 in the U.S.
found that very few estates made use of a ten-year payment extension, and, on the contrary, that with the exception of a few
large estates liquidity was sufficiently great as to avoid financial loss as a result of forced sales to meet tax liability.

In India in 1963-64, just under 50 per cent of the value
of estates assessed to duty was in the form of movable property.
Of that total of movable property, 53 per cent was held in a
form other than stocks, shares, debentures and business assets
including partnership and goodwill.[38] Given the average tax

rate indicated, there would appear to be little likelihood of forced liquidation of business assets. It is, in fact, to be expected that investors will tend to maintain sufficient liquid assets to meet liability if only because forced liquidation is likely to be a relatively painful process. The short payment period, interest charge on deferred liability and absence of an allowance for the effect on price of sale of the entire estate provide a strong incentive to maintain sufficient liquidity to meet total liability.

The improbability of a liquidity problem in India would, however, suggest that the asset composition of investment may be more conservative than in the absence of tax liability, and that the supply of funds available for risk investment may be diminished as a consequence. To the extent that potential assessees maintain a proportion of their estate in cash, savings accounts, bonds, etc., for the purpose of meeting tax liability, estate taxation has an opportunity cost, spread over the lifetime of the potential assessee, measurable in terms of risk investment foregone. This represents a cost to the economy as well as to the individual investor. Of estates assessed in 1963-64, 28 per cent of total value was in the form of government securities, cash, and life insurance.[39]

The cost to the economy is reduced to the extent that governments and financial institutions invest the funds diverted from risk investment. But risk investment is primarily the responsibility of the private sector in India; as a result of the maintenance of liquidity for payment of estate taxation, particularly a more severe tax with diminished exemptions, there is likely to be a net diminution in equity investment. The suggested lenient tax treatment for certain forms of assets, such as equity shares, productive plant and machinery, etc., may therefore be of crucial importance under severe tax rates and diminished exemptions. To such a policy might be added more lenient payment procedures, in particular a payment period extended from four years to ten years, and an allowance for the effect on price of forced sale.

A related argument, popular among U.S. critics of estate taxation, is that private risk investment is diminished to the extent that the tax law provisions encourage the creation of trusts and foundations which, in turn, maintain relatively conservative investment portfolios.[40] The encouragement of trust formation is unlikely to be of significant magnitude in India, in that favorable tax treatment of funds placed in trust is limited to exemptions of trust funds set up to provide for the marriage of dependent female relatives to a maximum of Rs. 10,000 for each such relative.[41]

In sum, the only significant effects of Indian transfer taxation on the private sector would appear to be, first, the diminished ability to save, and second, the incentive to relatively conservative asset portfolios as a result of rigorous payment requirements. These effects might be mitigated by more lenient tax treatment of particular forms of assets and by more generous tax payment provisions.

RE-APPRAISAL OF FORM AND STRUCTURE

Given the justification for transfer taxation on grounds of mitigating inequalities, the question remains whether the present conception of transfer taxation, comprised of a progressive gift tax levied on the donor and a progressive estate tax levied on the aggregate estate, constitutes the best method of implementing this equity objective. Henry Simons sums up this question succinctly:

> Death duties and gift taxes, in the main, are levies upon things or upon acts of transfer; they are essentially ad rem charges which take no account of the total circumstances of the recipient.[42] [Underlining added.]

This point is particularly apposite in the Indian case where gift tax is conceived of as a penalty on the act of transfer imposed on the donor, and estate tax is conceived of as a levy on the aggregate estate and takes no cognizance of the division of the estate determined by the legator, the proportion to be received by each legatee, or the economic circumstances of the legatees. Both gifts and inheritances represent accretions to the economic well-being of the recipient or recipients. Under the present Indian conception of transfer taxation a given sum donated to a very rich donee or to a very poor donee would incur exactly the same tax liability on the part of the donor. Equally, a given estate left to the rich man or to the poor man would be subject to identical tax liability in both cases.

The Inheritance Tax Method

In recognition of the inadequacy of a transfer tax system of the British, U.S., or Indian variety as a tool of mitigating inequalities, several tax jurisdictions employ an inheritance or succession tax in which tax liability is considered the responsibility of the recipient of the gift or inheritance and is graduated according to the amount of the transfer to each recipient; the aggregate size of the estate is thus of no consequence for the establishment of tax liability. In most cases the rates of inheritance tax appropriate to a particular case

also vary according to the relationship of the beneficiary to
the decedent, the rate structure being more moderate the closer
the relationship.[43] At a higher level of refinement the inheritance tax may be supplemented with a gift tax on inter vivos
transfers assessed on the donee and graduated according to the
amount transferred; the inheritance-gift tax technique is employed in both Germany[44] and Sweden,[45] both systems providing
for the cumulation of gifts for tax purposes.

The introduction of an inheritance-gift tax structure of
the Swedish or German variety in place of the present Indian
estate-gift structure, under which the amount of tax leviable
in respect of a particular transfer may vary widely according
to the aggregate size of the estate, would be unquestionably
desirable on equity grounds. The inheritance form of taxation
is based on the amount of the transfer and therefore is, at
least in terms of that particular accretion, in accordance with
the notion of "ability-to-pay."

In the Indian context there are, however, two objections
to the introduction of a cumulative inheritance tax system;
first, on grounds of revenue productivity, and, second, in
terms of the limited notion of equity attainable even under the
inheritance system.

Revenue

Where progressive tax rates are involved, inheritance tax
rates would have to be much more severe than estate tax rates
to recoup the same revenue. Where the rates are identical the
division of the estate into the various legatees' shares for
purposes of inheritance tax computation would result in a lower
average tax rate on each inheritance and thus on the total estate than if the rate structure had been applied to the unified
whole.[46] Moreover, it is customary in establishing inheritance
tax rates to make substantial discrimination in favor of those
closely related to the decedent. It is likely that the bulk of
inherited wealth would pass to direct heirs and thus be subject
to preferential tax treatment. The only way to compensate for
revenue loss under an inheritance tax system in India would be
to design a rate structure in which the lower bracket rates
were much more severe than under the present estate tax, and to
offer very limited concessions based on consanguinity. Equally,
from the point of view of the tax authorities, the revenue productivity of an estate tax system would be predictable with a
reasonable degree of accuracy on an actuarial basis. Revenue
under an inheritance tax is subject to the whims and vagaries
of the composition of final testaments.

Equity

On equity grounds an inheritance tax system, even of the refined German or Swedish variety, fails to take account, first, of gratuitous transfers received from more than one donor, and, second, of the personal circumstances of the donee other than as a recipient of gratuitous transfers. Averaging applies only to transfers from a particular donor and transfers from separate donors are separately taxed. The result of this separate treatment from different donors under a progressive tax system is a reduction in the average rate applicable to all transfers.[47] It would thus be possible for an individual to incur a larger tax liability on a transfer from a single donor than a second individual who received a larger aggregate sum from several donors. Equally, the inheritance tax system disregards all accretions to economic power or well-being other than gratuitous transfers, so that a given sum to two individuals with the same cumulative total of transfers incurs the same tax regardless of the fact that total net accretions from all sources to each of the two individuals may be greatly disparate.

The Accessions Tax Method

The inequity involved in taxing separately transfers from different donors is removed in the proposal to substitute a cumulative accessions tax[48] for the cumulative inheritance tax on gifts from one donor. The tax base under the cumulative accessions tax is changed from the aggregate of gifts and inheritance from one donor to the cumulative total of gifts and inheritance received by a donee over his lifetime. Tax liability in any one year would be computed by first computing liability at current rates on the aggregate taxable acquisitions of the taxpayer during current and prior years and then deducting from this figure the tax due at current rates[49] on the taxpayer's aggregate taxable acquisitions in prior years. From the point of view of the donee the tax consequences of gratuitous transfers are therefore identical whether received as inter vivos gifts or as inheritances, and regardless of the number of donors or legators involved.

In terms of potential revenue productivity, the accessions tax is preferable to the inheritance variety in that all gratuitous acquisitions of a particular donee are aggregated and are consequently subject to a higher average rate of tax under a progressive rate structure than if gifts from different donors were separately treated.

From the equity point of view, however, the accessions tax shares one significant defect with the inheritance tax principle in that tax liability is computed only in terms of acquisitions through gratuitous transfers and takes no cognizance of

accretions from other sources or the general economic circumstances of the taxpayer. There are two approaches to this
problem of basing tax liability on the total economic circumstances of the taxpayer rather than merely on cumulative accretions by gratuitous transfer. The first is to base tax liability on the wealth of the taxpayer; the second is to relate
liability to some measure of income. The irregularity and in-
divisibility of gratuitous transfers would necessitate some
system of averaging if transfers were included in the progressive income tax base in order to avoid horizontal inequity.
The effective choice of tax base is therefore between the <u>accu-
mulated stock of wealth</u> and a <u>cumulative measure of income</u>.

A Wealth Base

Mr. Kaldor has suggested a wealth base for use in India.[50]
Tax liability above a lifetime exemption of Rs. 10,000 was to
be determined on a progressive scale going from 15 per cent to
80 per cent of the transfer according to the net worth of the
taxpayer as determined for the annual tax on wealth. The initial attractiveness of this proposal is that it appears to provide as a tax base as a complete index of the economic circumstances of the taxpayer, in particular, including the accumulated total of wealth that an income base cannot comprise.

However, while the wealth tax base includes the accumulated
total of wealth it does not include cumulative accretions. It
includes, in fact, only that portion of accretions which has
been saved and omits from consideration that portion which has
been consumed. A cumulative income tax base includes all accretions to wealth over the period of cumulation; the longer the
period of operation of the tax the larger the proportion of
total accumulated wealth represented by these accretions. But
the cumulative income base also includes the probably larger
total of accretions <u>consumed</u>. Thus a transfer tax based solely
on accumulated wealth provides a direct disincentive to accumulation by penalizing saving.

An Income Base

The consumption plus net accretions to wealth definition
of income advocated in Chapter 3 would imply that gratuitous
transfers be completely integrated with other accretions for
income tax purposes. Gratuitous receipts constitute increments
in economic well-being in the same manner as income from other
sources and should be taxed in relation to all other income.
On equity grounds--in both horizontal and vertical terms--the
major criticism of proposals such as the cumulative inheritance
tax or the accessions tax was that such devices failed to consider the total increment in economic well-being of a given taxpayer and comprised, at best, cumulative gratuitous transfers

from all sources. The inclusion of gratuitous transfers in the
income base subject to progressive taxation ensures that individuals of very different total income circumstances pay very
different additional taxes by virtue of the same particular
receipts. There can be no case in horizontal equity for imposing the same tax on, say, Rs. 5,000 gifts to two individuals
one of whose cumulative income from all sources far exceeds
that of the other. Equally, there is no case in vertical
equity for taxing differently two individuals who receive gifts
of, say, Rs. 5,000 and Rs. 50,000 provided their cumulative
accretions from all sources gross of the above gifts are identical. The only legitimate distinction between gratuitous transfers and accretions from other sources is the irregular nature
of the former. The inclusion of gratuitous receipts in income
on an annual progressive tax basis would then penalize such
receipts solely as a result of their irregularity. However,
this difficulty is entirely removed by the cumulation of income
from all sources, including gratuitous transfers, for purposes
of computing progressive income tax liability.

Supplementary Levies

A minor disadvantage of simple aggregation of all gratuitous transfers in income from all other sources for tax purposes is the forfeiture of the opportunity to regard transfers
as peculiarly amenable to discriminatorily high rates because
of their fortuitous windfall nature.[51] To the case for treating transfers as part of income may thus be added the case for
supplementary levies. There are several variations on this
theme. Musgrave[52] and Shere[53] have argued that property rights
may be held to lapse at death and accordingly that on grounds
of equality of opportunity as between generations it is desirable to impose an estate duty on the estate as a whole before
consideration is given to taxing the shares going to individuals.

The acceptance of the principle that gratuitous transfers
represent income to the recipient would suggest, however, that
unless the equity base of the tax is to be seriously impaired,
any form of supplementary levy should take the form of incorporating in the recipient's income tax liability a penalty of
some kind for income of this nature.

The requirement of a satisfactory supplementary levy is
that it not conflict with the objective of relating tax liability following the receipt of transfers to the receipt of
income from all sources. This might be achieved in two ways,
the first in which the additional discrimination is identical
regardless of total income, the second in which the additional
discrimination is higher the higher is the total income of the
recipient.

The first method would involve the incorporation of transfers in income for tax purposes and the imposition of a supplementary levy or surcharge amounting to, say, 5 per cent of income accruing in the current year in the form of gratuitous
transfers. In this manner income tax liability depends on income accruing from all sources and will be higher (under a
proportional or progressive income tax) for the individual
whose total income is higher, but the additional discrimination
against gratuitous transfers is independent of income from
other sources.

The second method would employ as a supplementary levy,
say, 20 per cent of tax payable as a result of the inclusion
of gifts for the current year in income. The additional levy
would thus amount to 20 per cent of the difference between
total tax liability including gifts received in the current
year and total tax liability excluding current gifts. In this
manner the actual additional sum payable as a result of the
receipt of gifts is higher the higher is the taxpayer's total
income; this would follow from the progressive nature of the
income tax.

Revenue Productivity

The compelling case on equity grounds for the incorporation of gratuitous transfer in income is complemented by the
potential revenue productivity of such a system. The average
rate of estate duty in 1963-64 was only 8 per cent. The increase in rates in the 1964 Budget might be expected to raise
this average, but since the increased rates mainly apply to the
few large transfers it is unlikely that the average rate would
exceed 10 per cent; if the lower maximum rate applicable to
inter vivos transfers is also considered the average rate applicable to transfers in general would probably lie between 5-
10 per cent.

If transfers are incorporated in income and are thus added
to other income in order to determine the appropriate rate of
taxation (including the additional supplementary levy) it would
appear likely that the average rate of taxation of transfers
would be substantially greater than under the present system.
This probability is confirmed by U.S. experience which indicates
that those receiving transfers usually have high income from
other sources and would thus be subject to a high marginal rate
of tax. Evaluating the revenue productivity of taxing transfers as part of income a recent U.S. study estimates that the
average rate of tax transfers would rise from 5 per cent to 30
per cent.[54] The revenue productivity of taxing transfers as
part of income in India is estimated at from Rs. 2,200-4,400
million per annum.[55]

Effects on the Private Sector

Under the proposed system it would appear likely that disincentive effects on donors or legators would be less significant than under the present system in that tax liability falls entirely on the recipient of transfers and is thus only of indirect significance to the donor or legator. From the point of view of the recipient, transfers net of tax represent accretions unrelated to work, saving or investment, and the only possible disincentive effects might occur through a higher tax rate on earned income as a result of the inclusion of transfers in total income.

The consequences for economic growth of the diminished ability to save of transfer recipients as a result of taxation may be offset by the application to income in the form of transfers of the partial exemption scheme previously suggested. Particular provision would have, of course, to be made for the liquidity of assets problem, and preferential treatment afforded certain categories of productive assets.

CONCLUSION

Viewing the chapter as a whole, the conclusion would be that if the present conception of transfer taxation is to be continued, then considerations of equity and revenue productivity would necessitate the integration of gift and estate taxation and a system of cumulation for tax purposes. Revenue productivity would be more substantially increased, as would the contribution of transfer taxation to equity, by the full incorporation of transfers in cumulated recipient's income from all sources for income tax purposes.

NOTES TO CHAPTER 7

1. Constitution, Seventh Schedule, List 1, Entries 87-88; List 2, Entries 47 and 48.

2. Provision for such delegation is made in the Constitution, Article 252.

3. Government of India, Report of the Fourth Finance Commission, 1965 (Delhi: Manager of Publications, 1965).

4. Government of India, Estate Duty Act, 1953 (revised) (New Delhi: Ministry of Law, 1965).

5. The two-year period was eased to one year in the 1965-66 Budget, but restored in the 1966-67 Budget. Government of India, Memorandum Explaining the Provisions in the Finance Bill, 1966 (New Delhi: Ministry of Finance, 1966), p. 22.

6. Estate Duty Act, op. cit., Part III.

7. Memorandum Explaining the Provisions in the Finance Bill, 1966, loc. cit.

8. Government of India, Memorandum Explaining the Provisions in the Finance Bill, 1965 (New Delhi: Ministry of Finance, 1965).

9. Estate Duty Act, loc. cit.

10. Ibid., Part VII.

11. See particularly, I. S. Gulati, Capital Taxation in a Developing Economy (India) (Calcutta: Orient Longmans, 1957), Chapter 11; and N. Kaldor, Indian Tax Reform (New Delhi: Ministry of Finance, 1956), Chapter 5.

12. Government of India, Report of the Taxation Enquiry Commission (hereinafter TEC) (3 vols.; New Delhi: Ministry of Finance, 1953-54), Vol. II, p. 246.

13. Government of India, Gift Tax Act, 1958 (revised) (New Delhi: Ministry of Law, 1965).

14. Ibid., Chapter II.

15. Memorandum Explaining the Provisions in the Finance Bill, 1965, op. cit., p. 26.

16. Government of India, Government of India Budget for 1964-65, Finance Minister's Speech (New Delhi: Ministry of Finance, 1964), p. 444.

17. Government of India, Government of India Budget for 1966-67, Finance Minister's Speech (New Delhi: Ministry of Finance, 1966), p. 109.

18. Gift Tax Act, op. cit., Chapter II.

19. Ibid., Chapter III.

20. Ibid., Chapter VI.

21. Government of India, Draft Fourth Plan Material and Financial Balances (New Delhi: Planning Commission, 1966).

22. P. Pillai, "The Equalizing Effect of Estate Duty," Economic Weekly, XVI, No. 39 (September 26, 1964), 1569-74.

23. N. Kaldor, "Tax Reform in India," Economic Weekly, Annual Issue (January 1959), 195-98.

24. Estate Duty Act, op. cit., Part VI.

25. The revenue cost of net assessment may be seen from an arithmetical example: If gifts are subject to a 50 per cent tax rate a man with Rs. 150,000 might give Rs. 100,000 and pay the tax with the remaining Rs. 50,000. Had liability been gross, i.e., on Rs. 100,000 plus Rs. 50,000 tax liability, the tax payable on the gift would have been Rs. 75,000.

26. Harvard University Law School, International Tax Program, Taxation in the United States, World Tax Series (Chicago: Commerce Clearing House, Inc., 1963), pp. 249-68.

27. From Government of India, Report of the Committee on Distribution of Income and Levels of Living (New Delhi: Planning Commission, 1964), Table 3.25, p. 83, it was established that 57 per cent of the value of houses was possessed by householders whose houses exceeded Rs. 10,000 in value. Taking 57 per cent as an average for the amount of wealth in estates over the Rs. 10,000 exemption, and the total of wealth as Rs. 570,000 million (see Chapter 6), taxable wealth emerged as Rs. 325,500 million. Given that one generation in India is approximate 25 years, 4 per cent of taxable wealth was taken to pass each year by gift of one form or another, providing an annual taxable total of Rs. 13,000 million. The average tax rate was taken to be 10 per cent (probably a low estimate).

28. Government of India Budget for 1964-65, op. cit.

29. Committee on Distribution of Income, op. cit., Chapter 3.

30. Estate Duty Act, op. cit., Part II.

31. TEC, op. cit., Vol. II, p. 247.

32. J. M. Keynes, The General Theory of Employment, Interest and Money (London: MacMillan, 1960), pp. 372-74.

33. A. C. Pigou, A Study in Public Finance (London: MacMillan, 1947), pp. 138-46.

34. H. S. Bloch, "Economic Objectives of Gratuitous Transfer Taxation," National Tax Journal, III-IV (1950-51), 139-47.

35. Suppose an investor decides to acquire an asset worth Rs. 2,000 hoping that it will appreciate to Rs. 3,000 at death. If the gain is achieved and his estate is subject to a marginal rate of 60 per cent the net gain is reduced to Rs. 400. If, however, the asset depreciates to a value of Rs. 1,000, and the relevant marginal rate remains at 60 per cent, the gross loss of Rs. 1,000 is reduced after tax to a net loss of Rs. 400. Consequently the relative choice of gain or loss is unaffected. Should the lower value of the estate after the capital loss be subject to a lower marginal rate, say 50 per cent, then the gross loss of Rs. 1,000 is reduced to Rs. 500 after tax; thus loss offset is incomplete. The wide slabs subject to the same marginal rate would in most cases provide for automatic loss offset, and, by leaving unchanged the probability of gain or loss, provide no disincentive to risk investment.

36. Estate Duty Act, op. cit., Part VII.

37. C. Lowell Harriss, "Liquidity of Estates and Death Tax Liability," Political Science Quarterly, LXIV, No. 4 (1959), 533-59.

38. Government of India, All-India Estate Duty Statistics, 1963-64 (Delhi: Manager of Publications, 1966).

39. Ibid.

40. See, e.g., C. Lowell Harriss, "Economic Effects of Estate and Gift Taxation," in U.S. Congress, Committee on the Economic Report, Federal Taxation for Economic Growth and Stability (Washington: U.S. Government Printing Office, 1955), pp. 858-59. See also, J. K. Butters, L. E. Thompson and L. L. Bollinger, Effects of Taxation: Investment by Individuals (Boston: Harvard Graduate School of Business Administration, 1953), pp. 370-72.

41. Estate Duty Act, op. cit., Part III.

42. H. Simons, Personal Income Taxation (Chicago: University of Chicago Press, 1938), p. 128.

43. The varied inheritance tax structures used by the States in the U.S.A. are detailed in World Tax Series, Taxation in the United States, op. cit., pp. 241-48; and in Canada, by J. Harvey Perry, Taxation in Canada (Toronto: University of Toronto Press, 1960), pp. 193-96.

44. Harvard University Law School, International Tax Program, Taxation in the Federal Republic of Germany, World Tax Series (Chicago: Commerce Clearing House, Inc., 1963), pp. 179-96.

45. Harvard University Law School, International Tax Program, <u>Taxation in Sweden,</u> World Tax Series (Boston: Little, Brown and Co., 1959), pp. 126-39.

46. Suppose an estate of Rs. 30,000 is subject to an estate tax rate schedule of 10 per cent on the first Rs. 10,000, 25 per cent on the second Rs. 10,000 and 50 per cent on the third Rs. 10,000. Estate tax revenue would be Rs. 8,500 and the average rate of tax 20 per cent. If the estate is divided into three parts and taxed on an inheritance tax basis on the same rate structure, revenue would be Rs. 3,000 and the average rate of tax 10 per cent.

47. Suppose two individuals receive Rs. 1,000 from a given donor and that the cumulative liability of each recipient in respect of that donor is a tax rate of 50 per cent. Each would then pay Rs. 500 tax. Suppose, however, that another donor from whom no previous gifts had been received and that liability on a progressive scale was 10 per cent; tax paid on this transfer would then be Rs. 100. The average rate on transfer applicable to the first taxpayer would be 50 per cent whereas that applicable to the second on total transfers for the year would be 30 per cent.

48. H. J. Rudick, "What Alternative to Estate and Gift Taxes," <u>California Law Review</u>, XXXVIII (March 1950), 150-82.

49. The effect of changing tax rates over time on current liability is thus eliminated.

50. Kaldor, <u>Indian Tax Reform</u>, <u>op. cit.</u>, p. 16.

51. Cf., J. S. Mill's disapproval of progression in income taxation with his view that inheritance taxation should appropriate the entire estate with the exception of amounts required for the education of younger children. J. S. Mill, <u>Principles of Political Economy</u> (London: Longmans, Green and Co., 1923), pp. 224-26.

52. R. Musgrave, <u>The Theory of Public Finance</u> (New York: McGraw-Hill, 1959), p. 176.

53. L. Shere, "Discussion," on E. G. Keith, "How Should Wealth Transfers Be Taxed," <u>American Economic Review</u>, Papers and Proceedings (May 1950), 406-9.

54. E. Rolph and G. Break, <u>Public Finance</u> (New York: Ronald Press Co., 1961), pp. 257-71.

55. Taking 4 per cent of wealth--Rs. 22,080 million, as amount passing per annum and the average tax rate applicable

to such transfers, allowing for exemptions, allowances, etc.,
as from 10 per cent--20 per cent, the revenue potential works
out to Rs. 2,200-4,400 million.

CHAPTER TAX POLICY IN THE
INDIAN INSTITUTIONAL
SETTING

The revenue productivity of the tax system in a developing country depends to a considerable extent on the skill with which the tax system is adapted to the institutional framework.   In this context in India it is proposed to discuss the question of gold mobilization, compulsory savings, tax collections in kind, and a labor tax.

MOBILIZATION OF GOLD HOARDS

The private hoarding of gold has long been considered a socio-economic drain in India and early in this century writers such as G. Finlay Shirras[1] and J. Kitchin[2] stressed the magnitude of the problem.   J. M. Keynes also emphasized the baneful effects of the hoarding of gold and precious metals.[3]   More recently A. G. Chandavarkar has observed:

Gold hoarding is commonly held as the leading species of a wide spread genus of socially unproductive investment . . . which includes some traditional asset preferences such as the hoarding of currency, commodities, and the excessive accumulation of wealth in the form of land and luxury real estate.[4]

Recent tax measures of the Indian government emphasize the continuing nature of the problem.   Forward trading in gold was banned throughout the country as of November 14, 1962 (and in silver from January 10, 1963), and in line with the government's policy of bringing about a reduction in the demand for gold the exemption (up to Rs. 15,000) for jewelry under the Wealth Tax Act was withdrawn in the 1963-64 Budget.[5]   A widespread program of public exhortation was undertaken during and after the Sino-Indian border dispute to prevent further purchases of gold and to induce the release of existing stocks.[6]   As part of the same policy the government issued Gold Bonds, 1977 (on sale from November 12, 1962, to February 28, 1963); contributions under this Bond scheme were placed at Rs. 70 million.[7]   The 1965-66 Budget introduced a new flotation of 7 per cent Gold Bonds, available until May 31, 1965.[8]   Since November 1, 1966, a ban has been imposed on the possession of primary gold except by refiners, licensed dealers and goldsmiths, and a ceiling (2,000 grams for individuals and 4,000 grams for families) placed on the possession of gold ornaments.[9] In his study of Indian taxation Mr. Kaldor felt compelled to submit an extended defense of his wealth tax purely on the grounds that it would not, as his critics alleged, aggravate the problem of gold hoarding.[10]

The extent to which the market price of gold in India exceeds the parity price of Rs. 167 per ounce offers an indication of the present magnitude of the problem. From Independence through the First Plan the average price of gold in India was roughly Rs. 275 per ounce.[11] A deterioration in the situation is indicated by the upward trend in gold prices--the average price over the Second Plan was Rs. 311/oz., and Rs. 313/oz. over the Third Plan--and by the increase in the real value of gold vis-à-vis consumers' goods.[12]

Viewing the present privately-held stock of gold as a proportion of total household savings, gold hoarding might not appear to be a particularly serious problem. A 1961 study of the Indian savings pattern indicates that gold constituted 3.4 per cent of household saving and 0.2 per cent of total national income over the period 1950-59.[13] This confirmed the results of a similar study done in 1960; the latter also indicated that this particular form of savings grew at an annual average rate of 1.7 per cent.[14] Thus the problem must be kept in perspective and is clearly not of the magnitude supposed by many of the writers who regard gold hoarding as the root cause of Indian economic backwardness.[15] Nevertheless household saving constitutes over 80 per cent of total saving and the mobilization of the 3.4 per cent of household saving at present in the form of gold hoards would make a significant contribution to public developmental spending.

If gold is mobilized by some purchasing scheme there is, of course, no net quantitative addition to public spending; qualitatively however the availability of gold would make possible the purchase of scarce capital good imports. If, on the other hand, part of the supply of gold hoards is mobilized by a tax device which does not lead to a reduction in tax revenue or private savings from other sources, then there may be a net quantitative addition to resources available for public spending.

The actual amount of gold stocks presently held privately has been estimated by the Reserve Bank of India in 1958 at 105 million ounces.[16] At the 1957-58 average market price for gold of Rs. 289 per ounce the value of the stock would be Rs. 30,250 million. At the international price of gold (Rs. 167 per ounce) the value would be Rs. 17,500 million. This latter figure is equivalent to $3,675 million at the international price.[17]

The sum of $3,675 million is almost equivalent to the over-
all balance of payments deficit of the Second Five Year Plan
($4,500 million) and is equivalent to about half of the esti-
mated foreign exchange deficit of the Third Five Year Plan.
The real cost to India of holding gold is best emphasized by
drawing attention to this opportunity cost of holding such
hoards. H. T. Patrick concludes:

> . . . private hoarding of gold within a country is
> equivalent in terms of its command over the world's
> goods, to the hoarding of the most liquid foreign
> exchange which yields no return. . . . The oppor-
> tunity cost to the country is the usefulness of the
> foreign goods and services that have to be forgone.[18]

Such a cost is particularly onerous in the Indian case, which
is characterized by stagnant and relatively inelastic foreign
demand for Indian exports, highly income-elastic domestic private sector demand for imports of capital goods for development
purposes, and consequent built-in foreign exchange scarcity.
The magnitude of present gold stocks is such that their mobilization, though inevitably a once-for-all operation, even although phased over time, would constitute a vital increment of
resources in passing through the period of high import demand
and foreign exchange shortage in the early stages of development. This is the basic rationale behind a policy of gold
mobilization in India.

H. T. Patrick has also drawn attention to the fact that
the hoarding, domestic marketing and storage of gold, and its
processing into ornaments, requires the utilization of scarce
domestic resources, particularly skilled labor and entre-
preneurial talent.[19]

The gold problem in India may be envisaged in terms of a
"flow" (the need to prevent new private savings being directed
into purchases of gold imports), and in terms of a "stock" (the
need to mobilize present resources of gold and to shift the
composition of a given stock of private wealth in the economy
to a smaller proportion of gold and a larger proportion of productive imports). The flow component is of much less significance than the present gold stock. The import of gold is
officially forbidden, and domestic production is very small and
declining--monthly production in 1966 averaged just over 300
kilograms (about 10,000 oz.) as against just under 600 kilograms monthly in 1951.[20] The entire small and declining amount
produced domestically is directed into governmental monetary
gold stocks. The only increase in supply thus comes from
smuggling against which strict measures are taken. Such an
increase can, by its very nature, be only approximately estimated, but is thought to be of the order of Rs. 300-400 million

annually ($60 to $80 million).[21] Given an exhortation to in-
tensify measures to prevent smuggling, the supply of gold may
be regarded as approximately fixed. Accordingly, problems of
gold mobilization are essentially problems of the demand for
gold.

The demand for gold may be seen, first, in terms of a
transactions motivation; in other words, gold is desired as a
liquid asset. The liquidity of gold--the facility of exchang-
ing it for any other asset without delay or price reduction--is
reflected in the general willingness in India to accept gold as
payment for goods, as collateral for loans, and in the existence of organized markets for gold in the bullion and ornamental forms.[22] Gold is also of importance for special social or
religious reasons such as the provision of the marriage dowry
in terms of gold jewelry.[23]

Second, gold may be held in a precautionary sense as a
readily concealed form of wealth, and as a hedge against inflation.[24] Devaluation which increased the value of gold by 36.5
per cent overnight must certainly have increased the inflationary hedge motivation.

Third, gold may be held as a durable consumer good and
hoarding may thus be attributed to the psychic income accruing
from jewelry and ornaments. Opinion on this issue is virtually
unanimous.[25] H. T. Patrick observes:

It would appear that in India for millenia traditional social custom has so shaped individual
preference that gold is highly desired at all income levels for ornamental and status purposes as
a durable consumers' good from which a high degree
of psychic income derives.[26]

Chandavarkar would agree that "it is the role of gold as a durable consumers' good that affords the real clue to the phenom-
enon of gold hoarding in India."[27]

The demand for gold in terms of esteem and psychic income
presents considerable obstacles to attempted mobilization.
Demand in these terms is likely to be interest-inelastic and
traditional monetary methods of diverting gold into the banking
system or into interest-bearing securities are likely to be unsuccessful.[28] Equally, it is likely that the demand for gold
is quite price-inelastic. The lack of any consistent and determinate relationship between the price of gold and hoarding has
been shown;[29] the implications of such a condition is that yet
another traditional method of releasing hoards--by increasing
the government's buying price of gold--would be comparatively
unsuccessful. A final implication of the prestige demand for

gold is that this demand is likely to be highly income-elastic,
particularly in the upward direction. This may be illustrated
by the apparent close correlation of gold flows and prices with
periods of prosperity in the agricultural sector.[30]

The gold problem would thus appear to be of considerable
significance in the development context. The demand for gold
as a prestige durable consumers' good is likely to increase as
incomes increase, and such a demand is complemented by demand
for gold under the transactions and precautionary motives. The
precautionary motive would be particularly significant in the
context of inflationary price movements. Given the relatively
fixed supply of gold the market price may thus be expected to
rise. The increase in the price of gold then adds the motive
of capital appreciation to the demand for gold. As a consequence of the durable consumers' good aspect of the demand for
gold traditional monetary and price manipulation policies to
release hoards or limit demand are unlikely to be very successful.

It remains to consider tax devices to further the objectives of hoard mobilization and demand limitation.

Tax Devices for Gold Mobilization

One method suggested by Chandavarkar might offer some
promise. He proposes to issue import licences for capital
goods or essential consumer goods to such private importers as
are able to produce the requisite amount of gold from sources
known or accessible to them.[31] However, the potential profit
gained by the importer would have to be very high to offset the
loss incurred through the sale of gold at the international
parity price. Again, the fact that the bulk of hoarded gold
is in the form of jewelry and ornaments means that it could not
be easily converted into an acceptable exportable form.

The ultimate tax measure is, of course, confiscation by
the government of gold hoards. Direct confiscation would probably be unacceptable in the Indian political framework, but a
variation on this somewhat drastic theme might be possible. It
might be feasible to declare all private holdings of gold illegal and to institute government purchases by means of bonds of
existing gold stocks over a period of time at a price somewhere
between the going market rate and the international parity
price. This period of government purchase might be extended
over five years, with premium prices to early submissions.
After this initial period of five years the private ownership
of gold would be held to be strictly illegal and confiscatory
penalties enforced. A much milder solution of declaring ceil-
ings on holdings would be very difficult indeed to administer
because of the possibility of intra-family transfers, concealed

hoards and the incentive provided by the continued existence of the domestic market for gold.[32] The former more drastic solution would be much easier to administer but would necessitate a considerable public education program before it would achieve political respectability in a nation with a long tradition of gold usage as a store of value and a durable prestige consumers' good.

The use of incentives in the wealth tax rate structure to payment in gold by assessees offers a possibility of reaching the bulk of gold holdings in the upper income groups. A discount in assessment--say, 20 per cent--might be offered to all taxpayers who make payment in gold; provision might also be made for the acceptance of ornaments and jewelry. A variation on this theme might be the use of a once-for-all capital levy with strong financial inducements offered for tax payment in gold. Again, political acceptance would necessitate a consensus on the critical necessity of securing access to gold hoards as a means of international payment.

Provision of similar incentives to pay in gold might be incorporated in the estate tax structure. This latter method would seem to offer the best possible opportunity to demand payment in gold, insofar as wealth in this form is apparent and accessible, coupled with the offer of strong financial incentives to dishoard secret wealth held in the form of gold. The use of the estate tax would not introduce political difficulties but is a gradual process and may only be used in the present urgency to supplement other policies.

Conclusion

The successful implementation of a policy of gold mobilization cannot, of course, be achieved simply by the use of tax policy. A policy mix of fiscal and monetary devices and the application of social and cultural pressures of various kinds would be necessary to obtain the release of the greater part of gold hoards. Individual and social taste patterns would, indeed, have to be radically altered to enable such a scheme to be a complete success. A long-run solution to the problem of high income-elasticity of demand for gold might lie in the widening of consumer choice and the substitution of alternative durable consumers' goods--presumably with prestige or status connotations--for gold as objects of desirability. The fondness for gold is deeply ingrained however, and a diminution of such preference through the availability of substitutes is clearly of long-run significance and does not provide an immediate solution.

The conclusion of this section remains that the success of the Indian Plans may depend in large measure on the bridging of the foreign exchange gap in the initial stages of development.

The mobilization of even a portion of gold hoards would alleviate this problem, and attention must be directed in the formulation of tax policy to the fashioning of appropriate measures to
facilitate such mobilization.

COMPULSORY SAVINGS SCHEMES

The difficulties of conventional tax financing result in
part from the confiscatory label attached to taxation. The
consequent unpopularity of many tax measures, lack of public
co-operation, and constant need to review and modify the tax
structure in terms of possible deleterious effects on private
incentives, complicate the tax system and diminish the effectiveness and possible extent of conventional tax financing.
It may thus be desirable, and perhaps essential in the initial
period of development, to supplement voluntary saving and taxation by various quasi-fiscal devices such as compulsory saving.
If such schemes are viewed as essentially emergency in nature
and thus short run in application the mobilization of public
opinion may be considerably easier than under new avenues of
taxation. Equally, such schemes lack the confiscatory label
attached to taxation and thus might be extended beyond the
political limits of tax measures.

The term "compulsory savings" is taken to comprise such
devices as deferred pay schemes, compulsory insurance contributions of various kinds, compulsory purchases of government
bonds and annuities and compulsory provident or saving schemes.
Such procedures are not free from general disadvantages and
limitations.

First, for such schemes to be acceptable to the public
there must be a prospect of relative price stability. If the
government is considered unable to maintain stability and
planned development is thought likely to imply rapid price increases, then compulsory savings, unless compensated by a generous interest rate greater than the opportunity cost of such
funds (which would encompass the rate of increase in prices)
amounts to a form of taxation.

Second, there is always the possibility that compulsory
savings will simply be drawn from funds which would otherwise
have been voluntarily saved. In this sense the scheme is simply
transferring the right to dispose of savings from the private
to the public sector. There will almost certainly be some decline in private voluntary saving as a result of a compulsory
savings scheme of any magnitude, and the interest structure of
the compulsory scheme and other saving incentives generally
would have to be set up to maximize the extent to which

compulsory savings contributions represent a net increase in
the savings:income ratio.

Third, the burden of compulsory saving may, like taxes, be
shifted. In this fashion realized incidence may differ widely
from that intended. This is particularly undesirable if the
scale of progression in the scheme is distorted away from the
pattern envisaged as meeting the requirements of growth and
equity. Wage and price increases consequent on the scheme will
have the effect of shifting the burden in a manner that is not
consonant with fiscal and current Plan objectives. Measures
may thus have to be taken in the field of price and income
policy to offset such results.

Measures of compulsory saving have been advocated from
time to time in India since 1939 and some have been introduced.[33] A compulsory deposits scheme applicable to corpora-
tions--50 per cent of current profits in excess of Rs. 100,000
--was introduced in 1943 under the Excess Profits Tax and abolished as of March 31, 1946. Reintroduced in 1956 the scheme
was never fully implemented and was withdrawn in 1960.[34]

The TEC examined the possibility of a compulsory saving
scheme on the grounds that conspicuous consumption on the part
of high income groups was wasteful of scarce resources, inequitable in that it bore no relation to average living standards, and thus harmful to planning objectives, and recommended
the adoption of a scheme of surcharge-cum-compulsory deposits
applicable to income over Rs. 25,000. The suggested combined
surcharge and compulsory deposits deductions rose from 0.5 per
cent on income over Rs. 25,000 to 11.2 per cent for income
over Rs. 500,000; the compulsory deposit portion rose from 0.25
per cent to 5.60 per cent. The latter was to be refundable
only after 20 years--and then in the form of a twenty-five year
government bond--and only nominal interest was to be paid.[35]
This recommendation has never been implemented.

In the 1963-64 Union Budget a comprehensive scheme of compulsory savings was proposed.[36] The Compulsory Deposit Scheme
Bill, 1963, enabled the government to provide for compulsory
savings on the part of different groups on appropriate scales,
subject to certain maxima. The maxima were 50 per cent of the
basic land revenue on 1959-60 assessments for agriculturalists;
3 per cent of salary for employees who earn more than Rs. 1,500
per annum but are not liable to income tax; 0.33 per cent of
turnover of the preceding year for shopkeepers whose annual
turnover is Rs. 15,000 and who are not liable to income tax;
for those subject to taxes on professions, trades, callings or
employment, an amount equal to the amount of the relevant tax
payable by them during the year in which the deposit is required to be made; for income taxpayers whose residual after-tax

income does not exceed Rs. 6,000, an amount equal to 3 per cent
of the residual income, and in the case of those whose residual
income exceeds Rs. 6,000, an amount equal to 2 per cent of
residual income. These sums could be deducted from surcharge
or income tax payable by these groups. Deposits under this
scheme were not to be withdrawable for a period of five years
and carried simple interest at 4 per cent per annum. The
Finance Minister hoped to add Rs. 400 million to Central capital receipts on this account. The scheme proved to be a failure. The provisions in respect of land revenue payers, urban
immovable property holders and persons liable for sales tax were
never implemented, and the provision in respect of employees
not liable to income tax was abolished because of administrative
difficulty and political opposition. The scheme only added
Rs. 160 million to Union government capital receipts, and was
abandoned in the 1964 Budget.[37]

   Present measures in force in India consist mainly of the
Union and State Employees' Provident Funds, the recent extension of this scheme into other areas and the Annuity Deposit
scheme under the Union income tax. The total contribution to
the Union and State Employees' Provident Fund is approximately
Rs. 300 million annually. Various enactments of the last few
years have made contribution to a provident fund--at a usual
rate of 6.25 per cent of wage and salary--compulsory for employees and employers belonging to factories of a certain minimum size, coal mines and tea plantations.[38] However, only just
over two million contributors are encompassed by the scheme and
the present method of payment of benefit in a lump sum has some
apparent limitations. In the State of Uttar Pradesh a portion
of the low paid employees' contribution to a provident fund
is used as a compulsory life insurance premium, but this procedure has not been extended to other States as yet.

   It is hoped that the Annuity Deposit Scheme introduced in
1964 by Mr. Krishnamachari will be a greater success than the
Compulsory Deposit Scheme.[39] The 1964 scheme--still in opera-
tion--is much simpler and applies only to income brackets above
Rs. 15,000 per annum at rates varying between 5 per cent and
12.5 per cent. The amount of deposit made in any year is deductible in compiling the assessable income of the assessee for
that year, and deposits made in 1964-65 will earn just over 4
per cent interest per annum. Deposits are repayable in ten
equated annual installments of principal and interest commencing
one complete year after the year of assessment. Such repaid
deposits constitute assessable income. It was hoped to enhance
Union capital receipts by Rs. 670 million as a result of this
scheme; when losses resulting from the abolition of the Compulsory Deposit Scheme are included, however, the net accretion
was expected to be Rs. 570 million. Net receipts turned out to

be Rs. 403 million in 1964-65; for 1965-66 net receipts were Rs. 500 million, and Rs. 446 million are anticipated for 1966-67.[40]

The 1964 Annuity Deposit Scheme, which is limited to the upper income groups, has proved administratively simpler and politically more popular than its predecessor. The scheme is intended to curtail consumption by the upper income groups and thus raise the aggregate of saving; it is hoped that the cancellation of private saving will be substantial and that net savings--compulsory savings minus diminution in voluntary savings--will rise by around Rs. 500 million each year. Yet this plan, which indicates the possibilities of a well conceived compulsory savings scheme covers only a small group of taxpayers and makes a relatively small--approximately 4 per cent--addition to Union government capital receipts.[41]

An alternative, more productive, possibility might be the introduction of a much more comprehensive compulsory saving scheme, the scale of which will depend on whether it is viewed as a supplement or as an alternative to conventional tax measures. The scheme would comprise, first, the extension of the Annuity Deposit Scheme over the maximum possible range of taxpayers--in effect a massive scheme of deferred pay to finance the emergency circumstances of the "initial effort" period of planned growth; second, the increased use of compulsory purchases of government bonds, including here the possibility of mobilizing gold hoards; third the extension of the coverage of existent provident funds and pension and insurance schemes of various kinds.

The proposal made by J. M. Keynes in Britain in 1940 for a deferred pay or compulsory savings scheme was conceived in the emergency situation of wartime inflationary pressure.[42] The main provision of the Keynes proposal was a deduction from current wages and salaries to be credited to a savings account which would remain blocked for the duration of the war. This savings deduction would be in addition to the income tax and surtax withholding. The lowest income would be exempt from both deductions and would, in fact, be supplemented by family allowances in the case of married men. Although the lower income groups would contribute the bulk of the resources released by pay deferral, Keynes pointed out that at the end of the war it would be the wage earners, not the profit takers, who would emerge as the main holders--in the form of deferred-pay claims--of the newly created national debt. The long-run effect of the scheme would thus be redistributive.

The proposed scheme for India would envisage as the major provision a scheme of deferred earnings along the lines suggested by Keynes. The concern in India, as in the Keynesian case,

is to increase minimum standards of consumption from the subsistence level, but at all levels higher than this to prevent
income increased being entirely dissipated in the form of consumption. It is suggested that a structure of rates of deferred
earnings be super-imposed on the present Indian tax structure,
in such a way that the total deduction is sharply progressive
but that the rates of earnings deferral are only mildly progressive. The present Annuity Deposit Scheme might be integrated in the proposed comprehensive deduction plan. However,
the major change proposed would be to widen enormously the base
of the deduction. Administrative feasibility would suggest the
complete exemption of incomes below Rs. 1,500. It is accordingly postulated that incomes below Rs. 1,500 be exempted and
that incomes from Rs. 1,500 to Rs. 3,000 be subject to a 2 per
cent Annuity Deposit. From Rs. 3,001 to Rs. 10,000 the deposit
should be 3 per cent and from Rs. 10,001 to Rs. 15,000, 4 per
cent. Beyond this level the present Annuity Deposit rates
might be continued: 5 per cent between Rs. 15,001-Rs. 20,000;
7.5 per cent between Rs. 20,001-Rs. 40,000; 10 per cent between
Rs. 40,001-Rs. 70,000; and 12.5 per cent above Rs. 70,000. A
large part of receipts derived from this new Annuity Deposit
Scheme would come from the middle and lower income groups. The
suggested rates would be intended to supplement the standard
income tax and annuity deposit rates and in no sense to obviate
the need for increased tax rates, particularly in the middle
income groups. If the scheme were to be seen as an alternative
to increased income tax rates then the rates might be substantially increased across the board from a minimum of 5 per cent
up to a maximum of 20 per cent. The estimated annual revenue
productivity of the proposed system, seen as a supplement to
taxation, would be approximately Rs. 4,000 million.[43]

The system of repayment under the present Annuity Deposit
Scheme could be adapted to cover the wider scheme. Certainly
repayment must be phased over time; lump sum repayment would
defeat the purpose of the scheme and militate against price
stability. One slight modification of the present repayment
scheme might be adopted in present circumstances. Initial repayment, say for the first five years of the scheme, might be
deferred for two years rather than one. The present rate of
interest of slightly more than 4 per cent would seem adequate.

As in the Keynesian proposal it is suggested that the
sacrifice imposed may be extended much further under a scheme
of compulsory savings than under new tax measures. Provided
such a scheme is well publicized and clearly linked to the
urgency of the development problem there seems no reason why
the scheme should not be politically acceptable. This is particularly so because of the deliberate redistributive intent of
the scheme, which proposes, in fact, that in a relatively short

period of time the bulk of Indian government debt should pass
into the hands of the lower and middle income groups.

The general difficulties of compulsory savings schemes
would have to be resolved for the particular scheme proposed
for India. First, the successful implementation of stabilization policies of a fiscal and monetary nature is essential to
the success of the proposed scheme. In the nature of the
scheme the short period before repayment commences and the
relatively generous proposed interest rate should at least partially offset fears of inflationary losses in the value of
saving; the scheme itself is intended to make a significant
contribution to stabilization policy, and thus, in a sense,
should help to create the prerequisite psychological conditions for its continued successful implementation. Second, the
generous interest rate would have to be coupled to other saving
privileges, such as partial exemption from income tax of income
saved and invested in prescribed areas, in order to minimize
the diminution in voluntary savings consequent on the introduction of the compulsory scheme. Third, national price and incomes would have to be integrated with the scheme to counteract
attempts at shifting or re-allocation of the burden of the compulsory savings withdrawals.

Finally, and prima facie the most intractable problem,
there remains the question of administration. Insofar as the
scheme is applied to income taxpayers there seems little difficulty. First, deductions would be made from all salaries, interest and dividends through the present withholding scheme.
Second, for other income taxpayers the deduction would simply
be added at the end of the year to assessed tax liability, although the extension of withholding on a systematic basis offers
the most convenient method of collecting the deduction. For
those not liable to income tax Keynes advocated the same method
of collection as that used for social insurance, each insured
worker receiving a Deferred Pay card which would be stamped by
his employer.[44] Coverage by some form of provident, pension or
insurance scheme is growing rapidly but is not sufficiently
widespread in India to make the system proposed by Keynes immediately applicable. Statistics are very approximate for industrial workers and employees covered by provident fund and/or
pension schemes. B. Singh estimates this figure to be between
four and five million in 1960.[45] Life insurance figures are
available up to March 1965--total policies issued to that point
numbered 10.63 million.[46] This figure for life insurance is
growing very rapidly and has almost doubled since 1957. It
thus seems legitimate to postulate present coverage at roughly
twelve million, and, applying the same rate of growth to pension funds and employee insurance coverage, to estimate the
latter at six million. There will, of course, be some overlapping of coverage but it seems legitimate to assume that at

least fourteen million members of the working force are registered contributors to a savings, pension or insurance scheme of
some kind. This represents a relatively small percentage of
the working force of almost two hundred million, but does represent a much wider coverage than income tax assessees of just
over one million. For the estimated fourteen million who are
registered contributors to some withholding scheme the compulsory withdrawal under the new Annuity Deposit arrangements may
be administered through existing contributory provisions. The
remaining groups include workers not liable to income tax and
not contributors to a pension, provident or insurance fund,
and the agricultural population. Members of the former group
who are employees might be assessed by their employers using a
deferred pay card arrangement, the State governments being responsible for collecting the receipts from the employers.
Assessment of small self-employed individuals will be very
difficult but might be undertaken by extending the present income tax external survey procedures. For small retailers submission might be made under sales tax arrangements.

Government Bond and Annuity Sales

The second proposal under the comprehensive compulsory
savings scheme would be the increased use of compulsory sales
of government annuities and bonds. With regard to general
bond sales a rate of interest of 4, 5 or 6 per cent might be
paid according to the maturity date of the bond. There is no
reason why cash prizes may not be offered regularly--say, to
five thousand purchasers per annum. This scheme is used in
Britain--the so-called premium bond scheme--and has proved a
comparatively useful additional source of revenue; contribution
is purely voluntary under the British scheme. In India it may
be possible to acquire a considerable amount of resources by
the use of optional or semi-optional bond offers with strong
monetary inducements. In the Soviet Union there is no legal
compulsion but every worker is expected to purchase government
bonds equivalent to two or four weeks salary per annum. Deductions are at source and apparently the social pressure is such
that everyone contributes.[47] It may be necessary, however, in
India to make such purchases compulsory for certain groups,
particularly the middle income groups in the Rs. 3,000-Rs.
15,000 income range whose treatment under the present income
tax is relatively mild. Compulsory annual purchase of bonds
equivalent to, say, one or two weeks salary might be obliga-
tory for all employees and self-employed persons in this range.
The ulterior motivation here is again redistributive; this
point should be emphasized in publicizing the scheme.[48]

Provident Funds

Finally, the extension on a compulsory basis of existing provident, pension and insurance funds not only offers a ready method of administering the deferred earnings scheme, but is in itself a productive source of compulsory savings. It has been suggested above that only some fourteen million members of the work force contribute to a savings, pension or insurance scheme. It should be possible to extend coverage of these schemes on the model of State and Union Government Employees' Provident Funds which at present provide some Rs. 300 million per annum. I. M. D. Little has suggested integrating all present provident fund schemes into one integrated scheme; the redistributive aspect is emphasized in his scheme which suggests a scale of employee contributions increasing progressively with income, a scale of employer contributions falling progressively as incomes rise, and a scale of government contributions falling progressively as incomes rise and effective only at the lowest end of the income scale--up to an annual income of Rs. 3,000.[49]

Extended application of the Employees' State Insurance Act, 1948, might also be implemented. This Act applies to all perennial factories using power and employing twenty or more persons, and encompasses laborers and clerical staff with monthly earnings of up to Rs. 400. By the end of January 1966 the scheme covered 3,448,000 industrial workers in 249 centers in India. By the end of 1964-65 total (employers plus employees) contributions stood at Rs. 188.5 million.[50] A more comprehensive definition of the Act would broaden the group of employees covered.

The possibility of making life insurance in the Life Insurance Corporation of India (a nationalized industry) compulsory for all employees and self-employed might also be contemplated. Payment of premiums would be on the same basis as that suggested for the deferred earnings scheme. A cost-benefit analysis of such schemes would have to be worked out prior to the introduction to ensure net gains to the government. There seems no doubt that contributions would exceed payment by the government in the schemes outlined above. Other possible refinements such as the extension of the unemployment contribution or an old age pension fund are eminently desirable from a welfare point of view but should not be counted on as productive revenue sources. In any year payment by the government might exceed premiums, particularly in the case of unemployment insurance, thus defeating the object of compulsory saving. B. Singh has, however, suggested that the present creation of an old age pension fund, which would not begin paying until five years had elapsed would provide a useful immediate source of funds.[51] Other refinements suggested by Singh include a

crop insurance fund and the compulsory distribution of a portion of corporation dividends in the form of government savings
certificates.[52]

A comprehensive scheme of compulsory saving along the
lines suggested, the scale of which may be adjusted according
to whether the scheme is seen as a supplement to existing taxation or as an alternative to new taxes and increasing rates of
present taxes, might be of considerable assistance in furthering
the three major tax objectives.

TAX COLLECTIONS IN KIND

Roughly 40 per cent of consumption of all products in the
rural sector is transacted on a non-monetary basis.[53] Assessment in imputed monetary terms is of little value in cases
where the bulk of income accrues in kind, and the problem
arises of assessment of non-monetary income.

The difficulties inherent in the evaluation of subsistence
output and own production consumed have been examined in some
detail in a recent study of Nigeria.[54] This study is of relevance to all underdeveloped countries and indicates how arbitrary and approximate any monetary evaluation must be. The
final conclusion of the study is that retail prices in the
closest market offer the only reasonably satisfactory method of
evaluation, but even this criterion is admitted to be general
and approximate. Prices as between local markets may vary
widely and prices in one market may fluctuate over time; such
evaluation is therefore quite unsatisfactory as an equitable
basis for tax assessment. Even in an advanced country evaluation of benefits in kind may be extremely difficult, and raises
serious problems of horizontal equity.[55]

In India a benefit which is not convertible into money or
money's worth is not, conceptually, income and is excluded from
taxable income unless rendered specifically taxable by the Income Tax Act, as in the case of "perquisites" in lieu of, or
in addition to, salary.[56] Agricultural incomes are, of course,
excluded from the purview of the Income Tax Act and the various
State agricultural income taxes take no cognizance of benefits
in kind.

In sum, for those families whose income accrues almost
entirely or partially in kind evaluation and assessment in
monetary terms is futile in the former case--in that the farmer
has no means of meeting tax liability in monetary terms--and
conceptually complex and arbitrary in the latter case for that
part of the income accruing in kind. At the same time it is
reasonable to suppose that a proportion of these benefits in

kind does not simply represent a subsistence minimum, but may, in fact, represent a source of taxable income in a non-monetary sense. This is particularly true of families whose income is not entirely in kind, but may also be true of other areas where families will choose to remain in the non-monetary sector for the precise purpose of staying outside the pale of taxation. Indeed, much criticism of agricultural taxation reforms reflects a fear that families will choose to move back into the non-monetary sector in order to avoid tax liability.[57] Efficient implementation and comprehensive coverage of any new system of land taxation and agricultural income taxation may thus necessitate some form of taxation in kind.

The Association of In-Kind Taxation with Inefficiency and Totalitarianism

Taxes in kind are conventionally associated with inefficient tax collection. Available evidence would appear to invalidate this association. It has been shown by H. P. Wald that the two countries which at present obtain the highest percentage of total revenue from land taxes are Mainland China and South Korea.[58] Both countries obtain 24 per cent of total revenue from land taxation as against barely 9 per cent for India in 1954 (the fiscal year chosen by Wald for comparative purposes) and both rely primarily on collections in kind and on assessments based on gross harvest as recorded in land registers. Both China and Korea value in-kind collections at low official prices; were market prices to be used the percentage of total revenue constituted by land revenue would be much higher. It has been estimated that valuation at market prices in Korea in 1954 would reveal that between 40-45 per cent of total tax revenue came from the land tax.[59]

The effectiveness of land revenue collections in kind may also be illustrated by the proportion of the grain harvest taken by the government as tax payments. These figures are estimated to be 11 per cent in 1953 for Korea[60] and approximately 33 per cent for China.[61] With regard to India, the TEC estimated that land revenue in 1950-51 represented 1 per cent of the gross value of agricultural output.[62] The declining significance of land revenue in India since 1950-51, to around 5 per cent of total tax revenue of the Union and States in 1965-66, would suggest that the present figure for India might be considerably less than 1 per cent.

A second common belief is that collections in kind are usually associated with totalitarianism. The element of truth in this allegation lies in the indubitable fact that collections in kind imply a considerable degree of state control over the distribution and marketing of agricultural produce. Such a degree of control may, but need not, involve totalitarianism.

In the case of Mainland China the procedure doubtless involves
a large measure of government direction. The Soviet Union also
makes extensive use of special form of taxation in kind in the
agricultural sector, in the procedure whereby collective farms
and individual peasants are required to deliver a specified
proportion of their output to the state at a price well below
market value.[63] The difference between market price and
government-procurement price is seen as partly land rent and
partly tax in kind.

In-kind collections are, however, also employed with considerable success in Taiwan, which does not employ rigorous
method of compulsion,[64] and is also a feature of the Burmese
economy where the State Agricultural Marketing Board may be
seen as an instrument for taxation in kind.[65] In neither Taiwan or Burma may the degree of control involved be reasonably
described as totalitarian. This is also true of the Federation
of Financial Associations responsible for collection and storage of rice in South Korea; distribution is conducted by the
Ministry of Agriculture.[66]

The Canadian Wheat Board has powers under the Canadian
Wheat Board Act "to market, in an orderly manner, in the inter-
provincial and export trade, grain grown in Canada."[67] Its
powers include authority "to buy, take delivery of, store,
transfer, sell, ship or otherwise dispose of grain."[68] During
World War II all wheat going into commercial channels in
Canada was required to be marketed through the Wheat Board.
Although the Act was amended in 1947, the major wartime powers
of the Canadian Wheat Board were continued. A government board
in India on the same lines as the Canadian Wheat Board would be
sufficient to control the collection and distribution of grain
and thus adequate to collect taxes in kind.

The necessary administrative structure to implement a
policy of in-kind collection is, in fact, available in India.
The food crisis of the summer of 1964 led to the establishment
of the wholly Union government-owned Food Corporation of India.
This Corporation began operation on January 1, 1965, and has
branches in each State. It purchases foodgrains from producers
and from wholesalers at declared prices, handles imported foodgrains and has a monopoly of inter-State and long distance
movement of foodgrains in railways.[69] Additional measures include the statutory fixation of maximum prices of foodgrains
and the establishment of an Agricultural Prices Commission to
advise the Union government on a continuing basis on agricultural price policy.[70]

Advantages of In-Kind Taxation

In-kind taxes may provide more opportunities than cash taxes for influencing the composition of production.[71] By fixing the equivalency ratios between various crops from among which farmers have the option to pay taxes, the government may exercise a direct influence on the proportions of products grown.

Again taxes in kind would offer distinct advantages over cash taxes in a period of inflation. Although inflation has not been a general problem in India over the planning period, recent soaring food prices indicate clearly that taxes in kind would provide the government with insurance against loss of purchasing power of tax receipts in the event of price increases. The reintroduction of in-kind taxes in Korea and Taiwan was in large measure a response to the fiscal chaos caused by inflation.

Finally, in-kind collections permit the extensive use of buffer stocks by which the government can moderate local scarcities and discourage private speculative hoarding; thus the process of in-kind collection may contribute substantially to the price stability of agricultural products, and thus help to eliminate the inequity of artificial scarcities and speculative bottlenecks.

The experience of South Korea illustrates most of the above attributes of in-kind taxation. This productive and efficient method of tax collection ensured the stability of the purchasing power of tax receipts in a period of chronic inflation, permitted the government to mobilize a large percentage of agricultural income by way of taxation, and provided the necessary degree of control over the distribution and price of rice in a period of emergency. Using this procedure, "The Republic of Korea was able to achieve an exceptionally large increase in tax collections under extremely adverse circumstances."[72]

In-Kind Taxation in India

The persistence of a large non-monetized sector completely outside the scope of the present tax system in India makes the use of in-kind collections virtually essential if the full revenue potential of the agricultural sector is to be utilized. The general decline in the importance of in-kind taxation may be attributed in part to the increasing monetization of agriculture in most areas of the world. It is not suggested that collections in kind be a permanent feature of the Indian tax system. There indeed is the possibility that an extensive system of in-kind taxation may obstruct the process of monetization. In India this must be prevented by continued and extended

efforts to encompass the entire population in the monetary sector, through devices such as credit facilities in rural areas,
etc. As monetization becomes ubiquitous in the long run the
use of in-kind collection will atrophy and would be limited
only to those farmers whose presumptive income in monetary
terms is not sufficiently large to warrant the process of
assessment. But as a short-run emergency measure in-kind collection may offer a unique opportunity to tap a revenue source
otherwise beyond the pale of taxation. The proposed measure is
thus visualized as an essentially short-run expedient.

The form of taxation in kind must not only provide a wider
tax base and increased revenue, but must, particularly in the
present situation in the agricultural sector in India, provide
positive incentives to increased agricultural productivity.
This dual objective would best be attained by a procedure such
as was detailed in Chapter 5--i.e., a tax which left the reward
for additional effort undiminished. The in-kind tax base should
thus also be defined not in terms of actual output but in terms
of productive capacity and the tax would thus be based on
potential output in relation to some regional or local average.
As with monetary taxation the inefficient farmer whose production is less than the average for the region and/or for the
type of land concerned would be penalized, whereas the efficient
farmer would be correspondingly encouraged. Equally, in-kind
tax rates should be proportional in terms of potential output
for a given land size, but progressive in terms of difference
sizes of land holdings.

Arrangements for the reduction or remission of tax liability in the event of crop failures, and for the landlord:
tenant issue would be as detailed in Chapter 5. Administratively, in-kind taxation obviates complex assessment and valuation problems and might thus be implemented through the local
Panchayats.[73] It is suggested that the Panchayats assess and
collect the tax in kind locally under the supervision of a
Commission of each State government. National co-ordination
could be undertaken by a Commission of the Union government;
this would now obviously be done by the Food Corporation.

A scheme on the above lines would widen enormously the
base of agricultural taxation and substantially increase tax
revenue, would enhance the horizontal equity of agricultural
taxation by taxing a previously exempt group of taxpayers,
would offer the government a useful means of stabilizing food
prices and would thus further the control of inflationary pressures, and would provide a means of extending a tax system intended to promote directly increases in agricultural productivity.

A LABOR TAX

The use of compulsory or statutory labor requirements on government projects is of interest in India for two reasons. First, unutilized manpower may be the only taxable asset that large sections of the population possess, especially in the non-monetary sector, and a labor tax would thus extend the coverage of taxation and reduce the cost of government projects. This is particularly true of community development projects where the bulk of cost is attributable to labor. Second, unemployment remains very high in India and it may be contended that the opportunity cost of statutory labor drawn from the ranks of the unemployed is nil. Presumably some kind of subsistence allowance would replace wages on such projects involving the unemployed. The device would appear to have _prima facie_ attractiveness and Professor Enke concludes:

> The needs of community development are so great in most poor countries, and there is so much seasonal unemployment in many of them that levies on labor seem desirable and inevitable.[74]

A tax on rural labor has been advocated recently for use in India. The Report of the Congress Village Panchayat Committee recommended the use of a labor tax where efforts to enlist voluntary contribution had broken down.[75] The Santhanam Committee on local finance also recommended such a tax where voluntary contributions of cash or labor were insufficient for a particular project.[76] V. Gandhi has recently recommended a labor tax of five days labor a year--commutable into cash payments--to be levied on the entire rural sector.[77]

There is no question that unemployment and underemployment presently create a vast pool of unutilized labor in the Indian economy. The Fourth Plan estimated the number of underemployed in India generally, but mainly in the rural sector, at 16 million.[78] Gandhi suggests that in the agricultural sector labor is fully utilized for only about 65 per cent of the year.[79]

Given the high figures of unemployment and the predominantly labor-intensive character of most government projects, at least in rural areas, the conclusion would appear to be that some form of tax on labor would offer a ready means of financing community development projects in rural areas and minimizing labor costs of government projects in urban areas.

Before advocating conscriptive labor, however, it would seem appropriate to examine present practices in the utilization of surplus manpower. Since the end of the Second Five Year Plan the number of development Blocks--groups of villages --to which the community development program has been extended

has risen from 3,100 to 5,261, thus covering almost the entire
rural area of the country.[80] The emphasis of these projects
has been on agricultural development. Resources for community
development projects are drawn from the people and from the
government. For each Block area development schemes are conditioned by a qualifying scale of voluntary contributions from
people in cash or kind or labor. Voluntary contributions till
March 1965 amounted to Rs. 1,418.4 million, or approximately
32 per cent of government expenditure under this scheme.[81]

As a response to the national emergency, a scheme known
as the Village Volunteer Force was introduced in January 1963.[82]
The three-fold program of the Village Volunteer Force comprises
agricultural production, mass education and village defense.
A Defense Labor Bank has been set up in each village and considerable numbers of villagers have offered up to 12 days labor
a year under this scheme. It would then appear that a substantial amount of gratuitous labor is already being utilized
through a variety of development schemes.

The need to enlist the co-operation of the taxpayer is an
essential part of any tax policy. It may be argued that under
a labor tax it might be very difficult indeed to enlist the
required degree of co-operation, and that such a device might
go far to stifle enthusiasm for substantial volunteer projects
now under way. Conscript labor is notoriously inefficient
labor, and, with the best intentions, it would be difficult to
detach from the compulsory scheme the label of "slave" labor;
the political acceptability of the device might therefore be
doubtful.

The most profitable approach to this problem might be, as
an alternative, increased emphasis on volunteer projects of
various kinds, and the provision of assistance to the District
Zila Parishads,[83] Block Panchayat Samitis[84] and local Panchayats
to permit greater efficiency and co-ordination of activities.
The present administrative organization of the Community Development Program, with the emphasis on local effort, seems ideally
suited for the purpose.[85]

The need for integration, co-ordination and local planning
so as to encompass a wider range of activities and contributors
has, however, been emphasized.[86] A co-ordinated approach to
co-operative and community development projects might set targets for each District; below this level goals could be set for
each Block each of which comprises approximately 100 villages.
Within the Block the Block Panchayat Samiti could agree on tar-
get contributions of each village. It would then be the role
of each Village Panchayat to procure the required contributions
in cash and labor from the particular village. The Panchayats
and Panchayat Samitis might have the right to bring pressure to

bear on localities--if only by publicizing individual or village contributions--in order to maximize labor contributions to community development projects. In this sense labor contributions would become semi-optional and individuals would be under a certain amount of pressure to co-operate in the scheme.

The emphasis of the Plans to date has been on projects of community development involving a large measure of co-operative and voluntary effort. These schemes have been very successful and may be further improved by increased Union and State assistance and a variety of measures to co-ordinate and integrate local activities to enable the local bodies to enlarge the scope of voluntary contribution. At present when State assistance is offered for execution of such projects the expenses are shared by the Union and State governments equally in respect of recurring items and in the proportion of 3:1 in the case of non-recurring items. For productive works like irrigation reclamation of land, etc., necessary funds are advanced by the Union government to State governments in the form of loans. The Union government also bears half the expenditure on personnel employed by the States in Blocks.[87]

Increased Union and State participation, both financial and in the form of technical assistance in the formulation and co-ordination of District, Block and Village plans and targets, should make possible accelerated progress in the Community Development Scheme and the enlistment of greater quantities of voluntary labor. Financial incentives such as a rising scale of grants to Districts fulfilling agreed "community efforts" might also be employed.

The sense of this section would therefore be that a labor tax be examined with great caution and introduced only as a last resort. This somewhat negative recommendation on the use of a direct labor tax is made despite the recent positive recommendation by Gandhi, who estimated an annual return of Rs. 600 million by way of a labor tax of five days per year levied on the entire rural sector.[88]

Conclusion

The degree of labor co-operation and voluntary contribution presently achieved is an invaluable asset in the development program and should be retained if the various community projects are to be successfully implemented. A surplus of manpower--both rural and urban--provides immediate justification for labor-intensive government projects, and an opportunity for local bodies to enlist, wherever possible, such idle resources in development schemes. It does not necessarily provide the rationale for a labor tax, other than as a last resort. It is submitted that a more fruitful approach would provide for the

extension of the powers of local groups, at the Village, Block
and District levels, to encompass and bring pressure to bear on
wider range of contributors.

NOTES TO CHAPTER 8

1. G. Finlay Shirras, Indian Finance and Banking (London:
MacMillan, 1919), concluded that the value of gold in India in
1919 was Ł 361m. or approximately $1,400m.

2. J. Kitchin, submission to Government of the United
Kingdom, Report of the Royal Commission on Indian Currency and
Finance (3 vols.; London: 1926), Vol. III, pp. 534-35, estimated that between 1493 and 1924, 130 million ozs. of gold had
been hoarded by the Indian public.

3. J. M. Keynes, Indian Currency and Finance (London:
MacMillan, 1913); "India, as we all know already, wastes far
too high a proportion of resources on the needless accumulation of the precious metals" (p. 99).

4. A. G. Chandavarkar, "The Nature and Effects of Gold
Hoarding in Underdeveloped Economies," Oxford Economic Papers
(New Series), XIII (June 1961), 137-48.

5. Government of India, Government of India Budget 1963-
64, Finance Minister's Speech (New Delhi: Ministry of Finance,
1963).

6. See e.g., Government of India, India 1963 (Delhi:
Manager of Publications, 1964); "Be Vigilant" advertisement on
p. 106; "Do not buy gold. Give your gold for your country's
cause."

7. Government of India Budget 1963-64, Finance Minister's
Speech, loc. cit.

8. Government of India, Government of India Budget 1965-
66, Finance Minister's Speech (New Delhi: Ministry of Finance,
1965).

9. Economic Times (Bombay), November 3, 1966.

10. N. Kaldor, Indian Tax Reform (New Delhi: Ministry of
Finance, 1956), pp. 115-20.

11. "Estimates of Gold and Silver Stocks in India,"
Reserve Bank of India Bulletin (April 1958), 387.

12. A. Heston, "An Empirical Study of Indian Gold Prices," Indian Economic Journal, VIII, No. 3 (January 1961), 216, estimates that during the period 1952-59 the price elasticity of gold, relative to the consumer price index, was 1.6; i.e., the real value of gold, in terms of consumers' goods, rose over the period. The price figures for gold are taken from the Reserve Bank of India Bulletin (October 1967), 1361.

13. "Estimates of Saving and Investment in the Indian Economy, 1950-51 - 1958-59," Reserve Bank of India Bulletin (August 1961), 1205.

14. "Estimates of Saving in the Indian Economy," Reserve Bank of India Bulletin (March 1960), 326. The most recent study of Indian saving treats the household sector's holding of gold in the general category of consumer durable goods and provides no separate estimate of gold holdings. "Estimates of Savings and Investment in the Indian Economy," Reserve Bank of India Bulletin (March 1965), 314-33.

15. See e.g., N. S. Buchanan, "Deliberate Industrialization for Higher Incomes," Economic Journal (December 1946), 541; R. F. Kahn, "The Pace of Development," in The Challenge of Development (Jerusalem: Hebrew University, 1958), p. 185.

16. "Estimates of Gold and Silver," op. cit., p. 387.

17. This figure in U.S. dollars is, of course, unaffected by the 36.5 per cent devaluation of the rupee in terms of gold in June 1966.

18. H. T. Patrick, "The Mobilization of Private Gold Holdings," Indian Economic Journal, VII, No. 2 (October-December 1963), 178.

19. Ibid., p. 179.

20. Reserve Bank of Indian Bulletin (September 1967), p. 1269.

21. "Estimates of Gold and Silver," op. cit., p. 387. The domestic value of smuggled gold would, of course, be 36.5 per cent higher since the 1966 devaluation.

22. Patrick, op. cit., p. 118.

23. This custom persists in spite of official proscription.

24. P. T. Bauer and B. S. Yamey, The Economics of Underdeveloped Countries (Chicago: University of Chicago Press,

1958), define the role of trinkets and precious metals as "insurance against currency inflation" (p. 134).

25. See Kaldor, op. cit., p. 115 et seq.; Chandavarkar, op. cit.; Patrick, op. cit.

26. Patrick, op. cit., p. 181.

27. Chandavarkar, op. cit., p. 141.

28. Ibid., p. 141, quotes as an example the poor response to the Government of India 3.5 per cent National Loan Plan 1964 issued in 1954 which allowed the facility of tendering subscription in jewelry and ornaments. The revenue of Rs. 70 million from the 1963 Gold Bond scheme offers a more encouraging result. The latter, however, was issued at a time of national emergency.

29. Ibid., p. 143.

30. B. K. Madan, "The Role of Monetary Policy in a Developing Economy," Reserve Bank of India Bulletin (April 1961), 524.

31. Ibid., p. 148.

32. Though as indicated above, a policy of placing a ceiling on holdings of gold ornaments was introduced in November 1966.

33. This issue is detailed in B. Singh, "Compulsory Savings," Indian Economic Journal, VII (April 1960), 378-94.

34. Ibid., p. 382.

35. Government of India, Report of the Taxation Enquiry Commission (hereinafter TEC) (3 vols.; New Delhi: Ministry of Finance, 1953-54), Vol. II, pp. 143-45.

36. Government of India, Explanatory Memorandum on the Budget of the Central Government for 1963-64 (New Delhi: Ministry of Finance, 1963).

37. Government of India, Explanatory Memorandum on the Budget of the Central Government for 1964-65 (New Delhi: Ministry of Finance, 1964).

38. Singh, op. cit., p. 383.

39. Government of India, Government of India Budget, 1964-65, Finance Minister's Speech (New Delhi: Ministry of Finance, 1964).

40. Government of India, Government of India Budget for
1966-67 (New Delhi: Ministry of Finance, 1966). Receipts from
annuity deposits are for administrative purposes subsumed under
capital receipts rather than under current revenue.

41. Even this limited scheme is in jeopardy, the Finance
Minister having hinted strongly in his 1967-68 Budget Speech
that the withdrawal of the Annuity Deposit scheme was imminent.

42. J. M. Keynes, How to Pay for the War (Toronto:
MacMillan, 1940). A similar scheme has been suggested for the
U.S.A. See S. Slichter, "The Problem of Inflation," Review of
Economic Statistics, XXX (February 1948), 5. The Keynes scheme
was, in fact, introduced in Britain during the war and proved
comparatively successful. Subsequent repayment of "post-war
credits" by the government has, however, been less than expedi-
tious.

43. Approximately 75 per cent of income accrues to households whose income exceeds Rs. 1,500. Government of India,
Report of the Commission on the Distribution of Income and
Levels of Living (New Delhi: Planning Commission, 1964), Table
3.8, p. 71. Taking the average rate of annuity deposit as 4
per cent of income, total productivity works out to Rs. 4,000
million.

44. Keynes, op. cit., p. 43.

45. Singh, op. cit., p. 390.

46. Government of India, India 1966 (Delhi: Manager of
Publications, 1967), p. 212.

47. F. D. Holzman, Soviet Taxation (Cambridge: Harvard
University Press, 1955), pp. 200-208. "The bonds are usually
paid for by deductions from wages, as is the case with the income tax; such a payment procedure makes it much simpler to
exert compulsion upon recalcitrant workers" (p. 200).

48. The technique of bond sales might also be applied to
the problem of mobilizing gold hoards. Although there are many
difficulties here, in particular, the fact that gold confers a
considerable psychic income in India, and the recent 36.5 per
cent overnight increase in the domestic price of gold consequent on devaluation, it might be feasible to declare all private holdings of gold illegal and to introduce government purchases by means of bonds of existing gold stocks over a period
of time at a price lower than the market rate at the commencement of the scheme (the free market in gold would, of course,
have to be abolished) but higher than the international parity

price. This period of government purchase might be extended over five years with premium prices to early submissions.

49. I. M. D. Little, "Tax Policy and the Third Plan," in P. N. Rosenstein, ed., Pricing and Fiscal Policies, Studies in the Economic Development of India (London: George Allen and Unwin, 1964), pp. 30-76.

50. India 1966, op. cit., p. 384.

51. Singh, op. cit., p. 389.

52. Ibid, pp. 391-92.

53. M. I. T. Center for International Studies, The Non-Monetized Sector of Rural India (Cambridge: M. I. T. Press, 1956); "Thirty-nine per cent of consumption of all products was transacted on a non-monetary basis" (p. 5); TEC, op. cit., Vol. I, pp. 65-66, estimates that 37 per cent of total consumer expenditure should be represented by imputed value; 45 per cent of rural consumption was held to be of a non-monetary variety.

54. A. R. Prest and I. G. Stewart, The National Income of Nigeria, 1950-51 (London: H.M.S.O., 1953), pp. 12-15.

55. In the U.K. the law includes in the concept of income a benefit having money's worth even though it is only received in kind. Benefits in kind are listed as convertible (if it may be turned to money) or inconvertible (may only be enjoyed by the recipient). Subject to the special legislation of 1948-- aimed largely at company directors and highly paid employees-- inconvertible benefits are not taxable. The major reason for the failure to tax so called inconvertible benefits is the absence of any equitable universal method of evaluation; each case would therefore have to be treated on an ad hoc basis. Government of the United Kingdom, Report of the Royal Commission on the Taxation of Profits and Income, First Report, Cmd. 9474 (London: H.M.S.O., 1955), Chapter 8.

56. Harvard University Law School, International Tax Program, Taxation in India, World Tax Series (Boston: Little, Brown and Co., 1960), pp. 223-24.

57. A. R. Prest, Public Finance in Underdeveloped Countries (London: Weidenfeld and Nicolson, 1962), p. 130.

58. H. P. Wald, Taxation of Agricultural Land in Underdeveloped Economies (Cambridge: Harvard University Law School, 1959), p. 62.

59. H. P. Wald, "The Recent Experience of the Republic of Korea with Tax Collections in Kind," H. P. Wald and J. N. Froomkin, eds., Agricultural Taxation and Economic Development (Cambridge: Harvard University Law School, 1959), p. 429.

60. Ibid.

61. Wald, Taxation of Agricultural Land, op. cit., p. 64.

62. TEC, op. cit., Vol. I, p. 73.

63. Holzman, op. cit., pp. 82-86 and pp. 159-76.

64. W. Heller, "The Adaptation of Income Taxation to Agriculture in Underdeveloped Economies," in Agricultural Taxation and Economic Development, op. cit., p. 280.

65. J. Levin, "A Theory of Export Economies," unpublished doctoral dissertation, quoted in Wald, Agricultural Taxation and Economic Development, op. cit., p. 154.

66. Wald, "The Recent Experience of the Republic of Korea," op. cit., p. 428.

67. Government of Canada, Canada Year Book 1963-64 (Ottawa: Dominion Bureau of Statistics, 1964), p. 119; see also pp. 878-79.

68. Ibid.

69. Government of India, India 1965 (Delhi: Manager of Publications, 1966), p. 220.

70. Ibid.

71. Wald, Taxation of Agricultural Land in Underdeveloped Economies, op. cit., p. 155; also, G. S. Sahota, Indian Tax Structure and Economic Development (Bombay: Asia Publishing House, 1961), p. 54.

72. Wald, "The Recent Experience of the Republic of Korea," op. cit., p. 424.

73. Panchayats are local government bodies with administrative, civil and executive functions at the village level. There are over 200,000 Village Panchayats in India, covering approximately 99 per cent of the entire rural population. (India 1966, op. cit., p. 54.)

74. Enke, op. cit., p. 260.

75. Report of the Congress Village, Panchayat Committee (New Delhi: All-Indian Congress Committee, 1954), pp. 48-56.

76. "Financing Panchayats," Economic Weekly (February 7, 1963).

77. V. P. Gandhi, Tax Burden on Indian Agriculture, Harvard University Law School, International Tax Program (Cambridge: Harvard Law School, 1966), pp. 220-22.

78. Government of India, Fourth Five Year Plan--A Draft Outline (New Delhi: Planning Commission, 1966), p. 110.

79. Gandhi, op. cit., p. 221.

80. India 1966, op. cit., p. 185.

81. Ibid., p. 184.

82. Government of India, Third Five Year Plan--Mid-Term Appraisal (New Delhi: Planning Commission, 1963), p. 87.

83. The Zila Parishads are responsible for the implementation of the Community Development program in the Districts. They consist of elected representatives of the people.

84. The Panchayat Samitis are composed of the presidents of the local Village Panchayats and a few co-opted members.

85. The details of the Village, Block and District pattern of administration may be found in two essays in R. Braibanti and J. Spengler, eds., Administration and Economic Development in India (Durham, N.C.: Duke University Press, 1963); H. Tinker, "The Village in the Framework of Development," pp. 94-133; R. L. Park, "Administrative Co-ordination and Economic Development in the Districts of India," pp. 134-51.

86. Third Five Year Plan--Mid-Term Appraisal, op. cit., p. 85.

87. India 1966, loc. cit.

88. Gandhi, op. cit., p. 222.

9 CORPORATION INCOME TAXATION

DESCRIPTION

The Conception of the Corporation as a Separate Entity for Tax Purposes

The taxation of corporate income began in India with the first Income Tax Act of 1860.[1] Judicial decisions in India have always held that taxes paid by a corporation are paid by it as a separate entity and not simply on behalf of the share-holders.[2] The TEC also argued at some length the distinct economic as well as legal significance of corporations, and defended the suitability of corporations as separate subjects of taxation.[3]

Until the Budget of 1960-61, corporations were separately taxed only in a partial sense. A corporation was considered to pay income tax on behalf of its shareholders on dividends declared out of income on which the corporation itself had paid Indian income tax; each shareholder received a credit against his own income tax liability for the amount of tax paid on his behalf by the corporation. No credit on shareholder individual tax liability was granted for income tax paid on undistributed profits, nor was credit granted for supertax paid by a corporation on total profits. As of 1960-61 a corporation in India is regarded as a completely separate entity for purposes of taxation and no refund is allowed against individual tax liability for income tax and supertax paid by the corporation. The only link remaining between the corporation and personal income tax is the requirement on a corporation to act as a withholding agent for individual income tax due on dividend and interest income paid by that corporation.[4]

Classification of Corporations for Tax Purposes

The major legal distinction among corporations in India is into private and public limited corporations. Table 1 indicates the number and paid-up capital of public and private corporations in the corporate sector from 1950-65. The decline in numbers of public corporations reflects only the removal of moribund corporations from the corporation register. It is

TABLE 1

NUMBER AND PAID-UP CAPITAL OF PUBLIC AND PRIVATE CORPORATIONS IN INDIA, 1950-65

Year ending March 31	Public Corporations		Private Corporations	
	Number	Paid-up Capital Rs. Million	Number	Paid-up Capital Rs. Million
1950-51	12,568	5,665	15,964	2,089
1951-52	12,413	6,068	16,810	2,489
1952-53	12,055	6,288	17,257	2,688
1953-54	10,248	6,313	19,280	3,136
1954-55	10,056	6,613	19,569	3,083
1955-56	9,575	6,904	20,299	3,338
1956-57	8,810	7,146	20,547	3,630
1957-58	8,296	7,736	19,984	5,327
1958-59	7,760	7,841	19,719	7,257
1959-60	7,306	8,116	19,615	7,815
1960-61	6,745	8,761	19,363	8,485
1961-62	6,702	9,454	19,447	8,695
1962-63	5,994	10,869	19,530	10,983
1963-64	5,968	11,477	20,427	13,344
1964-65	5,978	12,860	20,675	13,502

Sources: Data for period 1950-51 - 1960-61 from S. Ambirajan, Taxation of Corporate Income in India (New York: Asia Publishing House, 1964), p. 86; subsequent data from, Government of India, India 1966 (Delhi: Manager of Publications, 1967), p. 209.

significant for tax policy, which taxes private corporations more rigorously, that private corporations, which are generally small and which have since 1950 always outnumbered public corporations, have now a higher total of paid-up capital than public corporations.

The classification of corporations for tax purposes is slightly more complex than the simple division into public and private. There are four major categories; first, corporations in which "the public are substantially interested," the total income of which does not exceed Rs. 50,000; second, corporations in which "the public are substantially interested," the total income of which exceeds Rs. 50,000; third, corporations in which "the public are not substantially interested"; fourth, foreign corporations, formally defined as corporations "which have not made prescribed arrangements for the declaration and payments of dividends within India."[5] Life insurance business is dealt with separately for income tax purposes, and may be regarded as a fifth category.

To be deemed a corporation in which "the public are substantially interested" a corporation must not be a private corporation, and at least 50 per cent of the corporation's equity share capital, carrying not less than 50 per cent of the voting power, must have been held unconditionally by the public throughout the previous year; equally, these shares must have been dealt with in recognized Indian stock exchanges, and at any time in the previous year not less than six persons should have controlled more than 50 per cent of the equity capital. The 1956-66 Budget broadened the definition to include subsidiaries (where at least 51 per cent of equity capital is owned by the parent corporation) of corporations defined in the above manner.[6] The definition of a corporation in which the public are not substantially interested was liberalized for certain categories of corporation in the 1966-67 Budget. For corporations mainly engaged in shipbuilding or in priority manufacturing activities (listed in Schedule 5 of the Income Tax Act) the test of substantial public interest is satisfied if 40 per cent of the equity--instead of the previous 50 per cent--is held by the government, public corporations, or members of the public. Equally, up to 60 per cent of the voting shares--as against not more than 50 per cent--may now be held by six or more persons.[7]

All private corporations are subsumed in the third category as corporations in which the public are not substantially interested.

Taxable Income

Total income of the corporation, as for individuals, for income tax purposes is the sum of all income under six

categories--salaries, interest on securities, income from property, profits and gains of business, profession or vocation,
capital gains, and income from other sources (a residual category including dividends, income from miscellaneous services,
royalties, etc.),[8] exclusive of exempt receipts which are not
included in total income (principally, allowances granted to
employees in connection with duties of employment and interest
on loans of various kinds),[9] and reduced by the deduction of
certain expenditures incurred in earning total income.   Into
this latter category fall losses under any of the six income
categories, which may be set off against income in any other
category which is taxable in the same year,[10] a comprehensive
list of specific current expenses, with a catch-all clause
covering all current expenses "laid out wholly and exclusively
for the purpose of the business,"[11] expenditures for life insurance, annuities and employee benefits, certain charitable
donations, and, finally, capital expenditures for business purposes.

     The category of capital expenditures includes depreciation
allowances and a development rebate. Depreciation is granted
for building, machinery, plant, or furniture owned by the taxpayer and used in his business, and for machinery, plant or
furniture which the taxpayer leases in return for "income from
other sources."[12] The two types of depreciation currently
allowed are normal depreciation, based on the useful life of
the asset, and extra-shift depreciation for the double-shift
working of machinery or plant, based on prescribed percentages
of the normal depreciation allowance.[13] Depreciation must be
calculated on the declining balance method--in which the prescribed percentage is applied to depreciated original cost,
thus concentrating the allowance in the early years--except in
the case of ocean-going ships where straight line depreciation,
in which an equal absolute amount of original cost is written
off each year, must be employed. The aggregate of depreciation
allowances is in all cases limited to the actual original purchase price of the asset to the taxpayer. A salient feature of
the depreciation provisions is that if there is not sufficient
income in any year to absorb the depreciation charges, the
deficiency can be carried forward indefinitely and set off
against profits of subsequent years. Prescribed depreciation
rates vary from 2.5 per cent to 40 per cent; the most common
rates for items of industrial machinery vary from 9-12 per
cent.

     A development rebate of a portion of the cost of new plant
and machinery was first provided in the Finance Bill 1955 as a
deduction from taxable income in the year of acquisition or installation of the asset. The development rebate was conceived
of as a bonus or special allowance of 25 per cent of the cost
of new plant or machinery over and above the normal recoupment

of their cost through depreciation allowances. The effect of the development rebate together with the depreciation allowances is to permit accelerated amortization of the cost of many new assets. Provision is made for the carry-forward for up to eight years of that portion of the development rebate which cannot be fully set off against net operating income for the year in which the development rebate is allowed.

The rate of development rebate is no longer uniform but is graduated according to a scale of priorities. Rates prevailing as of March 31, 1965, are 40 per cent of the cost of new ships and 35 per cent of the cost of new coal mining machinery, 25 per cent in respect of machinery or plant used for the business of shipbuilding or for the production of any one or more of the articles of priority industries listed in the new Fifth Schedule of the Income Tax Act, and 15 per cent in respect of plant and machinery in all other industries.[14]

Since the Finance Bill of 1958 the grant of a development rebate is constrained by two conditions--both slightly modified in subsequent Budgets; an amount equal to 75 per cent of the development rebate must be placed in a reserve account and utilized over an eight-year period only for the acquisition of assets for the undertaking or for investment in the undertaking; equally, the asset subject to development rebate may not be sold or transferred during the eight-year period.[15] The 1966-67 Budget reduced the required reserve percentage in the case of ship-owners from 75 per cent to 50 per cent.[16]

The 1967-68 Budget modified development rebate provisions in respect of expenditure on scientific research. New machinery or plant acquired and installed by an assessee after March 31, 1967, for the purpose of scientific research related to his business is eligible for development rebate at the priority rate of 35 per cent. Further, the amount of capital expenditure incurred by an assessee after March 31, 1967, may be completely written off for tax purposes in the year of its installation.[17]

The 1965-66 Budget introduced an additional specific development allowance for the tea plantation industry of 40 per cent of the cost of planting tea bushes in a new area, and 20 per cent of the cost of replanting tea bushes in an area already under cultivation.[18] These allowances were raised to 50 per cent and 30 per cent, respectively, in the 1966-67 Budget.[19]

Tax Rates, Rebates and Exemptions

A composite rate of income tax of 80 per cent was prescribed in the 1965-66 Budget, consequent on the integration of supertax with income tax (made up of pre-merger income tax at 25 per cent and supertax at 55 per cent) on income other than

capital gains.[20] This initial basic rate was, however, qualified by a wide series of exemptions and rebates.

The tax rate applicable to a particular corporation was
basically arrived at by deducting its allowable percentage rebate from the basic rate of 80 per cent. This somewhat complex
method of computation was discontinued in the 1966-67 Budget,
which stated directly the rate of income tax applicable to each
category of corporation. The basic rates specified in the 1966-
67 Budget were not altered in the 1967-68 Budget, and are as
set out below:

In the case of the Life Insurance Corporation
  of India,   52.5 per cent

1. In the case of a domestic corporation:

    (a) Where the corporation is one in which the public are
         substantially interested:

         i.   Where income does not
              exceed Rs. 50,000,   45   per cent

         ii. Where income exceeds Rs. 50,000,   55   per cent

    (b) Where the corporation is one in which the public are
         substantially interested:

         i.   In the case of an industrial corporation:[21]

              On income up to Rs. 1 million,   55   per cent
              On the balance of income,   60   per cent

         ii. In all other cases,   65   per cent

The rate applicable to category (a) ii. is subject to the
proviso that the income tax payable shall not exceed the aggregate of the income tax which would have been payable had the
income of the corporation been Rs. 50,000, and 80 per cent of
the amount by which its income exceeds Rs. 50,000.

2. In the case of a corporation other than a domestic
    corporation:

    (a) On as much of the income as consists of

         i.   royalties received from an Indian
              concern in pursuance of an agreement
              made by it with the Indian concern
              after March 31, 1961, or

ii. fees for rendering technical
     services received from an Indian
     concern in pursuance of an agree-
     ment made by it with the Indian
     concern after February 29, 1964,

     and where such agreement has in
     either case been approved by the
     Union government   50 per cent

(b) On the balance of income,   70 per cent.[22]

The rates specified are, in general, 5 per cent higher
than the effective rates in operation before the consolidation
of the rate structure in the 1966-67 Budget.

Until the 1966-67 Budget, the taxation of inter-corporate
dividends was also geared to the rebate system. As of 1966-
67, a deduction system is employed.   In calculating taxable
income a corporation may deduct the following percentages of
inter-corporate dividends received:

(a) 80 per cent of dividends received by a foreign
     corporation from an Indian corporation in which
     the public are not substantially interested and
     which is engaged in a Fifth Schedule priority
     activity,

(b) 60 per cent of dividends received by a foreign
     corporation from an Indian corporation other
     than the type referred to in (a) above, and
     dividends received by an Indian corporation
     from any other Indian corporation.[23]

Under pre-1966-67 provisions, certain corporations were
entitled to a special rebate of 10 per cent of tax payable in
respect of profits derived from the manufacture or production
of specified priority articles.   This rebate system has also
been abandoned, and has been replaced by the provision that
domestic corporations in which the public are substantially
interested, and whose income exceeds Rs. 50,000, are entitled
to a deduction, in the computation of taxable income, of an
amount equal to 8 per cent of their profits from the business
of generation or distribution of electricity or any other form
of power, or of construction, manufacture or production or
specified articles relating to priority industries.[24]

Until devaluation, all domestic corporations were eligible
for a 10 per cent rebate of income tax payable on profits
derived from export of goods and merchandise from India, and
an income tax rebate of 2 per cent of the value of certain

specified goods exported by a manufacturer or sold by him to
any other person in India and exported by the latter directly.[25]
This provision was withdrawn following devaluation. Two new
exemptions were introduced in the 1965-66 Budget and remain in
the Income Tax Act. First, a scheme was introduced for the
granting of Tax Credit Certificates to any corporation engaged
in the manufacture or production of any of the articles specified in the First Schedule of the Industries (Development and
Regulation) Act, 1951, for a period of five years from 1966-67.
The amount of the tax credit certificate will be calculated at
20 per cent of the additional corporation income tax including
surtax paid by any manufacturing corporation during the base
year, subject to a limit of 10 per cent of the over-all tax for
the year concerned. Equally, tax credit certificates are to be
provided to manufacturers who produce goods during any one or
more of the five financial years from 1965-66 in excess of
their production during the base year, at an amount not exceeding 25 per cent of the difference between Union excise duty
paid on these goods for the relevant year and the base year.[26]

In addition to the development rebate and depreciation
provisions, special provision is made in the Income Tax Act for
new industrial undertakings and hotels. Prior to the 1967-68
Budget, such concerns were entitled to a five-year "tax holiday,"
covering as much of their profits as did not exceed 6 per cent
of the capital employed in the undertaking. The 1967-68 Budget
provided that where any unused portion of the tax holiday exist-
ed at the end of the five-year period, an undertaking might
carry forward such unused portion for a further three years.[27]

A group of further taxes completes the tax coverage of
corporations. First, corporations in which the public are substantially interested are subject to a penalty tax on distributed profits, amounting to 7.5 per cent of that part of equity
dividends distributed or declared during the previous year
which exceed 10 per cent of the paid-up equity capital of the
undertaking. Prior to 1966-67, the provision relating to paid-
up capital applied only to corporations which had declared
their first dividend in the previous five years.[28]

Corporations in which the public are not substantially interested are, under Section 104 of the Income Tax Act, subject
to compulsory minimum distribution of profits, on penalty of a
penal tax on all undistributed profits. This provision is intended to offset the accumulation of private fortunes through
the loophole of incorporation. The specified statutory percentage of profits to be distributed is 60 per cent, except
where accumulated profits and reserves exceed the amount of
paid-up capital plus loan capital, or the value of fixed assets,
whichever is higher, in which case the rate is 90 per cent.
The penal tax rate is 50 per cent in the case of investment

corporations, 37 per cent in the case of trading corporations, and 25 per cent in the case of all other corporations. The 25 per cent rate was introduced in the 1965-66 Budget, in an attempt to promote reinvestment of profits; further, it was provided that the 90 per cent distribution requirement would not arise in the case of corporations other than trading and investment corporations until accumulated reserves exceeded twice the amount of paid-up capital, or the value of fixed assets, whichever was higher.[29] Manufacturing corporations are completely exempt from the requirements of Section 104.

All corporations are subject to tax on income in the form of realized capital gains. Short-term gains are included in other income and taxed at the rate of income tax applicable to such income. Long-term capital gains are taxed at 40 per cent on gains from land and buildings and 30 per cent on other gains. Capital gains realized by a domestic corporation in which the public are substantially interested, as a result of the transfer of operations to new areas are subject to tax relief, the proportion of capital gains tax relief being determined by the ratio of the cost of transfer of machinery, plant, etc., to new areas, to the total amount of capital gains, subject to a maximum of the amount of tax on capital gains. Equally the transfer of capital assets by a subsidiary corporation to its parent Indian corporation holding the entire share capital of the subsidiary, is not regarded as a transfer for purposes of capital gains taxation.[30]

Finally, all corporations are subject to surtax, introduced in 1964, which applies when the profits of corporations from all sources, reduced by income tax payable on them, exceed 10 per cent of the capital base or Rs. 200,000, whichever is higher. Surtax is levied at a uniform rate of 35 per cent of the entire corporation profits which exceed the specified level.[31] The capital base in this case includes paid-up capital, reserves, debentures and loans of all kind. In the case of a public corporation whose paid-up capital is not less than 25 per cent of the amount of its capital (including reserves) as ascertained for the purpose of surtax, the aggregate amount of liability of the corporation to income tax and surtax is limited to 70 per cent of total income for the relevant year.[32]

Until the 1966-67 Budget, domestic corporations of all kinds were subject to a further tax measure--a tax at the rate of 12.5 per cent of the face value of bonus shares issued to shareholders. This measure was discontinued in the 1966-67 provisions.[33]

Finally, until the 1967-68 Budget, the income tax structure provided a disincentive to amalgamation of corporations by taxing profits and capital gains considered to accrue as a

result of amalgamation. It was provided in the 1967-68 Budget
that amalgamation would not attract tax on such profits or
capital gains.[34]

It is proposed to appraise the present corporate tax system in India under six heads: revenue productivity; incidence;
equity; stabilization; effects on private sector; and, finally,
the question of integration of corporate with personal income
taxation.

APPRAISAL

Revenue Productivity

The possibility of resource mobilization through corporation income taxation is constrained in most underdeveloped
countries by the relatively small part of national income which
accrues to the corporate sector. Corporation income in India
averaged 2 per cent of national income over 1950-59 as against
13 per cent and 11 per cent in the U.K. and the U.S.A., respectively.[35]

Nevertheless, corporation income taxation has become of
crucial importance to the Union government--which does not have
to share such revenue with State governments--as the major
direct tax source. Table 2 traces corporation income tax revenue and total Union taxes on income and expenditure including
States' share of personal income tax receipts, and the former
as a percentage of the latter, from 1950-51 to 1965-66. From
1958-59 to 1962-63 corporation income tax revenue each year increased absolutely and relatively as a part of total income tax
revenue. The level of corporate tax revenue in 1965-66 is almost eight times that collected in 1950-51; the relative position of corporate tax revenue in total Union collections of
income tax has changed from slightly below one fifth to more
than one half.

Corporation income tax revenue also emerges as a relatively elastic revenue source. It will be recalled that the progressive personal income tax, which might have been expected
to be relatively elastic, was on the contrary relatively inelastic. The corporation tax on the other hand, turns out to
be a highly elastic revenue source. Table 3 sets out the
elasticity of corporation income tax revenue--defined as the
annual growth rate of that portion of revenue accruing other
than from tax changes--from 1955-56 to 1970-71, including in
the analysis the ex-ante estimates by the Planning Commission
of corporation tax revenue over the Fourth Plan.

TABLE 2

CORPORATION INCOME TAX REVENUE, 1950-66

Rs. million

Year	(1) Corporation Tax Receipts	(2) Union Income Tax Receipts including Corporation Tax Receipts	(3) (1) as per cent of (2)
1950-51 (Actuals)	404.9	2,119.8	19
1951-52 "	414.1	1,876.0	22
1952-53 "	438.0	1,852.0	25
1953-54 "	415.4	1,643.0	26
1954-55 "	373.3	1,595.9	23
1955-56 "	370.4	1,684.0	22
1956-57 "	511.8	2,029.2	25
1957-58 "	561.3	2,198.3	25
1958-59 "	543.3	2,263.4	24
1959-60 "	1,065.6	2,562.0	42
1960-61 "	1,110.5	2,793.3	40
1961-62 "	1,564.6	3,226.9	49
1962-63 "	2,215.0	4,076.6	54
1963-64 "	2,745.9	5,331.9	52
1964-65 "	3,140.5	5,806.0	54
1965-66 "	3,048.4	5,766.4	53

Source: Reserve Bank of India, Report on Currency and Finance, 1965-66 (Bombay: Reserve Bank of India, 1966).

TABLE 3

ELASTICITY OF CORPORATION TAX REVENUE, 1955-56 - 1970-71

1	2	3	4	5	6
Year	Actual Revenue (Rs.million)	Increase over previous year (Rs.million)	Anticipated increase due to Budget changes (Rs.million)	Increase due to built-in elasticity (3 minus 4)	Elasticity coefficient (5 as per cent of 2)
1955-56	370.4	141.4	0	141.4	38.17
1956-57	511.8	49.5	64.0	-14.5	-2.83
1957-58	561.3	-18.0	42.5	-60.5	-10.77
1958-59	543.3	522.3	0	522.3	96.14
1959-60	1,065.6	44.9	0	44.9	4.21
1960-61	1,110.5	454.1	0	454.1	40.88
1961-62	1,564.6	650.4	10.0	640.4	40.93
1962-63	2,215.0	530.9	20.0	510.9	23.07
1963-64	2,745.9	394.6	60.0	334.6	12.18
1964-65	3,140.5	-92.1	16.7	-108.8	-3.55
1965-66	3,048.4	351.6	-	351.6	11.53
(1966-67	3,400.0	270.0	-	270.0	7.94
Planning (1967-68	3,670.0	370.0	-	370.0	10.08
Commission (1968-69	4,040.0	440.0	-	440.0	10.88
Forecasts (1969-70	4,444.0	436.0	-	436.0	9.81
(1970-71	4,880.0				

Source: Reserve Bank of India, Reports on Currency and Finance for 1961-62 and 1965-66 (Bombay: Reserve Bank of India, 1962 and 1966).

284

From 1955-56 to 1965-66, the average elasticity of corporation tax revenue was 23.8. For the Fourth Plan period, the estimated elasticity averages 10.0.

Turning to the income-elasticity of corporation tax revenue, the coefficient relating built-in growth of tax revenue to growth of national income over 1955-56 to 1960-61 comes to 2.8. For the period 1960-61 to 1964-65, the coefficient is 2.7. These latter figures are somewhat higher than Sahota's estimate of income elasticity over 1950 to 1958 as 1.25.[36]

In a developing economy where corporate income is likely to become of greater relative significance in national income the importance of corporation income tax as a revenue source may be expected to increase substantially in absolute terms and, particularly in the Indian case where administrative problems have retarded the development of the personal income tax, probably in relative terms as part of direct tax revenue. Corporation taxation in India fulfills a vital role in the objective of mobilizing resources for public developmental spending. This defense is, of course, simply to link the "cynical rule of fiscal productivity . . . with the opportunistic maxim of administrative convenience,"[37] but nonetheless would present a formidable argument against modification of the tax structure which would drastically curtail corporation income tax revenue productivity. The development of an alternative revenue source of equivalent productivity would appear difficult; the only conceivable alternative presumably lies in indirect taxation which, it will be argued, does not offer the same possibilities as a means to the attainment of two other tax goals, equity and stabilization.

With regard to the possible increase of revenue productivity, it would be difficult to defend increased tax rates. Present rates in India, including allowances, exemptions and rebates of one kind or another are as high as those in developed countries,[38] and considerations of private sector growth would appear to preclude substantial general rate increases; the question might indeed be posed whether present rates are excessive. Two brief comments might, however, be apposite, the first on the complexity of the tax structure, the second on the question of deductible expenses.

On examining the layer structure of corporate taxation it is difficult to decide whether one is dealing with a highly sophisticated, sensitive tax structure or simply a nightmare of complexity which opens a multitude of avenues of evasion and avoidance for the initiated, and thus conflicts with horizontal equity as well as revenue productivity. Mr. Kaldor tends to the latter view:

> The company taxation provisions of India . . .
> are apt to strike a detached observer as a per-
> fect maze of unnecessary complications, the
> accretion of years of futile endeavour to recon-
> cile fundamentally contradictory objectives.[39]

Since Mr. Kaldor wrote, the situation has been improved by
the abandonment, in 1960, of refundability of the tax on distributed profits, the 1965 integration of income tax and supertax, and the removal of the rebate system in the 1966-67 Budget.
But the system remains incredibly complex, and the addition in
almost every Budget of new regulations, rates, exemptions, depreciation provisions, etc., has resulted in a corporation tax
system whose effects are almost impossible to establish with
any degree of certainty, and whose usefulness, therefore, as a
means to the attainment of the three major tax objectives is
difficult to ascertain.

The aggregation of five or six different taxes, super-
imposed on some dozen categories and sub-categories of corporation, the whole further complicated by a comprehensive and
often overlapping series of allowances, exemptions and incentives, would bear thorough and comprehensive re-appraisal, rationalization and simplification.

With regard to deductible expenses there would appear
little justification for the catch-all "wholly and exclusively
for the purpose of the business" clause[40] which, in effect,
provides an invitation to, at best, inflation and wastage in
business expenses, and, at worst, manipulation and deception in
defining taxable profits. Ad hoc adjustments were introduced
in the 1962, 1963 and 1964 Budgets limiting advertising, entertainment, travelling expenditure,[41] etc., but the general rule
persists and the complex agglomeration of specific expense
rules, modified in successive Budgets, has created a situation
of confusion in which manipulation can flourish. There is much
to be said for a rigorously defined general rule on purely
"functional" expenses which are "necessarily" as well as "wholly
and exclusively" incurred for business purposes. Specific exceptions should, of course, always be possible in a flexible
tax structure, but these should be sparingly and rigorously
defined in the framework of a simple functional definition of
deductible expenses.

Incidence

The contribution of a corporate income tax to equity and
stabilization, and the effects of such a tax on the private sector, depend on the incidence of the tax. Incidence may conven-
iently be divided into initial or short-run incidence and ultimate or long-run incidence--defining the long run as the period

in which adjustments in size of plant, location, etc., are
possible.

A tax on corporation income may be considered not to be
shifted if it is incident in the short run on either dividends
or undistributed profits. Alternatively the tax may be shifted
backwards to workers in form of lower wages or forward to consumers in the form of higher prices.

The traditional argument[42] has been that a tax on profits
cannot be shifted in the short run, in that under both competi-
tive and monopolistic conditions, neither marginal cost nor
marginal revenue are affected by the tax and, in consequence,
neither price nor output adjustments would be advantageous.

It would certainly seem likely that with wage determination through unions and government regulation there would be
little short-run backward shifting, though Musgrave points out
the possibility of union bargaining agreements which take into
account corporation after-tax "ability to pay."[43] With regard
to short-run price increases, it has been argued that in the
common oligopolistic market structure where group profits are
not maximized in a before-tax situation, the tax may be treated
as an expense item and be passed forward, first by the price
leaders and then by the other firms.[44]

The various mark-up and full cost pricing practices encourage the same type of adjustment so long as the firms treat
the tax as an element to be considered in the determination of
full-cost or mark-up percentage. There are many obstacles in
the way of complete shifting, such as the fact that the amount
of income tax per dollar of selling price of a product may vary
widely among firms, but it would seem that under the most prevalent type of competition and pricing partial short-run forward
tax shifting is almost inevitable. The degree of forward
shifting in any corporation is likely to be greater the more
inelastic is demand for the product of that corporation. Considerations such as those suggested above have led a recent
theoretical study to conclude that even in the short run the
corporation income tax is in large measure shifted forward to
consumers in the form of higher prices.[45]

The traditional argument on incidence has in some cases
continued that to the extent that the tax is confined to pure
profit it will exercise no influence on investment policies of
new or old firms. This long-run argument is difficult to de-
fend--in that corporate income taxes in practice are not confined to pure profit but also affect cost elements--and a
recent firm defender of minimal short-run shifting, R. Goode,
has conceded that, through investment adjustments, corporate
taxation in the long run is likely to increase the prices of

commodities in the production of which the corporate form is advantageous.[46]

To the extent that the initial incidence of the corporation income tax is at least partially upon corporation profits, the tax will reduce the rate of return on corporate investment. The reduction in undistributed profits diminishes corporate ability to reinvest, and the diminished return on investment may affect corporate reinvestment incentives. Equally, the so-called "double" taxation of dividend income lessens the relative attractiveness of, and the ability to direct funds to, equity investment.

The extent of long-run shifting, in sum, depends on the effect which the reduction in net profits after taxes has on the supply of equity capital. If there is a net reduction in the latter then a tax which is only partially shifted or not shifted at all in the short run will tend to be shifted to a greater extent in the long run in the form of higher prices to consumers for corporate products. On this conclusion there is some unanimity.[47]

Empirical evidence on shifting is conflicting. There have been two basic approaches to the analysis of shifting--the rate-of-return approach and the factor-shares approach.

Two studies in India using the rate-of-return approach suggest on the one hand complete short-run shifting,[48] and on the other hand partial short-run shifting of about one third of the corporate tax burden.[49] Simple rate-of-return studies have tended to neglect the influence of factors other than taxation on the rate of return, and a major U.S. study--by Musgrave and Krzyzaniak--sought to isolate the effects of corporate taxation from other exogenous variables influencing the rate of return.[50] The conclusion of this study was that, in the short run, the corporate tax was fully and in some cases over-fully shifted. Studies in India[51] and West Germany[52] using the method of the U.S. study confirm the thesis of complete short-run shifting. The adequacy of the approach in the U.S. study, particularly as to its usefulness in isolating the effects of the corporate tax on the rate of return, has been questioned, and a subsequent study, using the same basic method but with the addition of two further variables, reached the entirely opposite conclusion that there was zero short-run shifting, and that the tax rested entirely on capital owners.[53]

Studies of long-run shifting using the rate-of-return approach have generally been simpler and less sophisticated than that of Musgrave and Krzyzaniak, and have equally generally concluded that there is substantial shifting of the corporate tax in the long run.[54] These studies emphasize the long-run maintenance of stability in the after-tax rate of return, despite substantial increases in the corporate income tax.

The fact that a constant after-tax rate of return will not necessarily indicate shifting if the capital:output ratio is declining--i.e., capital is becoming more productive--over the period studied, generated a new method--the factor-shares approach. The premise of this approach is that the corporate tax is only shifted if the pre-tax share of profits in income originating in the corporate sector increases over time, regardless of the rate of return.

Two pioneering studies in the U.S. using this approach both reached the general conclusion that there was little shifting of the corporate tax burden.[55]

The most recent studies have sought to combine these two approaches. Using a model based on mark-up pricing and including the productivity of capital as an input in his model, R. J. Gordon concluded that there was, on the whole, little shifting of the corporate tax burden, as determined by either the rate-of-return or the factor-shares approach.[56] On the other hand, a recent Canadian study, using both approaches, concluded that there was 70 per cent short-run shifting.[57]

It is difficult, in the face of the mass of conflicting evidence available, to go further than Slitor's conclusion that "the issue of shifting and incidence of the corporate tax remains in a highly unsettled state."[58]

Equity

The contribution of the corporation income tax to vertical equity depends entirely on the incidence of the tax. Suppose, first, that the tax is borne solely by corporation profits, and is, for the sake of simplicity, equally divided between distributed and undistributed profits. In this case the Indian tax which does not permit refundability to a dividend recipient of corporation tax paid on distributed profits will tax more severely ("double tax") dividend income which--as has been indicated in Chapters 2 and 3--tends to be highly concentrated. Equally, the diminution in corporation reserves may diminish stock appreciation, again curtailing accretions of the upper income groups.

The tax would thus appear to exercise a progressive role in the tax system, though this effect is moderated because of the interrelated effect of the progressive personal income tax; the reduction in dividends received is partially offset by diminished personal income tax liability. Equally, the tax may exercise regressive effects among stockholders of various income

levels, taking a higher proportion of the income of the lower
income group stockholders. Goode has, however, demonstrated
that the tax structure as a whole in the U.S. is more progressive with the corporation tax than without it--on the crucial
premise of zero shifting.[59]

Suppose, on the contrary, that the tax is fully shifted
forward by way of higher prices. The tax becomes in this case
essentially a sales tax, inferior in its distribution of burden
to the standard sales tax because the burden is distributed un-
evenly and unpredictably on expenditures on various commodities.
To the extent that the tax becomes incident on low-income group
purchases, its over-all incidence may be regressive.

The conflicting evidence on shifting makes any firm conclusion on the vertical equity significance of the corporation
tax very difficult. The most reasonable procedure would seem
to be to assume that 50 per cent of the tax burden is shifted
and that 50 per cent rests on capital owners. On this assumption, the contribution to vertical equity implicit in the zero
shifting and "double" taxation of dividends argument would be
seriously compromised by the fact that 50 per cent of the corporate tax burden is assumed to be distributed in the manner of
a general sales tax on corporate products.

With regard to horizontal equity, zero shifting and non-
refundability imply differing tax burdens upon persons with the
same total income; increased vertical equity is thus compromised by diminished horizontal equity. Complete shifting would,
on the other hand, eliminate the horizontal equity problem, except insofar as equal income group household expenditure patterns differed as between commodities whose price rises and
those whose price does not rise as a result of the tax. The
net effect again is a compromise between the two extremes. On
equity grounds alone the probably diminished horizontal equity
as a result of a non-refundable corporation tax seems a small
price to pay for the possible increase in vertical equity.
This conclusion would seem particularly germane to the Indian
case.

Stabilization

Should the corporation income tax exercise a net inhibitory
effect on production, the implications of such a tax for inflationary control on the supply side would be undesirable.
The possibility of such an effect will be considered in the
next section, and the remainder of this section will examine
the manner in which the corporation tax influences stabilization
policy through changes in the level of aggregate demand.

If the tax is wholly borne by corporation profits the reduction in spending will occur through reduced corporation investment and reduced private consumption and investment by
dividend recipients. If the tax is wholly shifted the effect
is less predictable. It may reduce consumption (and so increase savings) to the extent that individuals no longer buy
higher priced articles, or it may merely change the composition
or consumption. To the extent that individuals continue to
purchase the higher priced articles their disposable income for
other consumption and/or saving is reduced. The effect on
spending is clearly more direct and predictable the smaller the
degree of shifting.

The effect on aggregate (consumption plus investment)
spending of the corporation tax in India is likely to be substantial. Corporation tax revenue is now the major direct tax
revenue source and is relatively large in relation to national
income. It has also been shown that corporation tax revenue is
relatively elastic. The tax has thus the two key prerequisites
of a built-in stabilizing measure; a relatively significant tax
base in relation to national income, and considerable responsiveness in the same direction as national income movements.

A measure of built-in flexibility, $\Delta T/\Delta Y$, where ΔT is the
change in corporation tax revenue, and ΔY is the change in
national income, over the period 1955-56 to 1964-65, comes to
0.0256, indicating that the change in corporation tax revenue
over the period was 2.56 per cent of the change in national income over the same period. The change in corporate tax revenue
is taken from Table 3, and abstracts from increases in revenue
due to budgetary changes in the corporate tax structure.
Though this figure is low by comparison with built-in flexibility coefficients in other countries,[60] there is little doubt
that a reduction in the coverage or in the rate structure of
the corporate income tax in India, or the introduction of a
refundability provision, would have the effect of diminishing
the stabilizing effectiveness of the tax system.

The present tax not only has significance in built-in
flexibility, but also as a discretionary stabilizing tool. The
virtual doubling of corporation tax revenue between 1962-63 and
1965-66, in part as a consequence of increased tax rates and a
widened tax base is evidence of the discretionary effectiveness
of corporation taxation. It will be recalled that the assumption of Table 3 was that the entire increase in revenue, other
than the amount predicted in the Budget, was due to built-in
elasticity. This maximum estimate of elasticity almost certainly underestimates the actual increase in revenue due to budgetary changes.

Perhaps the only undesirable implication of the corporation tax as a stabilizing tool would be that the curtailment in
spending may be at the expense of <u>investment</u> spending to a
greater extent than with other tax measures; it remains to consider this problem.

Effects on the Private Sector

Tax Splitting

If it is assumed that the corporation tax is only partially shifted in the short run, the question then arises how that
portion of the tax borne by corporate profits as a whole will
be allocated between distributed and undistributed profits. As
indicated previously, the Indian corporation tax attempts to
influence this allocation by discriminating against distributed
profits.

Evidence on India is inconclusive. The Ambirajan study
examined the accounts of Indian companies over the period 1939-
51 and 1951-59,[61] and indicates that in the former period of
slightly falling profits (15.8 per cent of total sales in 1939,
14.2 per cent in 1951) the tax provision increased from 3.1 per
cent of total sales to 4.4 per cent over the period, whereas
retained profits plus depreciation remained virtually constant
at 6.5 per cent. The increased tax provision had been made
possible by a reduction in dividends as a percentage of sales
from 6.2 per cent in 1939 to 3.3 per cent in 1951. Examination
of the second period 1951-59 of slightly increasing profits as
a percentage of sales reveals a fairly constant tax provision
(3.0 per cent of gross sales), a levelling out of the dividend
provision at a surprisingly constant 2.5 per cent, and a less
stable provision for undistributed profits (over-all average =
1.7 per cent) which, however, shows no marked upward trend;
provision for undistributed profits plus depreciation, on the
other hand, was fairly constant around 5 per cent. Ambirajan's
conclusion is that dividends are sticky below a certain percentage of sales and that further increases in taxation without
increases in profits would be at the expense of retained earnings.

This question of a low-level dividend equilibrium has been
postulated for Britain by Walker,[62] and by A. Rubner,[63] the
latter using this argument to deny the efficacy of discriminatory taxation of distributed profits. The argument as applied
to India would be that further taxation of corporations without
compensatory increases in profits will be borne by retained
profits, and that discriminatory taxation of distributed profits will merely lead to a larger provision from net profit
being allocated to distributed profits.

Examination of evidence from 1959-63 of selected public limited corporations would neither confirm nor deny the thesis, largely because profits have continued to increase. Table 4 indicates that over the period of rising profits as a percentage of sales (6.9 per cent to 8.1 per cent), the dividend provision was 2.8 per cent, 2.7 per cent, 2.9 per cent and 2.5 per cent, retained profits were steady at 1.7 per cent for the first three years and then fell to 1.5 per cent in 1962-63, and retained profits plus depreciation rose over the period from 4.5 per cent to 5.0 per cent.

Table 5 extends the analysis for 1955-60 to 333 selected private corporations. The issue in this case is complicated by the Section 104 legislation governing compulsory dividend distribution; the evidence, however, would suggest that the dividend base, if it exists, is very flexible and that it would be very difficult to conclude that increased taxation without increased profits would necessarily, beyond a certain point, be at the expense of retained profits.

The rationale of a discriminatory profits tax in India is that tax payment from retained profits is by definition at the expense of savings in toto, whereas taxation from distributed profits is at the expense of consumption and saving according to the appropriate propensities of dividend recipients. It seems reasonable to conclude that, at least as long as the profits:sales ratio is rising as quickly as the tax provision, as has been the case in recent years, the discriminatory tax on distribution may be presumed to exercise at the margin the intended disincentive effect on dividend distribution as against additions to corporate reserves. With regard to the present distribution of a portion of total tax burden on corporate profits, it seems plausible to postulate, as does Goode, that the tax provision is allocated in the same proportion between distributed and undistributed profits.[64]

Effect on Investment

The major criticism advanced against the corporation income tax has been that such a tax will have an adverse effect upon private investment. The adverse effect may occur as a result of the curtailment of the incentive and/or ability to invest. If the tax is shifted forward the disincentive effect is indirect and probably insignificant; it is limited to the reduced consumer demand for products whose prices have risen. To the extent that the tax is borne out of corporation profits, the disincentive effect may influence the individual investor through diminished return to risk, or corporate management through diminished returns to risk-bearing and expansion.

TABLE 4

PUBLIC CORPORATION SALES, PROFITS AND TAX

Rs. million

	Sales, Profits and Tax on 1001 Selected Public Limited Corporations		Sales, Profits and Tax on 1333 Selected Public Limited Corporations	
	1959-60		1961-63	
	1959	1960	1961-62	1962-63
1. Sales	23,389.0	26,364.6	28,287.5	31,255.9
2. Tax Provision	597.2	719.8	1,002.0	1,287.1
3. Profits before tax	1,643.1	1,876.6	2,313.5	2,542.0
4. Dividends	645.4	712.1	831.9	794.4
5. Retained Profits and Depreciation Provision	1,055.9	1,294.7	1,520.9	1,588.2
6. Retained Profit	391.5	444.7	479.7	460.5
2 as per cent of 1	2.5	2.7	3.5	4.1
3 as per cent of 1	6.9	7.1	8.1	8.1
4 as per cent of 1	2.8	2.7	2.9	2.5
5 as per cent of 1	4.5	4.8	5.3	5.0
6 as per cent of 1	1.7	1.7	1.7	1.5

Sources: Reserve Bank of India Bulletin (June 1962), p. 847; Reserve Bank of India Bulletin (July 1964), p. 873.

294

TABLE 5

PRIVATE CORPORATION SALES, PROFITS AND TAX

Rs. million

Profits of 333 Selected Private Corporations 1955-60						
	1955	1956	1957	1958	1959	1960
1. Sales	2,637.1	3,167.9	3,429.4	3,533.0	3,791.5	4,493.3
2. Tax Provision	64.9	89.3	106.9	123.0	121.6	142.5
3. Profits before tax	130.8	162.4	174.4	206.8	244.9	302.0
4. Dividends	45.9	51.5	50.6	67.7	81.6	100.1
5. Retained Profits and Depreciation Provision	63.7	70.6	76.3	68.5	99.2	124.3
6. Retained Profits	20.0	21.6	16.9	16.1	41.7	59.5
2 as per cent of 1	2.4	2.8	3.1	3.5	3.2	3.2
3 as per cent of 1	5.0	5.1	5.1	5.9	6.5	6.5
4 as per cent of 1	1.7	1.6	1.5	1.9	2.1	2.2
5 as per cent of 1	2.4	2.2	2.2	1.9	2.6	2.7
6 as per cent of 1	0.8	0.7	0.5	0.5	1.1	1.1

Source: Reserve Bank of India Bulletin (December 1962), p. 1920.

With regard to individual willingness to invest in equity stock the disincentive effect of the double taxation of dividend income is unlikely to be serious, particularly in that diminished dividend income will probably result in a lower marginal tax rate on the highest income bracket and thus a lower average effective rate on total income. The buoyancy of individual investment in corporate stock and debentures throughout the Third Plan period would seem to confirm the absence of serious effects on individual investment incentives.[65] The introduction of extended loss offset provisions for risk investment, as suggested in Chapter 3, should serve to eliminate any remaining disincentive effects on personal risk investment.

With regard to the incentives of corporate management, the return on risk investment is diminished by the proportional corporate income tax. It may again be useful to distinguish an income effect and a substitution effect. With indefinite loss offset under a proportional tax it is possible generally to eliminate the substitution effect against risk-taking,[66] leaving only the income effect which is positive in the direction of greater risk-taking. Theoretically, the higher the tax rate, the greater the positive incentive effect of a proportional tax to risk-taking. Of course, the operation of the income effect depends on the hypothesis that the marginal utility of income rises as income falls; this reasoning may not be fully applicable to corporate management. The income effect may therefore not be as great as in the case of an individual investor, but the net effect, given the elimination of the substitution effect through complete loss offset--present provisions in India only provide loss offset against other income taxable in the same year--should be, at worst, neutral, and, at best, slightly positive in the direction of risk investment.

Probably more serious is the effect of the tax on the ability to invest. A corporation income tax diminishes the funds available to corporations from both internal and external sources. The impact of the tax on retained net earnings is more direct than on external sources of funds and probably more serious, particularly as firms are in general more willing to undertake expansion with reserves than with funds obtained by borrowing or the sale of additional stock. This effect may be particularly severe on new enterprises which may have greater difficulty raising funds from outside sources. These firms may be the ones most likely to develop new products and new techniques, and the tax may thus be seen as exercising a dampening effect on economic development and as protecting existing firms against competition and so perpetuating monopoly positions.

There seems little doubt that a corporation tax on undistributed profits diminishes the percentage of national income saved more than most other taxes and may serve to harden

monopoly positions. On the other hand, the implications for
growth and competition are mitigated by several considerations.
First, the net initial diminution in private saving and investment consequent on the tax may be offset by considerations of
the effect of government expenditure of the tax revenue. In
effect, the situation appears less serious when viewed in a general rather than a partial sense. Equally, a corporation tax
does not strike the important source of internal financing represented by depreciation, depletion and amortization provisions.
These provisions in India are of a generous nature; Tables 4
and 5 indicate that provision for depreciation is a substantial
element in annual financing, usually as large as the sum of
retained and distributed profits. Finally, in addition to depreciation provisions, Indian tax law presently provides a comprehensive series of exemptions and allowances for expansion,
particularly for new enterprises, but also for expanded production by established enterprises.

The rationalization of exemption and allowance provisions
(which have tended to overlap), and the provision of extended
loss offset provisions, would help to offset any serious effects
which corporation income taxation might have on the incentive
and ability to invest in the private corporate sector. It
remains to consider depreciation provisions.

Depreciation provisions in India have been subject to criticism on the grounds that they are framed in terms of original
cost and thus are of steadily diminishing usefulness in an inflationary period, and that, accordingly, the system does not
provide adequate investment incentives. As indicated in the
first section of this chapter, the reform of the development
rebate system amounts to the introduction of a form of selective accelerated depreciation, but there is room for considerable further improvement.

The reform possibilities might take one of two forms. The
provisions for depreciation might be framed in replacement cost
terms--this is the primary argument of the private sector[67]--
or a much wider and more explicit scheme of accelerated depreciation provisions might be introduced, the latter at once
answering the problem of increasing capital costs and providing
an incentive to invest.[68]

A replacement cost depreciation system would presumably
incorporate either a common price index of some sort for all
the assets subject to depreciation provisions, or a series of
price indices for different broad categories of assets.

There are several disadvantages of a replacement cost system as against an accelerated depreciation system. First, a
replacement cost scheme confers a relatively greater benefit on

those firms earning a low rate of return on capital. The amount
of profit relieved of tax would be the same in the case of two
firms which had the same amount of capital assets subject to
depreciation, regardless of whether the total profit (and thus
in this case the rate of return) were greater in one case than
in the other.

Second, a replacement cost system would tend to favor
those firms with the oldest assets (on the assumption of a con-
tinual upward movement of prices), and there is a presumption
that these firms will not be the most dynamic or enterprising.

Third, there are considerable conceptual difficulties in
such a scheme, particularly the choice of price indices.

A scheme of accelerated depreciation, on the other hand,
has several distinct advantages. A scheme which provides for
the rapid write-off of capital assets for tax purposes, with,
say, a very large--perhaps 60 or 70 per cent--initial year
write-off, provides assistance at the most crucial time--when
the asset is being installed. The borrowing power of the firm
is correspondingly enlarged. Just as important, the provision
is greater, the greater the rate of net investment, and the
benefit now depends on the ratio of net investment to profits
rather than on the ratio of the stock of capital to profits as
in the replacement cost case.

Such a scheme will also provide an incentive to new capital formation, and will remove the discrimination against risk
investment inherent in any corporate tax system in which loss-
offset provisions are incomplete.

Accelerated depreciation provisions also constitute a
flexible fiscal tool for government. The rate of acceleration
can be increased or decreased according to the particular situation, and the introduction of such provisions to the corporate
tax structure would enlarge the role of the tax as a stabilization measure. The flexibility of accelerated depreciation provisions go beyond stabilization. In several countries, a differential rate of accelerated depreciation is employed as an
export incentive.[69]

In general, by concentrating relief on the key determinants
of investment--the liquidity of a firm and its willingness to
take risks--and by dint of its flexibility in stabilization and
as a dirigistic device, a scheme of selective accelerated depreciation would seem to be the better path of reform for Indian
depreciation provisions. The usefulness of accelerated depreciation in the U.S. has been recently confirmed.[70]

Corporation Financing Techniques

A corporation tax may not only affect the volume and pattern of investment, but may also affect the method of financing.[71] Under a corporation tax of the Indian variety, interest payments to bondholders are deductible whereas dividend payments are not. The tax, in effect, provides an incentive to bond issues as against stock flotations. Critics of the tax on this ground would then argue that increased reliance on bond issues might lift corporate fixed charges to a level which might cause financial stress and reserve depletion in a period of business slackness.

Empirical studies in the U.S. would suggest that the choice between stocks and bonds is not significantly affected by corporate taxation.[72]

Evidence on India, on the contrary, does suggest a move to debenture financing, although it is clearly difficult to isolate the corporate tax variable as a determinant of corporate investment. Table 6 indicates the structure of capital issues over the Second and Third Plans. Debenture issues amounted to just over 10 per cent of total issues between 1956 and 1960, and had risen to 20 per cent on average in the 1961-65 period. This might suggest that deductibility be extended to dividend payments, but this raises the whole issue of integration between the corporate and personal income tax, which constitutes the final section of this chapter.

Effect on Efficiency

A final possible effect of corporation income taxation might be that of lessening efficiency of operation and increasing wasteful and unnecessary expenditure. If corporations are subject to, say, a 50 per cent tax rate, the tax authorities bear one half of the cost of any unnecessary expenditure or inefficiency in operation. The tax authorities constitute, in effect, a sleeping partner in the sharing of risk. The problem may appear particularly significant if extended provisions for loss carry-over are introduced.

The net effect is difficult to forecast in that some firms may be stimulated by the tax to attain greater efficiency, in order to maintain old levels of profits after tax. Should the problem appear to be of significant dimensions it would be possible to introduce partial refunds and to depress risk-taking to the desired level; alternatively, differential treatment might be introduced for different types of risk-taking.

TABLE 6

CAPITAL ISSUES IN THE SECOND AND THIRD PLANS

Period	Total No. of Corporations	Ordinary Shares		Preference Shares		Debentures		Total	
		No. of Issues	Amount Rs.million	No. of Issues	Amount Rs.million	No. of Issues	Amount Rs.million	No. of Issues	Amount Rs.million
1956-60 (annual average)	315	260	1,353.0	90	308.0	27	193.0	377	1,851.0
1961-65 (annual average)	676	603	2,621.0	162	300.0	36	733.0	801	3,654.0

Source: "Capital Issues in the Private Section During the Third Plan," Reserve Bank of India Bulletin (June 1967), 719-39.

300

The Integration Issue

With the abolition of refundability in 1960, the Indian corporation income tax became completely separated from the personal income tax. The question of the integration of the two taxes is one to which much energy and ingenuity has been directed.[73]

Complete integration could be obtained only if the corporation is disregarded as a separate entity, all earnings of the corporation being taxed directly to the owners. In a similar manner to the treatment of registered partnerships in India, dividends to shareholders would be taxed as regular income to the shareholders, and undistributed profits allocated to individual shareholders and taxed to them, even though not currently received by them.

This ideal method presents some practical difficulties in the case of large corporations, as a result of the difficulty of allocating undistributed earnings and the fact that the individual shareholder has no influence on dividend policy and might be subjected to tax hardship (and disincentives) in cases where corporations retained large proportions of their earnings. The approach might well be considered in India, however, for small firms where earnings allocation would be relatively simple.[74]

Discussion on integration for large corporations is largely confined to schemes of partial integration designed to eliminate double taxation--at both the corporate and individual level--of dividend income. There are two basic approaches to this problem. The first, or dividend-received-credit scheme would allow the shareholder a credit for taxes paid by the corporation on that portion of profits paid out as dividends. There are several forms of this technique; the most sophisticated, employed presently in Britain and until 1960 in India, is the withholding principle in which the corporation acts as a withholding agent for taxes on shareholders' dividend income. The individual in turn subtracts from his total assessed tax liability that amount of tax paid by the corporation on his dividend income. This approach may be defended on grounds of horizontal equity and in terms of the increased supply of equity funds which might then become available. On the other hand, it does not affect the tax burden on the corporation, and it would be indefensible for that portion of corporation tax attributed to dividends but, in fact, shifted to workers or consumers. In the latter case relief would be given for double taxation which had not occurred.

A more satisfactory approach is the undistributed profits or dividend-paid-credit technique, in which corporations are

permitted to subtract amounts paid out as dividends--in the
same fashion as bond interest--in determining taxable income.
Dividend income to individuals would thus be treated as other
income, and the corporation tax would be confined to undistributed profits. Since distributed profits are not taxed at
the corporate level, the chances of shifting of the tax on distributed profits, and thus of an unwarranted bonus to shareholders when shifting occurs, would be eliminated. The incentive to debt financing would also be eliminated. This approach
combines the advantages of other partial integration approaches
on grounds of horizontal equity--through the elimination of
double taxation--with incentives to increased supply of equity
funds, without the disadvantages of the dividend-received-credit
approach. On the other hand, the reform would have several
serious disadvantages in the Indian case.

First, the revenue productivity of the corporation income
tax would be seriously curtailed. Table 4 indicates that the
larger proportion of corporation profits in India tends to be
allocated to dividends. The introduction of the dividend-paid-
credit form of integration would thus more than halve corporation tax revenue, and alternative sources of revenue would have
to be found.

Second, the progressivity of the tax depends entirely on
the double taxation of dividend income. The contribution of
the tax to vertical equity would thus be entirely eliminated by
integration.

Third, the diminished significance of corporation tax revenue as a proportion of national income and the diminished progressivity and thus, probably, income elasticity, would diminish the effectiveness of the tax as an automatic or discretionary stabilization tool.

Finally, a corporation tax on undistributed profits which
exempts (from the point of view of corporate management) distributed profits, would presumably provide an incentive, at
least at the margin, to increase dividend distributions at the
expense of retained profits. From a long-term standpoint such
a result might have adverse consequences for the rate of private
capital formation.

CONCLUSION

Analysis of corporation taxation suggests that the tax is
of considerable importance for the tax objectives of resource
mobilization, vertical equity and stabilization, and that, although the tax probably reduces funds available for private investment more than other tax sources, the variety of incentives

to new industries and expanded production, preferably extended
by provision of selective accelerated depreciation and extended
loss offset, should offset serious effects on private sector
growth. The possibility of partial integration was rejected on
grounds of revenue productivity, vertical equity and stabilization. On the other hand, it was suggested that there is a good
case for simplifying and rationalizing the present tax structure, in particular the accretion of exemptions and allowances,
and for simplifying and curtailing the present excessively
generous expenses provision.

NOTES TO CHAPTER 9

1. The historical development of the tax is traced in
S. Ambirajan, The Taxation of Corporate Income in India (New
York: Asia Publishing House, 1964), pp. 120-83. The terms
"company" and "corporation" are synonymous; for the sake of
consistency the term "corporation" will be employed throughout
this chapter.

2. Ibid., p. 127; see also Government of India, Report
of the Taxation Enquiry Commission (hereinafter TEC)(3 vols.;
New Delhi: Ministry of Finance, 1953-54), Vol. II, pp. 151-54.

3. TEC, loc. cit.

4. The process of transformation in the tax structure is
detailed in Harvard University Law School, International Tax
Program, Taxation in India, World Tax Series (Boston: Little,
Brown and Co., 1960), pp. 238-44.

5. Government of India, Finance Bill, 1967 (New Delhi:
Ministry of Finance, 1967), pp. 58-60. The Rs. 50,000 income
level, above which a concessionary tax rate is applicable, was
introduced in the 1966-67 Budget. The previous limit was
Rs. 25,000.

6. Government of India, Memorandum Explaining the Provisions in the Finance Bill, 1965 (New Delhi: Ministry of
Finance, 1965), p. 18.

7. Government of India, Memorandum Explaining the Provisions in the Finance Bill, 1966 (New Delhi: Ministry of
Finance, 1966), p. 14.

8. Government of India, Income Tax Act (revised up to
1965) (New Delhi: Ministry of Law, 1965), Chapter IV.

9. Ibid.

10. The only exception here is capital losses which may only be set off against capital gains. (Income Tax Act, op. cit., Chapter IV--the 1967-68 Budget permitted individuals but not corporations, to set off short-term capital gains against any other form of income.)

11. Income Tax Act, op. cit., Chapter IV, Section D.

12. Ibid.

13. Ibid.

14. Memorandum Explaining the Provisions in the Finance Bill, 1965, op. cit., pp. 16-17. The rates of 25 per cent and 15 per cent did not come into operation until March 31, 1967; until that date the pre-1965 standard rate of 20 per cent was continued. In the 1966-67 Budget, the list of priority industries was extended to include tea, newsprint and printing machinery.

15. Income Tax Act, op. cit., Chapter IV, Section D.

16. Memorandum Explaining the Provisions in the Finance Bill, 1966, op. cit., p. 11.

17. Government of India, Memorandum Explaining the Provisions in the Finance Bill, 1967 (New Delhi: Ministry of Finance, 1967), p. 10.

18. Memorandum Explaining the Provisions in the Finance Bill, 1965, op. cit., p. 17.

19. Memorandum Explaining the Provisions in the Finance Bill, 1966, op. cit., pp. 11-12.

20. As in the case of individuals, capital gains are divided into short-term and long-term. Tax rates will be detailed later in this chapter. All references to "income tax" will hereinafter refer to the composite tax.

21. Defined as a corporation mainly engaged in the business of generation or distribution of electricity or any other form of power, or in the construction of ships, or in the manufacture or processing of goods or in mining.

22. Finance Bill, 1967, op. cit., p. 28.

23. Memorandum Explaining the Provisions in the Finance Bill, 1967, op. cit., p. 20.

24. Ibid., p. 7; the qualifying income level was adjusted upward to Rs. 50,000 from Rs. 25,000 in the 1967-68 Budget.

25. Memorandum Explaining the Provisions in the Finance Bill, 1965, op. cit., pp. 10-11.

26. Ibid., pp. 15-16.

27. Memorandum Explaining the Provisions in the Finance Bill, 1967, op. cit., pp. 11-12.

28. Memorandum Explaining the Provisions in the Finance Bill, 1966, op. cit., p. 6.

29. Memorandum Explaining the Provisions in the Finance Bill, 1965, op. cit., p. 20.

30. Ibid., pp. 13 and 17.

31. The rate was reduced from 40 per cent to 30 per cent in the 1966-67 Budget. Government of India, Finance Bill, 1966 (New Delhi: Ministry of Finance, 1966), p. 24.

32. Government of India, Companies (Profits) Surtax Act, 1964 (New Delhi: Ministry of Law, 1964), Third Schedule.

33. Memorandum Explaining the Provisions in the Finance Bill, 1966, op. cit., p. 6.

34. Memorandum Explaining the Provisions in the Finance Bill, 1967, op. cit., pp. 14-17.

35. Ambirajan, op. cit., Appendix, p. 301. By 1964-65 corporation income tax revenue in India had fallen slightly to 1.5 per cent of national income.

36. G. S. Sahota, Indian Tax Structure and Economic Development (Bombay: Asia Publishing House, 1961), p. 15.

37. R. Goode, The Corporation Income Tax (New York: John Wiley and Sons, Inc., 1951), p. 26.

38. Ambirajan, op. cit., Appendix, p. 302.

39. N. Kaldor, Indian Tax Reform (New Delhi: Ministry of Finance, 1956), p. 85.

40. Income Tax Act, op. cit., Chapter IV, Section 39.

41. Government of India, Explanatory Memoranda on Budgets for 1962-63, 1963-64 and 1964-65 (New Delhi: Ministry of Finance, 1962, 1963 and 1964).

42. R. A. Musgrave, The Theory of Public Finance (New York: McGraw-Hill, 1959), p. 277, Note 1, lists the proponents of this argument--Edgeworth, Fisher, Cournot, Wicksell, etc.

43. Musgrave, op. cit., pp. 282-85.

44. Ibid., pp. 281-82; see also C. Shoup, "Incidence of the Corporation Income Tax: Capital Structure and Turnover Rates," National Tax Journal, I, No. 1 (March 1948), reprinted in R. A. Musgrave and C. Shoup, Readings in the Economics of Taxation (London: George Allen and Unwin, 1959), pp. 322-29.

45. C. Cosciani, The Effects of Differential Tax Treatment of Corporate and Non-Corporate Incomes (Paris: European Productivity Agency of the OEEC, February 1959).

46. Goode, op. cit., pp. 71-72.

47. Musgrave, op. cit., p. 286; J. F. Due, Government Finance (Homewood, Ill.: Irwin, 1959), p. 227; D. Bodenhorn, "The Shifting of the Corporation Income Tax in a Growing Economy," Quarterly Journal of Economics, LXX (November 1956), 563-80.

48. V. D. Lall, "Shifting of Tax by Companies," Economic and Political Weekly (May 6, 1967), 839-49.

49. Ambirajan, op. cit., pp. 224-29.

50. M. Krzyzaniak and R. Musgrave, The Shifting of the Corporate Income Tax (Baltimore: Johns Hopkins Press, 1963).

51. G. S. Laumas, "The Shifting of the Corporation Income Tax--A study with Reference to Indian Corporations," Public Finance, 21 (1966), 463-72.

52. K. W. Roskamp, "The Shifting of Taxes on Business Income: The Case of the West German Corporations," National Tax Journal, XVIII (1965), 247-57.

53. J. G. Cragg, A. C. Harberger and P. Mieszlowski, "Empirical Evidence on the Incidence of the Corporation Income Tax," Journal of Political Economy, 75 (1967), 811-21.

54. E. M. Lerner and E. S. Hendriksen, "Federal Taxes on Corporate Income and the Rate of Return in Manufacturing 1927-1952," National Tax Journal, IX (1965), 193-202; R. E. Slitor,

"The Enigma of Corporate Tax Incidence," Public Finance, XVIII (1963), 328-52.

55. M. A. Adelman, "The Corporate Income Tax in the Long Run," Journal of Political Economy, LXV (1957), 151-57.

56. C. Hall, Jr., "Direct Shifting and the Taxation of Corporate Profits in Manufacturing," American Economic Review, Papers and Proceedings (1963), 258-71.

57. R. J. Levesque, The Shifting of the Corporate Income Tax in the Short Run, Studies of the Royal Commission on Taxation (Ottawa: Queen's Printer, 1966).

58. Slitor, op. cit.

59. Goode, op. cit., pp. 73-97.

60. Musgrave, op. cit., pp. 501-17; R. Goode, The Personal Income Tax (Washington, D.C.: The Brookings Institution, 1964), pp. 259-93 and Appendix E, pp. 345-54.

61. Ambirajan, op. cit., pp. 229-40. In the subsequent summary of the Ambirajan study, the term "tax provision" is to be understood in the sense of "tax liability."

62. D. Walker, "Some Economic Aspects of the Taxation of Companies," Manchester School, XXXII (1954), 1-36.

63. A. Rubner, "The Irrelevancy of the British Differential Profits Tax," Economic Journal, LXXIV, No. 294 (June 1964), 347-59.

64. Goode, op. cit., p. 100.

65. "Capital Issues in the Private Sector During the Third Plan," Reserve Bank of India Bulletin (June 1967), 719-39.

66. Musgrave, op. cit., p. 320. The existence of a substitution effect is, of course, predicated on the assumption that the ratio of probability-weighted returns is altered by the tax. The substitution effect would not be eliminated even with complete loss offset, in such situations as the following: of two corporations, one earns nil profits in the first two years, Rs. 250,000 in each of the third and fourth years, and nil profits in the final year. The second corporation loses Rs. 250,000 in each of the first two years, earns Rs. 250,000 in each of the second and third years, and earns nil profits in the final year. Taxable income of the first corporation would then be Rs. 500,000 and that of the second would be nil.

67.   Report on Conference of Tax Executives (New Delhi: Federation of Indian Chambers of Commerce and Industry, 1966).

68.   This issue is examined at length in A. R. Prest, Public Finance in Theory and Practice (London: Weidenfeld and Nicolson, 1960), pp. 319-39.

69.   H. D. Sourie and R. K. Pandey, Export Incentives in Developed and Developing Countries (New Delhi: Indian Institute of Foreign Trade, 1967). France, Japan and Switzerland employ accelerated depreciation as an export incentive.

70.   N. B. Ture, Accelerated Depreciation in the United States, 1954-60 (New York: Columbia University Press, for the National Bureau of Economic Research, 1967).

71.   The most extensive discussion of this problem is to be found in D. T. Smith, Effects of Taxation: Corporate Financial Policy (Boston: Harvard University Graduate School of Business Administration, 1952).

72.   Smith, op. cit., pp. 285-89; G. E. Lent, "Bond Interest Deduction and the Federal Corporation Income Tax," National Tax Journal, II (June 1949), 131-41.

73.   R. Goode, op. cit., Chapter 10, and, "Alternative Approaches to the Integration of the Corporate and Individual Income Taxes," Proceedings of the National Tax Association (1947), 134-45; J. R. Petrie, The Taxation of Corporate Income in Canada (Toronto: University of Toronto Press, 1952), see p. 203, Note 2, for extensive bibliography, and discussion in Chapter 8.

74.   Complete integration has, however, been recently proposed for use in Canada. See Government of Canada, Report of the Royal Commission on Taxation (Ottawa: Queen's Printer, 1966), Vol. 4.

CHAPTER **10** INDIRECT TAXATION

THE MAJOR INDIRECT TAXES

Indirect taxes (taxes on commodities and transactions) are imposed in India by the Union government and by all of the States. The Union government levies a sales tax on inter-State sales, manufacturers' and producers' excise taxes, and import and export duties; the States levy general sales or purchase taxes, excise taxes on alcoholic beverages and drugs, entertainment taxes, electricity duties, and taxes on sales or purchases of specific commodities. It is proposed to consider only the major indirect tax measures at the Union and State levels: customs duties, Union and State excise duties, and State sales tax.

Customs Duties

The Union government levies both import and export duties under its constitutional allocation of tax powers.[1] These duties supplement export and import controls as instruments of international trade policy, in addition to their standard revenue function; import duties are, indeed, classified in the Budget revenue statement according to whether their primary function is protective or as a source of revenue.[2] The procedural provisions of customs law are set out in the Customs Act 1962; the rates of duty are prescribed in the Indian Tariff Act of 1934. Exemptions and rate changes made by the Union government under the Indian Tariff Act are published in the Gazette of India; twice each year the current rates and exemptions are published by the Department of Commercial Intelligence and Statistics in Indian Customs Tariff, which contains the import and export tariff schedules and schedules of rates for Union excise taxes.

Import Duties

The First Schedule to the Indian Tariff Act of 1934 provides the rates of import duty for commodities in twenty-two classes; for each commodity the duty is listed as "protective," "revenue," or "preferential revenue." The list has been extended and the 1965-66 Indian Customs and Central Excise Tariff distinguishes eighty-seven classes of commodities. Most of the

duties are now ad valorem, the tariff having been rationalized
in the Finance Bill, 1965, although some of the ad valorem duties are made specific by the fixing of the tariff values of
the commodities to which they apply. Specific duties, either
alone or in addition to ad valorem duties, are applicable to
some commodities, and in certain cases the duty is the higher
of the ad valorem or the specific duty. Since imported goods
are not subject to Union excise duty, the import duty on certain commodities contains an additional levy--separately listed
as a "countervailing duty"--based on the excise tax levied on
similar commodities manufactured or produced in India.

Prior to devaluation, the basic rate of duty was 60 per
cent on most intermediate and raw materials (other than primary
raw materials), and 40 per cent on machinery and primary raw
materials. Rates were much higher on consumer goods, generally
100 per cent, but ranging as high as 200 per cent. Following
devaluation the revised rates are generally, 27.5 per cent on
machinery and primary raw materials, 50 per cent on other raw
materials, 60 per cent on processed materials and intermediate
goods, and 100 per cent (unchanged) on consumers' goods.

The 1963-64 Budget introduced a 10 per cent surcharge on
the duty otherwise payable on all dutiable articles; this surcharge was retained up to the 1965-66 Budget; in the 1966-67
and 1967-68 Budgets provision for the surcharge was retained,
although in both Budgets all goods were exempted from the additional charge.

A further regulatory customs surcharge of 10 per cent ad
valorem was introduced on February 17, 1965, on all imported
goods except foodgrains, fertilizers, pesticides, books and
accessories for family planning; the regulating surcharge has
not been levied since devaluation, though provision for its
levy has been made on an annual basis in all subsequent Budgets.
Certain food products, raw materials for industry, agricultural
implements, specified types of machinery, and fuel oils were
exempt or taxed at lower rates while the surcharge was in operation.

Protective duties are imposed for a limited period specified in the tariff schedule at rates recommended by the Tariff
Commission--a permanent body appointed in 1952 to recommend
industrial protection policy. Protective duties are presently
levied on several categories of commodities including: heavy
chemicals; metals other than iron and steel; raw silk; machinery
other than sewing machines; cycles and cycle parts; coal-tar
dyes; motor vehicle parts; and a final miscellaneous category.
Rates are, with very few exceptions, ad valorem, and often vary
greatly within one category; on electrical machinery parts, for
instance, rates range from 10 per cent to 95 per cent. Other

typical rates are 65 per cent to 75 per cent on chemicals and
dyes, and 30 per cent to 40 per cent on metals. Protective
duties are frequently levied at lower rates than revenue duties
on associated articles.

The Indian Tariff Act provides for entry of certain goods
from the U.K. and other affiliated countries under "Commonwealth Preference" at favored rates--generally ten percentage
points--less than the normal ad valorem duty. Preferential
rates, either complete exemption or rates lower than 20 per
cent, are also accorded to certain goods imported from Burma.

India is a member of the General Agreement on Tariffs and
Trade (GATT) and duties on certain commodities are bound under
the Agreement; duties so bound have also been extended to non-
signatories of GATT, since the Indian tariff contains no "most
favored nation" rate other than Commonwealth Preference. Duties bound in GATT, and all other duties of a non-preferential
nature, are termed "standard rates," and are separately listed
from the "preferential rates" applicable to Burma and Commonwealth countries.

The Union government is empowered to exempt any commodity
from the import tariff in whole or in part, or to fix or revise
the tariff values of any commodities, by notification in the
Gazette of India; the major notifications of general application issued under this power refer to the reimportation of
goods previously imported, the reimportation of goods exported
less than three years previously, and goods imported by a person on change of residence.

Export Duties

Of minor significance before 1946, export duties were imposed on a substantial number of commodities after 1946, in
part to provide revenue, but primarily to control the import of
inflation, to stabilize prices in the internal market, and to
discourage the export of raw materials used in Indian manu-
facture.3

Revenue from export duties had diminished to insignificance
by 1965-66, and it would have been accurate to suggest that the
export duty in India had been virtually replaced by the export
subsidy. Devaluation in 1966 altered the situation, and export
duties were imposed on a group of twelve commodities. Eleven of
the duties were specific and one ad valorem. As might have been
expected, the export duty on four of these commodities was considerably reduced in the 1967-68 Budget, and further reductions
may be expected as the initial impact of devaluation disappears.

As in the case of import duties the Union government has the power to exempt goods or reduce rates by notification; thus, black pepper, iron and steel products, manganese ore and vegetable oils have been exempted; the Union government also has emergency powers to levy or increase export duties by notification, subject to the approval of Parliament.

In addition to export duties, excise duties or cesses are levied on the export of certain commodities. The latter category has been greatly reduced in recent years in accordance with the official policy of export promotion.

If imported goods are reexported or shipped as ship's stores within two years, seven eighths of the import duty which has been paid on the goods is refunded under the "drawback" principle.

The 1965-66 Budget noted that exporters were still subject to various taxes--States sales taxes, local octroi, etc.--and provided for tax credit certificates to exporters of up to 15 per cent of the value of exports; the exact quantum of assistance varied as between different commodities, and could be used for payment of taxes or refunded in cash to the assessee to the extent that their value exceeded tax liability.[4] In any event, the provision was withdrawn following devaluation.

The administrative and procedural provisions of all Acts relating to customs duties have now been consolidated in the Customs Act, 1962. Customs duties are administered by the Central Board of Revenue, which has the power to make rules for that purpose. Collectors of customs, assisted by deputy collectors, assistant collectors and customs officers, are appointed by the Union government and are assigned to the principal ports and foreign frontiers.

Excise Duties

An excise tax is best seen as a true commodity tax, rather than as a transactions tax, since it is essentially imposed on the production of a commodity, and collected at the factory, rather than on the actual sale of the commodity. In this sense, an excise tax is distinct from a retail sales tax, the latter being strictly a transactions tax. Both taxes are, of course, intended to be shifted forward to consumers and are therefore ultimately incident on consumption.

To the extent that an excise tax is completely shifted forward, the final burden or incidence is distributed in proportion to consumption expenditures on the tax articles. Excises intended to fulfill the latter general function may be termed luxury excises. Excises based on the desire to curtail the

consumption of commodities whose use results in costs to society over and above those incurred in their production and/or to
penalize consumers who persist in purchasing the taxed commodities may be termed sumptuary excises (the alcohol and tobacco
excises are the classic examples of this category). Excises
based on the principle of allocating tax burden in relation to
benefits received from government expenditure may be termed
benefit excises. Finally, excises employed as allocationary or
rationing devices to curtail the use of scarce and/or essential
commodities, may be termed diversionary excises. These categories are not, of course, mutually exclusive, and elements of
all four principles are apparent in Indian Union and State
excise duties.

Union Excise Duties

Union excise duties are imposed under the Constitutional
provision which reserves to the Union government the exclusive
power to impose excise taxes on tobacco and all other goods
manufactured or produced in India, except alcoholic beverages
and narcotics, the taxation of which is reserved to the States.[5]
The imposition and collection of the duties are governed by the
Central Excises and Salt Act of 1944, as amended from time to
time. The first excise duty in India was levied in 1894, and
the device was extended to a wider range of articles in the
1930's during World War II, and, particularly, following the
recommendations of the TEC in 1953-54.

For the fiscal year 1967-68 revenue is anticipated from
duty on seventy-two categories of commodities, although the
major sources of revenue are motor spirit, kerosene, sugar,
tobacco, matches, tires and tubes, cotton fabrics and yarn,
tea, diesel oils, paper, motor vehicles, and iron and steel
products.[6] Duties are imposed principally at specific rates,
only a few categories and subcategories of commodities being
currently taxed at ad valorem rates. The tax is not applicable
to imported or exported commodities and the Union government is
authorized to grant total or partial rebates on tax paid under
the Central Excises and Salt Act on exported goods.

As suggested above, while excise duties are intended to be
borne by the ultimate consumers of the taxable goods, for administrative convenience and feasibility the taxes are imposed
on and collected from manufacturers, in the case of manufactured goods, and on curers and wholesale dealers, in the case
of unmanufactured goods. Control by the authorities is strict,
involving close supervision of manufacture, and, in the case of
tobacco, of warehousing and transport. Revenue from Union excise duties must be shared with the States, which, in accordance with the recommendations of the Fourth Finance Commission,
receive 20 per cent of revenue from all Union excise duties.

The Additional Duties of Excise (Goods of Special Importance) Act, 1957, provides for the levy and collection of additional duties on sugar, tobacco, cotton fabrics, silk fabrics,
woollen fabrics, and rayon or artificial silk fabrics, manufactured in India. These duties are in addition to the duties
payable under the Central Excises and Salt Act, 1944, and replace, by agreement with the State governments, the sales tax
levied by them on these commodities. The entire net proceeds
of these additional duties, other than 1 per cent in respect of
Union territories, is distributed to the States. Each State is
guaranteed under this head the income derived by it from the
sales tax on these commodities in the financial year 1956-57.

Under the Finance Act, 1964, Special Duties of Excise
ranging from 10 per cent to 33 1/3 per cent of the basic duty
were levied on around forty articles chargeable to duty under
the Central Excises and Salt Act, 1944, notably dyes, motor
spirit, and diesel oils (10 per cent), tobacco, tea, coffee,
cosmetics and cement (20 per cent), and silk fabrics, radios,
and motor cars (33 1/3 per cent). The list of special duties
was reduced and rates diminished in several cases in the 1964
and 1965 Finance Bills; no changes in Special Excise coverage
or procedures were introduced in 1966 and 1967. These special
duties are exclusively for Union purposes and are not shared
with the States.

A number of other benefit excises are levied by the Union
government upon designated industries for the purpose of defray-
ing the costs of government activities undertaken on behalf of
the industry taxed. A small number of these taxes are supplementary to the Union excise duty on the same commodities. Thus
a tax is levied at varying specific rates per bale of cotton
produced or per yard or square yard of certain natural and
synthetic fabrics manufactured, in order to finance research,
dissemination of information and other activities beneficial to
the industries. The same is true of a supplementary specific
tax on vegetable oils. Finally, certain commodities, not subject to the Union excise, are subject to special small excise
levies or cesses at specific rates on the benefit basis. Salt,
coal, copra, oil and oil-seeds, iron ores, and rubber are subject to such specific cesses.[7]

Union excises are administered by the Central Board of
Revenue through Collectors of Union Excise who are the heads of
excise departments. Each department normally supervises the
administration and collection of the tax for at least one State,
and is divided into divisions; the latter are divided into
circles, which, in turn, are comprised of ranges, which are the
basic units of excise tax administration.[8] The Union government
is given broad authority to make rules for the administration

of excise duties, and, by notification, to exempt from duty in whole or in part any excised goods.

State Excise Duties

State governments are empowered to levy excise taxes solely on alcoholic liquors for human consumption, and on opium, Indian hemp, and other narcotics.[9] Excise taxes on medicinal and toilet preparations containing alcohol or narcotics are imposed by the Union government but are collected by and accrue entirely to the States.[10] Opium, Indian hemp and other narcotics are subject to excise tax at varying rates in all States which have not prohibited their sale. Opium consumption has been closely controlled by the Union government, which has a monopoly on its production. Since 1959, pursuant to a resolution of the All-India Opium Conference of 1949, all sales of opium, except for medicinal or scientific purposes, have been prohibited, though sales of other narcotics continue to be a matter of State option.

Alcoholic liquors are subject to State excise tax, at varying but uniformly high specific rates, in all those States which have not adopted a policy of prohibition. The Union government, as early as 1905, adopted a policy of sharply restricting liquor consumption which later became a constitutional directive to the States to "endeavour to bring about prohibition of consumption" of all intoxicating liquors or drugs, except for medicinal purposes.[11] The Indian State excise tax on alcoholic liquor is perhaps the only sumptuary excise in existence which would not be legitimately subject to Henry Simons' eloquent denunciation on grounds of the hypocrisy of the alleged moralistic objective.[12] The 1905 resolution in India specifically stated that "all considerations of revenue must be absolutely subordinated" to the end of deterring consumption,[13] and, in spite of the fact that the liquor excise is a major independent revenue source for most States--second only to land revenue until 1950-51, and still third to the States sales taxes and land revenue--the policy of prohibition initially enjoyed considerable success. Complete prohibition was at one point in force in Gujarat, Madras and Maharashtra, and prohibition covered 60 per cent and over of the population in Kerala, Andhra Pradesh, Mysore, and Orissa. Partial prohibition for certain districts and/or at certain times was in effect in Uttar Pradesh, and only in Punjab West Bengal and Rajasthan was little progress reported.[14]

The revenue implications were serious and, in these terms, the TEC was divided on the desirability of the rapid extension of prohibition.[15] Present (Fall, 1967) indications are that revenue scarcity has prevailed over social concern, and that the trend to prohibition has been almost completely halted, and

in some significant instances reversed. It may therefore be
hoped that the States will again be able to rely on the liquor
excise for a significant and probably increasing proportion of
their revenue.

Sales Taxes

A sales tax, as distinct from an excise tax, is a true
transactions tax, and, further, is generally imposed on the
sale of a wide range of goods and services. A universal or
general sales tax would cover the sale of all goods and services; a selective sales tax covers only specified or selected
goods and services. In practice, most sales taxes are not general but exhibit varying degrees of selectivity; this is true
of all the sales taxes levied by the Indian States. Another
broad distinction made in India is between a sales tax proper
and a purchase tax. A tax assessed on the aggregate sales of
a registered dealer and collected from that dealer, is called
a sales tax. If, on the other hand, the tax is assessed on the
aggregate of a dealer's purchases, irrespective of his sales,
it is referred to as a purchase tax. The sales tax is levied
only on dealers, whereas the purchase tax is occasionally levied
directly on consumers in the case of conspicuous articles of
consumption.

A sales tax on motor fuel and lubricants was first levied
in Madhya Pradesh in 1938 and the first general sales tax was
introduced in Madras in 1939. Presently all of the States levy
a sales tax of one form or another. The Constitution, as
adopted in 1950, gave the States exclusive power to impose
taxes on the sales of all goods except newspapers.[16] Services
are excluded from the ambit of the sales taxes.

The Constitution also precluded any State from taxing any
sale or purchase taking place either outside the State or in the
course of the import or export of goods into or out of India.[17]
All these provisions have remained in force. Two other provisions adopted in 1950--that precluding the States from taxing
goods in the course of inter-State trade and that requiring the
assent of the President for the taxation by a State of sales or
purchase of any goods which might be declared by Parliament to
be "essential for the life of the community"[18]--have since been
modified. The difficulties regarding taxation of inter-State
sales resulted in the passage of the Constitution (Six Amendment) Act of 1956, which gave Parliament exclusive power to tax
sales in inter-State trade, but required the assignment of the
proceeds to the States in which the taxes were levied. The provision requiring presidential assent for the taxation of "essential" goods was repealed in the Central Sales Tax Act of 1956,
but the Constitution (Six Amendment) Act of the same year authorized Parliament to impose restrictions and conditions on

the taxation by the States of sales or purchases, whether or not in inter-State commerce, of goods declared by Parliament to be of special importance in inter-State trade or commerce.[19]

The Central Sales Tax Act lists thirteen raw materials to be considered in the latter category, restricts taxes on these commodities to a single-point levy at a special rate (not over 3 per cent), and requires that any tax paid on a sale of any of these commodities in a State be refunded if the goods are subsequently sold in the course of inter-State commerce.

General Structure of Sales Taxes

The various sales taxes differ widely in their intended incidence and operation.[20] In each system the most important characteristic is the point or points between production and retail sale at which the tax is levied, since this affects the qualifications of taxpayers, the classes of goods subject to the tax, rates of tax, and administrative procedures. The evolution and character of the sales tax system in each State has been conditioned by economic structure, financial needs, and adaptation to constitutional amendment.

In general terms, States which are characterized by substantial urban trade and significant industrial and manufacturing activities have tended to adopt a single-point tax imposed at only one point between production of goods and their sale to a consumer, and usually on a limited group of dealers. In these States, a relatively high rate of tax is imposed on taxable sales and a large number of essential goods and basic raw materials are usually exempt. The incidence of a single-point tax is closely controlled, in accordance with the largely urban commercial economy in which it operates. States with predominantly rural economies, on the other hand, have generally adopted multi-point sales taxes, imposed on every sale between production of the goods and their sale to the ultimate consumer. Since the incidence of such taxes is not controlled--so that the number of occasions on which different products are assessed before the retail level may vary considerably--the rates of tax are relatively low, exemptions are few, and most dealers are subject to the tax. A variety of factors, including changing economic structures, revenue needs, revenue structures, and tax evasion, have prompted many States to adopt mixed features of both the single-point and multi-point sales taxes, and to add such novel features as the purchase tax (defined above). The over-all impression is one of great variety and considerable complexity.

Broadly speaking, multi-point sales taxes are presently levied in Andhra Pradesh, Bihar, Kerala, Mysore and Uttar Pradesh, and single-point taxes are levied in Assam, Jammu and

Kashmir, Madhya Pradesh, Orissa, Punjab, Rajasthan and West
Bengal. With the exceptions of Madhya Pradesh and Rajasthan,
the latter group of States levy tax on the last sale.

Tax Liability

Although the Union and State sales taxes are intended to
be borne by the ultimate consumer of taxable goods, the taxes
are imposed on and collected from registered dealers--under the
State sales tax laws, registration is required of all dealers
whose annual gross receipts exceed the mimimum limits established for tax liability--and only a registered dealer is entitled to collect the tax payable to him from a purchaser.
Most of the States impose sales tax liability for intra-State
sales only on dealers whose annual gross receipts ("turnover")
exceed prescribed limits.

Limits for wholesalers and retailers under single-point
systems (Rs. 50,000 in West Bengal) are generally higher than
under multi-point systems (Rs. 7,500 in Madras) in which the
taxes are smaller but are applied to each transfer of goods
from production to consumption. The average exemption level is
Rs. 10,000.[21] A few States prescribe limits for importers and
manufacturers which are lower than the general limits for wholesalers and retailers.

Under the Central Sales Tax Act, every dealer is required
to pay tax on his inter-State sales. The amount of sales tax
liability is determined by applying the applicable rate of tax
to the "sales price" of the goods at the time of sale. Under
the Central Sales Tax Act, the "sales price" of taxable goods
is the amount paid or payable as consideration for the goods,
reduced by any cash discounts allowed under normal practices
of the trade. Sales price under the State Acts is determined
in a similar manner.

Taxable Goods

The State taxes apply to sales of all kinds of tangible
movable property. They do not apply to sales of real estate or
to sales of intangibles such as actionable claims or securities.
As previously indicated, they do not cover newspapers, services
of all kinds, and intra-State sales of goods which have been
declared by Parliament to be of special importance to inter-
State trade. Various classes of goods are exempted, either
by law or State government notification, from the State sales
taxes.

In general, States which impose single-point taxes exempt
the necessaries of life and raw materials. Exemptions are
much fewer under the multi-point taxes; since most of the

essential goods do not change hands frequently between production and consumption, the total burden on them resulting from
the low rates of tax at each stage under multi-point sales
taxes is low, and the need for exemptions, which are difficult
to administer, is therefore less. Exemptions of sales of certain goods at specified stages under a multi-point system are
used in some States to effect concessionary rates of tax. The
exemptions granted under the various State laws may be classified as: necessaries or essential goods--mainly foodstuffs and
industrial raw materials; goods subject to high taxes under
other laws of the State or Union government, e.g., tobacco,
goods produced by small scale (cottage or village) industries;
and various miscellaneous exemptions.[22] The Central Sales Tax
Act--governing inter-State sales--applies to all sales of tangible movable property except newspapers, and expressly excludes sales of intangibles.

Tax Rates

The rates at which the State sales taxes are levied depend
on whether the tax is a single-point or a multi-point tax and
on the nature of the goods sold. The rates applicable to each
sale under single-point system are generally higher than under
multi-point systems, although the total of taxes imposed from
producer to consumer under a multi-point system may be as high
as the tax under a single-point system. Exemptions and concessionary rates vary widely between States. So-called luxury
goods, such as motor cars, radios, electric appliances, watches
and cosmetics are taxed at higher rates than other goods in
most States.

Among the single-point States the general rate of sales
tax varies. It has been fixed at 4 per cent in Assam, Madhya
Pradesh and Rajasthan, 5 per cent in Orissa and West Bengal
and 6 per cent in Punjab. The minimum rate is 0.5 per cent
and the maximum rate generally 10 per cent. In regard to
foreign liquor the rate is higher still: in seven States it is
more than 20 per cent.

In the States where a multi-cum-single-point tax system is
prevalent, i.e., in Andhra Pradesh, Bihar, Kerala, Madras,
Mysore and Uttar Pradesh, the general rate of multi-point tax
is 2 per cent except in the case of Bihar where it is 0.5 per
cent. In some States like Madras and Mysore a special rate of
1 per cent is imposed on the sale of foodgrains whereas in
Andhra Pradesh a higher rate of 3 per cent is levied on the
articles of food and drinks sold in hotels, restaurants, etc.
In Uttar Pradesh unlike other States, there are many special
rates between 0.25 per cent and 3 per cent depending upon the
nature of commodities. The minimum rate of single-point tax

in multi-cum-single-point States fluctuates between 0.5 per
cent and 3 per cent.

The Central Sales Tax Act prescribes the special rates
previously indicated, on intra-State sales of goods declared
of special importance in inter-State trade, and also prescribes
the rate of tax on inter-State sales. The latter rate is 3 per
cent raised from 2 per cent in the 1966-67 Budget.[23]

The State sales taxes are administered by State departments established solely or principally for that purpose. In
general, each department consists of a commissioner, his deputies and tax officers, collectors, or inspectors. In most
States, taxes are assessed by the tax officers or collectors,
and the commissioners and their deputies have an appellate function. Under the Central Sales Tax Act, the tax on an inter-
State sale is assessed and collected by the State which has
jurisdiction over the sale in the same manner as its own taxes
on intra-State sales.

An Outline of State Sales Taxes

Procedures in each State are as follows:

Andhra Pradesh Sales tax in Andhra Pradesh is levied under the
Andhra Pradesh General Sales Tax Act, 1957. This provides for
a basic multi-point levy at the rate of 2 per cent at every
point of sale except in respect of certain goods specified in
three schedules appended to the Act. The tax on the scheduled
goods is levied at a single-point only ranging from 0.5 per
cent to 10 per cent. The taxable turnover in goods other than
declared goods is also subject to an additional tax at 0.25 per
cent in respect of the dealers whose total turnover for the
years is Rs. 3 lakh or more. The Andhra Pradesh system does
not provide for any concession or remission of tax on sales of
raw materials, etc., to a manufacturer, or on sales of finished
products to an exporter who purchases such products for export
out of India.

Assam The Assam Sales Tax Act, 1947, prescribed a single-point
levy in the State at the last point of sale. The general rate
of tax is 4 per cent. There are certain goods which are taxable at the rate of 10 per cent while the rate of tax on declared goods is 20 per cent. A few items have been transferred
to be taxed at the same rate but at the first point of sale
under a separate law called the Assam Finance (Sales Tax) Act,
1956. None of these Acts provides for any concession from
sales tax on sales to exporters. Sales of goods including raw
materials to a manufacturer registered under the Act are exempt
from tax if the goods purchased are used in the manufacture of
taxable goods.

Bihar The Bihar Sales Tax Act, 1959, provides for the levy of
tax on multi-point-cum-single-point basis. The rate of general
sales tax is 0.5 per cent at every point of sale; in addition
a tax of 4 per cent is levied at the last point when the goods
leave the sector of registered dealers. Declared goods and
certain specified goods are taxed only once inside the State
at the rate of 2 per cent and 10 per cent, respectively. The
Act provides that the sale to a registered dealer who purchases
goods including raw materials for use directly in the processing manufacture of goods for sale would be taxed at the concessional rate of 1 per cent. The Act also provides that the
turnover of a dealer relating to sale of goods to a registered
dealer who purchases for the purpose of exports of such goods
out of India would not be subjected to the special sales tax
of 4 per cent. No concession is allowed by the State government under the Central Sales Tax Act on inter-State sales preceding the export transaction.

Gujarat and Maharashtra The Bombay Sales Tax Act, 1959, as
adopted by the State of Gujarat and Maharashtra after the bi-
furcation of the former State of Bombay, is in operation in
these two States. Separate amendments to the original Act have
been made in Gujarat and Maharashtra which have made for slight
differences in the system prevailing in the two States. The
basic structure which is still common provides for a schedule
of taxfree goods, the levy of tax at the single-point at the
first stage of sale by the producer or importer in the State on
a bulk of items imported in the State or produced in medium- or
large-scale industries. On a few commodities there is a single-
point tax at the penultimate stage of sales by the wholesaler or
semi-wholesaler to the retailer. On a few scheduled items and
on all residuary items there is a two-point tax which is levied
at the state of the first sale and then at the stage of the penultimate sale. In addition, in respect of these items the retailer pays a retail turnover tax at the rate of 0.5 per cent.

In both the States there is provision for registration of
dealers. There is also provision for authorization of dealers
engaged in exports. Sales to such authorized dealers are
exempt from the tax on the certificate that the goods are exported outside the States within a period of nine months,
either by themselves or by another dealer to whom they may have
sold them.

There are certain concessions in tax available to manufacturers on their purchase of goods required in the manufacture
of goods for sale. In Maharashtra, manufacturers who have obtained a recognition certificate are entitled to purchase their
requirements for use in the manufacture of taxable goods at a
concessional rate of 1 per cent on all articles taxed at the
higher rate. In Gujarat, manufacturers holding the recognition

certificate can buy all such goods liable to tax at rates in
excess of 2 per cent, free of tax. However, in respect of purchases of machinery and spare parts and goods taxable at the
rate of 2 per cent or less no concession is available in these
two States under the Central Sales Tax in respect of inter-State
sales made to exporters in other States.

Jammu and Kashmir The Jammu and Kashmir General Sales Tax Act,
1962, imposes a tax on fifty-four items named in the State
government's notification at rates ranging from 1 per cent to
10 per cent. No concession from the sales tax is allowed by
the State government on sales of raw materials to manufacturers
or on sales of finished products to exporters who export such
products out of India.

Kerala The Kerala General States Tax Act, 1963, imposes a
liability to pay tax on a multi-point basis on all sales of
goods at the rate of 3 per cent. Declared goods and certain
other items are taxed at rates ranging from 1 per cent to 10
per cent at the first point of sale or at the last point of
purchase in the State. There are three items, namely liquor,
motor spirit other than petrol, and petrol on which the rate of
tax is 50 per cent, 20 per cent and 15 per cent, respectively.
Sales of certain goods mentioned in the Act to a manufacturer
in the State are taxable at a concessional rate of 1 per cent
if such goods are used as component parts of the goods manufactured for sale. No concession from the tax is allowed in the
State on transactions preceding the actual export.

Madhya Pradesh The Madhya Pradesh General Sales Tax Act, 1958,
provides for the levy on a single-point basis at 4 per cent on
the first point of sale. Declared goods and a few other goods
are taxed at the last point of sale; the rate of tax ranges
from 1 per cent to 10 per cent. Tax on raw materials sold to
a manufacturer for use in the manufacture of major export commodities is levied at the rate of 1 per cent. The State government grants a refund of local sales tax and exemption from
Central sales tax on the local/inter-State sale immediately preceding the actual export transaction of the following goods:

        i.   Minerals
       ii.   Shellac
      iii.   Vegetable oils
       iv.   Hides and skins
        v.   Oil cakes   and
       vi.   Carpets

Madras Sales tax in Madras is governed under the provisions of
Madras General Sales Tax Act, 1959. The Act provides for the
levy of tax on the purchase of a number of goods and on the
sale of others. The rate of tax is generally 2 per cent multi-

point, but declared goods and certain specified articles are taxed on a single-point basis at rates ranging from 1 per cent to 10 per cent. No concessions from tax are generally allowed by the State government on raw materials used in the manufacture of finished products, but there is a provision under which in respect of the sale of goods mentioned in the first schedule of the Act by a dealer to another for use by the latter as a component part of any other goods mentioned in that Schedule which he intends to manufacture inside the State for sale, the tax liability is reduced to 1 per cent. This concession is available only for an article which forms an identifiable constituent of the finished product. There is no concession on the sale to or purchase by exporters of goods exported by them out of India.

Mysore Mysore has a multi-point system of sales tax governed by the provision of the Mysore Sales Tax Act, 1957. The rate of tax is 2 per cent on all sales of goods. A few goods are subject to purchase tax also, while certain goods are taxed at a single point only at rates ranging from 0.5 per cent in the case of bullion to 10 per cent in the case of certain specified goods. No concession of sales tax or purchase tax is allowed on raw materials used in the manufacture of finished products or on goods purchased by exporters for export out of India.

Orissa The Orissa Sales Tax Act, 1947, provides for the levy of tax on the last point of sale. The general rate of tax is 5 per cent. Certain specified goods are taxed at the rate of 10 per cent while in respect of certain others, the rate is only 1 per cent. No concession is allowed in the State on sales of raw materials to manufacturers or on sales of finished products to exporters who export such goods out of India.

Punjab The Punjab General Sales Tax Act, 1948, provides for levy of tax on the last point of sale. The general rate of tax is 6 per cent. In addition, a surcharge of 1 per cent is levied on a temporary basis for a specific purpose under the Punjab Temporary Taxation Act, 1962. Certain specified goods are taxed at the rate of 10 per cent whereas the rate of tax on declared goods is 2 per cent. A lower rate has also been fixed in respect of certain goods. Sales to a manufacturer (registered under the Act) of such goods as are specified in the registration certificate and are required for use in the manufacture in the State of Punjab of any goods for sale are allowed tax free. The State government also allows exemption from local sales tax on sales of goods to a registered dealer who purchases them for the purpose of export out of India. No concession is allowed under the Central Sales Tax Act on inter-State sales preceding the actual export transaction.

Rajasthan Sales tax is levied under the Rajasthan Sales Tax Act, 1956, on a single-point basis generally at the first point of sale. Certain goods are taxed on the last point also when they leave the registered sector. The general rate of tax is 4 per cent, although certain goods are taxed at lower rates. Sales of raw materials (including fuel and lubricants) to manufacturers under the Act are taxable at the concessional rate of 1 per cent. The State government also allows exemption from local and Central sales tax on the transaction immediately preceding the export of the following goods:

    i. Oilseeds
   ii. Raw wool
  iii. Cotton and
   iv. Mica

Uttar Pradesh The scheme of taxation under the Uttar Pradesh Sales Tax Act, 1948, is essentially multi-point, the general rate of tax being 2 per cent. However, certain goods specified by the State government are taxed on a single-point basis, either at the point of the last or the first sale or purchase, at different rates not exceeding 10 per cent. The State government does not allow any concession on sales of raw materials to manufacturers, but it allows full rebate of local sales tax and complete exemption from Central Sales Tax on the transaction immediately preceding export of the following goods:

     i. Tea
    ii. Jute goods
   iii. Mica
    iv. Mineral ores (metallic)
     v. Spices
    vi. Vegetable oil
   vii. Raw wool
  viii. Hides and skins (raw
          and tanned leather)
    ix. Raw cotton
     x. Walnuts
    xi. Sandalwood oil
   xii. Carpets and rugs
  xiii. Silk and silk manufactures
   xiv. Sports goods
    xv. Sewing machines and accessories
   xvi. Bicycles and accessories
  xvii. Diesel engines
 xviii. Oil pressure lamps and
   xix. Electric fans

West Bengal The Bengal Finance (Sales Tax) Act, 1941, provides for levy of tax at the last point of sale in the State. The general rate of tax is 5 per cent. Certain goods are taxable

at lower rates (the minimum rate being 1 per cent except for
gold of not less than 90 per cent fineness for which the rate
is 0.5 per cent), while luxury goods are taxed at a rate of 10
per cent. Some of the goods which have been taken out of the
purview of the above Act are taxed under the West Bengal Sales
Tax Act, at the first point of sale in the hands of importers
and manufacturers. All sales of goods (including raw materials)
to a manufacturer who is a registered dealer under the Act and
who purchases such goods for use in the manufacture of goods
for sale whether locally, outside the State or outside India,
are exempt from tax. The scheme of levy in the State being
such, sales of finished products to an exporter who is registered under the 1941 Act, are also exempt and do not bear local
sales tax. However, no concession is allowed under the Central
Sales Tax on inter-State transactions preceding the actual export sale.

Union Territories The only Territory requiring consideration
is Delhi--in others there is either no sales tax or no significant export. Delhi has adopted the West Bengal Sales Tax system as provided in the Bengal Finance (Sales Tax) Act, 1941.

REVENUE PRODUCTIVITY

General Considerations

The importance of the four major indirect tax measures--
customs, Union excise duties, State excise duties, and the
State sales tax--in the aggregate of Union and State revenue is
apparent from available statistics. Table 1 indicates revenue
from these four tax measures over the planning period, and their
relative significance, separately and in aggregate, as a proportion of total (Union and States) tax revenue.

The major indirect tax measures constituted over 50 per
cent of total tax revenue in 1950-51 and 64.5 per cent in 1965-
66. The increasing aggregate figure conceals significant disparities in the changing relative significance of the different
tax measures. Customs revenue, which constituted 25 per cent of
total tax revenue in 1950-51 now amounts to only 15 per cent.
Customs revenue in 1965-66 is accounted for almost entirely by
import duties, revenue from which has increased fairly rapidly
since 1960-61; export duties, which provided roughly 8 per cent
of total tax revenue in 1950-51 provided only 0.06 per cent in
1965-66.

The most important indirect tax source is now Union excise
taxation, which accounted for 11 per cent of total tax revenue
in 1950-51 and 31 per cent in 1965-66. Revenue from State excise duties indicates the fiscal cost of prohibition, accounting

TABLE 1

REVENUE FROM MAJOR INDIRECT TAXES (1950-61 - 1965-66)

Rs. million

	1950-51	1955-56	Total First Plan Period	1956-57	1960-61	Total Second Plan Period	1961-62	1962-63	1963-64	1964-65	1965-66	Total Third Plan Period
1. Customs												
a. Imports	1,077.0	1,279.8	6,483.0	1,405.2	1,546.1	6,984.2	1,982.2	2,384.2	3,342.5	4,046.4	5,476.9	17,232.2
b. Exports	473.6	377.6	2,643.7	286.7	131.2	1,043.5	126.9	96.0	33.7	24.3	21.4	302.3
c. Net Receipts (after refunds, etc.)	1,571.5	1,677.0	9,157.1	1,732.3	1,700.3	8,176.5	2,122.5	2,459.6	3,347.4	3,975.0	5,389.7	17,294.2
2. Union Excise Duties (including additional excise duties and States' share)	675.4	1,452.5	5,172.6	1,904.3	4,163.5	15,339.9	4,893.1	5,988.3	7,295.8	8,015.1	8,979.2	35,171.5
3. State Excise Duties	494.0	451.0	2,300.0	464.0	531.0	2,420.0	586.0	628.0	728.9	845.4	963.7	3,752.0
4. General Sales Tax	544.0	801.0	3,104.0	966.0	1,425.0	5,824.0	1,631.0	1,875.0	2,454.1	2,950.9	3,385.7	12,296.7
5. Total (Union and State) Tax Revenue (from all sources)	6,384.0	7,675.7	35,831.7	8,894.6	13,549.4	56,017.3	15,379.7	18,549.8	23,133.9	25,852.2	29,023.7	111,939.3
1(c)+2+3+4 as per cent of 5	53.04	58.42	55.07	57.01	57.72	58.01	60.03	59.03	59.84	61.12	64.51	60.90
1(c) as per cent of 5	24.63	21.85	26.14	19.48	12.54	14.59	13.80	13.26	14.47	15.38	18.57	15.10
2 as per cent of 5	10.59	18.93	14.44	21.42	30.73	27.38	31.80	32.28	31.56	34.67	30.94	32.25
3 as per cent of 5	7.74	5.88	6.42	5.22	3.92	4.32	3.81	3.39	3.15	3.66	3.32	3.46
4 as per cent of 5	8.53	10.43	8.66	10.86	10.52	10.40	10.60	10.10	10.62	12.76	11.66	11.15

Source: Reserve Bank of India, Report on Currency and Finance, 1961-62 and 1965-66 (Bombay: Reserve Bank of India, 1962 and 1966).

for 8 per cent of total tax revenue in 1950-51, but only 3 per
cent in 1965-66. Revenue from sales tax amounted to 8.5 per
cent of total tax revenue in 1950-51, and over 11 per cent in
1965-66; the growth of sales tax revenue has thus been steady
but not as spectacular as that of Union excise duties.

Customs Revenue

Table 2 sets out some estimates of the elasticity--the
annual growth rate of revenue other than from budgetary changes
--of customs revenue over the period 1955-56 to 1970-71, including Planning Commission forecasts of revenue over the
Fourth Plan. Over the period 1955-56 to 1965-66, for which ex
post statistics are available, the elasticity of customs revenue averages 10.5; this aggregate figure conceals a period of
relatively slow revenue growth up to 1960-61.

The latter point is confirmed by calculation of the income
elasticity of customs revenue. Over the period 1955-56 to 1960-
61, the actual growth of customs revenue was Rs. 33.3 million,
less than the Rs. 82.7 million predicted as a result of budgetary changes. Growth of revenue as a result of built-in elasticity was therefore negative. From 1960-61 to 1964-65, the
income elasticity coefficient of customs revenue comes to 1.096,
indicating that the built-in rate of growth of customs revenue
barely exceeded the growth rate of national income.

The relatively slow growth of customs revenue can be attributed to several factors. First, revenue from export duties
has now diminished to insignificance. Second, the substitution
of prohibitively high protective duties for revenue duties on a
wide range of industrial products after World War II substantially reduced customs revenue. This policy was supplemented
until the middle 1950's by an extensive series of import quo-
tas. Third, the contribution of alcoholic beverages to import
revenue has become insignificant as a result of prohibitive
rates, import control and prohibition. Fourth, measures to
promote industrialization have included the lowering of duties
on industrial raw materials, capital goods and machinery. Increases in rates on "luxury" consumer goods have failed to compensate for industrial concessions. Fifth, closely related to
the previous point, the increasing significance of relatively
lightly taxed industrial materials and exempt foodgrains in the
Indian import mix has curtailed the rate of increase in revenue
from imports.[24] Finally, India's obligations under GATT which
limit duties on a substantial range of consumer goods, and the
preferential treatment accorded to Commonwealth countries and
Burma, have a substantial revenue cost.

The TEC was pessimistic concerning the possibility of increasing import revenue, particularly in terms of the need to

TABLE 2

ELASTICITY OF CUSTOMS REVENUE, 1955-56 -- 1970-71

1 Year	2 Actual Revenue (Rs.million)	3 Increase over Previous Year (Rs.million)	4 Anticipated Increase due to Budget Changes (Rs.million)	5 Increase due to Built-in Elasticity (3-4) (Rs.million)	6 Elasticity Coefficient (5 as per cent of 2)
1955-56	1,667.0	65.3	-5.0	70.3	5.31
1956-67	1,732.3	67.6	0	67.6	3.90
1957-58	1,799.9	-417.0	60.0	-477.0	-26.50
1958-59	1,382.9	178.2	0	178.2	12.88
1959-60	1,561.1	139.2	27.7	111.5	7.14
1960-61	1,700.3	422.2	25.0	397.2	23.36
1961-62	2,122.5	337.1	293.0	44.1	2.08
1962-63	2,459.6	887.8	83.2	804.6	37.71
1963-64	3,347.4	627.6	803.9	-176.3	-5.27
1964-65	3,975.0	1,414.7	63.7	1,351.0	33.98
1965-66	5,389.7	1,510.3	145.0	1,365.3	25.32
1966-67	6,900.0	660.0	-	660.0	9.57
1967-68	7,560.0	760.0	-	760.0	10.06
1968-69	8,320.0	-270.0	-	-270.0	-3.24
1969-70	8,050.0	-340.0	-	-340.0	-4.22
1970-71	7,710.0				

Sources: Reserve Bank of India, Reports on Currency and Finance for 1961-62 and 1965-66 (Bombay: Reserve Bank of India, 1962 and 1966); Government of India, Draft Fourth Plan Material and Financial Balances (New Delhi: Planning Commission, 1964).

offer concessions to industrial raw materials and capital goods.[25] Recent trends toward increased imports of exempt foodgrains, and continued protectionism would also appear to augur ill for the revenue productivity of import duties, and the reciprocal benefits received under the preferential arrangements and GATT would probably prevent any radical changes in these policies.

However, the policy of taxing lightly industrial raw materials and machinery was modified in the 1963-64 Budget which also increased the standard rate to 60 per cent and radically increased duties on "luxury" consumer goods. The 1963-64 Budget provided in addition for a comprehensive 10 per cent surcharge, which continued through 1964-65 and 1965-66, and remains in the statutes although operationally in abeyance in 1966-67 and 1967-68. An additional 10 per cent regulatory surcharge, intended partly to discourage imports and partly as a revenue source, was introduced in 1965-66, but has been in abeyance since devaluation. As a result of these changes, revenue from import duties more than doubled between 1962-63 and 1965-66.

It is difficult to forecast the future of customs duties as a revenue source. It may be expected that the export duties introduced after devaluation will be reduced and ultimately abolished, but import duties have proved surprisingly productive in the last few years. The revenue motive is, of course, only one of the objectives of import duties, and there is doubtless a limit to the extent to which duties can be raised with the revenue objective in mind, before a revenue duty inadvertently becomes a protective duty. On balance the scope for increased duties would not now appear to be wide, except perhaps in the event of further tightening of the policy of favoring industrial requirements.

The Planning Commission forecasts reflect concern over the growth of customs revenue (Table 2). Revenue is expected to continue to increase until 1968-69, after which it is expected to fall absolutely, and quite sharply.

Union Excise Duties

Table 3 sets out the elasticity of Union excise duties between 1955-56 and 1970-71, including Planning Commission forecasts of revenue over the Fourth Plan. Over 1955-56 to 1965-66, the average elasticity (annual rate of revenue growth other than from Budget changes), of Union excise duties was 12.1. The forecast elasticity for the Fourth Plan averages 9.7.

Turning to income elasticity of excise revenue, the income elasticity coefficient over the period 1955-56 to 1960-61 comes

TABLE 3

ELASTICITY OF UNION EXCISE GROSS COLLECTIONS, 1955-56 - 1970-71

1	2	3	4	5	6
Year	Actual Revenue (Rs.million)	Increase over Previous Year (Rs.million)	Anticipated Increase due to Budget Changes (Rs.million)	Increase due to Built-in Elasticity (3-4) (Rs.million)	Elasticity Coefficient (5 as per cent of 2)
1955-56	1,452.5	451.8	88.2	363.6	25.02
1956-57	1,904.3	831.9	249.0	582.9	30.61
1957-58	2,736.2	393.2	490.0	-96.8	-3.54
1958-59	3,129.4	477.1	28.3	448.8	14.34
1959-60	3,606.5	557.0	208.0	349.0	9.68
1960-61	4,163.5	729.6	217.3	512.3	12.30
1961-62	4,893.1	1,095.2	309.0	786.2	16.06
1962-63	5,988.3	1,307.5	361.6	945.9	15.80
1963-64	7,295.8	719.3	1,221.1	-501.8	-6.88
1964-65	8,015.1	964.1	191.5	772.6	9.64
1965-66	8,979.2	420.8	-79.8	500.6	5.58
1966-67	9,400.0	1,160.0	-	1,160.0	12.31
1967-68	10,560.0	940.0	-	940.0	8.90
1968-69	11,500.0	1,130.0	-	1,130.0	9.82
1969-70	12,630.0	1,490.0	-	1,490.0	11.80
1970-71	14,120.0				

Sources: Reserve Bank of India, Reports on Currency and Finance for 1961-62 and 1965-66 (Bombay: Reserve Bank of India, 1962 and 1966); Government of India, Draft Fourth Plan Material and Financial Balances (New Delhi: Planning Commission, 1964).

to 1.7; the corresponding figure for 1960-61 to 1964-65 is 1.8. These are, it will be recalled, maximum estimates of built-in elasticity, which probably explains the disparity between the above estimates of income elasticity and Sahota's estimate of 1.16 over the period 1950-59.[26]

An analysis by the Central Excise Reorganisation Committee suggests that the increase in excise revenue over the period 1938-39 to 1961-62 is attributable to the following factors: 16 per cent due to increased consumption, 57 per cent due to increased rates, and 24 per cent due to additional coverage.[27] Built-in elasticity in this latter study therefore remains significant, but is of considerably less significance relative to rate increases than the previous estimates would suggest.

What is surprising is the relatively low revenue significance of increased coverage. Of total excise tax revenue in 1965-66, 60 per cent came from duties on those commodities taxed before 1963-64, 25 per cent from those commodities taxed for the first time between 1953-54 and 1959-60, 1 per cent from those taxed for the first time in 1960-61, and 14 per cent from those taxed for the first time since 1960-61. So those duties in operation before the Second Five Year Plan are roughly twice as productive as those introduced in the Second Five Year Plan, and this latter group is roughly twice as productive as those taxed for the first time in the Third Five Year Plan.

The moral of the story would seem to be that action to increase excise revenue should concentrate on rate increases. Since most rates are specific, it is difficult to ascertain at first glance the pattern of relative burden. Table 4 sets out the forty groups of articles subject to excise duties with the specific rates translated into ad valorem rates for 1964-65, 1965-66, and 1966-67. The wide variation in ad valorem rates is illuminating. Although rates range to more than 300 per cent, two thirds of commodities are taxed at effective rates of less than 20 per cent. In this group are many items of personal, even luxury, consumption, e.g., internal combustion engines, electric motors, silk fabric, motor vehicles, wireless sets, etc., on which rates might be substantially increased. It would also seem likely that a general conversion of rates to ad valorem terms would, in addition to making effective tax burden more immediately apparent, impart a considerably greater intrinsic elasticity to excise revenue. This follows since ad valorem rates mean that tax revenue shares automatically in price increases, whereas specific rates do not. This recommendation is made despite the contrary view of the Central Excise Reorganisation Committee.[28]

TABLE 4

EXCISE DUTIES IN AD VALOREM TERMS,
1964-65, 1965-66 and 1966-67

Tariff Item No.	Commodity	Basic (per cent)	1964-65 Additional (per cent)	Total (per cent)
(1)	(2)	(3)	(4)	(5)
1.	(i) Sugar V.P.	30.3	9.7	40.0
	(ii) Sugar Khandsari (N)) Sugar Khandsari (S))	10.7	1.2	11.9
2.	Coffee	13.1	-	13.1
3.	Tea	14.5	-	14.5
4I.	Unmanufactured Tobacco	95.4	6.1	101.5
II.	Cigarettes	46.9	8.8	55.7
III.	Cigars & Cheroots	25.7	4.8	30.5
6.	Motor Spirit	319.1	-	319.1
	Power Alcohol	-	-	-
7.	Kerosene (i) Superior	131.6	-	131.6
	(ii) Inferior	85.4	-	85.4
8.	Refined Diesel Oil	343.0	-	343.0
9.	Diesel Oil N.O.S.	191.3	-	191.3
10.	Furnace Oil	72.6	-	72.6
11.	Asphalt Bitumen	27.0	-	27.0
11A.	Petroleum Products N.O.S.	5.0	-	5.0
12.	V.N.S. Oils (Processed)	6.0	-	6.0
13.	Vegetable Products	18.0	-	18.0
14.	Paints and Varnishes	17.8	-	17.8
14A.	Soda Ash	4.8	-	4.8
14B.	Caustic Soda	6.1	-	6.1
14BB.	Sodium Silicate	18.0	-	18.0
14C.	Glycerine	5.2	-	5.2
14D.	Synthetic Organic Dyestuffs	15.0	-	15.0
14DD.	Synthetic Organic Product	-	-	-
14E.	Patent or Proprietory Medicines	7.9	-	7.9
14F.	Cosmetics	30.0	-	30.0
14G.	Acides (Sulphuric)	7.4	-	7.4
14H.	Gases	50.0	-	50.0
15.	Soap	8.5	-	8.5
15A.	Plastics	24.0	-	24.0
15AA.	Organic Surface Active Agents	-	-	-
15B.	Cellophane	20.0	-	20.0
16.	Tyres	42.0	-	42.0
16A.	Rubber Products	22.7	-	22.7
16B.	Plywood	8.7	-	8.7
17.	Paper	23.1	-	23.1
18.	Rayon & Synthetics Fibres and Yarn	39.7	-	39.7
18A.	Cotton Yarn	9.2	-	9.2
18B.	Woollen Yarn	17.9	-	17.9
19.	Cotton Fabrics (i) Mills	15.7	5.9	21.6
	(ii) Powerloom	4.7	1.8	6.5

Basic (per cent)	1965-66 Additional (per cent)	Total (per cent)	Basic (per cent)	1966-67 Additional (per cent)	Total (per cent)
(6)	(7)	(8)	(9)	(10)	(11)
23.7	7.1	30.8	33.0	7.0	40.0
9.2	1.0	10.2	11.5	1.0	12.5
8.1	-	8.1	6.8	-	6.8
10.5	-	10.5	9.7	-	9.7
9.2	-	9.2	8.2	-	8.2
83.5	5.8	89.3	91.9	5.7	97.6
48.3	8.1	56.4	55.5	8.3	63.8
-	-	-	-	-	-
331.6	-	331.6	280.1	-	280.1
32.7	-	32.7	N.A.	-	N.A.
172.1	-	172.1)	114.8	-	114.8
133.8	-	133.8)			
328.6	-	328.6	266.5	-	266.5
166.7	-	166.7	123.4	-	123.4
92.3	-	92.3	87.1	-	87.1
40.1	-	40.1	36.8	-	36.8
13.3	-	13.3	13.5	-	13.5
3.9	-	3.9	2.4	-	2.4
6.0	-	6.0	3.5	-	3.5
15.6	-	15.6	10.9	-	10.9
4.3	-	4.3	3.8	-	3.8
4.1	-	4.1	4.3	-	4.3
20.0	-	20.0	23.1	-	23.1
4.2	-	4.2	4.0	-	4.0
15.0	-	15.0	15.0	-	15.0
-	-	-	15.0	-	15.0
6.7	-	6.7	6.5	-	6.5
30.0	-	30.0	30.0	-	30.0
10.0	-	10.0	10.0	-	10.0
50.0	-	50.0	59.8	-	59.8
9.9	-	9.9	10.1	-	10.1
24.0	-	24.0	24.0	-	24.0
-	-	-	10.0	-	10.0
20.0	-	20.0	20.0	-	20.0
45.8	-	45.8	45.0	-	45.0
24.0	-	24.0	24.0	-	24.0
7.0	-	7.0	6.3	-	6.3
21.1	-	21.1	17.9	-	17.9
40.0	-	40.0	31.8	-	31.8
8.0	-	8.0	4.9	-	4.9
16.5	-	16.5	16.5	-	16.5
19.2	5.5	24.7	18.0	5.6	23.6

continued

333

TABLE 4 (cont.)

Tariff Item No.	Commodity	1964-65 Basic (per cent)	Additional (per cent)	Total (per cent)
(1)	(2)	(3)	(4)	(5)
21.	Woollen Fabrics	5.8	4.5	10.3
22.	Rayon or Art Silk Fabrics	3.5	1.9	5.4
22A.	Jute manufactures	12.7	-	12.7
23.	Cement	42.0	-	42.0
23A.	Glass and Glassware	13.6	-	13.6
23B.	Chinaware	12.9	-	12.9
23C.	Asbestos Cement Products	9.6	-	9.6
25.	Iron in any crude form	12.5	-	12.5
26.	Steel Ingots	10.1	-	10.1
26A.	Copper and Copper Alloys (i) in crude form) (ii) Manufactures) (iii) Pipes and Tubes)	9.7	-	9.7
26AA.	Iron or Steel Products	6.0	-	6.0
26B.	Zinc	9.9	-	9.9
27.	Aluminium	8.5	-	8.5
27A.	Lead	-	-	-
28.	Tin Plates and Tinned Sheets	19.3	-	19.3
29.	I.C. Engines	7.3	-	7.3
29A.	Refrigerating & Air Conditioning Applicances	26.8	-	26.8
30.	Electric Motors	9.4	-	9.4
31.	Electric Batteries	16.7	-	16.7
32.	Electric Bulbs & P.L. Tubes	12.4	-	12.4
33.	Electric Fans	11.4	-	11.4
33A.	Wireless Receiving Sets	15.2	-	15.2
33B.	Electric Wires and Cables	6.1	-	6.1
34.	Motor Vehicles	13.4	-	13.4
37.	Cinematograph Films Exposed	10.9	-	10.9
37A.	Gramophone and Parts	7.9	-	7.9
38.	Matches	144.8	-	144.8
39.	Footwear	11.5	-	11.5
40.	Silk Fabrics	7.0	4.2	11.2
	ALL COMMODITIES	24.30	1.84	26.14

Basic (per cent)	1965-66 Additional (per cent)	Total (per cent)	Basic (per cent)	1966-67 Additional (per cent)	Total (per cent)
(6)	(7)	(8)	(9)	(10)	(11)
6.0	4.8	10.8	6.0	4.8	10.8
2.5	1.5	4.0	2.3	1.3	3.6
7.8	-	7.8	7.3	-	7.3
23.8	-	23.8	19.5	-	19.5
13.8	-	13.8	13.8	-	13.8
12.6	-	12.6	12.5	-	12.5
10.0	-	10.0	10.0	-	10.0
11.1	-	11.1	14.0	-	14.0
16.0	-	16.0	13.5	-	13.5
15.0	-	15.0	17.0	-	17.0
18.0	-	18.0	20.0	-	20.0
10.0	-	10.0	10.0	-	10.0
21.0	-	21.0	16.2	-	16.2
9.5	-	9.5	15.0	-	15.0
10.0	-	10.0	10.0	-	10.0
-	-	-	15.0	-	15.0
24.0	-	24.0	24.0	-	24.0
7.8	-	7.8	8.2	-	8.2
28.4	-	28.4	28.0	-	28.0
8.8	-	8.8	8.2	-	8.2
16.7	-	16.7	16.7	-	16.7
12.4	-	12.4	9.7	-	9.7
11.0	-	11.0	9.4	-	9.4
12.0	-	12.0	11.3	-	11.3
6.3	-	6.3	N.A.	-	N.A.
12.0	-	12.0	12.0	-	12.0
10.0	-	10.0	10.0	-	10.0
15.0	-	15.0	20.9	-	20.9
141.6	-	141.6	136.0	-	136.0
-	-	-	-	-	-
-	-	-	-	-	-
24.9	1.5	26.4	23.9	1.2	25.1

Sources: Reserve Bank of India, Report on Currency and Finance, 1965-66 (Bombay: Reserve Bank of India, 1966); Government of India, Monthly Statistics of the Production of Selected Industries of India, (Delhi: Manager of Publications).

The surcharge and special excise duties introduced in 1963 and retained in modified form in subsequent Budgets have sought to avoid taxing essential foodstuffs and intermediate goods and to tax more rigorously consumption goods considered of a non-essential nature, such as motor cars and electric appliances. The only exception to this general rule has been the increased tobacco tax. Given the presumption that excise taxes are borne by the consumer for whom they are intended, it follows that what has been attempted in an approximate manner over recent Budgets is the establishment of an excise tax structure which is progressive with respect to increases in national income, in that it taxes more heavily goods for which the income elasticity of demand is likely to be relatively high.

It might be possible to maximize the revenue productivity of excise taxation by planning tax rates on the basis of extrapolations of consumer demand as incomes increase. By taxing on the basis of anticipated income-elasticity of demand, the responsiveness of excise taxation to income changes can be maximized. It would seem preferable to set up a scheme of excise taxation on a scientific basis which maximizes potential elasticity than to seek the same result by a series of surcharges, special duties, and the selection of commodities on an ad hoc basis. Such a procedure would dispense in part with the invidious distinction of commodities into "luxuries" and "necessities," and would provide a basis for systematic consistent review of tax rates and coverage.

The major difficulty with the suggested procedure lies in the fact that a proportion of excise taxation (and of other indirect tax measures) cannot be attributed to final consumption goods but impinges on goods intermediate in the production process. For these goods it is difficult to allocate excise taxes to various income groups on the basis of their estimated expenditure patterns. The procedure is far from being, however, statistically inconceivable, and a recent Indian study has, in fact, suggested a comprehensive list of commodities arranged according to the proportion of total expenditure incurred by the lowest income group--which is the reverse order to that in which these commodities offer scope for increased rates on the basis of income elasticity.[29] On the basis of National Sample Survey data on consumption patterns, W. Malenbaum has calculated the income elasticity of demand of five income groups in ascending order for ten categories of commodities.[30] On the basis of such a study a more rational, consistent and elastic excise tax system, insofar as it relates to consumers' goods, might be derived.

A possible method of reform of excise duties not yet considered at length in India would be to replace the whole series of Union excise duties by a tax on value added.

A tax on value added might best be described as a sophisticated turnover tax, where the cumulative tax factor is
removed by taxing each transaction only in respect of the addition to sale value which has occurred in the stage immediately
prior to the transaction in question. The tax base for any
entrepreneur would then be the sale price of his output less
the cost of materials and other inputs. The tax collected
under the value-added approach would be identical to that collected under a general retail sales tax, assuming the same rate
of tax.

A value-added tax is generally thought of as an alternative to a retail sales tax. In general, since the anticipated
revenue under a value-added tax would be the same as under a
retail sales tax, the value-added approach seems simply to
spread the direct impact of the tax over a larger number of
firms, and therefore to add unnecessarily to the complexity of
collecting a given amount of revenue. This point is particularly apposite when the value-added tax is being considered as
an alternative to an excise tax system levied at the factory
stage. Further, one of the advantages of the value-added approach, its neutrality as between commodites, might be seen as
a disadvantage in India, where the excise tax system is employed
as a very effective tool of dirigistic tax policy.

State Excise Duties

Over the First and Second Plans revenue from State excises
was virtually stagnant absolutely, and, in consequence, declined rapidly in relative significance. No attempt has been
made to calculate elasticity over this period. With the apparent beginnings of the disintegration of prohibition in the
Third Plan--a process which accelerated rapidly in 1967 and
1968--the liquor excise has begun again to demonstrate its
standard usefulness as a revenue source.

Allowing--with only slight inaccuracy--the entire increase
in revenue over the Third Plan as attributable to built-in revenue growth, the elasticity of State excises from 1961-62 to
1965-66 averages 13.25. From 1961-62 to 1964-65, the income
elasticity of State excises is a remarkable 1.6.

In the stagnancy of the early figures and the rapid growth
of the later figures lies an unequivocal sermon on the fiscal
costs of prohibition. It would have been more rational in the
first place to gear the pace of prohibition to the availability
of alternative revenue sources. Since prohibition appears to
be disintegrating, there can be little but rejoicing in State
Finance Ministries, whether or not there be concern elsewhere.

Sales Taxes

A problem endemic to federal States is that of inelastic revenue structures at the State level in the federation. To this rule India was no exception until the development of sales taxation after World War II. The great significance of sales taxation in India is that it has provided a relatively elastic and productive independent revenue source to the States. This feature of sales taxation has recently led an eminent U.S. economist to advocate widely extended use of sales taxation at the State level.[31]

Table 5 sets out the elasticity of State sales tax revenue over the period 1955-56 to 1970-71, including Planning Commission forecasts of revenue over the Fourth Plan. From 1955-56 to 1965-66, the elasticity--annual rate of growth of revenue other than from Budget changes--of sales tax revenue averaged 11.13. The expected growth rate over the Fourth Plan is 5.49.

As to income elasticity, the coefficient over the period 1955-56 to 1960-61 was 1.29--a very respectable figure indeed, but far exceeded by the remarkable performance of sales tax revenue over the Third Plan period from 1960-61 to 1965-66, when the coefficient was 2.37.

Discussion of means of increasing the revenue productivity of the sales taxes may be divided into two heads: first, the type of sales tax which should be employed, and, second, the question of taxation of services.

Examining the different sales tax structures from the point of view of revenue productivity, the TEC pointed out that the object of a multi-point tax was to levy a relatively low rate tax on the majority of articles of consumption and on a large number of dealers, whereas the object of a single-point tax was to levy a relatively high rate tax on the majority of articles--though with a significant list of exemptions--and on a limited number of dealers.[32] The sales tax structure recommended by the TEC as most effective in terms of revenue productivity was a combination of multi-point and single-point levies. Each State should levy on all dealers having a turnover greater than Rs. 5,000 a multi-point low rate (0.05 per cent) tax without exemptions and should complement the turnover tax with a single-point levy--preferably at the retail stage--on dealers above a relatively high turnover limit; the single-point levy should exempt household necessaries and should be levied at higher rates on "luxury" goods.[33]

There is little question that a combination of turnover tax and single-point levy would offer for most States a higher revenue productivity than at present. There are two qualifications

TABLE 5

ELASTICITY OF STATE SALES TAX REVENUE, 1955-56 - 1970-71

1	2	3	4	5	6
Year	Actual Revenue (Rs.million)	Increase over Previous Year (Rs.million)	Anticipated Increase due to Budget Changes (Rs.million)	Increase due to Built-in Elasticity (3-4) (Rs.million)	Elasticity Coefficient (5 as per cent of 2)
1955-56	800.6	0	20.0	-20.0	-0.25
1956-57	800.6	367.1	40.0	327.1	4.09
1957-58	1,073.7	43.1	20.0	23.1	2.15
1958-59	1,116.8	126.9	35.7	91.2	8.17
1959-60	1,243.7	180.7	11.0	169.7	13.64
1960-61	1,424.4	207.0	5.3	201.7	14.17
1961-62	1,631.4	243.8	53.0	190.8	11.69
1962-63	1,875.2	578.9	60.0	518.9	27.68
1963-64	2,454.1	496.8	111.0	385.8	15.72
1964-65	2,950.9	434.8	28.4	406.4	13.77
1965-66	3,385.7	904.3	410.0	494.3	14.60
1966-67	4,290.0	440.0	-	440.0	10.26
1967-68	4,730.0	470.0	-	470.0	9.94
1968-69	5,200.0	720.0	-	720.0	13.85
1969-70	5,920.0	370.0	-	370.0	6.25
1970-71	6,290.0				

Sources: Reserve Bank of India, Reports on Currency and Finance for 1961-62 and 1965-66 (Bombay: Reserve Bank of India, 1962 and 1966); Government of India, Draft Fourth Plan Material and Financial Balances (New Delhi: Planning Commission, 1964).

which might, however, be added. First, the turnover tax has
serious economic implications which will be examined later in
this chapter. Second, it is by no means certain that a single-
point tax at the retail level would be most productive in terms
of revenue in India. For the majority of States a sales tax
levied at the manufacturing or whole sale stage--at a higher
rate, of course, than had the tax been levied at the retail
stage--might produce more revenue if only by dint of its
greater administrative feasibility. A. R. Prest has pointed
out that a reform of the British Purchase tax which would levy
the tax at a retail rather than wholesale stage would multiply
the number of collecting points tenfold and the work of collection more than tenfold.[34] In most States the levy of a tax at
the retail level would necessitate the assessment of a very
large number of taxpayers who keep very rudimentary accounts.[35]
Perhaps the best system, strictly from the point of view of revenue productivity, would be a combination of the suggested
turnover tax and a relatively high rate single-point tax at the
latest stage up to retail sale at which assessment is administratively feasible.

     One of the major defects in sales taxation in India and
elsewhere has been its nearly exclusive application to tangible
commodities. The constitutional provision empowers the States
to tax only sales of "goods." The TEC, reviewing the matter
briefly, suggested that sales of services would be administratively difficult to assess, and recommended no change in the
constitutional provision.[36] The administrative argument is
important but not decisive; it would not be unfeasible to in-
sist on the issue of receipts for a wide range of personal services and consumer repair services where presently no written
document--the basis for tax--changes hands. Equally, there are
many recreational and amusement services where taxation of pur-
veyors on the basis of sales medical services or rental payments, and services to business, might be excluded, but the
widening of the State sales tax net to encompass a wide range
of personal, repair and amusement services offers one significant possibility of increasing sales tax revenue, and inciden-
tally, furthering the pursuit of vertical equity in that higher
income groups, on average, spend greater percentages of their
income on services.[37]

                              EQUITY

     In examining the contribution of indirect taxation to the
mitigation of inequalities, the initial premise will be that
indirect taxes are completely shifted forward and are borne by
consumers in proportion to their consumption expenditure on the
taxed goods. It will be argued that this assumption is something of an over-generalization but suffices as a legitimate

first approximation to indirect tax incidence; this is the premise on which recent incidence studies in India by the TEC and
the Ministry of Finance were based.[38] From the initial premise
it follows that an examination of the indirect tax element in
the price of purchases by various income groups would indicate
the degree of progressivity of indirect taxation.

The usual assumption concerning the incidence of indirect
taxation is one of regressivity, based on the observation that
the proportion of income constituted by consumption expenditure
is inversely related to the absolute level of income. M. Friedman has recently denied that consumption expenditure is a declining function of absolute real income, and has suggested
that consumers spend on the basis of normal or "permanent income,"[39] defined as the average income a consumer expects over
the long term. Friedman contends that given a sufficiently
long period of income receipt and consumption, the consumption:
income ratio would be the same for all levels of income. Were
this hypothesis to be true, the regressivity of indirect taxation would be more apparent than real, and proportionality
would seem a more likely incidence.

Friedman's hypothesis is valuable in suggesting that an
accurate measure of incidence would probably have to consider
expenditure patterns over a period longer than one year, but
statistical studies would not validate the central hypothesis
of a constant consumption:income ratio,[40] and the National
Sample Survey, TEC, and Ministry of Finance evidence on consumption patterns would strongly support the validity of a negative correlation between the proportion of income spent on
consumption and the level of income.

On the assumption of complete forward shifting several
U.S. studies have developed the view that indirect taxes may be
levied with considerable precision as to burden distribution
among individual income levels, and particularly, in reference
to the general sales tax, have suggested that possible regressivity can be removed or moderated by the exemption of food
purchases, household utilities, etc.[41] If the indirect tax
measure which is likely to be most regressive can be thus modified, it would seem likely that a mix of indirect taxes which
includes selective excise taxation and import duties with a
wide series of exemptions and discrimination against high-
income group purchases might be set up with a theoretically
progressive incidence, and thus serve as a means of mitigating
inequalities.

Recent studies of progressivity in India confirm this latter possibility and suggest that the indirect tax system was
progressive in 1953-54 and had become more so by 1958-59.[42]
Table 6 collates the results of the two studies. The proportion

of consumer expenditure paid in indirect taxes rose from 3.6
per cent in 1953-54 to 5.7 per cent in 1958-59 (Table 6b). The
rise was accounted for mainly by increased coverage of Union
excises and States sales taxes and affected both urban and
rural households (Table 6a). The proportion of consumer expenditure paid in indirect taxes by different expenditure
groups rose progressively from 2.4 per cent to 5.5 per cent in
1953-54 and from 3.1 per cent to 9.3 per cent in 1958-59 (Table
6b). Column 7, Table 6b, indicates that the increase in the
percentage of consumer expenditure paid in indirect taxation
was greater the higher the monthly expenditure group, in effect,
that the degree of progressivity had been accentuated over the
period. Another study of indirect tax incidence in 1955-56 in
India--using the same assumption that complete forward shifting
occurs--found that indirect taxes accounted for 2 per cent of
the income of the lowest income groups and 6 per cent of the
top income groups.[43]

By introducing either universal food exemptions into the
State sales tax structure or a credit refund system based on
family size and similar to a family allowance system,[44] and by
a procedure such as that suggested in the second part of the
first section of this Chapter of basing excise tax coverage and
rates on scientific extrapolations of consumer expenditure patterns and taxing at progressively higher rates those articles
purchased by successively higher income groups, it would appear possible to substantially increase the progressivity of
indirect taxation and its usefulness as a means of mitigating
inequalities.

The latter conclusion must, however, be qualified by the
approximate nature of the initial premise of complete forward
shifting. Even if complete forward shifting is assumed,
D. Dosser has shown that different and changing taste patterns
make the assumption of automatic movements of consumer purchases as incomes rise to groups of more highly taxed goods,
necessarily general and imprecise.[45] Hansen has, similarly,
drawn attention to the capricious horizontal incidence of indirect taxation on consumers in equal circumstances, and has
shown that in the U.S. families of the same size and income
were subject to considerably different tax burdens depending on
a variety of different circumstances, such as rural or urban
habitat, racial or ethnic characteristics, or simply wide variations in individual preferences in allocating expenditure.[46]

Again on the assumption of forward shifting--i.e., adjustments only on the "income uses" side through changes in relative prices of commodities bought by the consumer--J. F. Due
has shown that the degree of forward shifting will depend on
the type of tax involved and a variety of other circumstances,
in particular the level of production at which the tax is

TABLE 6

TAXATION AND HOUSEHOLD EXPENDITURE

(a) Tax as Percentage of Rural and Urban Household Expenditure

	1953-54		1958-59	
	Rural Households	Urban Households	Rural Households	Urban Households
All Indirect Taxes	2.9	5.9	4.4	9.3
Union Taxes	1.8	3.5	3.1	6.0
State Taxes	1.1	2.4	1.3	3.3

(b) Tax as Percentage of Consumer Expenditure

Monthly Household Expenditure Groups (Rs.)	1953-54			1958-59			
	1 Rural	2 Urban	3 All-India	4 Rural	5 Urban	6 All-India	7 (6 minus 3)
1- 50	2.2	3.6	2.4	2.5	5.8	3.1	0.7
51-100	2.4	4.5	2.7	3.6	7.1	4.3	1.6
101-150	2.6	5.1	3.1	4.1	8.0	5.1	2.0
151-300	2.8	5.1	3.3	4.8	9.0	5.9	2.6
301 and above	4.1	8.2	5.5	6.9	13.8	9.3	3.8
All Households	2.9	5.9	3.6	4.4	9.3	5.7	2.1

Sources: Government of India, Report of the Taxation Enquiry Commission (3 vols.; New Delhi: Ministry of Finance, 1953-54), Vol. I, pp. 69-70; Government of India, Incidence of Indirect Taxation, 1958-59 (New Delhi: Ministry of Finance, 1960), pp. 10-13.

343

imposed, the method of marketing the product and the possibility
of pyramiding over a series of intermediate stages between production and consumption, the particular circumstances of the
firm or industry on the product of which the tax is imposed,
the structure of the market for the product, the elasticity of
demand for the product and the period of time considered.[47]

A general analysis of tax incidence would also have to take
account of adjustments on the "income sources" side--changes
in the market value of consumers' services. Changing relative
factor prices will affect consumers' real income and may cause
an ultimate pattern of incidence quite different to that intended. The Brown-Rolph hypothesis[48] indeed contends that sales
taxes work to restrict the output of taxed goods and to raise
their prices, but also increase the output of exempt goods and
lower their prices; there is thus no general price change.
Sales taxes are thus like taxes on factors of production, and
the groups suffering a reduction in real income may be owners
of resources employed in the taxed industries, owners of resources on which consumers economize as a result of spending
more for the sales-taxed goods, or owners of resources which
compete with either of these groups. Given a sufficiently com-
petitive economy, the burden of sales tax will be distributed
like that of a general factor income tax with a proportional
rate.

The Brown-Rolph hypothesis is based on fairly limited assumptions, in particular, that aggregate money expenditure and
total real output are unchanged by the imposition of the tax,
and the hypothesis has been generally criticized.[49] Nonetheless, it follows that the general conception of indirect taxation leading only to adjustments on the "income uses" side is
strictly an approximation.

The conclusion of this section is that while a structure
of indirect taxation based on extrapolated expenditure patterns
may have a significant effect on the over-all progressivity of
the tax structure, the uncertainty concerning ultimate incidence
makes indirect taxation at best an imprecise and approximate
means of mitigating inequalities.

STABILIZATION

The significance of indirect taxation as a means of curtailing aggregate demand lies in deterring consumption through
an initial once-for-all increase in price of the taxed commodity. Indirect taxation is particularly significant in the
growth context in India in that, at least directly, the diminution in demand is purely at the expense of consumption rather
than investment. The potential stabilizing effectiveness of a

mode of taxation is a function of the size of tax revenue in
relation to national income, movement of tax revenue in the
same direction as national income changes, and the degree of
responsiveness of tax revenue to changes in national income.

A measure of built-in flexibility--change in tax revenue
other than from Budget changes, over change in national income
--comes to 0.055 for the aggregate of customs revenue, Union
excises, and State sales taxes, over the period 1955-56 to
1964-65, indicating that the change in revenue from the major
indirect taxes constituted 5.5 per cent of the change in national income over the same period. The most important of the
indirect taxes are, of course, Union excises, the increased revenue from which constituted 3.3 per cent of the change in national income. The changes in customs revenue and State sales
were both 1.1 per cent.

Given the relatively high flexibility coefficient, and the
fact that a large proportion of the flexibility of Union excises is the consequence of heightened rates and, to a lesser
extent, coverage, it follows that indirect taxation in India
offers an effective tool of both discretionary and automatic
stabilization. A system of import duties, sales taxes and excise taxes set up to maximize responsiveness to income changes,
with increased rates and coverage geared to movements in wholesale or consumer prices by a pre-determined statutory automatic
formula (formula flexibility), would offer increased effectiveness as a means of correcting inflationary price trends.

The effectiveness of the present indirect tax system in
countering inflation is hindered by the specific nature of most
Union excise duties. A general conversion of all excise tax
rates to an ad valorem basis would make for responsiveness of
excise tax revenue to price as well as consumption changes,
would increase the built-in automatic stabilizing effectiveness
of excise taxation, and would diminish the need for tax widening (through increased coverage) and deepening (through increased rates).

Import duties serve as a stabilizing tool in the same manner as other indirect tax measures by restricting the demand
for consumer goods, particularly those of a non-essential nature. A role of particular importance for import duties, especially at the present juncture where a series of general surcharges and rate increases have all but cancelled the relatively low rates offered to machinery, capital goods and raw materials, might be, in the context of inflationary pressure, to
offer reduced rates on key industrial inputs of a machinery or
raw material nature in an attempt to break supply bottlenecks.
Export duties may serve as a means of preventing the import of
inflation from abroad, and export duties on jute, cotton

textiles and black pepper were effectively levied for this purpose in India during the Korean War.[50] The duty on tea was not
increased in accordance with an export promotion policy; significantly, increased duty on tea would probably have been ineffective in any event because of the relative inelasticity of
demand for tea and the consequent incidence of the tax on
foreign buyers.[51] The same situation largely nullified the
effectiveness of an anti-inflationary export duty on tea in
Ceylon during the Korean War.[52]

EFFECTS ON THE PRIVATE SECTOR

Assuming that indirect taxes are completely shifted forward, their effect on private saving is largely indeterminate.
On one hand, to the extent that consumers continue to purchase
the taxed commodities, their ability to save is diminished. On
the other hand, by increasing the cost of present consumption
relative to present saving, indirect taxation provides a positive incentive to save. Increased private saving would, of
course, be a measure of diminished potential tax revenue to the
public sector. On balance, it would seem likely that no serious
effects on private saving may be expected from indirect taxation.
Similarly, there is no disincentive to invest intrinsic to indirect taxation except in the unlikely case where investment
income is intended solely for consumption.

With regard to the incentive to work, progressive indirect
taxation which falls on the commodities with a high income
elasticity of demand which individuals are likely to purchase
with their marginal earnings, may have detrimental effects on
work incentives.[53] On the other hand, such a substitution
effect may be more than compensated by an income effect which
would induce individuals to work harder in order to be able to
purchase the desired commodities irrespective of the tax. To
the extent that indirect taxation is shifted backwards to factor owners the effect on saving, investment and work is even
more uncertain; though, as the Rolph thesis suggested, the effect is most likely to be similar to that of a proportional income tax and, therefore, not to be of serious consequence for
additional work, saving or investment.

Excise taxes of a non-sumptuary nature are basically revenue devices; revenue maximization implies no change in buying patterns. There will, of course, probably be some re-
allocationary effect on the consumption pattern. It would,
however, be difficult to argue that any such change was necessarily undesirable; indeed if non-essential consumers' goods
are penalized, it is arguable that in the context of limited
means the change is likely to be desirable. Excise taxes may
also, of course, be used as deliberate interventionist devices

to divert scarce resources to particular ends considered of a priority nature; this would be accomplished by discriminatory taxation of commodities in particular uses. To the extent that excise taxes are borne by factor owners the re-allocationary effects are unpredictable.

There are two effects of the Indian excise tax structure which may be considered undesirable. First, the taxation of raw materials and goods used as industrial inputs may deter or modify investment decisions; the ultimate incidence of such a tax is unpredictable and will be distributed in a manner which is unlikely to bear any relation to consumer expenditure on the taxed goods. Wherever revenue considerations permit, it would be desirable to remove or reduce to relatively low levels all excise taxes on raw materials and industrial inputs; with the exception of the very high rates on steel products, most industrial inputs are taxed at sufficiently low rates to make the abolition of the duty of minor revenue significance.

Second, the imposition of excise duties at the manufacturing level makes some pyramiding of the tax almost inevitable; the resultant price increases to the consumer are likely to be in excess of the tax revenue collected, the excess depending on the "mark-up" procedures used at the wholesaling or retailing level. There is substantial evidence of pyramiding in the Canadian manufacturers' sales tax.[54] Since the manufacturing or wholesale levels are the only stages at which the Indian excise taxes can be levied in practice, the only means of avoiding the excess burden of pyramiding would be to link price control measures to excise tax policy.

Import duties which are protectionist in nature fall under the larger objective of the planned composition and magnitude of domestic industrial development. Insofar as such duties are successful in curtailing the importation of foreign goods, domestic resources will be diverted into the protected areas. Viewing the attainment of planning objectives as the optimum allocation of resources, such intended diversion may be considered desirable. As indicated previously, many ostensibly protective duties in India are levied at moderate rates, comparable to revenue duties on associated articles, and may be presumed to operate essentially as revenue duties.

To the extent that revenue duties are levied on final consumers' goods, possible re-allocationary effects are similar to those of excise taxes. As with excise taxes, the taxation of industrial inputs is of great importance in India, particularly in terms of the recent tariff surcharges and rate increases. The consequent increased cost of domestic investment must be weighed carefully against the revenue objective.

The effect of <u>sales taxes</u> on the private sector depends
largely on the point between production and consumption at
which particular sales taxes are imposed. It will be recalled
that a multi-point turnover tax at low rates was recommended by
the TEC on revenue grounds. This recommendation bears serious
reconsideration in terms of the economic effects of such a tax,
examples of which may be found only in the Soviet Union[55] and
West Germany.[56] The turnover tax in its pure form discriminates severely against non-integrated business concerns, makes
sub-contracting in manufacturing costly, encourages integration
directly, and assists large firms at the expense of small ones.
Although modifications have been introduced in most of the
Indian States to lessen discrimination, they seriously complicate tax administration. The comprehensive nature of the tax
makes exemptions of any categories of final product very difficult and may have serious effects on the use of industrial raw
materials. Finally, a turnover tax results in substantial
variation of burden on different commodities because of differences in the average number of transactions through which
goods pass.

In terms of economic effects, probably the most desirable
form of sales tax is one levied at the retail level. Only the
retail form allows the collection of a uniform percentage of
tax on all consumption expenditures, permits the relatively
simple introduction of exemptions and provides no incentive to
integration; likewise a retail levy avoids the pyramiding which
may occur under a manufacturers' or wholesale levy.

On balance, the economic effects of a turnover tax and the
administrative considerations previously discussed suggest that
perhaps the basic form of sales tax adopted by the Indian
States might be a wholesale level tax at reasonably high rates
with comprehensive exemptions on a relatively small number of
dealers, supplemented by a general tax at low rates with few
exemptions, imposed, however, strictly at the retail level.

CONCLUSION

Indirect taxation in India presently provides an elastic
and productive source of revenue for public spending. The revenue productivity of Union excises might be increased by increased rates on a wide range of commodities, use of <u>ad valorem</u>
rates, the establishment of tax rates and coverage on the basis
of extrapolations of consumer expenditure, and the taxation
at progressively higher rates of articles with successively
higher income elasticities of demand. Such a change would
also enhance the efficacy of indirect taxation as a means of
mitigating inequalities and would serve as a tool of formula
flexibility in containing inflation. The economic effects of

excise taxation on the private sector are unlikely to be serious; the two most serious problems are the taxation of producers goods and the problem of pyramiding. Considerations of revenue productivity suggest that the form of sales taxation adopted by the Indian States should be a combination of a turnover tax and a single-point retail levy. The economic implications of turnover taxation would, however, suggest that reliance should preferably be placed on a combination of a high rate wholesale levy and a low rate general levy at the retail level.

NOTES TO CHAPTER 10

1. Constitution, Seventh Schedule, List 1, Entry 83.

2. Government of India, Explanatory Memorandum on the Budget of the Central Government for 1965-66 (New Delhi: Ministry of Finance, 1966), pp. 16-17.

3. Government of India, Report of the Taxation Enquiry Commission (hereinafter TEC) (3 vols.; New Delhi: Ministry of Finance, 1953-54), Vol. II, pp. 272-75.

4. Government of India, Memorandum Explaining the Provisions in the Finance Bill, 1965 (New Delhi: Ministry of Finance, 1965), p. 11.

5. Constitution, Seventh Schedule, List 1, Entry 84.

6. Government of India, Explanatory Memorandum on the Budget of the Central Government for 1967-68 (New Delhi: Ministry of Finance, 1967), pp. 22-23.

7. Ibid., p. 24.

8. Harvard University Law School, International Tax Program, Taxation in India, World Tax Series (Boston: Little, Brown and Co., 1960), pp. 464-68.

9. Constitution, Seventh Schedule, List 2, Entry 51.

10. Constitution, Article 286; Medicinal and Toilet Preparations (Excise Duties) Act, 1955.

11. Constitution, Article 47.

12. H. Simons, Personal Income Taxation (Chicago: University of Chicago Press, 1938), pp. 39-40, Note 22: "Many liberal persons defend levies like the Tobacco Tax [and liquor

tax] on grounds that [these articles] are not necessities--that
poor people may or can avoid the burden by not consuming the
commodity. This position invites two comments. First, it is
hardly accurate to say that no burden is involved in getting
along without the commodity. Second, it seems a little absurd
to go around arguing that poor people could or ought to do
without tobacco [or liquor], especially if [they are] taxed, in
the face of the facts that they simply do not do anything of
the kind, that the [commodities] were selected for taxation
because they were not expected to do so, and that the government would not get much revenue if they did. The plain fact,
to one not confused by moralistic distinctions between necessities and luxuries, is simply that [sumptuary excises] are the
most effective means available for draining government revenues
out from the very bottom of the income scale." Presumably the
Union tobacco excise in India would fall under this denunciation.

13. TEC, op. cit., Vol. III, p. 130.

14. Government of India, India 1966 (Delhi: Manager of
Publications, 1967), pp. 106-10.

15. TEC, op. cit., Vol. III, pp. 138-40.

16. Constitution, Article 246, and Seventh Schedule,
List 2, Entry 54.

17. Constitution, Article 286.

18. Constitution, Article 286.

19. Constitution, Article 286 (amended).

20. A detailed study of the structure and operation of the
variety of sales taxes levied by all the States is available in
TEC, op. cit., Vol. III, pp. 1-33 and 141-62. A complete
account of present sales taxes is available in K. Chaturvedi,
The Principles of Sales Tax Laws (Calcutta: Eastern Law House
Private, Ltd., 1967). "Intended incidence" is sometimes referred to as the "impact incidence" of the tax, i.e., the pattern of legal obligations to pay the tax. In this description
of the general tax structure, "incidence" refers to "intended"
as distinct from "final" incidence.

21. TEC, op. cit., Vol. III, pp. 141-62. See also
Chaturvedi, op. cit., for details of present procedures in each
State.

22. Chaturvedi, op. cit.

23. Government of India, Memorandum Explaining the Provisions in the Finance Bill, 1966 (New Delhi: Ministry of Finance, 1966), p. 24.

24. This question is examined at some length in TEC, op. cit., Vol. II, p. 255 and adjoining chart.

25. Ibid., p. 262.

26. G. S. Sahota, Indian Tax Structure and Economic Development (Bombay: Asia Publishing House, 1961), p. 15.

27. Government of India, Report of the Central Excise Reorganisation Committee (Delhi: Manager of Publications, 1963), p. 68.

28. Ibid., p. 213.

29. H. F. Lydall and M. Ahmed, "An Exercise in Forecasting Consumer Demand and Taxation Yields in India in 1965-66," Indian Economic Review, V, No. I (August 1961), 313-32.

30. W. Malenbaum, Prospects for Indian Development (London: George Allen and Unwin, Ltd., 1962), pp. 179-82.

31. J. K. Galbraith, The Affluent Society (Boston: Houghton Mifflin, 1958), pp. 315-16. Galbraith's advocacy of the measure is tied to his theory of social imbalance; the sales tax, as the most effective way of diverting resources to the public sectoi, would help to correct that balance.

32. TEC, op. cit., Vol. III, p. 8.

33. Ibid., pp. 63-66.

34. A. R. Prest, Reform for Purchase Tax, Hobart Paper, No. 8, Second Edition (London: Institute of Economic Affairs, 1963), p. 30.

35. Administrative difficulties led C. S. Shoup et al. to recommend a general sales tax at the wholesale level in Venezuela. See C. S. Shoup et al., The Fiscal System of Venezuela --A Report (Baltimore: Johns Hopkins Press, 1959), pp. 303-12.

36. TEC, op. cit., Vol. III, p. 35.

37. The extension of sales taxation on revenue and equity grounds to services has been advocated in the U.S.A. by J. F. Due, "Retail Sales Taxation in Theory and Practice," National Tax Journal, III (1950), 314-25, and by D. C. Morgan, Retail

Sales Tax (Madison: University of Wisconsin Press, 1964), pp. 120-39.

    38.   TEC, op. cit., Vol. I, p. 45; Government of India, Incidence of Indirect Taxation in India, 1958-59 (New Delhi: Ministry of Finance, 1961), p. 6.

    39.   M. Friedman, A Theory of the Consumption Function (Princeton: Princeton University Press, for the National Bureau of Economic Research, 1957).

    40.   I. Friend and I. B. Kravis, "Consumption Patterns and Permanent Income," American Economic Review, XLVII (May 1957), 536-55; L. R. Klein and N. Liviatan, "The Significance of Income Variability on Savings Behavior," Bulletin of the Oxford University Institute of Statistics, XIX (May 1957), 151-60; T. Mayer, "The Permanent Income Theory and Occupation Groups," The Review of Economics and Statistics, XLV (February 1963), 16-22; I. Friend and S. Schor, "Who Saves," The Review of Economics and Statistics, XLI (May 1959), 213-48.

    41.   D. G. Davies, "An Empirical Test of Sales-Tax Regressivity," Journal of Political Economy, LXVII (1959), 72-78, and "Commodity Taxation and Equity," Journal of Finance, XVI (1961), 581-90; J. W. McGrew, "Effect of a Food Exemption on the Incidence of a Retail Sales Tax," National Tax Journal, II (1949), 362-67; R. R. Hansen, "An Empirical Analysis of the Retail Sales Tax with Policy Recommendations," National Tax Journal, XV (1962), 1-13.

    42.   TEC, op. cit, Vol. I, pp. 45-84; Incidence of Indirect Taxation in India, 1958-59, op. cit.

    43.   Lydall and Ahmed, op. cit., p. 320.

    44.   D. C. Morgan, op. cit., pp. 132-39.   A refund through the personal income tax would be of little use because of very low income tax coverage.

    45.   D. Dosser, "Tax Incidence and Growth," Economic Journal (1961), 41-63.

    46.   Hansen, op. cit., p. 13.

    47.   J. F. Due, Government Finance (Homewood, Ill.:   Irwin, 1959), Chapter 17, also The Theory and Incidence of Sales Taxation (New York: King's Crown Press, 1942), and Sales Taxation (London: Routledge and Kegan Paul, 1957).

    48.   H. G. Brown, "The Incidence of a General Output or a General Sales Tax," Journal of Political Economy, XLVII (April

1959), 254-62; E. Rolph, "A Proposed Revision of Excise Tax Theory," Journal of Political Economy, LX (April 1952), 102-17, and The Theory of Fiscal Economics (Berkeley: University of California Press, 1954), Chapters VI-VIII; see also E. Rolph and G. Break, Public Finance (New York: Ronald Book Co., 1961), pp. 287-309.

49. See, particularly, D. C. Morgan, op. cit., pp. 107-19; C. A. Hall, Jr., review of Public Finance, by Rolph and Break, in American Economic Review, LII (March 1962), 267-69; R. A. Musgrave, The Theory of Public Finance (New York: McGraw-Hill, 1959), pp. 347-71.

50. TEC, op. cit., Vol. II, pp. 276-77.

51. Ibid., p. 275.

52. C. E. Staley, "Export Taxes in Ceylon," Public Finance, XIV-XV (1959-60), 249-68.

53. This point is developed by A. R. Prest in Public Finance in Underdeveloped Countries (London: Weidenfeld and Nicolson, 1962), p. 26, and in Reform for Purchase Tax, op. cit., p. 14.

54. J. F. Due, Government Finance, op. cit., p. 294.

55. P. J. Pettibone, "The Soviet Turnover Tax," Public Finance, XIX, No. 4 (1964), 361-82.

56. "The German Umsatzsteuer," in OEEC, The Influence of Sales Taxes on Productivity (Paris, 1958), pp. 85-102.

CHAPTER **11** TAX
ADMINISTRATION

It is not the object of this section to discuss, even
cursorily, the entire system of fiscal administration in India.
Such a formidable task has been adequately undertaken on several
occasions and is well documented.[1] Further, this chapter will
not be concerned with the entire budgetary process, but merely
with the administrative criteria applicable to budget implementation on the revenue side.

The primary responsibility for tax formulation and administration in the Union government lies with the Department of Revenue in the Ministry of Finance, but its functions are delegated to the Central Board of Revenue. The Board consists of the
Secretary of the Department of Revenue, acting as chairman, and
four Joint Secretaries of the Department of Revenue as members.
Apart from its role in the formulation of tax measures, the
Board supervises the administration of Union taxes and performs
additional functions assigned to it under the various tax Acts.
Through the Commissioners of Income Tax, the Board directs and
controls the administration of income, wealth, gift and--until
the 1966-67 Budget--expenditure taxes. Through corresponding
tax officers the Board administers Union excise duties, estate
taxation, and customs duties.

Administrative difficulty is primarily a problem of direct
taxation, and therein of personal direct taxation. It is in
this area that the major difficulties of tax assessment, enforcement, collection and administration generally are to be
found, as the literary evidence amply attests.[2] Attention will
then be mainly directed to personal direct taxation, but administrative difficulties in corporation taxation and in customs
and excise taxation will also be examined briefly, and those of
sales taxation at some length.

The discussion will be framed in terms of the general revenue productivity criterion of minimizing collection costs to
both tax collector and taxpayer, but will also be extended to
include the view, introduced in Chapter 2, that the criterion
of minimizing administrative cost be qualified, first, by the
fact that such an injunction may conflict with the other tax
objectives of growth, redistribution, and stabilization, and,
second, by the notion that it might be desirable to extend the

marginal cost of tax administration (defined as the cost of a
unit extension of administrative facilities) beyond marginal
revenue productivity (defined as the additional revenue consequent on the extension of the administrative facilities by one
unit), in the short run in order to minimize, in the long run,
administrative costs per unit of revenue. In effect, present
administrative machinery and procedures cannot be construed as
constituting absolute parameters on the development of a more
elastic, sophisticated tax system.

PERSONAL DIRECT TAXATION

It is proposed under this head to consider specific administrative reforms for wealth and income taxation, to consider at some length the problem of income tax avoidance and
evasion, and to elaborate the notion of a comprehensive self-
checking return for personal direct taxation.

Wealth Taxation

Behind all income--with the exception of vocational or
professional incomes--lie physical or monetary assets; equally,
most property yields income or profit of some kind. Assessment
of both income and property thus provides a large measure of
reciprocal cross-checking and increases the administrative
efficiency of the tax system. There are, however, two major
administrative difficulties under the existing net wealth tax.

The first is the issue of wealth tax evasion through failure to report possession of assets. Possible means to curtailment of such evasion would include the establishment of a Central Records Office for the listing and valuation of urban
property (along the lines suggested by the Local Finance
Enquiry Committee in 1951)[3] and the registration of ownership
of government securities at the Reserve Bank.

To date, the only relationship between registration procedures under the Indian Registration Act, 1908, and tax liability, is Section 230A of the Income Tax Act which requires the
sanction of an Income Tax Officer as to satisfaction of liability to income, wealth, gift and expenditure taxes, before a
transfer of property of value greater than Rs. 50,000 may be
registered.

The second problem is that of valuation of assets. It is
axiomatic that a tax on current value must encounter more
severe problems of valuation than a tax based on income or receipts in that no transaction is involved in the current value
case. The exemption of corporations from wealth tax liability
removes the most intractable valuation problems but difficulties

remain, in particular in the case of personal assets, etc., not generally marketed.

At present in India the value of an asset is the price it would command on an open market on the valuation date, this value being determined by a Wealth Tax Officer from whose decision appeal can be made to an Appellate Assistant Commissioner and thence to an Appellate Tribunal.[4] This appeal system would appear to be adequate for the elimination of the inequities of arbitrary assessment in cases where no clear market value is apparent, and to provide some recourse where the taxpayer's initial assessment of liability is rejected by a Wealth Tax Officer.

Valuation problems would, however, be greatly eased by the establishment of Mr. Kaldor's proposed Central Valuation Department[5] (under the Central Board of Revenue) and an array of regional and sub-regional offices; such a co-ordinating agency might serve to reduce the number of contested valuations and thus lessen the amount of appellate work. The possible use of a capital levy would accentuate the need for a Central Valuation Department.

Income Taxation

The problems to be examined under this head are, first, some general administrative points; second, the most desirable means of collection; third, the problem of the administration of the proposed averaging system; fourth, the problem of inadequate accounting records and the assessment of relatively small income recipients, and, fifth, the critical problem of avoidance and evasion.

The recent studies by a U.S. Internal Revenue team[6] and by Mr. Bhoothalingam[7] have focused on several general administrative points, and steps have been taken to at least begin implementation of their recommendations. This writer disagrees with the recommendation that the use of annuity deposits in the income tax structure be abolished. The case for a scheme of compulsory savings in India has been made in Chapter 8, and requires no reiteration.

The recommendation that discrimination against unearned income be abolished is, however, undoubtedly a good one. This essay has argued strongly for an elaborate system of incentives to save and invest, and it would be absurd to argue on the one hand for such incentives, and on the other to advocate discriminatory treatment of earnings from such employment of resources. Quite apart from the incentive question, the definition of income advocated in Chapter 3 generally requires that income of all sorts from all sources be treated in an identical manner. Recent Budgets have moved toward the elimination of the unnecessary distinction.

The 1967-68 Budget also saw the introduction of two further measures advocated in the studies referred to above-- the application of tax changes prospectively, and the introduction of a "functional" system of income tax administration.

As of 1967-68, the practice of applying budgeted tax rates retrospectively to incomes of the past year was abandoned; all changes in tax law and rates will henceforth be applied prospectively. The rationale of tax incentives depends, in their first year of operation, entirely on prospective application, and this reform removes an anomaly from the tax system.

Following a highly successful project by the U.S. Internal Revenue team, it was proposed in the 1967-68 Budget to expedite income tax assessment and improve collections by adopting the so-called functional system of tax administration. Under the previous system the Income Tax Officer was responsible for the entire range of functions in respect of a particular group of assessees: under the functional system particular functions are assigned to different Income Tax Officers. The major advantages of the new scheme are specialization and concentration of senior staff on only the most important functions and cases. If the results of the pilot projects are repeated in the rest of the country the huge backlog of assessments--over two million cases as of March 31, 1966--involving tax of Rs. 640 million[8]--may begin to be seriously dealt with.

The withholding system of collection employed with regard to salaries, income from dividends and interest on securities-- and, since the 1967-68 Budget, interest on deposits, loans and other borrowings[9]--is unquestionably the most efficient collection method employed, from the point of view of both assessor and assessee, and the system might be extended wherever possible to wage recipients and to professional fees of all kinds.[10] In the case of those assessees for whom withholding is not possible, such as self-employed individuals, the present system of quarterly advance payments of tax liability should be extended as widely as possible. The percentage of income tax revenue submitted in the form of advance payments rose from 33 per cent in 1948-49[11] to 45 per cent in 1963-64,[12] and this technique of installment collection has received the blessing of the TEC.[13]

The two possible income averaging schemes suggested were those of Vickrey and Holt. The economic advantages of the latter are complemented by greater administrative simplicity. The Holt scheme does not involve extended record-keeping for the taxpayer, nor does it involve the tax authorities in complex assessment problems. Vickrey's scheme, on the other hand,

provides a table of rates for each year of operation of the tax
and would present formidable checking and assessment problems,
particularly in the context of changing tax law. The computation of tax liability by the taxpayer on the basis of extended
records and elaborate interest computation would seem unduly
complex from the taxpayers' viewpoint.

The inadequacy of taxpayer accounting records entails a
substantial amount of arbitrary assessment, for instance, of
small retailers' incomes.[14] The development of a relatively
simple accounting form, the monthly completion of which would
be mandatory, and subject to inspection, would facilitate tax
assessment. For other than small assessees (income below
Rs. 7,500) the Direct Taxes Administration Enquiry Committee
(DTAEC) recommended that minimum accounts should be prescribed
for all trades, businesses and vocations.[15] No action has been
taken on this recommendation. For small assessees the DTAEC
recommended the compulsory completion of a special, relatively
simple form, accompanied by special charts and ready-reckoners,
and the provision of a special Income Tax Office staff to
assist assessees.[16] No action has been taken on this recommendation either and the possible role of such a procedure in a
new system of tax administration, based on a comprehensive tax
return, will be examined later in this chapter.

The major administrative problem is the curtailment of
avoidance and evasion. In this section the terminology will be
defined, estimates of the magnitude of evasion presented, present policy in India outlined, and possible reforms suggested.
The TEC defined the concepts of avoidance and evasion unequivo-
cally:

> Leakage in revenue may occur either through a
> deliberate distortion of facts relating to an
> assessment after the liability has been incurred,
> or by so arranging one's affairs before the lia-
> bility is incurred as to prevent its occurence or
> to reduce the incidence of the tax within the
> framework of the existing legislation. The former
> set of transactions is usually referred to as
> "evasion" and the latter as "avoidance," . . .
> Both avoidance and evasion result in loss of reve-
> nue to [the] Government, but the former has the
> colour of legality about it. In the net result,
> the burden on the honest citizen increases pro
> tanto.[17]

It is clear that the difference between avoidance and
evasion is only one of degree; both offend the spirit of the
law although the former may technically conform to its letter.
Procedures to alleviate one will also diminish the other, but

it may be said that evasion is the more serious problem.
Avoidance may be dealt with by removing ambiguities in the definition of the tax base, plugging the numerous loopholes in
the law and by meticulous drafting of new legislation. The
prevention of evasion, on the other hand, requires the above
measures and also rigorous enforcement and strict administration of tax provisions, and the use of a variety of techniques
to promote accurate disclosure, both through voluntary disclosure systems and through severe punishment of offenders
"pour encourager les autres."

Among the devices employed to dodge taxation the TEC lists
under evasion the following procedures: omission to report
taxable income, fraudulent changes in account books, maintenance of multiple sets of account books, opening of bank
accounts under assumed names, securing of contracts in the
name of figureheads or non-existent persons, and keeping transactions out of account books. Under avoidance are suggested:
the creation of corporate institutions to escape liability to
personal income tax, the use of charitable trusts for the same
purpose, the constitution of trusts and family partnerships and
the transference of income-earning assets to one's wife and
children for fractioning income for tax purposes.[18]

It is very difficult by the very nature of the problem to
estimate the extent of tax evasion. Professor Kaldor in 1956
made some estimates of evasion in India on the basis of tenta-
tive figures of the distribution of national income submitted
by the Indian Statistical Office. He concluded that the amount
of income tax lost through evasion amounted to between Rs. 2,000
million and Rs. 3,000 million for the year 1953-54.[19] A con-
temporaneous, and more thorough study by the Central Board of
Revenue reached the much more modest estimate for the same year
of Rs. 200-300 million.[20] Mr. Kaldor's figures included much
that the Central Board of Revenue counted as avoidance rather
than evasion, but even apart from this it does appear that his
estimates are on the high side. This suspicion is echoed by
the DTAEC:

We are of the opinion that the quantum of evasion,
though undoubtedly high, is not of the magnitude
indicated by Professor Kaldor in his report.[21]

The DTAEC reported that of the 1,058 cases investigated by
the Income Tax Investigation Commission concealed income of the
order of Rs. 450 million was discovered and taxes and penalties
levied to the extent of Rs. 294.2 million.[22] The Voluntary
Disclosure Scheme of 1951 dealt with 20,912 cases, and imposed
additional taxes and penalties amounting to Rs. 110 million,[23]
and up to March 31, 1967, the 1951 and subsequent Voluntary

Disclosure Schemes had yielded Rs. 2,271.7 million of concealed income.[24]

Investigation by the Department of Revenue under Section 34 of the Income Tax Act, which permits the reopening of past cases, in the fiscal year 1958-59 resulted in additional tax and penalties of Rs. 156.40 million from concealed incomes amounting to Rs. 311.0 million in some 27,343 cases investigated.[25] Each year the office of the Comptroller and Auditor General of India publishes statistics of evasion for the preceding year. The most recent statistics available are for 1965-66, when penalties were levied in 24,165 cases under Section 271 of the Income Tax Act, which specifies procedures in the event of concealment of income. A total of concealed income of Rs. 207.6 million was discovered, against which penalties of Rs. 45.9 million, and extra tax of Rs. 76.05 million were levied.[26]

The above figures are, however, only of attempted and detected evasion. The quantum of undetected evasion is certainly considerably higher, especially bearing in mind the inadequacy of trained staff to cope with the problem.[27]

In his analysis of the income elasticity of the Indian tax structure Sahota reaches some interesting conclusions on the extent of evasion.[28] Over the period 1951-52 to 1957-58 he shows that gross income tax receipts have increased at only 0.6 per cent per annum as against a rise of 2.2 per cent per annum in national income and 3.5 per cent per annum in incomes originating in the urban sector (which pays virtually the entire present income tax). An ingenious piece of statistical analysis is then attempted to indicate the theoretical extent to which tax yields should increase; and he shows that the elasticity built into the income tax structure is such that a 1 per cent increase in the incomes of taxpayers should lead to a 1.82 per cent increase in tax yields.[29] The realized figure of 0.6 per cent falls far short of this goal. To illustrate the actual extent of evasion he applies 1957-58 tax rates to the initial year 1951-52 and the final year 1957-58 to estimate the theoretical increase in tax yields resulting from built-in flexibility in the tax structure (tax rates are assumed constant throughout). His findings show that income tax yields due to built-in factors should have increased by 28.2 per cent, whereas they actually fell by 6.53 per cent, giving a total shortfall, over the seven years, of 34.7 per cent. Sahota concludes that widespread tax evasion is the prime cause of the inelasticity of income tax revenue.[30]

A similar, but much shorter, study has argued that of expected personal income tax yield in 1960-61 over 1950-51, only

43 per cent was collected, the 57 per cent shortfall being accounted for by avoidance and evasion.[31]

Present Policy

The existence of large-scale evasion vitiates a system of income taxation, and the importance of adequate administration and legal measures to combat evasion cannot be over-emphasized. The procedure of enquiry and investigation in India at present is relatively complex.[32] There are two groups of arrangements for investigation; the first may be designated administrative measures to trace assessees who have come within the purview of income tax but have as yet failed to send in returns, and to verify the accuracy of returns submitted by present assessees; the second falls under the heading of special arrangements to deal with cases of substantial evasion.

Investigations under the first head are carried out by external survey, the exchange of information collected from the records of existing assessees available in the Income Tax Department, and the collection and collation of information obtained from outside sources, including informers.

"External survey" consists of door-to-door inquiry in cities, towns and large villages by Inspectors of the Department of Revenue at regular intervals, usually once every three years. This work appears to have been conspicuously successful.[33] "Internal survey" and exchange of information refers to the system of cross-verification whereby Assessing Officers check transactions recorded in an assessee's records by reference to the records of another party or to other information available in the Department. Apparently such work is understaffed and is badly in arrears.[34]

The regional agencies for the collection, collation and distribution of information from outside sources are the Special Investigation Branches, one of which is located in each of the eighteen Commissioners' offices. These branches collect information from a variety of sources, official and non-official.[35] Information of an inter-State character is gathered, collated and disseminated to the Special Branches by the Director of Investigations attached to the Central Board of Revenue. Under this Director is the Collation Branch located in Madras which collects information from the various Departments of the Union and State governments and quasi-governmental bodies concerning payments to contractors, and also collates the returns of companies showing dividend payments of over Rs. 5,000. This information is submitted to Income Tax Officers.[36]

Another source of information relating to the nefarious activities of taxpayers is the informer. Rewards are given

under conditions laid down by executive instructions.[37] Rewards
are at the discretion of the government, reach a maximum of 2.5
per cent of the resultant gain to revenue and are generally
paid only after the tax had been collected. Although subject
to much disapproval on the grounds that the system encouraged
blackmail,[38] the DTAEC confirmed that substantial revenue has
been derived in this manner and vindicated the procedure.[39]

Apart from the administrative procedures there are special
arrangements for investigation into cases of substantial evasion. First, there are four Central Commissioners of Income
Tax in Bombay, Calcutta, Delhi and Madras, who have no specific
regional jurisdiction but examine any assessment that is specifically allotted to either of them which the Central Board of
Revenue has decided warrants special examination. The work of
these Commissioners has proved quite effective but is substantially in arrears.[40] Second, there are presently twenty-eight
so-called Special Circles scattered over the country and responsible to the Central Commissioner's charges; to these Circles
are assigned cases requiring detailed investigation.[41] Third,
in January 1966 four intelligence units were set up in Calcutta,
Madras, Bombay and Delhi to collect and process information on
evasion for use by the Central Commissioners.[42] Finally, on
the recommendation of the Income Tax Investigation Commission,
a Directorate of Inspection (Investigation) was set up in 1952
to undertake and co-ordinate investigations in difficult and
complicated cases of tax evasion. This Directorate exercises
technical supervision and control of the twenty-eight Special
Circles and also co-ordinates the investigation work of the
Commissioner's offices.[43]

The investigations of these various groups are conducted
under a variety of powers conferred by the Income Tax Act. Of
particular importance are Section 34, which provides the power
to re-open past cases, the recently amended powers of Income
Tax Officers which permit the entering and searching of any
building or place and the seizing of books or accounts or other
documents relevant for assessment purposes[44]--this amendment
was in pursuance of the recommendations of the TEC[45]--and the
power to call for a statement of assets and liabilities of an
assessee on a particular date. This so-called net worth statement is permitted under Section 22(4) of the Income Tax Act.[46]
Until the 1964-65 Budget the secrecy provisions of the Income
Tax Act prohibited disclosure of assessment records. Mr. Krishnamachari's 1964 Budget removed this limitation, in accordance
with the recommendation of the DTAEC,[47] and in spite of an exhortation against such a procedure by the TEC.[48]

The 1964-65 Budget of the Union government extended widely
the provisions for expediting tax collection, countering tax
evasion and bringing tax offenders to book more effectively.

The inducement of 1 per cent discount on taxes paid before the
first of January of the assessment year and the penalty of 2
per cent interest if no return is filed or tax paid by December
31 of the assessment year, introduced in the Finance Act of
1963, were found to have been ineffective in ensuring the payment of tax on a self-assessment basis. The new legislation
included increased penalty for late returns, a tightening of
the provisions regarding concealment of income, the provision
of extensive powers of search, and the abolition of the secrecy
provisions prohibiting disclosure of information in the assessment records.[49]

The general structure of the deterrent system remains,
however, unchanged and relatively gentle.[50] Penalties are at
present calculated with reference to the amount of tax demand
raised against the assessees. The various direct tax acts provide that in cases of concealment of income, wealth, expenditure, gifts, etc., or deliberate furnishing of inaccurate par-
ticulars in regard to them, penalties up to a maximum of one
and one half times the amount of tax sought to be evaded may be
levied.

In addition to monetary penalties, various acts of omission and commission are subject to prosecution under Sections
51 and 52 of the Income Tax Act and corresponding sections of
the other direct tax acts--until 1964-65 prosecution might not
be brought on the same facts under which a monetary penalty had
been imposed; this restriction was removed in the 1964-65 Budget. Imprisonment of not less than six months and up to two
years may be imposed in cases brought to prosecution under the
various direct tax acts.[51] Significantly, the maximum monetary
penalty is seldom levied and even the moderate penalties levied
by assessing officers are often reduced by the appelate authorities to nominal amounts. The DTAEC commented succinctly:

Non-levy of deterrent penalties has been an important factor in encouraging evasion. . . . In actual
practice, even a 10% penalty is not ultimately levied
in many cases.[52]

Similarly, prosecution is rarely resorted to. The DTAEC pointed
out that not a single person had been convicted for an offense
against the Income Tax Act in the last ten years, and that pre-
liminary hearings had been initiated in only a very small number of cases.[53] An examination of the annual Audit Reports of
the office of the Comptroller and Auditor General reveals that
no prosecutions had occurred up to March 31, 1966.

Such a policy of leniency is apparently based on the belief that the tax authorities will fare better if they encourage offenders to voluntarily confess offenses by permitting

exemption from penalties rather than threaten dire consequences as a deterrent to evasion. This is the principle of the British "confession method," enacted in Section 504 of the U.K. Income Tax Act 1952. A formal scheme of Voluntary Disclosure was, in fact, operated by the Union government from May to October 1951. The principle of the scheme was informally maintained, however, and the DTAEC reported that by the end of 1958-59 some 21,000 cases had been settled in this way with an addition to revenue of Rs. 109.8 million.[54] The 1965-66 Budget formally provided for another three-month voluntary disclosure period from March 1 to May 31. Under this scheme, an individual who has failed to disclose his income to the authorities before March 1, 1965, was allowed to declare his income up to May 31, 1965. The rate of tax payable was to be 60 per cent of such income, or 57 per cent for declarants who paid the tax in March 1965. Provision was made under the scheme for granting immunity to the declarant from any assessment or re-assessment of the income declared by him, and maintaining secrecy as to his identity.[55] The revenue significance of these Voluntary Disclosure schemes to date has been indicated earlier in this chapter.

Reforms: General

Various further administrative reforms appear to be necessary if the proposed tax system is to function effectively in a growing Indian economy.

The recent abrogation of the secrecy provisions in the direct tax acts is a desirable amendment. There are several excellent precedents. In Sweden the "publicity principle" is of great importance in the tax field. While details of tax declarations must be kept secret, the official assessment lists, showing the amounts of assessable income as determined by the assessment boards, are public documents. Regular figures of income and wealth of firms and individuals are thus available.[56] Equally, every citizen must declare his income when he is registered under the National Registration Law which is necessary for social security purposes. This register is open to inspection by members of the public. In Norway figures of wealth and income of taxpayers are available for public inspection, and the French government regularly publishes a list of taxpayers and tax paid. Finally, in Italy the published figures include declared income and official estimates, which enables the public to see such a gap as may exist.[57] The DTAEC recommended the use of this publicity principle in India,[58] and the recent legislation goes far to implement this recommendation, though there is no reason why the principle should not be further extended on the Italian model, publishing both declared and assessed income. A further recommendation of the DTAEC--publication of the names of all persons on whom penalties of more than Rs. 5,000 have been levied[59]--has not been implemented.

There seems no reason why the Australian precedent of publication of all offenders should not be followed. In the U.S. also,
considerable publicity is given to the discovery of tax frauds
and to the punishment meted out to offenders.

The relatively mild penalties meted out to tax evaders
in India have been indicated. Professor Kaldor drew particular
attention to, and was sharply critical of, this policy of moderation; given the relatively low probability of detection in
India (he suggests one chance in ten) he calculated that to be
a real deterrent the penalty imposed should be more than 900
per cent of the sum evaded rather than 150 per cent.[60] The TEC
also examined this problem and suggested raising the maximum
penalty to three times the tax evaded.[61] However, the DTAEC
concluded that the present 150 per cent penalty would suffice[62]
and the maximum penalty has remained at that level. The DTAEC
did advocate an immutable statutory scale of penalties beneath
the maximum figure to counter appellate leniency; this recommendation has been ignored. What might be effective would be
a rigorous statutory scale of penalties commensurate with the
magnitude of the offense and reaching a maximum of five times
the amount of tax evaded, as occurs in Sweden.[63] There is
really no valid reason for a statutory maximum, and provision
might be made for a discretionary statutory order by the Minister of Finance waiving the maximum.

The question of prosecution might also be approached with
far greater vigor. The supine record of action under the
appropriate section of the direct tax acts has already been
indicated. The DTAEC was adamant on this issue:

> . . . failure to institute prosecution even in clear
> cases of tax evasion, cannot, in our opinion, be
> justified. . . . We feel that in all cases of
> deliberate concealment, where there is sufficient
> evidence, the Department should as a rule, resort
> to criminal prosecution.[64]

The Committee did not, however, believe that the maximum periods
of imprisonment should be raised,[65] but did suggest the creation
of a specialized Enforcement Branch in each Commissioner's office; no action has been taken on the latter recommendation.

There seems no reason why relatively severe penalties
should not be levied against this peculiarly culpable offense.
In the U.S., criminal prosecution of willful evasion is frequently resorted to under code Section 7201 which carries a fine of
$10,000 or imprisonment for not more than five years or both.[66]
In Sweden, criminal prosecution is also common for tax offenses.
A scale of rigorous fines corresponding to the nature of the
offense may be levied as may prison sentences culminating in

two years hard labor.[67]   The American precedent of a five year
maximum would suggest a model for the Indian system.   Prosecution should also be an automatic statutory procedure.   This
essay would echo the spirit of Mr. Kaldor's summary:

> I feel quite certain that very heavy penalties
> and prosecution with a great dea. of publicity
> is an infinitely more effective method of dealing
> with tax evasion than the policy of deliberate
> leniency and avoidance of public disclosure fol-
> lowed in Britain and India.[68]

Specialized enforcement officers--along the lines suggested by
the DTAEC[69]--attached to the Commissioner's offices should be
available for such prosecution, and this function might now be
discharged by the four intelligence units described above.

What is suggested, however, is that rigorous enforcement
of tax obligations and severe punishment of offenders be accompanied by the increased use of the "confession" or "voluntary
disclosure" method for a specified monthly period every two or
three years.   This method has been reasonably successful in
Britain and in 1951 in India, has been tried again in 1965, and
should be a useful statutory feature of the Indian tax system
provided severe retribution is meted out to continued concealment after the regular amnesty period.   The risk of dishonesty
would then be considerable, the effective inducement to probity
higher, and the incentive to utilize the regular--biennial or
triennial--period of very moderate penalties, say, 25 per cent
of tax evaded, substantially increased.   The suggestion is made
despite the feelings of both the TEC[70] and the DTAEC[71] to the
contrary.

Mention has been made of the power under Section 22 of the
Income Tax Act to call for a "Net Worth" statement.   The TEC
recommended that such a statement should be compulsory under
the law every three years.[72]   What might be more effective
would be the increased use of this power on a random sample
basis every year, and the enactment of a compulsory universal
submission every three years.

A few very general recommendations along the lines suggested by the DTAEC might be effected.   It was proposed that the
present Directorate of Inspection should be renamed the Directorate of Inspection and Intelligence and should assume the
formal functions of collecting, collating and disseminating
to the various Commissioner's offices all such information as
would be useful in determining the correct tax liability of the
assessee.   Such a Directorate should employ specialists in particular areas, professions or industries to investigate these
fields.[73]   This seems a desirable suggestion; it would be

useful to co-ordinate and formalize the present intelligence work done, particularly since the recent creation of the four regional intelligence units. Again it was suggested that the work of the Collation Branch and the extent of internal and external surveys should be intensified and improved. This set of suggestions involves increased expenditure on personnel training. The present shortage of personnel is regarded as a major cause of evasion.[74]

Related to personnel training is the question of public education. The DTAEC talked generally about the need for public education and made a detailed list of suggestions under the somewhat ambitious title of "Arousing Public Conscience."[75] The recommendations covered public education through press, radio and film of the real object of taxation, and a presentation of clear evidence that tax revenue was not squandered, deprivation of convicted evaders of the right to official patronage or recognition of any kind, increased prosecution and publicity of cases, and the enlistment of the co-operation of professional associations and civic leaders.[76] The exhortation to increased publicity and public education is of great significance in the Indian situation.

Reforms: A Comprehensive Personal Direct Tax Return

A major step to administrative refinement in Indian direct taxation and to the prevention of evasion would be the introduction of a comprehensive self-checking direct tax return along the lines suggested by Mr. Kaldor.[77] Mr. Kaldor recommended that the taxation of income--defined to include capital gains and all increases in wealth--a net wealth tax, an expenditure tax, and gift and inheritance taxes be enacted and combined in a comprehensive, self-checking return. The Indian government has enacted most of these recommendations in a piecemeal fashion--a capital gains tax in 1956, a net wealth tax in 1957, an expenditure tax in 1957 (suspended in the 1962-63 Budget, reintroduced in the 1964-65 Budget, and abolished in the 1966-67 Budget), and a gift tax in 1958. The capital gains tax is reported on the return of personal income tax (although long-term gains are treated as a separate entity and taxed at concessionary rates) but the other direct taxes are all reported separately; there is thus no provision as yet for a comprehensive return.

The self-checking system proposed by Mr. Kaldor has two aspects--the first relating to the reconciliation of the accounts for different taxes paid by the same taxpayer and the second relating to the proposed voucher system for capital transactions by means of which the reported transactions of one taxpayer could be verified against the reported transactions of another. In regard to the checking of an individual return

Mr. Kaldor stressed that the requirement of furnishing a complete set of accounts, i.e., a statement of total wealth at the beginning of the year, all accruals during the year by way of gifts, bequests, winnings and all forms of taxable income, the application of these to personal expenses and investments, and a complete statement of the resulting asset picture at the end of the year, would make the concealment of income or property and the falsification of accounts much more difficult.[78]

The second aspect, the cross-checking of property transactions, would be achieved by the allotment to each taxpayer of a code number, and the compulsory registration--using a duplicate system of vouchers--of all property transactions and cash payments over a certain sum (Rs. 10,000) which are not made for goods and services.[79] To reinforce this system Mr. Kaldor advocates compulsory auditing of all accounts above certain minimum limits. He is cognizant of the shortage of trained accounting staff in India but suggests that the minimum be fairly high initially and be lowered as staff become available.[80]

Such a system goes far in the direction of self-enforcement, but is not a completely closed system. It will not prevent evasion if both parties to a transaction gain by understatement or concealment. Thus under the Kaldor system the seller of a capital asset will gain by reporting its sale, thus providing a check on concealment or understatement by the buyer; but in the case of a transfer of goods, both buyer and seller may gain from falsification of accounts--the buyer reducing his expenditure tax and the seller his income tax.

Higgins has devised a means of closing this gap and ensuring that this system is, in fact, completely self-enforcing, so that any individual failing to report one taxable transaction will find that either his tax liability under another head has been increased or that the transaction has been reported by the other party who will gain by so doing.[81] This tightening of the system is accomplished by adding to the Kaldor system of personal taxation and corporate income and wealth taxation a penal tax on excess inventories and a general sales or turnover tax. Specific investment incentives are included in the system and Higgins points out that the only possible means by avoiding tax liability under his system would be either by buying goods or assets without reporting or detection and later selling without reporting or detection, or by reporting false sales and later selling without reporting or detection.[82]

The refinements suggested by Higgins are subject to modification in the Indian setting--particularly in that the general sales tax is collected and retained by the States--but do not present insuperable additional difficulties to the administration of the Kaldor proposals. There is no reason why in all possible cases the annual sales tax statement by those engaged in trades, businesses and professions, should not be incorporated in the return suggested by Kaldor.

The possibilities of using a comprehensive return are indicated by the experience of Sweden and Ceylon. In Sweden a comprehensive return is submitted by individual taxpayers covering the national income tax, the national tax on net wealth--which includes all real and financial property with few exceptions[83]--and the local income tax. Corporations and other bodies not subject to the wealth tax submit a return covering national and local income tax.[84] The taxpayer's declaration is merely an information form, tax assessment being computed by the tax authorities.[85] A system of vouchers for property transactions, similar to Kaldor's proposal for use in India, is also employed.[86]

Ceylon has gone further than India in implementing the Kaldor proposals.[87] The system adopted in 1959 includes a revised income tax (including capital gains), a personal tax incorporating a wealth tax, an expenditure tax and a gift tax, and a revised estate duty.[88] Although the self-checking aspect of this system of interlocking direct taxes was emphasized as a major objective,[89] the full Kaldor proposals to ensure self-enforcement have not been implemented. First, the comprehensive return covers only the taxes comprised in the new personal tax. Second, there is no system of registration for property transfers and cash transactions over a certain minimum. Because of these deficiencies the opportunities for cross-checking are diminished and rendered administratively more difficult. However, as Goode has indicated,[90] even with these inadequacies, a considerable amount of cross-checking is still possible, given administrative endeavor and a degree of taxpayer compliance, because of the interlocking nature of the taxes.

Administrative Feasibility

Objections to the introduction of the comprehensive self-checking system in India are mainly on administrative grounds. The DTAEC after what appears to be a very perfunctory examination declared:

We consider that such a system would throw an undue volume of work and is unworkable under the conditions existing in India today.[91]

This view has been echoed by A. R. Prest.[92]

It may be readily conceded that the amount of administrative work involved in setting up the proposed system would be

considerable. However, there are several reasons why the above
objections would not appear to be decisive. First, the adoption of the proposed system--of a Kaldor-Higgins model specifically adapted to the Indian constitutional situation--need not
involve even in the short run more administrative work than the
present administration of the complex direct tax structure under which the return for each direct tax is submitted individu-
ally. In the long run the use of the new system with automatic
statutory provisions and individual code numbers should involve
considerably less work than the extension of the present system, and lower costs per unit of revenue derived.

Second, Indian administrative ability may have been seriously underestimated. The withholding system of tax deduction
at source for certain types of income was introduced during
the last war and has worked very well.[93] The technical complexity of administering such a system has been clearly described,[94]
and Indian ability to successfully implement the withholding
scheme would augur well for the possibilities of successful administration of the comprehensive self-checking return.

Third, the belief that the present Indian system is self-
checking and that there is no need to improve the scheme may be
shown to be fallacious. The DTAEC concluded:

> Almost the same object is achieved at present by
> the collecting of information from the registration
> offices and other sources every year. . . . [Thus]
> the present integrated scheme of taxation is itself
> self-checking in character and should, in the long
> run, provide sufficient information to the taxing
> authorities to put to the test the returns and state-
> ments of the assessees regarding their income, wealth,
> etc.[95]

Quite apart from the clearly enormous administrative task of
compiling and collating information from half a dozen separate
returns, this method is not self-checking. The multiplicity of
returns involved would make checking the return of an individual
taxpayer much more difficult and there is no system of automatic
property transference registration to provide for cross-checking
as between taxpayers. R. M. Eigner has shown that the present
returns in India could be used--with the multiplicity of labor
envisaged above however--as a checking mechanism for the individual taxpayer only if the dates for the reporting of opening
and closing net wealth and the periods for the reporting of income and expenditure are co-ordinated.[96]

Fourth, much of the criticism on administrative grounds is based on the belief that such a system would be incomprehensible to, and would place a great burden of inconvenience upon, the taxpaying group. To offset possible inconvenience three procedures might be undertaken:

First, the comprehensive return might in the first few years be confined to middle and upper income groups whose annual income exceeds Rs. 7,500. For assessees with incomes below this level the DTAEC proposal (previously detailed) for the assessment of small income recipients might be introduced.

Second, it is suggested that in the early years of the tax the Swedish procedure be adopted of submission by the taxpayer of an information return only; the entire tax computation would be done by the tax authorities.[98] This is a concession to taxpayer convenience which results in greater administrative responsibility, and implies the use of regional assessment boards; this might be accomplished in India by extending the role of the sixteen regional Commissioners of Income Tax.[99]

Third, given the relative complexity of the proposed system in India there might be established a National Tax Board (in Sweden the riksskattenamnden)[100] to provide a forum where taxpayers may obtain advance decisions on the tax consequences of proposed transactions. Such a body would also issue general directives and instructions for the guidance of regional assessment boards and taxpayers generally, and would serve to interpret and explain the new system of taxation in its relation to the Plans. The Board would conduct taxpayer education schemes and publicity on the role of taxation in planned development, and would assist the Central Board of Revenue in Delhi in investigating and checking evasion and avoidance, particularly in the field of inter-State problems. The Board might also co-ordinate the work of the Directorate of Intelligence and Inspection, the Collation Branch, and external and internal survey work.

Finally, it is arguable that the present situation in India, where the number of assessees is relatively small is ideal from the point of view of the proposed plan. It should be possible to overcome initial administrative difficulties before the tax net is widened to encompass a larger number of taxpayers. Such a policy would be consonant with the definition of administrative efficiency in a dynamic sense which would justify short-run expenditure on administration, perhaps greater than immediate returns, in order to minimize revenue costs in the long run.

Reforms: The Black Money Problem

None of the reforms suggested above provides a complete
answer to the "black money" problem, although the completely
self-checking return would make the acquisition of black money
--cash concealed or hoarded in some manner or another for purposes of tax evasion--much more difficult. The techniques for
the acquisition of black money are many and various, and reveal
the incredible ingenuity of the taxpayer--an ingenuity which is
invariably ignored by those opposed to tax reforms of any complexity!--in devising means to evade his tax obligations.

The best, perhaps the only feasible, method of discourag-
ing the acquisition of black money--there is no way, other than
by search and seizure, of getting at existing hoards--would be
simply to require that all payments above a specified level--
as low as is administratively feasible--be made by cheque.
Then after, say, a two-year period, all large bills, say, over
Rs. 100, would be demonetized. The threat of demonetization
and the uncertainty as to which bills would be demonetized
would discourage cash hoarding, since the demonetization operation would render useless hoards of demonetized bills, unless
presented at a government tax office. Something certainly must
be done, since the black money techniques of tax evasion are a
spreading and continuing drain on tax revenue, and since hoards
are almost invariably used for entirely non-functional conspicuous consumption, such as elaborate homes.

CORPORATION INCOME TAXATION

One of the theoretical advantages of corporation income
taxation is its relative administrative simplicity. The corporation as a taxable entity does not present the assessment
problems encountered in personal direct taxation; evasion is
thus unlikely. However, the present overlapping structure of
exemptions, allowances, and special provisions create a situation which may permit the manipulation and re-definition of income by certain corporations in such a way as to avoid taxation,
and which almost certainly have a cost in terms of inconvenience
and difficulty to all corporations in computing tax liability.
The simplification and rationalization of existing exemptions,
allowances and privileges of all kinds would thus be necessary
to minimize opportunities for corporate tax avoidance and inconvenience to corporations through computational difficulties.

CUSTOMS AND EXCISE TAXATION

With regard to customs taxation, there would appear to be
two salient problems, both dwelt on in some detail by the TEC.

The first is the question of appellate procedures, the second the issue of smuggling.[101]

At present the final appellate authority for customs and excise taxation is the Central Board of Revenue, which, al- though a separate statutory body is, for all practical pur- poses, part of the Department of Revenue in the Ministry of Finance. A considerable body of evidence was submitted to the TEC suggesting that the final appellate authority for customs and excise should be a quasi-judicial body independent of the Ministry of Finance such as the Appellate Tribunal, which is the final court of appeal for income, wealth, expenditure and gift taxation.[102] The TEC recommended that revision petitions against the Central Board of Revenue should, in fact, be to such a quasi-judicial Tribunal,[103] and there would seem to be an excellent case for final review of an impartial judicial nature. To date the recommendation has been ignored.

The issue of smuggling was discussed in the examination of the gold mobilization problem and the need for rigorous control stressed. The TEC was aware of the problem in the wider sense and pointed out that smuggling "constitutes not only a loophole for escaping duties but also a threat to the effective fulfil- ment of the objectives of foreign trade control."[104] The TEC suggested designating smuggling a criminal offense, recommended extensive powers of search, seizure, and interrogation under a revised Customs Act, the transfer of the onus of proof to the accused, and suggested that the present ban on the use by a customs officer in legal proceedings of information discovered in discharge of his duties be removed.[105] These proposals have been largely implemented in the Customs Act, 1962.

With regard to excise taxation the suggested appellate re- vision would also be applicable. The administration of Union excise taxation is stringent and generally effective.[106] Con- trol is exercised by Excise Officers who are resident in fac- tories in the case of manufactured articles, or who visit plan- tations regularly in the case of unmanufactured articles such as tobacco. Regulations with regard to licensing of assessees, the furnishing of bonds of surety, and the provision of monthly returns and daily stock accounts are thorough and comprehensive. Excise officers also have broad powers of entry, detention, and search, and failure to comply with the regulations may result in a fine up to Rs. 2,000 or six months imprisonment, or both. The administrative arrangements are costly--up to 4.5 per cent of total duties collected--but were considered eminently justi- fied by the TEC.[107] Excise taxation is unquestionably the most effectively administered major revenue source; perhaps the only possible weakness is the statutory limit on the fine for rule violation. It might be more effective to introduce a scale of

fines consonant with the magnitude of the offense, perhaps
reaching, in a similar fashion to that suggested for income
taxation, a maximum of five times the amount of tax evaded.

SALES TAXATION

The period of assessment in most States is one year,
though shorter periods of assessment are prescribed in a few
States for dealers who are thought likely to attempt evasion.
Where returns have not been furnished or where the Sales Tax
Officer is dissatisfied with the returns, he is entitled to
assess the dealers on an arbitrary basis. Equally, most States
permit Sales Tax Officers wide powers of entry, search, seizure
and detention, and usually provide for the re-opening of assessments on the availability of fresh information. The higher tax
authorities are the final court of appeal in most States on
sales tax issues, though quasi-judicial Appellate Tribunals
constitute the final appellate authority in several States.
The principal offenses under State Sales Tax Acts are: carrying on business without registration (or possessing a license
where necessary), failing to furnish returns, failing to pay
tax when due, providing false accounts or information, and the
obstruction of Sales Tax Officers in discharge of their duties.
The acts provide fines, imprisonment up to six months, or penalty taxes for these offenses. A continuing offense usually
draws an additional daily fine of Rs. 50 as long as the offense
continues.[108]

There are three major demerits of the assorted sales tax
systems.[109] A first major difficulty is the complexity and
ambiguity of rules and regulations, for instance, in the framing of exemptions and special regulations, as a result of which
bona fide interpretations by dealers are challenged and/or
rejected by the authorities. A second virtually universal com-
plaint is delay in assessment; dilatoriness in assessment penalizes the honest dealer who is unable to obtain necessary
evidence, etc., and diminishes taxpayer morale. From the point
of view of the tax authorities, a third problem in most States
is the neglect of inspection and investigation procedures,
which are usually conducted by the assessment staff. The TEC
recommendation for a separate inspection staff, who would also
serve in a liaison capacity between authorities and dealers,
has as yet been ignored by most States; a related suggestion
for the establishment of an Intelligence Section in each State
Sales Tax Department to provide thorough statistical material
has also been neglected.

In such a setting of generally ambiguous law, dilatory and
often arbitrary assessment, and inadequate inspection and general taxpayer alienation, tax evasion constitutes a serious

problem. The standard methods of evasion are the manipulation
of accounts, suppression of evidence of transactions (usually
through customer:dealer collusion) falsification of entries,
failure to register, splitting of business to reduce turnover
below the taxable limit, changing the place and/or name of the
firm, etc.[110] Unambiguous framing of tax law, prompt assessment on the basis of adequate statistics, and thorough inspection would go far to offset such evasion.

Perhaps, however, the most important desiderata are inter-
State co-operation and exchange of information, and the establishment of as much uniformity and simplicity as possible between different States as to sales tax law, regulation, tax
rates, exemptions, penalties, etc. The ad hoc development of
sales tax law in each State has produced a complex and varie-
gated pattern which provides unnecessary difficulties for dealers and facilitates tax evasion.

With regard to appellate procedures there is a good case
for extending the recommended excise tax procedure to sales
taxation, by setting up quasi-judicial Appellate Tribunals in
each State to act as final arbiter on tax grievances.

CONCLUSION

It has been suggested that inadequate present administration cannot provide the parameters around tax reform and that
increased present administrative cost is necessary to minimize
administrative costs in the long run. A variety of procedures
were proposed to minimize the problems of avoidance and evasion, in particular, a comprehensive self-checking tax return
covering all personal direct taxes and the sales tax. Devices
such as a National Tax Board, and tax assessment and computation by the tax authorities, would serve to mitigate taxpayer
inconvenience. With regard to indirect taxation the major remaining problems would appear to be inadequate appellate procedures, excise tax penalties, ambiguity in tax law, dilatory
assessment, and lack of inter-State co-ordination in the forms
and procedures of the sales tax.

NOTES TO CHAPTER 11

1. Government of India, Report of the Taxation Enquiry
Commission (hereinafter TEC) (3 vols.; New Delhi: Ministry of
Finance, 1953-54), Vol. II, Chapters 4, 6, 12 and 13, and Vol.
III, Chapter 5, pp. 67-76, examine the administrative difficul-
ties of the major direct and indirect forms of taxation in India;
Government of India, Report of the Direct Taxes Administration

Enquiry Committee, 1958-59 (hereinafter DTAEC) (Delhi: Manager of Publications, 1960), an extensive survey of the administration of direct taxation; Harvard University Law School, International Tax Program, Taxation in India, World Tax Series (Boston: Little, Brown and Co., 1960), especially pp. 64-72 for a summary of tax administration in general and Chapter 13 for income tax administration; B. R. Misra, Indian Federal Finance (Bombay: Orient Longmans, 1960), Chapter 7; R. N. Bhargava, The Theory and Practice of Union Finance in India (London: George Allen and Unwin, 1956), Chapter 9; and, most recently, Foreign Tax Assistance Staff, U.S. Internal Revenue Service, Report on Tax Administration in India (Delhi: USAID, 1964).

2. DTAEC, op. cit., and TEC, op. cit., Vol. II, Chapters 12-13.

3. Government of India, Local Finance Enquiry Committee (Delhi: Manager of Publications, 1951); the idea was revived by Mr. Kaldor in "Indian Tax Reform," op. cit., p. 23.

4. Government of India, Wealth Tax Act, 1957 (New Delhi: Ministry of Law, 1958), Chapter 6.

5. N. Kaldor, Tax Reform in India (New Delhi: Ministry of Finance, 1956), p. 25. Mr. Kaldor again revives here a suggestion of the Local Finance Enquiry Committee.

6. Report on Tax Administration in India, op. cit.

7. Government of India, First Interim Report on Rationalization and Simplification of Direct Taxation Laws (New Delhi: Ministry of Finance, 1967).

8. Government of India, Office of the Comptroller and Auditor General, Audit Report (Civil) Revenue Receipts 1967 (Delhi: Manager of Publications, 1967), p. 76.

9. Government of India, Memorandum Explaining the Provisions in the Finance Bill, 1967 (New Delhi: Ministry of Finance, 1967), pp. 4-5.

10. The TEC considered this matter and rejected it for the rather odd reason that the need for a refund scheme under universal withholding would inconvenience taxpayers and that firms withholding tax might not forward the funds to the tax authorities (Vol. II, pp. 225-26). The popularity of withholding among taxpayers has been proved in Britain and the supervision of firms acting as withholding agents should not be difficult; Government of the United Kingdom, Report of the Royal Commission on the Taxation of Profits and Income, Second Report, Cmd. 9105 (London: H.M.S.O., 1955), pp. 106-7.

An attempt to extend withholding to professional fees in the
1966-67 Budget was withdrawn after a storm of protest.

11. TEC, op. cit., Vol. II, p. 226.

12. Government of India, All-India Income Tax Revenue
Statistics, 1963-64 (Delhi: Manager of Publications, 1967),
All-India Statement 3.

13. TEC, op. cit., Vol. II, pp. 226-27.

14. TEC, op. cit., Vol. II, p. 212, indicates that in
99.8 per cent of the cases of retail traders the Income Tax
Officer rejects the accounts on the grounds that the stock
lists have not been proved.

15. DTAEC, op. cit., p. 21.

16. Ibid., p. 15.

17. TEC, op. cit., Vol. II, pp. 189-90.

18. Ibid., p. 190.

19. Kaldor, op. cit., p. 186.

20. DTAEC, op. cit., p. 148.

21. Ibid.

22. Ibid.

23. Ibid.

24. Economic Times, Friday, July 7, 1967.

25. DTAEC, loc. cit.

26. Audit Report (Civil) Revenue Receipts 1967, op. cit.,
p. 80.

27. TEC, op. cit., Vol. II, p. 189.

28. G. S. Sahota, Indian Tax Structure and Economic
Development (Bombay: Asia Publishing House, 1961), pp. 41-51.

29. Ibid., p. 43.

30. Ibid., pp. 50-51.

31. R. K. Sehgal, "Extent of Tax Evasion and Avoidance, An Estimate," Economic and Political Weekly (July 22, 1967), pp. 1301-2.

32. The procedure is detailed in DTAEC, op. cit., Chapters 7-8, pp. 146-240; see also TEC, op. cit., Vol. II, Chapters 12-13, pp. 189-248.

33. TEC, op. cit., Vol. II, pp. 191-92, especially Table I, p. 191; DTAEC, op. cit., p. 151.

34. DTAEC, op. cit., pp. 152-53.

35. Ibid., p. 153.

36. A detailed account of Collation Branch work is presented in TEC, op. cit., Vol. II, pp. 190-92.

37. TEC, op. cit., Vol. II, pp. 193-94; DTAEC, op. cit., pp. 165-66.

38. Government of India, Report of Income Tax Investigation Commission (Delhi: Manager of Publications, 1947), p. 137, reported in TEC, op. cit., Vol. II, p. 194.

39. DTAEC, op. cit., p. 166.

40. Ibid., pp. 154-55. The charges in Delhi and Madras were opened in 1965.

41. Ibid.

42. Hindustan Times (Delhi), Friday, July 7, 1967.

43. Ibid., p. 153. The writer had the privilege in 1967 of an interview with Mr. R. D. Shah, the Director of the Income Tax Directorate of Inspection (Investigation).

44. Ibid., p. 159.

45. TEC, op. cit., Vol. II, pp. 201-2.

46. Ibid., pp. 202-3.

47. DTAEC, op. cit., pp. 184-86.

48. TEC, op. cit., Vol. II, p. 203.

49. The details of the new legislation are as follows: "Firstly, every return of income filed by an assessee under the

Income Tax Rules, will carry an affirmation about the correct-
ness instead of the declaration as hitherto; this is expected
to ensure a greater measure of care and truthfulness in the
declaration of income. Secondly, tax due . . . will have to be
deposited within one month of the submission of the return,
failing which the assessee will have to pay a substantial penalty, i.e., for assessees whose net tax liability exceeds Rs.
500, the penalty for default will be up to 50% of the tax liability. Thirdly, the existing provisions concerning concealment of income are proposed to be amended; in the new provision
where the income returned by a person is less than 90% of the
assessed income, the assessee should be deemed to have concealed
his income unless he proves his bona fides. Fourthly, it is
proposed to take extensive powers to search evaded wealth; income tax authorities will be empowered to survey, search, seize
books of accounts or documents, place marks of identification
on them, etc. If an assessee in any particular year is found
to be the owner of money, bullion or other valuable articles
not recorded in the books of account, but fails to explain
satisfactorily the source of acquisition of the money, bullion,
etc., the money and the value of such articles will be deemed
as his income for that year. Fifthly, it is proposed to abolish the provisions in the Income Tax Act and other direct taxes
enactments prohibiting the disclosure of information contained
in the assessment records." "Government of India Budget, 1964-
65," Reserve Bank of India Bulletin (March, 1964), 294.

50. DTAEC, op. cit., pp. 167-76; TEC, op. cit., Vol. II,
p. 202; Kaldor, op. cit., pp. 113-14.

51. The minimum period of imprisonment and the maximum
period of two years were introduced in the 1965-66 Budget.
Prior to this legislation, only a maximum (six months in the
Income Tax Act, and one year in the other direct tax acts) was
specified.

52. DTAEC, op. cit., p. 67.

53. Ibid., p. 170.

54. Ibid., p. 177.

55. Government of India, Memorandum Explaining the Provisions in the Finance Bill, 1965 (New Delhi: Ministry of
Finance, 1965), pp. 11-12.

56. Harvard University Law School, International Tax Program, Taxation in Sweden, World Tax Series (Boston: Little,
Brown and Co., 1959), pp. 50-51.

57. DTAEC, op. cit., p. 185, details various schemes.

58. Ibid., p. 153.

59. Ibid.

60. Kaldor, op. cit., pp. 113-14.

61. TEC, op. cit., Vol. II, p. 202.

62. DTAEC, op. cit., p. 168.

63. Taxation in Sweden, op. cit., p. 601.

64. DTAEC, op. cit., p. 170.

65. Ibid., p. 172.

66. Harvard University Law School, International Tax Program, Taxation in the United States, World Tax Series (Chicago: Commerce Clearing House, Inc., 1963), p. 1265.

67. Taxation in Sweden, loc. cit.

68. Kaldor, op. cit., p. 114.

69. DTAEC, op. cit., p. 172.

70. TEC, op. cit., Vol. II, p. 304.

71. DTAEC, op. cit., p. 177.

72. TEC, op. cit., Vol. II, p. 298.

73. DTAEC, op. cit., pp. 155-56.

74. Ibid., p. 149.

75. Ibid., pp. 187-88.

76. Ibid.

77. Kaldor, op. cit., pp. 53-61.

78. Kaldor, op. cit., p. 13.

79. Ibid., pp. 53-55.

80. Ibid., p. 110.

81. B. Higgins, Economic Development (New York: Norton, 1959), pp. 524-44.

82. Ibid., p. 528.

83. Taxation in Sweden, op. cit., pp. 625-26.

84. Ibid., p. 556.

85. Ibid., pp. 583-84.

86. Kaldor, op. cit., Appendix B.

87. Kaldor, Suggestions for a Comprehensive Reform of Direct Taxation, Sessional Paper IV (Colombo, Ceylon: Government Press, April, 1960).

88. See R. Goode, "New System of Direct Taxation in Ceylon," National Tax Journal, XIII (December 1960), 329-40.

89. Speech of the Ceylon Minister of Finance in the House of Representatives, April 7, 1959, published by the Department of Information of Ceylon.

90. Goode, op. cit., p. 337.

91. DTAEC, op. cit., p. 163.

92. A. R. Prest, Public Finance in Underdeveloped Countries (London: Weidenfeld and Nicolson, 1962), p. 130.

93. TEC, op. cit., Vol. II, p. 226.

94. Royal Commission on the Taxation of Profits and Income, op. cit., Part I.

95. DTAEC, op. cit., p. 163.

96. R. M. Eigner, "Indian Income, Wealth and Expenditure Taxes; Integration and Administration," National Tax Journal, XI-XII (1958-59), pp. 151-64.

97. Ibid., p. 160.

98. Taxation in Sweden, op. cit., pp. 582-83.

99. Taxation in India, op. cit., pp. 66-67.

100. Taxation in Sweden, op. cit., pp. 602-12.

101. TEC, op. cit., Vol. II, pp. 318-26.

102. Government of India, Income Tax Act (revised up to 1965) (New Delhi: Ministry of Law, 1965), Chapter XX.

103. TEC, op. cit., Vol. II, p. 319.

104. Ibid., p. 320.

105. Ibid.

106. Government of India, The Central Excises and Salt Tax Act, 1944 (New Delhi: Ministry of Law, 1964).

107. TEC, op. cit., Vol. II, p. 323.

108. The system of offenses and penalties is set out for each State in Taxation in India, op. cit., pp. 447-52; in TEC, op. cit., Vol. III, pp. 14-16; and in K. Chaturvedi, The Principles of Sales Tax Laws (Calcutta: Eastern Law House Private Ltd., 1967).

109. TEC, op. cit., Vol. III, p. 67.

110. Ibid., p. 75.

CHAPTER **12** TAXATION AND
ECONOMIC DEVELOPMENT:
GENERAL CONCLUSIONS

The financing of economic development is primarily a
"bootstraps" operation. Developing countries must to a very
large extent finance internally their development programs.
The primary means of internal financing available to such countries is taxation.

The tax structures in the various developing countries
differ widely, but a group of central principles has emerged
in the preceding detailed examination of taxation in India. It
is proposed, first, to survey these principles, and, second, to
examine the policy inferences with respect to individual tax
heads.

The first principle is that the objectives of the tax system, and the relationship between these objectives, be clearly
established. The primary objectives, it was argued, are growth,
equity, and stabilization.

All developing countries share, by definition, the problem
of increasing the rate of growth of national income. The better index of economic growth is, of course, per capita rather
than national income, but these magnitudes are related through
the rate of growth of population, which is not considered to
be amenable to conventional tax devices. Where there is no
system of family welfare payments, and the vast majority of the
population are beyond the pale of the personal income tax, it
is difficult to envisage how the population dimension can be
treated through the tax side of the budget system.

To further the growth of national income, taxation must
increase the proportion of national income directed to development spending, defined as investment in the private sector, and
investment plus consumption expenditures of a developmental
nature in the public sector. On the one hand, taxation must
claim an increasing share of national income, and as large a
proportion as possible of that tax revenue must be channelled
into developmental spending. On the other hand, it is essential not only to minimize the opportunity cost of increased
tax revenue in terms of private saving (and therefore investment) foregone, but to incorporate in the tax system a system

of incentives designed to promote directly an increased ratio
of saving to income in the private sector. In sum, a tax system oriented to the growth objective must minimize the extent
to which increases in national income are directed to private
consumption and public sector consumption of a non-developmental
nature.

The policy of providing incentives to private sector saving and investment, and, possibly, to work of certain kinds,
constitutes an active policy of fiscal dirigism. The principle
of neutrality, whereby the tax system seeks to avoid inter-
ference in the private allocation of resources, is defensible
in a developed economy, but, it has been argued, is of little
relevance to the problem of economic development.

In addition to a system of incentives to save, invest and
work, it has been argued that the tax system in developing
countries may be designed to promote the desired use of resources by taxing in terms of "potential" resource use. This
principle is of great importance in agriculture, where the tax
base may be defined as "average potential output," and in the
case of wealth taxation, where the net wealth tax effectively
taxes on an assumed average rate of return on capital, penalizing, respectively, the inefficient farmer on the one hand, and
the hoarder and the conservative investor on the other.

Finally, the importance of a revenue-productive tax system
which finances public sector developmental spending, and which
at the same time incorporates the required incentives to private
sector behavior, means that the conventional principle of administrative simplicity must be seen in a dynamic sense--in relation to the requirements of a growth-oriented tax system, and
thus in terms of minimizing administrative costs per unit of
revenue in the long run from a developed, sophisticated tax
system.

The over-all equity objective was defined to include the
fundamental principle of horizontal equity--defined as the
equal treatment for tax purposes of taxable entities in equal
economic circumstances, except insofar as unequal treatment is
a deliberate aspect of dirigistic tax policy--and the objective
of vertical equity--defined as the moderation of inequalities
of income, wealth and opportunity.

Although there is seldom disagreement on the principle of
horizontal equity, it is frequently argued that a redistributive tax policy designed to promote the objective of vertical
equity will conflict with the objective of promoting private
sector growth, and that, accordingly, the vertical equity objective be relegated to the status of a long-term aspiration.
There is no question that a redistributive tax policy which

retards growth will be self-defeating, and it was argued that the necessary reconciliation between the private sector growth and vertical equity objectives might best be attained by the introduction of the principle of "functionalism" into the tax structure. Such a principle would provide for concessionary treatment, within an over-all progressive tax system, for income or wealth used for specified priority investment purposes. In this manner, "functional" inequalities would be tolerated, while non-functional inequalities--inequalities of consumption in the case of the income tax, and inequalities of unproductive wealth in the case of wealth taxation--would be moderated.

The actual degree of income and wealth inequality toward which the tax system--in conjunction with the expenditure side of the budget--must aspire, will reflect the political consensus at any given time as to the desirable state of income and wealth distribution. Inequality of opportunity reflects in large measure the perpetuation of income and wealth inequalities from one generation to another as a consequence of inadequate taxation of gratuitous transfers. There is no functional justification for such inequality--except perhaps on the issue of the sale of family businesses to pay tax, and this issue can be separately provided for--and the problem can best be solved by radical reform of estate and gift taxation.

The question of reducing unemployment and underemployment may be subsumed in developing countries under the growth objective. The stabilization objective may therefore be defined essentially as the prevention of inflationary price increases. The body of evidence suggests that a rate of price increase beyond a rather low minimum--certainly not higher than 5 per cent per annum--retards the rate and distorts the pattern of growth, and worsens the redistributive problem.

It is, of course, important in a growing economy to permit price increases in growing sectors in order to attract resources to these areas. Since equivalent price reductions in declining areas are unlikely, some upward pressure on the general price level may be expected as a result of what has been referred to as "functional" instability. Inflationary price increases, unlike functional price increases, tend to be cumulative and pervasive in nature. It is equally important to ensure that measures to promote stability not conflict with the growth objective. To this end, the functional exemptions and concessions referred to above under the vertical equity objective will serve to ensure that reductions in aggregate spending are primarily at the expense of consumption spending rather than investment spending.

Having defined a consistent set of objectives, and geared the tax system to the pursuit of these objectives, the second principle follows that the tax system which best realizes the given objectives will be that system which is best adapted to the peculiar institutional circumstances of a particular country. Several examples of such adaptation were adduced in the Indian case. The system of agricultural taxation suggested was geared to the structure of Indian agriculture, and provided a means of taxing those farmers who could meet tax obligations in monetary terms, and an in-kind tax procedure for those whose transactions were primarily outside the monetary sector. Further measures adapted to particular Indian requirements--and it should be emphasized that these requirements will differ widely between developing countries--were a scheme for the mobilization of gold hoards, and a comprehensive compulsory savings proposal. The use of a labor tax was also examined, and considerable caution in its use urged. This question of particular institutional circumstances focuses attention on the hazards of generalizing on tax policy recommendations for developing countries.

The third basic principle applies only to developing countries with a federal system of government, and requires that each level of government have adequate resources to discharge its expenditure responsibilities, that particular taxes be collected by that level of government which can do so most efficiently, and that a system of revenue sharing--subject to continuing review in the light of changing circumstances--be established to reconcile resources and responsibilities. Such a procedure is particularly important since, traditionally, the second level of government in federal organizations--the State or Province--is responsible for expenditure areas which tend to be very elastic in the development process, yet has access directly only to tax measures which tend to be relatively inelastic. It is, on the other hand, essential to ensure that the lower levels of government do not fail to utilize their tax means to the full, and to this end it is appropriate in a federal organization to develop some indices of relative tax capacity and tax effort.

The fourth principle may be regarded in one sense as an extension of the notion of horizontal equity to require inter-sectoral balance in the tax system. There are several historical cases--particularly in pre-revolutionary Russia and Meiji Japan--where inter-sectoral imbalance was deliberately used as an instrument of development, the agricultural sector being required essentially to finance industrial growth. The problem in many contemporary developing countries is quite the reverse. For a variety of reasons--often largely administrative--the relative tax burden on the agricultural sector tends to be light, the heavier tax burden falling on the more rapidly

growing urban, industrial sector. India is a classic example
of this problem, and a variety of measures were suggested to
rectify the situation.

The final general principle must be somewhat vaguely
couched. It is that <u>direct tax measures are, almost by definition, more sensitive, more selective policy instruments than
indirect tax measures, and can be geared more specifically to
the given tax objectives</u>. It is a matter of historical record
that the direct:indirect tax ratio increases with economic development and increasing fiscal sophistication. This is not to
deny the very great revenue importance of excise taxes and general sales taxes in developing countries, nor to deny that such
taxes can be developed and refined to a great extent--some such
refinements were explored at length in the Indian case--but
simply to suggest that it is the easier, but not the best
route, to fall back increasingly on the administratively simple
and revenue-productive indirect tax measures, at the cost of
failing to develop in the best and most rapid manner more
sophisticated direct tax measures. India again provides a
classic example of such a policy; the direct:indirect tax ratio
has, in fact, been falling quite sharply over the planning
period.

In developed countries the progressive personal income tax
is generally an elastic and productive revenue source; is an
extremely flexible device, in that a variety of forms of selectivity, discrimination, etc., can be introduced into the tax if
so desired; tends to be the most useful tax device in stabilization policy, in terms of both built-in stabilization and as
a discretionary stabilization device; and, finally, by dint of
its progressivity, is considered the most appropriate tax
device for the pursuit of vertical equity.

In developing countries, on the other hand, the personal
income tax generally has a very limited coverage, frequently
is inapplicable to the agricultural sector--for either constitutional or administrative reasons--and tends to be subject to
widespread avoidance and evasion. For these reasons, the personal income tax plays a less significant role in the tax
structure than in developed countries.

It was argued in the Indian case, and the argument is
valid in a general sense, that part of the reason for the inadequate coverage of the personal income tax is the excessively
narrow definition of income. It was proposed that the more
appropriate definition would be a comprehensive one--essential-
ly consumption plus increase in net worth over the appropriate
tax period. This would encompass accretions to economic well-
being of all kinds in the tax base, including capital gains,
windfall receipts, and all gifts and bequests received.

It was further argued that the exemption level for personal income tax tends to be defined so as to exclude the vast majority of taxpayers. The coverage of the tax could be greatly widened by the definition of the exemption limit at the lowest possible level of administrative feasibility. Such widened coverage would be of considerable revenue significance even if those at the widened lower end of the scale were subject only to the minimum tax rate of, say, 5 per cent.

It was established in the Indian case that tax rates on middle-income groups were also very moderate, and that rate increases across this group would enhance the revenue productivity of the income tax, and would make it a more effective device for the pursuit of equity and stabilization.

The possible detrimental effects of increased coverage and increased rates, particularly on middle-income groups, may be offset by the partial exemption from income tax of income used for saving and investment in specified priority areas, and income earned in specified priority occupations, and, further, by the introduction of extended loss-offset provisions and the cumulation of income for tax purposes.

The comprehensive definition of income implies the complete inclusion of capital gains in the definition of income. It was, however, argued in the Indian case that the concessionary treatment of long-term gains might be maintained as an investment incentive. Further, the partial exemption scheme for income saved and invested, and the proposed averaging and extended loss-offset provisions would be extended to income in the form of long-term capital gains.

The relative tax burden on the agricultural sector tends to be light, and certainly to be incommensurate with the priority investment position generally afforded agriculture in developing countries. The three major tax objectives require both increased revenue productivity from agricultural taxation, and increased agricultural productivity. The most appropriate means in the long term of reconciling these two aspects would be an agricultural income tax based on ascertained net income and qualified by a series of exemptions and allowances for reinvestment, etc. Assessment problems in the short term suggest that the first step to a solution might lie in a device already used in several developing countries--an extended land tax which would be progressive in terms of land size but proportional in terms of average potential output for each land size. The tax would be refined by the introduction of structural flexibility and personal allowances. The notion of taxing on the basis of average potential output might also be extended in the form of an in-kind tax to those agriculturalists whose transactions were mainly outside the monetized sector.

An annual tax on net wealth is envisaged more in the nature of an additional income tax on income from capital than as a tax on capital itself. The tax is particularly useful in that it taxes on an assumed average rate of return on capital, thus providing an incentive to high-yield risk investment and a disincentive to hoarding and conservative investment. Again the notion of "functionality" might be introduced into the tax by specifying a series of assets which were either exempt or were treated at concessionary rates.

A capital levy, on the other hand, is a genuine tax on capital, and might offer a useful additionl revenue source to developing countries in two senses: first, in the form of a moderate levy--up to 5 per cent--payable immediately, and designed to finance an emergency situation, and, second, in the form of a more severe levy, up to, say, 40 or 50 per cent, payable by installments over twenty to thirty years, and designed to provide a substantial revenue increment over the payment period, and to effect a radical diminution in wealth inequalities.

The expenditure tax has recently been abolished in India, but it has been argued that such a tax has an important role to play in developing countries. The particular functions of the tax are to curtail the extent to which increases in income are directed to conspicuous consumption instead of saving, to diminish consumption inequalities, to assist in curtailing consumption demand in an inflationary situation, and, finally, to act as an integral part of a self-checking personal direct tax system. The effectiveness of the tax will depend on a much more severe definition of exempt expenditure for tax purposes than that previously employed in India.

The existing estate and gift taxes in India and in developing countries generally--indeed, also in most developed countries--have not proved to be productive revenue sources, and would appear to have made little contribution to the diminution of inequalities of opportunity between generations. Within the standard structure of separate estate and gift taxes, the most effective reform would be the complete integration of gift and estate taxation into one transfer tax levied on a cumulative basis, and the use of an over-all sharply progressive rate structure in the transfer tax. More liberal tax payment procedures and preferential tax treatment for "functional" assets would serve to moderate any adverse effects of the proposed changes on the private sector.

The optimal reform on both equity and revenue grounds would be of a more radical nature, and would go beyond such variants as the accessions tax to suggest the full incorporation of all

gratuitous transfers--whether testamentary or _inter vivos_--in
the cumulated taxable income of the recipient.

For many developing countries corporation income taxation
is a more important revenue source than personal income taxation.   In India, the corporation income tax has proved to be a
relatively elastic and productive revenue source.   Further, a
separate, non-integrated corporation tax contributes to vertical equity--on the assumption that at least a portion of the
tax is borne by capital owners--by taxing dividends and curtailing stock appreciation, and by dint of broad coverage and
elasticity, is of great significance in automatic and discretionary stabilization policy.

The major disadvantage of the corporation tax is that it
probably reduces funds for investment more than any other tax.
However, this effect may be moderated by the introduction of
extended loss-offset provisions and the use of selective accelerated depreciation (the latter is to be preferred to the often-
suggested alternative of replacement cost depreciation).

The proposal to integrate either fully or partially the
personal and corporation income taxes has merit only on grounds
of horizontal equity, and, it was argued, would considerably
reduce the contribution of the corporate income tax to revenue
productivity, vertical equity and stabilization.

Indirect tax measures are generally the most important
revenue sources in developing countries, although it has been
argued that the attainment of the three tax objectives requires
increasing use of direct tax measures.

Revenue from customs has traditionally formed a large part
of indirect tax revenue in developing countries, although in
India the role of customs has been overshadowed by Union excise
duties.   The requirements of foreign exchange, and the need for
imports, particularly of capital goods, suggest that customs
revenue is likely to decline as a proportion of total tax revenue, and that increasing reliance be placed on domestic indirect tax measures.

Union excise duties have proved to be the most elastic and
productive revenue sources in the Indian tax system.   Their
productivity and elasticity might be increased, it was argued,
by substantial rate increases in a wide variety of goods, and
by planning tax rates on consumer goods on the basis of extrapolations of consumer expenditure.   An alternative proposal of
a Union value-added tax, which would have the same revenue effect as a Union retail sales tax, was rejected on the grounds
that excise duties were more useful instruments of dirigistic
tax policy.

At the State level in India, and indeed in most federal states, the primary indirect source of revenue is the general sales tax. On economic grounds, the least desirable form of the retail sales tax is the turnover tax. The optimal form is probably the sales tax levied at the retail level, although, on administrative grounds, there is much to commend a tax levied at the wholesale level.

It has been argued that the principle of administrative efficiency must be defined in developing countries in a dynamic sense. The major administrative problem in India, and in most developing countries is that of avoidance and evasion, particularly of personal income taxation. It was argued that a major step toward the elimination of evasion would be the use of a comprehensive, self-checking personal direct tax return, including income (comprehensively defined), wealth and expenditure returns on one self-checking form.

SELECTED BIBLIOGRAPHY

SELECTED BIBLIOGRAPHY

Books and Pamphlets

Ambirajan, S. The Taxation of Corporate Income in India. New York: Asia Publishing House, 1964.

Baran, P. The Political Economy of Growth. New York: Monthly Review Press, 1962.

Bauer, P. T. and B. S. Yamey. The Economics of Underdeveloped Countries. Chicago: University of Chicago Press, 1957.

Bhargava, R. N. The Theory and Practice of Union Finance in India. London: George Allen and Unwin, 1956.

Braibanti, R. and J. J. Spengler, eds. Administration and Economic Development in India. Durham, N.C.: Duke University Press, 1963.

Butters, J. K. and J. Lintner. Effects of Federal Taxes on Growing Enterprises. Boston: Harvard University Graduate School of Business Administration, 1945.

Butters, J. K. and L. E. Thompson and L. L. Bollinger. Effects of Taxation: Investments by Individuals. Boston: Harvard Graduate School of Business Administration, 1953.

Casey, W. J. and J. K. Lasser. Tax Sheltered Investments. New York: Business Reports, Inc., 1951.

Chaturvedi, K. The Principles of Sales Tax Laws. Calcutta: Eastern Law House Private Limited, 1967.

Chelliah, R. J. Fiscal Policy in Underdeveloped Countries. London: George Allen and Unwin, 1960.

Choudhury, R. The Plans for Economic Development in India. Calcutta: Bookland Private Ltd., 1959.

A Conference of the Universities--National Bureau Committee for Economic Research. Public Finances: Needs, Sources and Utilization. Princeton: Princeton University Press, 1961.

Cosciani, C. The Effects of Differential Tax Treatment of Corporate and Non-Corporate Income. Paris: European Productivity Agency of the O.E.E.C., February 1959.

Crane, R. I. Aspects of Economic Development in South Asia. New York: International Secretariat, Institute of Pacific Relations, 1954.

Dasgupta, A., A. Sen and J. Sengupta. Planning and the Plans. Calcutta: Postgraduate Book Mart, 1961.

Dastur, S.E., Damania, H. M. and Dastur, J. E. Direct Tax Laws 1966-67. Bombay: N. M. Tripathi Private Limited, 1966.

Due, J. F. Government Finance. Revised Edition. Homewood, Ill.: Irwin, 1959.

_____. Sales Taxation. London: Routledge and Kegan Paul, 1957.

_____. Taxation and Economic Development in Tropical Africa. Cambridge: MIT Press, 1963.

_____. The Theory and Incidence of Sales Taxation. New York: King's Crown Press, 1942.

Enke, S. Economics for Development. Englewood Cliffs, N.J.: Prentice Hall, 1963.

European Productivity Agency of O.E.E.C. The Influence of Sales Tax on Productivity. Paris: 1958.

Friedman, M. A Theory of the Consumption Function. Princeton: Princeton University Press, 1957.

Galbraith, J. K. The Affluent Society. Boston: Houghton Mifflin, 1958.

Gandhi, V. P. Tax Burden on Indian Agriculture. Cambridge: Harvard University Law School, 1966.

Ghosh, S. The Financing of Economic Development. Calcutta: The World Press, Ltd., 1962.

Goode, R. The Corporation Income Tax. New York: John Wiley and Sons, Inc., 1951.

_____. The Individual Income Tax. Washington, D.C.: The Brookings Institution, 1964.

Gulati, I. S. Capital Taxation in a Developing Economy (India).
    Calcutta: Orient Longmans, 1957.

Gulati, I. S. and K. S. Gulati. The Undivided Hindu Family:
    A Study of its Tax Privileges. Bombay: Asia Publishing
    House, 1962.

Hall, C. A., Jr. Effects of Taxation; Executive Compensation
    and Retirement Plans. Boston: Harvard University Press,
    Bureau of Business Research, 1951.

Hansen, B. The Economic Theory of Fiscal Policy. London:
    George Allen and Unwin, 1958.

Harvard University Law School, International Tax Program. Taxa-
    tion in Australia. World Tax Series. Boston: Little,
    Brown and Co., 1958.

_____. Taxation in Brazil. World Tax Series. Boston:
    Little, Brown and Co., 1957.

_____. Taxation in the Federal Republic of West Germany.
    World Tax Series. Chicago: Commerce Clearing House,
    Inc., 1963.

_____. Taxation in India. World Tax Series. Boston:
    Little, Brown and Co., 1960.

_____. Taxation in Mexico. World Tax Series. Boston:
    Little, Brown and Co., 1957.

_____. Taxation in Sweden. World Tax Series. Boston:
    Little, Brown and Co., 1959.

_____. Taxation in the United Kingdom. World Tax Series.
    Boston: Little, Brown and Co., 1957.

_____. Taxation in the United States. Chicago: Commerce
    Clearing House, Inc., 1963.

Heller, J. and Kauffman, K. M. Tax Incentives for Industry in
    Less Developed Countries. Cambridge: Harvard University
    Law School, International Tax Program, 1963.

Henderson, H. D. Inheritance and Inequality--A Practical
    Proposal. London: The Daily News, Ltd., 1936.

Hicks, J. R., V. K. Hicks and L. Rostas. The Taxation of War
    Wealth. Oxford: Oxford University Press, 1941.

Hicks, U. K. Public Finance. London: Pitman, 1947.

Hobson, J. A. Taxation in the New State. London: Methuen and Co., Ltd., 1919.

Holmans, A. E. United States Fiscal Policy, 1945-1959--Its Contribution to Economic Stability. London: Oxford University Press, 1961.

Holzman, F. D. Soviet Taxation. Boston: Harvard University Press, 1955.

International Monetary Fund. Economic Development with Stability. A Report to the Government of India. Washington, D.C., 1953.

Joshi, C. N. The Constitution of India. London: MacMillan, 1961.

Kaldor, N. An Expenditure Tax. London: George Allen and Unwin, 1959.

_____. Indian Tax Reform. New Delhi: Government of India, Ministry of Finance, 1956.

_____. Suggestions for a Comprehensive Reform of Direct Taxation. Sessional Paper IV. Colombo, Ceylon: Government Press, April 1960.

Keynes, J. M. The General Theory of Employment, Interest and Money. London: MacMillan, 1960.

_____. How to Pay for the War. Toronto: MacMillan, 1940

_____. Indian Currency and Finance. London: MacMillan, 1913.

Khan, C. H. Personal Deductions in the Federal Income Tax. Princeton: Princeton University Press, 1960.

Khan, N. A. Problems of Growth of an Underdeveloped Economy. Bombay: Asia Publishing House, 1961.

Krzyazniak, M. and R. Musgrave. The Shifting of the Corporation Income Tax. Baltimore: Johns Hopkins Press, 1963.

Lakdawala, D. T. Justice in Taxation in India. Bombay: The Popular Book Depot, 1946.

_____. Taxation and the Plan. Bombay: Popular Book Depot, 1964.

Levy, M. E. Income Tax Exemptions. Amsterdam: North-Holland
     Publishing Co., 1960.

Lewis, W. A. Theory of Economic Growth. London: Unwin, 1963.

Long, C. D. The Labor Force Under Changing Income and Employ-
     ment. Princeton: Princeton University Press, 1958.

Malenbaum, W. Prospects for Indian Development. London:
     George Allen and Unwin, 1962.

Maxwell, J. A. Tax Credits and Intergovernmental Fiscal
     Relations. Washington: The Brookings Institution, 1962.

McCulloch, J. R. Taxation and the Funding System. Edinburgh:
     A. & C. Black, 1891.

Mehta, J. K. and S. N. Agarwala. Public Finance in Theory and
     Practice. Allahabad: Kitab Mahal, 1949.

Meyer, J. R. and R. R. Glauber. Investment Decisions, Economic
     Forecasting and Public Policy. Boston: Harvard University
     Press, 1964.

Meyer, J. R. and E. Kuh. The Investment Decision. Cambridge:
     Harvard University Press, 1957.

Mill, J. S. Principles of Political Economy. Edited by
     W. J. Ashley. London: Longmans, Green and Co., 1923.

Misra, B. R. Indian Federal Finance. Bombay: Orient Long-
     mans, 1960.

M.I.T. Center for International Studies. The Non-Monetized
     Sector of Rural India. Cambridge: M.I.T. Press, 1956.

Morgan, D. C. Retail Sales Tax. Madison: University of Wis-
     consin Press, 1964.

Musgrave, R. A. The Theory of Public Finance. New York:
     McGraw-Hill, 1959.

Musgrave, R. and C. Shoup. Readings in the Economics of Taxa-
     tion. London: George Allen and Unwin, 1959.

National Committee of Applied Economic Research. Taxation and
     Private Investment. New Delhi, 1961.

Perry, J. Harvey. Taxation in Canada. Toronto: University of
     Toronto Press, 1960.

Petrie, J. R. The Taxation of Corporate Income in Canada.
    Toronto: University of Toronto Press, 1952.

Pigou, A. C. A Study in Public Finance. London: MacMillan,
    1947.

Prest, A. R. Public Finance in Theory and Practice. London:
    Weidenfeld and Nicolson, 1960.

_____. Public Finance in Underdeveloped Countries. London:
    Weidenfeld and Nicolson, 1962.

_____. Reform for Purchase Tax. Hobart Paper, No. 8,
    Second Edition. London: Institute of Economic Affairs,
    1963.

Prest, A. R. and Stewart, I. G. The National Income of Nigeria,
    1950-51. London: H.M.S.O., 1953.

Rolph, E. The Theory of Fiscal Economics. Berkeley: Universi-
    ty of California Press, 1954.

Sahota, G. S. Indian Tax Structure and Economic Development.
    Bombay: Asia Publishing House, 1961.

Sanders, T. H. The Effects of Taxation on Executives. Boston:
    Harvard University Graduate School of Business Administra-
    tion, 1951.

Sastri, K. V. S. Federal-State Fiscal Relations in India.
    London: Oxford University Press, 1966.

Seligman, E. R. A. Progressive Taxation in Theory and Practice.
    Princeton: Princeton University Press, 1908.

Seltzer, L. H. The Nature and Tax Treatment of Capital Gains.
    New York: National Bureau of Economic Research, 1951.

Shehab, F. Progressive Taxation. Oxford: The Clarendon
    Press, 1953.

Shirras, G. Finlay. Indian Finance and Banking. London:
    MacMillan, 1919.

_____. Science of Public Finance. 2 vols. Third Edition.
    London: MacMillan, 1936.

Shoup, C. S. et al. The Fiscal System of Venezuela: A Report.
    Baltimore: Johns Hopkins Press, 1959.

Shultz, W. J. The Taxation of Inheritance. Boston:
    Houghton Mifflin, 1926.

Simons, H. Personal Income Taxation. Chicago: University of
    Chicago Press, 1938.

Smith, D. T. Effects of Taxation: Corporate Financial Policy.
    Boston: Harvard University Graduate School of Business
    Administration, 1952.

Smith, D. T., ed. The Limits of Taxable Capacity. Princeton:
    Tax Institute Inc., 1963.

Taylor, P. E. The Economics of Public Finance. New York:
    MacMillan, 1961.

Thomas, P. J. The Growth of Federal Finance in India. Madras:
    Oxford, 1937.

Tinbergen, J. Centralization and Decentralization in Economic
    Policy. Amsterdam: North-Holland Publishing Co., 1954.

_____. On the Theory of Economic Policy. Amsterdam:
    North-Holland Publishing Co., 1952.

Tripathy, R. N. Federal Finance in a Developing Economy.
    Calcutta: The World Press, Private Ltd., 1960.

_____. Fiscal Policy and Economic Development in India.
    Calcutta: The World Press, 1958.

_____. Local Finance in a Developing Economy. New Delhi:
    Planning Commission, 1967.

Vickrey, W. Agenda for Progressive Taxation. New York:
    Ronald Press, 1947.

Wald, H. R. Taxation of Agricultural Land in Underdeveloped
    Economies. Cambridge: Harvard University Law School,
    1959.

Wald, H. P. and J. N. Froomkin, eds. Agricultural Taxation and
    Economic Development. Cambridge: Harvard University Law
    School, 1954.

Wedgwood, J. The Economics of Inheritance. London: G. Rout-
    ledge & Sons, Ltd., 1929.

Willis, J. The Mitigation of the Tax Penalty on Fluctuating or
    Irregular Incomes. Toronto: Canadian Tax Foundation,
    1951.

Periodical Articles and Parts of Books

Baer, W. "Inflation and Economic Growth: An Interpretation of the Brazilian Case," Economic Development and Cultural Change, XI (October 1962), 85-97.

Baykov, A. "The Economic Development of Russia," Economic History Review (December 1954), 137-49.

Bhatia, R. J. "Inflation, Deflation and Economic Development," IMF Staff Papers (November 1960), 101-14.

Bloch, H. S. "Economic Objectives of Gratuitous Transfer Taxation," National Tax Journal, III-IV (1950-51), 139-47.

Bodenhorn, D. "The Shifting of the Corporation Income Tax in a Growing Economy," Quarterly Journal of Economics, LXX (November 1956), 563-80.

Boulding, K. E. "The Fruits of Progress and the Dynamics of Distribution," American Economic Review, XLIII (May 1953), 473-83.

Bravman, J. "Equalization of Income Tax," Columbia Law Review, L (January 1950), 9.

Break, G. F. "Income Taxes and Incentives to Work; An Empirical Study," American Economic Review, XLVII (September 1957), 529-49.

Bronfenbrenner, M. "The Japanese Value-Added Tax," National Tax Journal, II (March 1950), 298-313.

Brown, E. Cary. "Mr. Kaldor on Taxation and Risk Bearing," Review of Economic Studies (October 1957), 114-22.

Brown, H. G. "The Incidence of a General Output or a General Sales Tax," Journal of Political Economy, XLVII (April 1959), 254-62.

Buchanan, N. S. "Deliberate Industrialization for Higher Incomes," Economic Journal (December 1946), 534-48.

David, M. "Economic Effects of the Capital Gains Tax," American Economic Review, LIV (May 1964), 288-99.

Davies, D. G. "Commodity Taxation and Equity," Journal of Finance, XVI (1961), 581-90.

_____. "An Empirical Test of Sales-Tax Regressivity," Journal of Political Economy, LXVII (1959), 72-78.

Dorrance, G. S. "The Effect of Inflation on Economic Development," IMF Staff Papers (March 1963), 1-31.

Due, J. F. "A General Sales Tax and the Level of Employment: A Reconsideration," National Tax Journal, II (1949), 122-30.

_____. "Retail Sales Taxation in Theory and Practice," National Tax Journal, III (1950), 314-25.

Eigner, R. M. "Indian Income, Wealth and Expenditure Taxes: Integration and Administration," National Tax Journal, XI-XII (1958-59), 151-64.

Federal Reserve Bank of New York. "Inflation and Economic Development," Monthly Review of the Bank (August 1959), 122-27.

Fisher, J. "Taxation of Personal Income and Net Worth in Norway," Economic Journal (1918), 38-58.

Friedman, Milton. "A Monetary and Fiscal Framework for Economic Stability," in his Essays in Positive Economics, Chicago: University of Chicago Press, 1953, 64-94.

Friend, I. and I. B. Kravis. "Consumption Patterns and Permanent Income," American Economic Review, XLVII (May 1957), 536-55.

Friend, I. and S. Schor. "Who Saves?" The Review of Economics and Statistics, XLI (May 1959), 213-48.

Froomkin, J. "A Program for Taxation and Economic Development --The Indian Case," Economic Development and Cultural Change, VI (January 1958), 129-42.

Gerschenkron, A. "The Rate of Growth in Russia Since 1885," Journal of Economic History, Supplement VII (1947), 144-74.

Goheen, J., M. N. Srinivas, D. G. Garve, and M. Singer. "India's Cultural Values and Economic Development--A Discussion," Economic Development and Cultural Change, XII (October 1958), 1-12.

Goode, R. "Alternative Approaches to the Integration of the Corporate and Individual Income Taxes," Proceedings of the National Tax Association (1947), 134-45.

_____. "The Income Tax and the Supply of Labour," Journal of Political Economy, LVIII (October 1949), 428-37.

Goode, R. "New Systems of Direct Taxation in Ceylon," National Tax Journal, XIII (December 1960), 329-40.

Gopal, M. J. "Towards a Realistic Tax Policy for India," Indian Economic Journal, VII (January 1959), 281-326.

Gulati, I. S. "A Note on the Capital Gains Tax in India," Public Finance, XVIII (1963), 101-7.

Hagen, E. E. and A. G. Hart. "Problems in Timing and Administering Fiscal Policy in Prosperity and Depression," American Economic Review (May 1948), 417-51.

Haig, R. M. "The Concept of Income--Economic and Legal Aspects, in the Federal Income Tax," New York, 1921. Reproduced in R. A. Musgrave and C. S. Shoup. Readings in the Economics of Taxation. London: George Allen and Unwin, 1959.

Hall, C. A., Jr. Review of "Public Finance" (Rolph and Break), American Economic Review, LII (March 1962), 267-69.

Hansen, R. R. "An Empirical Analysis of the Retail Sales Tax with Policy Recommendations," National Tax Journal, XV (1962), 1-13.

Harriss, C. Lowell. "Economic Effects of Estate and Gift Taxation," Federal Taxation for Economic Growth and Stability. Washington: U. S. Government Printing Office, 1955, 855-63.

_____. "Liquidity of Estates and Death Tax Liability." Political Science Quarterly, LXIV (1959), 533-59.

Head, F. G. "The Case for a Capital Gains Tax," Public Finance, XVIII (1963), 220-49.

Heller, W. "The Adaptation of Income Taxation to Agriculture in Underdeveloped Economies," in Agricultural Taxation and Economic Development. Cambridge: Harvard University Law School, 1954, 270-84.

_____. "Investors' Decisions, Equity and the Capital Gains Tax," Federal Tax Policy for Economic Growth and Stability. Washington: U. S. Government Printing Office, 1958, 381-84.

_____. "The Use of Agricultural Taxation for Incentive Purposes," in Agricultural Taxation and Economic Development. Cambridge: Harvard University Law School, 1954, 117-88.

Heston, A. "An Empirical Study of Indian Gold Prices," Indian Economic Journal, VIII (January 1961), 204-26.

Hicks, U. K. "Direct Taxation and Economic Growth," Oxford Economic Papers, New Series, VIII (1956), 302-17.

Hinrichs, H. H. "Dynamic Regressive Effects of the Treatment of Capital Gains on the American Tax System during 1957-59," Public Finance, XIX (1964), 73-85.

Holt, C. C. "Averaging of Income for Tax Purposes, Equity and Fiscal Policy Considerations," National Tax Journal, II (December 1949), 349-61.

Ike, Nobutaka. "Taxation and Landownership in the Westernization of Japan," Journal of Economic History, VII (November 1947), 160-82.

Johnston, B. F. "Agricultural Productivity and Economic Development in Japan," Journal of Political Economy (December 1951), 498-534.

Kahn, R. F. "The Pace of Development," The Challenge of Development. Jerusalem: Hebrew University, 1958, 169-82.

Kaldor, N. "The Income Burden of Capital Taxes," Review of Economic Studies, IX (1942). Reproduced in R. A. Musgrave and C. S. Shoup. Readings in the Economics of Taxation. American Economic Association Series. London: George Allen and Unwin, 1959, 393-415.

_____. "Role of Taxation in Economic Development," Essays in Economic Policy, Vol. I, London: Duckworth, 1954, 225-54.

_____. "Tax Reform in India," The Economic Weekly, Annual Number (January 1959), 195-98.

_____. "Tax Reform in India," Essays in Economic Policy, Vol. I. London: Duckworth, 1964, 217-19.

Khan, N. A. "Resource Mobilization from Agriculture and Economic Development in India," Economic Development and Cultural Change, XII (October 1963), 42-54.

Khusro, A. M. "Taxation and Agricultural Land--A Proposal," The Economic Weekly, Annual Number (February 1963), 275-82.

Klein, L. R. and N. Liviatin. "The Significance of Income
    Variability on Savings Behavior," Bulletin of the Oxford
    University Institute of Statistics, XIX (May 1957), 151-60.

Lakdawala, D. T. "An Expenditure Tax," Indian Economic Journal,
    III (April 1956), 331-40.

Lent, G. E. "Bond Interest Deduction and the Federal Corpora-
    tion Income Tax," National Tax Journal, II (June 1949),
    131-41.

Lerner, E. M. and E. S. Hendriksen. "Federal Taxes on Corporate
    Income and the Rate of Return in Manufacturing, 1927-1952,"
    National Tax Journal, IX (September 1965), 192-202.

Little, I. M. D. "Direct Versus Indirect Taxes," Economic
    Journal (September 1951). Reprinted in R. A. Musgrave and
    C. S. Shoup. Readings in the Economics of Taxation.
    London: George Allen and Unwin, 1959, 123-31.

_____. "Tax Policy and the Third Plan," Institute of Eco-
    nomic Growth (1959), mimeograph. Reproduced in Prices
    and Fiscal Policies--A Study in Method. Edited by P. N.
    Rosenstein-Rodan. London: G. Allen and Unwin, 1963,
    30-76.

Long, C. D. "Impact of the Federal Income Tax on Labor Force
    Participation," Federal Tax Policy for Economic Growth and
    Stability. Washington: U. S. Government Printing Office,
    1955, 153-66.

Lydall, H. F. and M. Ahmed. "An Exercise in Forecasting Con-
    sumer Demand and Taxation Yields in India in 1965-66,"
    Indian Economic Review, V (August 1961), 313-32.

McGrew, J. W. "Effect of a Food Exemption on the Incidence of a
    Retail Sales Tax," National Tax Journal, II (1949) 362-67.

Madan, B. K. "The Role of Monetary Policy in a Developing Eco-
    nomy," Reserve Bank of India Bulletin (April 1961), 521-27.

Madhavan, M. "Inflation and Economic Development--A Case Study
    of India," Indian Economic Journal, X (January 1963), 257-
    66.

Marget, A. W. "Inflation--Some Lessons of Recent Foreign Ex-
    perience," American Economic Review (May 1960), 205-11.

Marshall, A. "The Equitable Distribution of Taxation," in
    A. C. Pigou, ed. Memorials of Alfred Marshall. New York:
    Kelley and Millman, Inc., 1956, 347-52.

Maynard, G. "Inflation and Growth in Latin America," Oxford
    Economic Papers, New Series, XV (March 1963), 63-65.

_____. "Inflation and Growth--Some Lessons to be Drawn
    from Latin American Experience," Oxford Economic Papers,
    New Series, XIII (June 1961), 184-202.

Mayer, T. "The Permanent Income Theory and Occupation Groups,"
    The Review of Economics and Statistics, XLV (February
    1963), 16-22.

Merrett, A. J. "Capital Gains Taxation; The Accrual Alter-
    native," Oxford Economic Papers, New Series, XVI (July
    1964), 262-74.

Mitra, Ashok. "Tax Burden for Indian Agriculture," R. Brai-
    banti and J. Spengler, eds. Administration and Economic
    Development in India. Durham, N.C.: Duke University
    Press, 1963, 281-303.

Nakamura, J. I. "Growth of Japanese Agriculture, 1875-1920,"
    W. W. Lockwood, ed. The State and Economic Enterprise in
    Japan. Princeton: Princeton University Press, 1965, 249-
    324.

Nash, M. "Social Prerequisites to Economic Growth in Latin
    America and South East Asia," Economic Development and
    Cultural Change, XII (April 1964), 316-18.

Papke, J. A. "Michigan's Value-Added Tax After Seven Years,"
    National Tax Journal, XIII (December 1960), 350-63.

Patrick, H. T. "The Mobilization of Private Gold Holdings,"
    Indian Economic Journal, VII (October-December 1963), 177-
    98.

Peacock, A. T. "Built-in Flexibility and Economic Growth," in
    Stabile Preise in wachsender Wirtschaft. Edited by
    G. Bombach. Tübingen: J. C. B. Mohr, 1960.

Pettibone, P. J. "The Soviet Turnover Tax," Public Finance,
    XIX (1964), 361-82.

Phelps-Brown and M. H. Browne. "Distribution and Productivity
    under Inflation," Economic Journal (March 1960), 42-81.

Pigou, A. C. "A Special Levy to Discharge War Debt," Economic
    Journal (1918), 38-58.

Pillai, V. R. "A Basic Tax on Land; The Travancore Experiment,"
    Indian Journal of Agricultural Economics, V (March 1950),
    185-90.

_____. "The Equalizing Effect of Estate Duty," Economic
    Weekly, XVI (September 26, 1964), 1569-74.

Prakash, O. "An Indian View of the Expenditure Tax."
    Manchester School, XXVI (January 1958), 48-67.

Prest, A. R. "The Expenditure Tax and Saving," Appendix 2,
    Chapter 2 in his Public Finance in Underdeveloped Coun-
    tries. London: Weidenfeld and Nicolson, 1962, 53-62.

_____. Review of Kaldor's "An Expenditure Tax" in Economic
    Journal, LXVI (March 1956), 116-20.

Raj, K. N. "Resources for the Third Plan: An Approach," The
    Economic Weekly, Annual Number (January 1959), 30-34.

Ranis, G. "The Financing of Japanese Economic Development,"
    Economic History Review, Second Series, XI (April 1959),
    440-54.

Rao, V. K. R. V. "Changes in India's National Income," Capital:
    Annual Review of Commerce, Trade and Industry. Calcutta,
    Supplement of December 1954, pp. 15-17, quoted in
    W. Malenbaum, Prospects for India's Development. London:
    George Allen and Unwin, 1962.

_____. "Economic Growth and Rural-Urban Income Distribu-
    tion, 1950-61," The Economic Weekly, XVII (February 20,
    1965), 373-78.

Ratchford, B. U. and P. B. Han. "The Burden of the Corporate
    Income Tax," National Tax Journal, X (December 1957), 310-
    24.

Rolph, E. "A Proposed Revision of Excise Tax Theory," Journal
    of Political Economy, LX (April 1952), 102-17.

Rubner, A. "The Irrelevancy of the British Differential Profits
    Tax," Economic Journal, LXXIV (June 1964), 347-59.

Rudick, H. J. "What Alternative to Estate and Gift Taxes,"
    California Law Review, XXXVIII (March 1950), 150-82.

Sarien, R. G. and O. P. Sawla. "The Capital Gains Tax in India,"
    Canadian Tax Journal, II (September-October 1903), 451-57.

Shere, L. "Discussion," on E. G. Keith, "How Should Wealth Transfers be Taxed," American Economic Review (May 1950), 406-9.

Shoup, C. S. "Incidence of the Corporation Income Tax: Capital Structure and Turnover Rates," National Tax Journal, I (March 1948). Reprinted in R. A. Musgrave and C. S. Shoup, Readings in the Economics of Taxation. London: George Allen and Unwin, 1959, 322-29.

Singh, B. "Compulsory Savings," Indian Economic Journal, VII (April 1960), 378-94.

Slichter, S. "The Problem of Inflation," Review of Economic Statistics, XXX (February 1948), 5.

Slitor, R. E. "The Enigma of Corporate Tax Incidence," Public Finance, XVIII (1963), 328-52.

Somers, H. M. "Reconsideration of the Capital Gains Tax," National Tax Journal, XIII (December 1960), 289-309.

Staley, C. E. "Export Taxes in Ceylon," Public Finance, XIV-XV (1959-60), 249-68.

Steger, W. A. "Averaging Income for Tax Purposes; A Statistical Study," National Tax Journal, IX (June 1956), 97-114.

Stevens, R. D. "A Review of Measures of Farm Income for International Use," Indian Journal of Agricultural Economics, XVIII (October-December 1963), 1-20.

Sundelson, J. W. "Report on Japanese Taxation by the Shoup Mission," National Tax Journal, III (March 1950), 104-20.

Vickrey, W. "Expenditure, Capital Gains and the Basis of Progressive Taxation," Manchester School of Economic and Social Studies, XXV (January 1957), 1-25.

Von Laue, T. H. "The High Cost and the Gamble of the Witte System: A Chapter in the Industrialization of Russia," Journal of Economic History (1953), 156-72.

Wai, U Tun. "The Relation Between Inflation and Economic Growth," IMF Staff Papers (October 1959), 302-17.

Wald, H. P. "The Recent Experience of the Republic of Korea with Tax Collections in Kind," in Agricultural Taxation and Economic Development. Cambridge: Harvard University Law School, 1954, 424-34.

Walker, K. "Some Economic Aspects of the Taxation of Companies," Manchester School of Economic and Social Studies, XXXII (January 1954), 1-36.

Wertheimer, R. G. "Tax Incentives in Germany," National Tax Journal, X (1957), 325-38.

Willemson, M. A. "The Effect Upon the Rate of Private Savings of a Change from a Personal Income Tax to a Personal Expenditure Tax," National Tax Journal, IX (1956), 48-71.

Government Publications

British White Paper on Employment Policy. Cmd. 6527. London: H.M.S.O., 1944.

Canada Year Book 1963-64. Ottawa: Dominion Bureau of Statistics, 1964.

Government of Canada. Report of the Royal Commission on Taxation. 6 vols. Ottawa: Queen's Printer, 1966.

Government of India. The Additional Duties of Excise (Goods of Special Importance) Act, 1957. New Delhi: Ministry of Law, 1964.

_____. All-India Estate Tax Revenue Statistics, 1963-64. Delhi: Manager of Publications, 1966.

_____. All-India Expenditure Tax Revenue Statistics, 1963-64. Delhi: Manager of Publications, 1966.

_____. All-India Gift Tax Revenue Statistics, 1963-64. Delhi: Manager of Publications, 1966.

_____. All-India Income Tax Revenue Statistics, 1963-64. Delhi: Manager of Publications, 1967.

_____. Audit Reports (Civil) on Revenue Receipts, 1963-67. Delhi: Manager of Publications, 1963-67.

_____. Budget Papers (including Explanatory Memoranda), 1958-59 - 1967-68. New Delhi: Ministry of Finance, 1958-67.

_____. The Central Excises and Salt Act, 1944. New Delhi: Ministry of Law, 1964.

Government of India. The Central Sales Tax Act, 1956. New
    Delhi: Ministry of Law, 1966.

_____. The Constitution of India. Delhi: Manager of
    Publications, 1967.

_____. The Customs Act, 1962. New Delhi: Ministry of Law,
    1963.

_____. Estate Duty Act, 1953 (revised). New Delhi:
    Ministry of Law, 1965.

_____. Estimates of National Income 1948-49 - 1962-63. New
    Delhi: Central Statistical Office, 1964.

_____. The Expenditure Tax Act, 1957. New Delhi: Ministry
    of Law, 1965.

_____. First Interim Report on Rationalization and Simpli-
    fication of Direct Taxation Laws. New Delhi: Ministry of
    Finance, 1967.

_____. Gift Tax Act, 1958 (revised). New Delhi: Ministry
    of Law, 1965.

_____. Incidence of Indirect Taxation in India, 1958-59.
    New Delhi: Ministry of Finance, 1961.

_____. The Income Tax Act 1961. New Delhi: Ministry of
    Law, 1966.

_____. India 1963. Delhi: Manager of Publications, 1964.

_____. India 1964. Delhi: Manager of Publications, 1965.

_____. India 1965. Delhi: Manager of Publications, 1966.

_____. India 1966. Delhi: Manager of Publications, 1967.

_____. The Indian Tariff Act, 1934. New Delhi: Ministry
    of Law, 1966.

_____. Outline of Direct Taxes in India. New Delhi:
    Ministry of Finance, 1960.

_____. Planning Commission. Appraisal and Prospects of the
    Second Five Year Plan. Delhi: Manager of Publications,
    1958.

_____. Planning Commission. Plan Resources and Outlay: A
    Review. Delhi: Manager of Publications, 1959.

Government of India. Planning Commission. Review of the First
        Five Year Plan. Delhi: Manager of Publications, 1957.

_____. Planning Commission. Third Five Year Plan--Mid-Term
        Appraisal. Delhi: Manager of Publications, 1963.

_____. Planning Commission. Third Five Year Plan--Summary.
        Delhi: Manager of Publications, 1962.

_____. Problems of the Third Plan. Delhi: Manager of
        Publications, 1961.

_____. Report of the Central Excise Reorganisation Comittee.
        Delhi: Manager of Publications, 1963.

_____. Report of the Commission on the Distribution of In-
        come and Levels of Living. New Delhi: Planning Commis-
        sion, 1964.

_____. Report of the Committee on Prevention of Corruption.
        New Delhi: Ministry of Home Affairs, 1964.

_____. Report of the Direct Taxes Administration Enquiry
        Committee, 1958-59. Delhi: Manager of Publications, 1960.

_____. Report of the Fourth Finance Commission, 1965.
        Delhi: Manager of Publications, 1965.

_____. Report of Income Tax Investigation Commission.
        Delhi: Manager of Publications, 1965.

_____. Report of the Study Team on Prohibition. 3 vols.
        New Delhi: Planning Commission, 1964.

_____. Report of the Taxation Enquiry Commission. 3 vols.
        New Delhi: Ministry of Finance, 1953-54.

_____. Reports of the Public Accounts Committee, 1960-61 -
        66-67. New Delhi: Lok Sabha Secretariat, 1961-67.

_____. The Wealth Tax Act, 1957. New Delhi: Ministry of
        Law, 1965.

Royal Commission on the Taxation of Profits and Income. Cmd.
        9474. London: H.M.S.O., 1955.

Royal Commission on the Taxation of Profits and Income. Second
        Report, Cmd. 9105. London: H.M.S.O., 1955.

United Nations Secretariat, Department of Economic Affairs.
        Public Finance Survey: India. New York, 1951.

U. S. Congress, Committee on the Economic Report. Federal Tax Policy for Economic Growth and Stability. Washington, D.C.: United States Government Printing Office, 1955.

U. S. Congress, House Committee on Ways and Means. Income Tax Revision. Washington, D.C.: United States Government Printing Office, 1960.

U. S. Government. Report of the Commission on Money and Credit. Englewood Cliffs, N.J.: Prentice Hall, 1961.

U. S. Internal Revenue Service. Report on Tax Administration in India. New Delhi: USAID, 1964.

ABOUT THE AUTHOR

James Cutt has taught at the University of Toronto and is now an Assistant Professor of Economics at York University in Toronto. He studied Economics at the University of Edinburgh and did his post-graduate work at the University of Toronto. His major interests are public finance, quantitative methods and development economics.